T0354356

JENNIFER VANICA

COURAGEOUS PHILANTHROPY

GOING PUBLIC IN A CLOSELY HELD WORLD

COURAGEOUS PHILANTHROPY
GOING PUBLIC IN A CLOSELY HELD WORLD

Cover:
"Children's Wall" and "The Dragonfly,"
Art Wall and Sculpture by Jean Cornwell Wheat
Located at Market Creek Plaza
Photography by Jean Savage

Illustrations:
Artistic Drawings by Joni Vanica
Photography by Jean Savage and William Jones

People Whose Images are in the Drawings:
Roque Barros
Chip Buttner
Leigh Chapman
Kurtis Laifaiga Leilua
Alejandro Meraz
Maya Payne
Dylan Solomon
Jose Venegas
Breanna Zwart

Architectural Drawings:
Courtesy of Hector Reyes

iUniverse books may be ordered through booksellers or by contacting:

iUniverse
1663 Liberty Drive
Bloomington, IN 47403
www.iuniverse.com
1-800-Authors (1-800-288-4677)

ISBN: 978-1-5320-5191-3 (sc)
ISBN: 978-1-5320-5190-6 (e)

Library of Congress Control Number: 2018907619

Print information available on the last page.

iUniverse rev. date: 09/19/2018

This book is dedicated to Joe Jacobs
and the residents of the southeastern
San Diego neighborhoods

CONTENTS

FOREWORD
by Angela Glover Blackwell

Creativity, will, and motivation are essential in making change. The capacity to harness imagination, envision possibilities, engage teams with honesty and authenticity, and have ownership of action are the elements necessary to ensure that change does, indeed, endure. In the pages that follow, Jennifer Vanica recounts the remarkable story of the partnership between the Jacobs Family Foundation and the residents of San Diego's southeastern Diamond Neighborhoods that has become a model of what creative and unwavering partnerships can achieve: Market Creek Plaza.

I first met Jennifer in 2001. At the time, my organization, PolicyLink, had embarked on its own journey of Lifting Up What Works®. Our aim was to find and share the unique yet ultimately replicable work in communities that provide lessons for practice and policy through a focus on local leaders who are shaping solutions to economic and social problems in historically disinvested communities and communities of color. The PolicyLink team met with Jacobs Center staff, sat in on community meetings, and observed closely just how honestly and openly everyone related to one another. We saw how decisions were made about what residents wanted — a supermarket was first on the list and foremost in this neighborhood that had long gone without one. The look, feel, selection of tenant participants in planning, and ultimately the design and implementation of a pioneering IPO creating literal ownership of the growing Market Creek project unfolded through teams of community members using a shared decision-making process.

What started for Jennifer as a two-week consultancy with the Jacobs Family Foundation eventually became a twenty-year commitment to support *people* — the community residents as they organized, engaged one another, debated, and changed the *place* — with all the opportunities and amenities the people who lived there needed and wanted. The foundation and the community were changed by the transformative power of working across race, class, age, gender, and cultural identity in an inclusive and participatory process.

This is the story that *Courageous Philanthropy* tells.

But there is also a second, parallel story that emerges in these pages. That is a chronicle of how a foundation, an institution inherently associated with power and privilege — can and must own its own change. The foundation must do so by understanding that building an inclusive society shouldn't just be a program priority for funding; it needs to be self-directed and start from within.

This second story examines how a foundation can be an equal partner when it adopts an uncompromising commitment to inclusion and equity in decision-making, seeing itself in the larger and interconnected ecosystem of change, and being willing to risk changing who they have been — both institutionally and individually.

In telling this story, Jennifer looks at the ways in which her team struggled and grew in their effort to be self-reflective in the face of "historic processes and policies that can inhibit innovation, sustain silo approaches, and unintentionally disempower residents in the disinvested communities foundations seek to support." It calls for foundations to end the debate about the engagement of residents in community change and realize the centrality of those residents to the process. It is a message poignantly captured in a line from a community team meeting: "Don't do about me without me."

This is a long way from the policies that surrounded urban renewal in the 1950s that led to large-scale displacement of people, the isolation and dividing up of neighborhoods with freeways, and what was referred to as "slum clearance." Proposed as solutions to the devastation caused by long-term discrimination, disinvestment, and historic disparities, little thought or concern was given to the voices of residents in deciding the future of their neighborhoods. Resident participation needs to be more than a box to check for points on a state or federal proposal; it is critical to solid decision-making as public deliberation is critical to our democracy.

Throughout the Market Creek experience, the eagerness of citizens to participate paved the way to outcomes exemplifying what can happen when philanthropy is aligned with community, determined to ensure equity, unafraid to share power, and committed to strengthening democracy by lifting the voice of those living change on the ground. Equity means just and fair inclusion into a society in which all can participate, prosper, and achieve their full potential. It demands that the wisdom, voice, and experience of people living in disinvested communities or communities of color are authentically engaged in determining and achieving the outcomes they desire. Without equity, community redevelopment can improve a physical place but leave the people behind, stifle broad creativity, bring economic benefit only to a few, and lead to a homogeneous community, or displace many. Equity enables everyone, including the most vulnerable in our society, to share in the opportunities many take for granted.

As an observer of the committed struggles and the outstanding achievements that are hallmarks of Market Creek, I can attest to the ways in which Joe Jacobs' vision of ownership and values of "risk, respect, responsibility, and working in relationship" were creatively adhered to and operationalized during his lifetime. Those from many parts of the country who knew or worked with him will recognize these values throughout *Courageous Philanthropy*. Impacting people across the country who interacted with him or participated in learning exchanges with the Market Creek teams, these values are important and enduring principles for foundations that are stepping up and supporting communities' creative visions for change in small towns, large cities, and everywhere in between.

I hope that *Courageous Philanthropy* will be widely read and its messages about creating meaningful change are shared and adopted. They are messages of hope and possibility that are sorely needed today.

— *Angela Glover Blackwell is Founder in Residence, PolicyLink, the national research and action institute that advances racial and economic equity by Lifting Up What Works®*

ACKNOWLEDGEMENTS

The transformation of historically disinvested communities requires ownership. Culture might eat strategy for lunch,[1] but it's ownership that nourishes inspired action and creates enduring change.

The Market Creek experience, as it came to be known, was a place-based effort in southeastern San Diego that sought to turn a hundred years of arms-length community-foundation relations upside down to see what could happen if the closed circle of philanthropic decision-making was opened up to the broader public and if resident teams took ownership of action. It moved resident engagement into uncharted territory, amping up the volume on resident voice and culminating in a large-scale community-owned venture. It challenged and changed the foundation to "go public" in every sense of the word.

It was a risk. A big risk. And given that, my gratitude is amplified for all that were involved and invested.

In helping me reflect back on the twenty-year period, I am grateful to the many residents, partners, and teammates who took time out to sit down and talk about the impact of the experience on their lives, share how that impact rippled through their community and extended families, and pinpoint amazing, challenging, and priceless moments of our time together. In addition to giving me this time, several also were advance readers and advisors on the manuscript.

I am also grateful to the many colleagues from around the country who shared what they observed about the Market Creek experience, the state of place-based community change, and the need to open up the field of philanthropy to greater inclusion of residents as partners.

In particular, I want to thank the Jacobs Center for Neighborhood Innovation for its two-decade-long commitment to exploring a new relationship for philanthropy in community change; The California Endowment for providing funding to reflect and write, encouraging me to dissect and share the many lessons of leading the Village at Market Creek work; PolicyLink and the Aspen Institute Roundtable on Community Change, which challenged me to think beyond Market Creek to the next generation of community change leaders who could benefit from all that worked and didn't; and to the James Irvine Foundation, which by honoring me with the James Irvine Leadership Award affirmed the commitment of the many resident leaders who dared to navigate uncharted waters and construct a platform of joint action and collaborative leadership unlike any we had ever experienced before.

These five organizations, along with the enormously creative and talented team I had the privilege of working with for so many years at the Jacobs Center, inspired me to lift up at least a few of the many stories and lessons I experienced while working at the intersection of race, place, class, gender, faith, organizing, philanthropy, development, securities law, and politics.

I also want to thank my husband, Ron Cummings, who was my steadfast editor and sounding board in structuring and writing this book and my life-long learning partner on the topic of teamwork. Twenty-five years ago, we decided to go into business together, testing our ability to truly partner. Disagreements taught us how to keep our hearts open to learning through differences. And by staying steady through uncomfortable moments and opening up to what we might not want to hear, we learned what it meant to really listen. This teamwork was rich with lessons, among them the realization that partnership is powerful, our strengths complement each other's, and our differences help us see in our blind spots. With Ron, I learned the fundamental truths of being and working in relationship:

- It is challenging to align on *what* and agree on *how* – but worth the effort;
- Trust is earned;
- Communication is hard;
- Listening and learning are everything;

- If you are asking people to reach for change, you have to reach for and risk your own; and
- In the best relationships, both are changed forever.

Lastly, I am grateful to Joe Jacobs, the all-in angel-entrepreneur-philanthropist who was open to new ways of doing the work of foundations and who asked me to step up to the plate and swing for the fences. He taught me to reach for the dreams that are born of daring, greet each day with the courage that inspired action demands, take my lumps, hold my ground, and pass the lessons on.

Because of him, with his great spirit of risk-taking, I had the opportunity to work side-by-side and in relationship with thousands of incredible people and partners with whom we shared decision-making and with whom we "went public." By fighting our way through differences, disappointments, and set-backs to hard-won successes, we got to experience the profound hope, caring, and energy for action that are the cornerstones of enduring change. And for a moment in time, we opened the doors of philanthropy to Inclusion, Participation, and Ownership — an IPO like no other.

INTRODUCTION

―――――――――――――― ▪▪

LESSONS FROM A DO-TANK

INTRODUCTION

"To go fast, go alone. To go far, go together."

— African Proverb

Toward Building a New Narrative Together

Everyone has a story. Ask anyone their story and you will find yourself in the midst of an intriguing, almost always surprising, assumption-breaking journey into someone else's life. To invite someone's story is to enter a new dimension. It is an invitation to shake your world view. My last community convening in August 2011, I was in the room with 400 stories.

In a sea of vibrant textiles and earth-toned mud cloth, there was this buzz — an energy that comes with checking in on friends, sharing a nod of respect, hugging and catching up on where the stories left off — before sitting down for the work to start. This was a space that filled itself up through the sharing of stories.

The Lost Boy of Sudan. The Lao mother who fled war, moving from country to country to find work. Survivors of shootings, prison, and Jim Crow. The woman who had been sold by her father to a husband for $100. A small-town farm girl who ran away from home to work on a reservation. Skin tones of all colors and shades, different religions, different languages. Some who endured unbearable sorrow. Some who grew up feeling less than, colonized, forced to assimilate. Others whose stories centered on surprise, the shock of being wrong about what they assumed about other people, a learning journey causing them to let go of old thinking.

As I stood and took it all in, I realized that perhaps the most important question I had asked for the past decade and a half was "what is your story?" It had changed everything. That night, we broke bread. We shared. We laughed. We loved. We built enduring friendships. To this gathering, people brought their smiles and smarts, refreshing the hope in our hearts on the hot August evening. Some would call it sacred space. A place of where everyone was valued and validated. To me, it was community.

Communities also have stories. They have more than one narrative. Rich histories. The amalgamation of thousands of journeys to one place. And like people, communities are constantly changing. They grow, thrive, stagnate, decline, or re-generate in reaction to a range of internal and external factors which impact the human experience.

Foundations have stories also. Stories that represent the very best of our human nature and the very worst.

Behind each one is an extraordinary story about risk-taking and wealth-building, about sharing what we have with those who have less or are challenged more, and about believing in our shared destiny.

At the same time, as a field, there is the embedded story of a class society controlled by the elite, concentrated financial power behind spreading the values of a dominate culture, and the promotion of "ruling-class interests" which have often worked against the interests of minorities and indigenous people throughout the world.[2]

Its history is one of a closed circle. And while chartered to act in the public interest, the public voice is largely missing.

But as the wealth gap grows, we are being called to rethink old narratives, adopt new ways of being and knowing, open up to greater equity and inclusion, connect across differences, and think as much about how we will go about the process of change as the changes we should make.

In changing the trajectory of a disinvested community, those of us in the foundation sector have known for a long time that incremental strategies and isolated projects are not enough. The magnitude and complexity of the challenges require us to break out of thinking we can somehow "fund" or "professionally staff" our way through the entrenched issues of our day, simply refining the current model of how foundations, non-profits, and communities interact.

The most significant asset we have at our fingertips — and have always had — for igniting inspired social change is the wisdom, creativity, and experience of everyday people choosing to express and strengthen their human and cultural connection to each other, to the communities they call home, and to the issues they care about. And yet, for the most part, our philanthropic and political responses to disinvested neighborhoods have been to either separate people from their historical communities in order to "change the place," as we did with Urban Renewal, or to define the people who live there as consumers of social services and try to "change the people."

With the pioneering efforts of daring teams over the last 20 years, comprehensive community initiatives to connect people and place were funded, market-based strategies for social change were introduced, and tool kits were diversified. Greater collaboration, spawned by "collective impact"[3] and supported by "backbone organizations," continues to gain momentum. But despite these, we still largely discuss the need to scale strategies for social change by closing gaps in services, investing in projects that have guaranteed outcomes and income streams, and aligning "stakeholders" defined for the most part as institutional partners.

These efforts, however, have been pointing us in a new direction. They tell us that we need to go beyond traditional public-private partnerships to a new construct. We need to build strong platforms for joint action, de-silo efforts, coordinate networks of significant scale, create sacred spaces, balance individual and community interests, blend social justice and market strategies, matrix resources, and lead collaboratively. We need to re-imagine the non-profit and foundation of the future — both strategically and structurally.

This will demand something very different of the next generation of community change leaders. These leaders will have to rearrange the existing elements in the ecosystem in a way that is no longer defined by organizational boundaries. They will have to be adept at working with a high level of uncertainty. And they will need the heart necessary to embrace learning, survive in a world of complexity and critics, and endure the change process itself.

To step into this new future, we must step out of the safety of what we think we know and be willing to live the questions. And that requires courage. The courage to leave what is familiar and re-see, reinterpret, and redefine the ecosystem and the nature of our relationships within it. To invite and embrace each other's stories. To build a new narrative together — one that raises the volume of the voice of everyday citizens.

Philanthropy in an Open Field

For twenty years I worked for the family foundation launched by Joe and Vi Jacobs. I thought I was on a two-week consulting assignment to help the family put its grantmaking agenda and funding guidelines in place when in 1992 South Central Los Angeles burned. Following the acquittal of the police officers that were videotaped beating Rodney King, riots left 53 dead and over 2,000 injured. The philanthropic field ignited with discussions of racism, police brutality, violence, and in particular, the economic conditions in South Central that led to the uprising.

Joe Jacobs, at that time, was still the Chairman of the Jacobs Engineering Group, which had its worldwide headquarters in Pasadena, California. He wanted to roll up his own sleeves and personally work toward addressing economic conditions. He believed strongly that if people in South Central had owned the businesses and were participating in our country's prosperity, this would not have happened.

My two-week assignment would turn into a 20-year journey that would always, despite its many twists and turns, stay centered on economic prosperity and ownership.

At first, the firm I ran with my husband, Ron Cummings (VanicaCummings & Associates) would become the Jacobs Family Foundation's technical assistance partner, supporting selected entrepreneurial non-profits. This capacity-building support was linked strategically to the grantmaking of the family foundation.

An operating foundation, the Jacobs Center for NonProfit Innovation, was incorporated in 1995 to provide more flexibility in the roles we could play, and VanicaCummings' group of associates became the initial "Jacobs Team." Ron and I set aside our company to lead the work of the new Jacobs Center.

In 1997, five years after LA burned and still questioning how to help kick-start economic vibrancy, a change was needed. Aware that organizational grants, even when linked to capacity-building, could not address the large disparities in health, education, and access to jobs and their underlying causes, the foundation board decided to put the Jacobs Center offices in a disinvested area of San Diego where learning partnerships with several non-profits were in progress and embark on a journey to conduct an up-close-and-personal trial-and-error look of philanthropy in community change.

As a team trying to operationalize Joe's deep belief in the dignity of all people, we knew that we could "no longer act as patrons,"[4] as Margaret Wheatley has so aptly framed our deep desire to pay others to do our learning. Seeking to change ourselves as an institutional construct of power and privilege, we faced challenging questions. Is it possible to be a philanthropic partner that is not patronizing? Is it possible to create a structure for community transformation that truly respects the people who live there? Is it possible to level the playing field of decision-making? And most importantly, is it possible to create the conditions for ownership so that our actions, as Joe would put it, don't become corrosive, or as Peter Block would put it, don't become "coercive or wishfully dependent on the transformation of others?"[5]

To answer these questions, we would have to open up and let go of how place-based philanthropy had always been done. We would have to understand our own need and ability to change. And, out of honor and respect for the residents of the community we chose to move into, graciously embrace the lessons they would teach us.

It was a voyage into uncharted waters, flipping a century of philanthropic/community relations on its ear by no longer assuming charitable foundations should be at arm's length or set the agenda. The community partnership that was forged was based on the idea that deep connections, powerful relationships, and teamwork might stand a better chance to change things than the philanthropic model being used to support neighborhood revitalization at that time.

The neighborhood where we would move was experiencing the all too common impact of racism and disinvestment — gangs and youth violence, methamphetamine trafficking, a 40 percent high-school-drop-out rate, and widespread blight. As partners, we would ask residents to step out of their homes to address the decades of disinvestment, help us learn how to be a more effective partner in supporting change, and — together — create a new community and philanthropic narrative.

Starting with the initial goals of securing a major grocery store and getting rid of a contaminated factory site, resident teams would work with the foundation to bring down the barbed wire fence that surrounded the decaying property and bring up a commercial project that they would plan, design, build, manage, and ultimately own — Market Creek Plaza.

The teams that spawned Market Creek Plaza would turn it into a platform for large-scale civic action focused on the goal of transforming a "field of brownfields" in to San Diego's "place-to-be" for multicultural food, art, and entertainment. Fueled by the energy of hundreds of residents serving on teams, by 2010 the ten-acre Market Creek Plaza was generating $50 million in annual economic activity, over 25,000 people were attending cultural events and activities, and an expanding community vision called for turning another 50 acres of untended, unused, and blighted land into new homes, businesses, jobs, services, and entertainment venues — the Village at Market Creek.

Throughout the project, we would ask ourselves *"What does it really take?"* and document what it did take to honor people's voices broadly and keep community change from being blocked or short-lived.

Working side-by-side with residents in an open and inclusive process would require me to rethink everything I thought I knew about leadership. It would teach me to suspend my own world view long enough to listen and let go of preconceived ideas about how things should unfold. It would require me to find the pulse and consensus points and put support behind a community of engaged citizens on their agenda rather than a pre-determined foundation agenda. Most importantly, it would teach me that each of us — both personally and professionally — must own our own change.

It was a bold undertaking inspired by Joe Jacobs and his commitment to entrepreneurship, risk-taking, and ownership. From my earliest conversations with Joe, he wanted his family foundation to be deeply rooted in risk-taking, testing new tools, and assuming shared responsibility for change. He wanted our work to be about achieving a deep understanding of how change happens by risking what we had, sharing what we learned, and then going out of business as a one-generation foundation.

It would be philanthropy in the open — open to new world views and ways of working, open and transparent in our teamwork with residents, and free to explore the open field of ideas residents brought to the table. Nothing was off limits.

Going "Public"

The Jacobs Center was set up to be an institute of applied learning. As Darren Walker, President and CEO of the Ford Foundation, framed it — we were a "do-tank." Joe Jacobs wanted to go beyond theory to figuring out practice. He wanted to be up-close-and-personal and experience the work in real time. He wanted to be all about ownership.

At the launch of the Jacobs Center, much had been written about the consequences of foundations controlling the development of social policy without engaging the broader public, but little headway had been made in changing how this unequal power dynamic plays out for communities that are the target of place-focused philanthropy. Despite being chartered to act in the public interest, no mechanism existed for foundations to actually invite the "public" into decision-making about what was in its best interest, making it easy to undermine the fundamental premise of self-determination and democracy by setting the policy agenda, determining what strategies and activities get funded, and controlling the narrative.

Our work was to figure out how to "be public" and "go public."

Could we use, design, or refine planning methods that would promote shared decision-making and distribute the ownership and accountability for change? Could we create an opening for people to get real about what is standing in the way of change without the influence of financial control? Could we figuratively and literally share the risks and rewards of the change that occurred?

We were on the search for the practices and principles of enduring change — change that has staying power after an initiative goes away — and the secret to that, we believed, lay in the community gaining control of both decisions about their community and assets that could be leveraged for future change.

If "closely held" corporations have a small, tightly-knit group of shareholders, operating as a closed circle of people who benefit and have control, we would figure out how to "go public" and open up to a large network of people with ownership — of the planning, the implementation, and the assets.

Lessons from the Do-Tank

By amplifying community voice and creating a platform for diverse perspectives, we believed that highly-charged deliberation and teamwork would accelerate innovation. This meant we had to be adept at change, able to operate in a world of multiple realities, including those that confronted our own beliefs, work collaboratively as leaders among peers, and build a culture that encouraged risk, tolerated failure, and loved learning.

Our work was to listen, plan, act, and reflect on a fast rotation and then apply that learning in real time, not waiting for mid-course corrections. In this environment, relationships were challenging, complex, and close; everyone's potential was seen as a gift; human behavior was not expected to be predictable; and most importantly, people knew that if a risk were necessary, I would have their backs. And I knew Joe would have mine.

I used to tell people, if running a traditional foundation was classical, then Jacobs was jazz. It was improvisational, could run ahead on a gut feel, and could be at peace with paradox. But we all knew that for it to be music and not noise, we needed to be careful listeners and move to a common theme and beat. Inspired and guided by John Kao's masterful work Jamming, we knew that as an R&D experiment in philanthropy — which was posing the question *What would it take?* — we needed both "free expressiveness and disciplined self-control, solitude in a crowded room, acceptance and defiance, serendipity and direction."[6]

The many lessons of this journey is what this book is about.

For social change practitioners on the search for structures and strategies for complex community change, it is an up-close look at the conditions for leading, the practices and principles for managing cross-disciplinary work, the need for blending types of capital, and the process for moving large-scale civic action.

And it is a story of the lived experience of community change on the ground — much of it told through the voices of residents, stakeholders, and partners. It is a look at the people, the personal nature of the work, the roadblocks and challenges, and the power of participation and ownership to ignite the will and motivation of ordinary people to achieve extraordinary dreams.

It is also a case study for and about institutional philanthropy — the need to be self-reflective in the face of historic processes and policies that inhibit innovation, sustain silo approaches, and unintentionally undercut the gifts and talents of everyday residents in the disinvested communities we seek to support. And it is a story, told through the lens of my personal experience in leading a charitable foundation and my journey of discovery and learning about how we owned our own change — deeply listening and respecting the voices of residents and endeavoring to democratize philanthropy by creating a platform for shared decision-making and co-investment.

For the next generation of social impact investors, it is also the story of an angel-entrepreneur-philanthropist — Joe Jacobs — and the level of risk and endurance required to support the economic growth and revitalization of our country's disinvested communities. While all of the Jacobs family members on the board were highly engaged and active participants in the direction and decisions of the foundation and its courageous philanthropy, I have chosen to share this experience as a story of my personal relationship with Joe, the lessons he shared, his deep and abiding belief in the power and possibility of people to create change, and a commitment to ownership that fed incredible passion, innovation, and inspired action.

Ultimately, <u>Courageous Philanthropy: Going Public in a Closely Held World</u> is a call to action to end our debate about the engagement of residents in community change and realize their central position in it. Inclusion, shared power, and democracy aren't just ideals; they are practices.

In a time when power and privilege set the agenda for change and everyday citizens don't believe their voices count more than money — either in the polling booth or in philanthropy — we need to shed the contradiction that those who control private wealth within foundations are building power in marginalized communities by determining what policies, what programs, and what opportunities are in other people's best interest. There is no pathway to enduring social change unless people determine for themselves what is in their best interest. They must have ownership.

To do this, philanthropy must own its own change. Recognizing that building an inclusive society starts now and starts with us, we need to open up the closed circle of voices we value by:

- Making it our moral imperative to no longer "do about me without me," supporting the growing momentum and desire of everyday residents to be civically engaged;
- Creating intentional structures for community ownership — both figurative and literal — to unleash innovation, feed endurance, and raise expectations for change;
- Developing practices that allow disinvested communities to physically develop in ways that promote "form following culture;"[7]
- Preparing mechanisms to matrix money across types of capital — including community capital — making our own foundation dollars bounce in the communities we serve, in order to achieve leveraged economic development; and lastly,
- Becoming uncompromising in our need to be open, attentive, thoughtful, and respectful in how we start, stop, or change our

commitments to community "initiatives," given their deep roots in relationships, emotional ties, and hard-earned trust.

While these can't fully address the imbalance of power, they can move the needle toward enduring community change, in which residents of historically disinvested communities have a voice, can weigh options in a deliberative process that is biased toward action, and can heal across differences.

During the 20 years that I worked for the Jacobs Foundations, I was aware of the many people on whose shoulders I was standing. Many of the community change structures and strategies that were developed evolved by pushing their work forward. I also embraced many learning partners, some people I only met in books, and others who graced my days with real life stories that pushed us forward. They were my lifeline for understanding what it meant to lead — not with answers — but questions and for helping me understand, that in addition to having something important to give, I also had something important to learn about what it means to be fundamentally human.

As a learning organization — a do-tank — there were countless lessons. In the book, I share many of the actual ah-ha moments that occurred and what they taught us about what endures and about endurance. It is my hope in writing this book that these lessons may point the next generation of social change leaders in new directions, and that some of the strategies will push forward with new teams in new locations.

A Journey of Risks and Rewards

To "go public" is to share ownership — with all of its risks and all of its rewards.

For me, the journey to align philanthropy with the soul of democracy by lifting up the chorus of voices within the communities we seek to serve as worthy, mindful, and equal at the table, risking both real relationships and large-scale action, and using failure as a foundation for discovery-based learning was simultaneously professional and personal, urgent and patient, complex and simple, intentional and intuitive, guided and organic.

It is the story of change not always happening the way we'd like it to — through grand initiatives, catalytic grants, and astute theories — but through turbulent interactions and simple acts of kindness. It is also the story about how change is most often derailed, not through faulty program designs and poor implementation, as we expected, but rather through pettiness, politics, and the human drive to revert to what is comfortable...because it's hard. Hard to step out of norms. Hard to change the ecosystem of how funders, non-profits, and residents in communities interact. Hard to change the power dynamic of money. Hard to admit you are complicit. Hard to let go of control. And hard to stay the course when things get difficult, confusing, and messy.

Stepping out of long-established norms invites detractors and makes you a lightning rod for criticism. For me personally, this was a learning journey into the dynamics of actually <u>enduring</u> change — learning what it takes to rally the will to work day-by-day at the heart of change, dealing with overwhelming barriers and unrelenting nay-sayers. It was about mustering the courage to walk on uncertain paths with an indefatigable will, the ability to withstand critics, an unmoving set of operationalized values, and an unsinkable spirit.

Hurt and disappointment — this is the risk.

But opening up philanthropic process to include residents as partners and co-investors is also the story of ordinary people being capable of extraordinary things. When human creativity is unleashed, relationships are nourished, and dreams are nurtured, people believe that anything is possible and easily step into personal and collective responsibility for change. When people truly own change, they go after it in a way that is whole-hearted and enduring.

Staying power — this is the reward.

Throughout the last 20 years, I have heard a range of responses to the idea of large-scale resident voice as the centerpiece of place-based philanthropic efforts. I have heard colleagues adamantly exclude residents from planning, saying that they don't want resident involvement because "people don't have experience" or "it will mess up our program designs." On a more moderate front, I have heard colleagues say "we want community feedback, but we only have room for one parent or one student on the leadership cabinet so it feels like tokenism," uncertain about how planning can include both institutional partners and large-scale civic participation. I also heard colleagues say things like "moral and ethical arguments aside, it seems to be getting better results."

For the Market Creek teams, it became clear that residents <u>do</u> have critical experience, their expertise will <u>save</u> our program designs, there are planning methods and structures that can get us <u>beyond tokenism</u>, and last but not least — results aside, we should be doing it exactly because it <u>is</u> the moral and ethical thing to do.

As a premise of our democracy, those affected by decisions need a voice in those decisions. And that demands that we let go of the idea that a group representing only power and privilege should try to stimulate social change without opening the door to having their own worldview challenged.

We need to be in the room together — courageously having the conversations that can truly create change. As the African proverb so astutely notes, "to go far, we must go together."

OWNING
CHANGE

INNOVATION STARTS HERE

1

RABBIT IN A DOG RACE

"It may be when we no longer know what to do,
we have come to our real work,
and that when we no longer know which way to go,
we have begun our real journey."[8]

— Wendell Berry

Who Owns Change?

If you ask people who owns change, everyone looks around the room.

No one.

When we started our community building work, it appeared that residents had grown tired of waiting for government to initiate change and had given up, finding the sheer scale of disinvestment disheartening and disempowering.

For the few people who did turn out to try to make a difference, the plot always seemed to thicken. They described their participation in plan after plan. Start and stop. Start and stop.

Then every time they passed a boarded-up building, they felt disrespected and angry — not just from all the broken promises — but because the hope of investment, as one young man shared with me, had been "dangled in front of them over and over like the rabbit in a dog race."

Resources — dangled just out of reach.

Those in the public sector also had no ownership of changing the conditions left behind in the wake of disinvestment. If they did have a specialized grant, they drove that specific agenda, and most — despite the irony of being in the "public" sector — saw engaging residents as a mandated requirement to be tolerated.

Foundations also had no long-term ownership. At that time, foundations were expected to be at arms-length in order to be objective, which resulted in not having to — and not getting to — grapple with the barriers that stand in the way of change day-in and day-out.

Grants required long lead-times (often as long as the grant period itself), needed predictable outcomes (nothing too risky), had to be solicited by the foundation itself (making many in disinvested areas feel excluded from the in-crowd), had little or no flexibility built in, and put the burden on the grantee for both implementation and sustainability, which road on finding another funder before the grant ran out.

Directors of non-profits, responding to RFPs, expressed that they felt constrained having to come to a table that was already set. In 1996, I interviewed fourteen non-profits working in an economic development collaboration. Each one shared that they knew from the beginning that the project wouldn't work but felt powerless to change the course that had been set. They were saddened that their own working knowledge and creativity were almost never taken into account and that their ability to course correct routinely was just not possible with the constraints of the funding streams within which they had to work.

This was the landscape of social change people described: services got provided, clients got counted, communities got studied, initiatives came and went, and transformational work never had a chance to take root.

By 1991, I'd been around San Diego philanthropy for 15 years and admired our city's amazing track record of building top-ranked medical and educational facilities, endowing great scientific and research institutions, and developing an internationally-acclaimed zoo. But during that 15 years and the 15 before it, San Diego's older urban southeastern neighborhoods had only gotten worse — despite private grants, block grants, and 200 non-profits, religious organizations, associations, and other groups working in a one-mile radius.

Something wasn't working.

2

A COMMUNITY, A WILDCAT, AND A CULTURE OF INNOVATION

---

*"While most people see the risks of taking action,
innovators see the risk of inaction."*

— Rensselaerville Institute, "Assumptions for Innovation"

A Community

"You know you are in a disinvested neighborhood if you are located off the Martin Luther King, Jr. Freeway, Highway, Street, or Boulevard. Pick any city."

The man was right. His neighborhood was one of the neighborhoods in southeastern San Diego that was just off the MLK Freeway, but it could have been in any city. Take any MLK thoroughfare and you'll find yourself in a community of color with an area median income half of the surrounding city, with no grocery store and a history of disinvestment.

The story of the Diamond — ten neighborhoods of southeastern San Diego named for the loosely-shaped diamond outline of the Diamond Business Improvement District — in the early 1990s read like many others around the country, highlighting the challenging and cyclical narrative of change.

With her old abandoned industrial properties, the Diamond told a story about maquiladoras and the struggle for jobs along the border. Her toxic waterways channeled in concrete painted a picture of the historic obsession for containing mother nature. Drug trade tucked in her vacant, contaminated commercial buildings and families crowded into single rooms put a spotlight on her critical shortage of jobs and housing. And her gradual decline into blight exposed the underlying story of San Diego segregation and the common and unjust narrative of race and real estate.

Stripped of all opportunity and investment, racism and economic isolation left her laid out on the bed, slowly and progressively getting worse, until — tagged as the "Four Corners of Death" — people in other parts of San Diego would turn their heads because to look her in the face would be to admit being complicit for this large-scale disinvestment.

But there is another story to be told about these neighborhoods.

I'm not sure why this struck me so deeply or remained in my memory so long, but in high school I read John Steinbeck's novel Cannery Row. I stopped almost immediately on one line to read it over and over. The inhabitants of Cannery Row, Steinbeck wrote, "are, as the man once said, 'whores, pimps, gamblers, and sons of bitches,' by which he meant everybody. Had the man looked through another peephole he might have said, 'saints and angels and martyrs and holy men,' and he would have meant the same thing."[10]

As a teenager I was so moved by the book I hitchhiked from my small Ohio farm town to California to stand on the streets of Cannery Row.

I no longer want to read the narrative of disinvested communities as the story of the plight of the poor, uneducated, and disenfranchised as conditions caused by being dropouts, druggies, teen moms, gang homies, and ex-cons. This is not the lens — or "peephole" as Steinbeck framed it — I want or choose to look through.

The story of this community and of Market Creek — the project that was shaped through a long-term learning partnership between a foundation focused on ownership and residents who came together to tackle the impossible, improbable, and infeasible challenges their neighborhood faced — is a story about a community of graceful teachers and creative spirits, people of faith, deep histories of fighting their way through life's difficulties, great bandwidth for caring, extraordinary respect for the gifts and talents of those around them, and the grounded human resilience that comes from expressing their experience through dance, song, and the breaking of bread.

This is a community of caring and collaborative fighters from cultures all over the world, who are leaders as Marshall Ganz so simply defines them— people willing to "accept responsibility for enabling others to achieve purpose under conditions of uncertainly."[11]

These are people who came forward and chose change when staying with the status quo was easier. People who had the guts to try something different, take risks, and stay the course over a long period of time without assurances. People who stepped into purposeful action against gale-force critics, willing to embrace every barrier, one after another, refusing to give up or give in, acting with confidence in a culture of reflection and fun.

When people from around the country ask me if it was horrible working around so much blight, all I can say looking back on it is —

I would have hated to have missed it.

A Wildcat

"Hell, there are no rules here, we're trying to accomplish something."

If this hadn't been a Thomas Edison quote, I would have thought it came from a conversation with Joe Jacobs.

Joe was a full-faced man with a massive brow and thin wavy hair. He was striking in appearance with his large nose, distinct ear lobes, and a wonderful double chin his grandchildren called his waddle. But what you noticed first was his welcoming smile, his openness, and genuine love for people and ideas. "Sweet Lovable Joe," he would call himself. Then he would laugh. He was approachable, unassuming, comfortable in this own skin and at ease with everyone with whom he came in contact.

Joe had a boyish curiosity that drove him, a chemical engineer by training but a seven-year-old boy with a chemistry set inside. He never lost his love for learning. And his devotion to discovery made him fall in love with cooking, baking, wine-making, and figuring out human nature.

He was a mind-racing search-for-meaning conversation — challenging, unabashed, willing to talk about any topic, including race and class — a topic that many men of his era seemed to want to avoid at all cost. He loved grappling with issues, ideas, and understanding people. And while he kidded about being able to speak "a thousand well-chosen words on any subject at any time," he was more likely to be in a debate. The back-and-forth tug of war of words and thought were his signature.

"People like Joe Jacobs have their own separate genre within philanthropy," noted Ralph Smith, former Executive Vice President of the Annie E. Casey Foundation, speaking admiringly of what he dubbed "wildcat" philanthropy. "This kind of risk-taking in philanthropy, which most people in a stewardship role feel compelled to avoid," he shared, "can only be practiced by the wealth-makers themselves."

Ralph, who was a long-time friend and advocate of our work, had coined the term "wildcat philanthropist" after getting to know Sam Gary, the founder of the Piton Foundation. Sam was in the oil and gas exploration business. Wildcatters drill for oil in areas not known for oil production. Sam loved to talk about the science, instinct, intuition, and risk-taking that drilling in an unproven area takes. For risks like this, Sam would say, "you look at the science, but then you have to make a decision and expect that you'll miss more than you hit. The majority of holes you drill are going to be dry and you have to accept that." He would also add that "drilling half way doesn't get you anything." When you take a risk of that scope and scale, you go for it — win or lose.

Wildcatters are all-in.

"If I look back on the half dozen riskiest things we have done at Casey," Ralph continued, "none come close to Market Creek Plaza."

Joe Jacobs was the "man in the arena" that Theodore Roosevelt described in his famous speech delivered in Sorbonne, Paris, in 1910 about daring greatly. He believed that success could only be measured against the real prospect of failure and that above all it was important to risk action.

Honored by the United Nations and given the Hoover Medal by the White House, Joe loved addressing the most pressing and challenging problems of his time. He wrote extensively — articles, editorials, and books — and taught himself cooking, baking bread, and making wine. Well into his 80's, he pursued a goal of learning the piano. A learner to the very end, Joe believed that life was to be lived at bat up at the plate, that you needed the courage every day to swing for the fences, and that if you practiced the fundamentals, all else would follow.

I was in a rare spot. I was in the fortunate and uncommon position to lead a foundation created by an all-in, give-while-you-live, wildcat philanthropist that intuitively knew the level of risk had to match the level of change the community was after. Too often in the field of social change, we talk about the level of money being mismatched to the scope and scale of the change we are seeking. But we've missed the more important ingredient — the level of risk.

"This genre of wildcat philanthropist takes us to the next level," Ralph Smith reflected. "The fear of failure has risen in today's evidence-based environment, so more than ever we need to encourage and embrace a new generation of pioneers."

In cultivating and encouraging risk-taking, Joe believed that "the emphasis has too often been on results" and "not enough stress placed upon the values inherent in the way in which one gets those results."[12] For success, he believed, leadership should keep its eye on <u>how</u> the game is played, not always what the end-result or bottom-line should be.

At that time (and perhaps even more so today), it was uncommon in foundations to hear people talk about risk, let alone placing a priority on operationalizing a set of values rather than driving home a set of predetermined results.

Could a philanthropic organization care more about the *how* than the *what*?

He wanted to design a way of helping that was based on dignity, respect, and breaking cycles of dependency. This meant we had to confront the irony of how the very ask-give relationship reinforces the sense of dependency, entitlement, disrespect, and lack of trust. Without addressing the "have and have-not" dynamic, we would never be able to fully address philanthropy's potentially corrosive and emotional complexity.

At that time, terms like social entrepreneur, impact investor, and venture philanthropist hadn't moved onto the landscape, but all of these terms suited Joe. He was a risk-taker and wanted his philanthropy to convey this in its approach.

We would be guided by the determination to operationalize a set of core values around **respect, relationship, responsibility, and risk**. These "Four R's" would become the core principles by which we would work, respecting and valuing what each person could bring to the table, working in relationship, being responsible to and not for, and putting ourselves in the risk position, accepting the possibility of failure.

A Culture of Innovation

"What business are you in?" Joe would ask.

He loved to tell the story that in the Lebanese culture people would never ask you what job you had; they would ask you what business you were in. It was at the core of Joe's sense of himself as an entrepreneur.

But in thinking about shaping a philanthropic agenda that mirrored Joe's entrepreneurial spirit, this question — simple enough — about what business we were in pushed us. In the early 1990s, most of us in foundations thought of ourselves as grantmakers.

But since a grant is a single tool, not a business identity, Joe's question — *what business are you in?* — along with the conversations that followed, challenged us to get clear about our purpose and then let ourselves think expansively and without limits when considering the tools we could bring to the table.

Throughout the history of institutional philanthropy from the time it was provided a corporate structure under the tax law (something some of the first multi-millionaires fought for in the early 1900s), what was intended to be a flexible nongovernmental structure for improving the quality of life for people had for the most part focused on only one tool — the cash grant — embedded within a larger sustainability framework that provided the mechanism for the long-term preservation and control of assets.

With economic development as a goal and not a grantmaking area of interest, we were confronted with the question about whether or not grants were even the best way to achieve it. If our mission was to build wealth and wealth-building takes the ability to leverage assets, not just income, it stood to follow that we should be leveraging our assets and not just our income.

The questions we began to pose were focused on the irony of wanting social innovation and change, while being rigid about our own structure, process, and tools. If one tool didn't work, we needed to create another. If our corporate structure didn't allow what we needed to get done, we needed to form another. If something didn't fit in our guidelines, we needed to feel free to change the guidelines. If something was stopping us, we wanted to make sure it wasn't a rule of our own making.

"You might strike out, but be OK with it", Joe would say. "If you don't swing, you will never hit the ball."

Often when I entered his office, he pointed to his statue of Babe Ruth and would read the inscription about Babe Ruth striking out 1330 times. He loved it. Like the stories of Thomas Edison and the Wright Brothers, who were undaunted by setbacks, the story of Babe Ruth swinging for the fences spoke to Joe and his deep-seeded belief that the most important element of success was not being afraid to fail.

The longer I knew Joe the more I realized that this was not just a lesson in playing the odds, like a venture capitalist who knows he's not going to hit every ball but is betting on the home run. It was more than that.

It was a lesson in daring, endurance, risk-taking, and most of all — courage. The courage to stand in there and not back away from the plate. The courage to steady yourself for the swing at the exact moment your very humanness makes you want to flinch or freeze.

Until I met Joe, I had found the non-profit world's never-ending need to solve the most depressing and entrenched issues of our day, at best, exhausting. At its worst, I found it demeaning, demanding, disrespectful, and thankless. So often non-profit leaders are the marathoners who run alone. They are people who run without water stations, protein snacks, music, or fans rooting them on. They just run.

But Joe made the experience of grappling with the impossible, improbable, and infeasible truly different. Energizing, instead of depleting. More often than not, the work to transform communities fails because we fail to champion our change-makers. To hand water to the marathoners. To say good job, don't give up, don't lose faith, look what you have done already, you can do this. Or better yet — we can do this! To challenge people to take risks, trust their instincts, reignite their creativity, and refresh or restore the will to change the future. And to remind them to celebrate every success, no matter how small.

For the 13 years I worked for Joe before he passed away, I was invigorated at every turn by challenging debates and the struggle to find that ever-moving sweet spot between structure and creative break-through. I was further energized by never having to waste a moment of time wondering about hidden agendas or worrying if we would be expected to make a policy, program, or conventional practice take priority over how we treated people.

I always knew Joe had my back. I knew if I got hit at the plate, he would be the first to pat me on the back, hand me an icepack, and say "good try!" Then he'd wait a minute or two and say "if you're still breathing, get back up to bat!"

This was his greatest gift.

He was an all-cards-on-the-table guy. He didn't like closed sessions of the board, confidential conversations, and people criticizing each other behind their backs. Get the critics in the middle of the room. If there's a problem, go to lunch. Confused about something? Call. A culture of risk demands a culture of openness and respect. He knew there was too much opportunity for people to get hit in their blind spots not knowing they weren't seeing the whole picture. Even if you don't like what people say, you'll like that they said it.

Joe was also thoughtful about the underlying values that stimulated risk-taking, created trust, supported teamwork, and made people "exultant," as he put it in his autobiography, <u>Anatomy of an Entrepreneur: Family, Culture, and Ethics</u>, "in attacking the ever-present enemy — failure."[13] He wrote about how his journey and his drive to reach for seemingly unattainable goals were deeply rooted in a commitment to family and community. As the child of an immigrant family, Joe believed that stepping out with courage is best done when supported by the power of close, trusting relationships. He also felt the tension between individualism and community. Wanting to belong and wanting to remain separate, achievement realized in a personal financial sense and success defined by animating long-held cultural values — these must be embraced and balanced.

His book would serve as the guiding document to inform the values of the foundation. It would be a foundation set up to encourage both personal responsibility and collective action. It would embrace risk-taking as a core value and nestle it inside a culture of trust and close relationships. It would look at business "as an expression of culture and morality" and see the importance of working at the intersection of social responsibility and market-driven approaches.

Joe believed that being an entrepreneur was in no way heroic. "I had no brilliant flashes of inspiration, no spectacular recognition of market need, no marvelous coincidence of being in the right place at the right time. I [simply] slugged it out in my chosen profession."[14]

My work to do with the foundation was to build a culture of risk-taking, undaunted by not having the right answer at the right time in the right place, but able to "slug" things out. A culture that waited for no one to come to solve problems but embraced them as opportunities. A culture that was not afraid of critics, conflict, or tension, tolerated no whiners, and thrived on impatience, pressure, and problem-solving.

As a one-generation foundation focused on "R&D" — the applied study of the "how" of philanthropy — we would organize our work around *strategies,* which were intended to keep pushing into pioneering territory, evolving, changing, and innovating, as opposed to *programs,* which carry with them the connotation that they will be refined, polished, and institutionalized.

We would abandon titles like Program Officer, the 5 percent rule, silo areas of interest, and traditional methods of determining the feasibility of investments, shedding anything we believed could kill innovation. We would come to define our primary customer not as the non-profit, but everyday citizens, and focus intensively on listening to them on what was needed, how it should be prioritized, who the extended partners should be, and the best path for building a future of inclusion and opportunity.

When Joe and I were beginning our work together, a report from the Rensselaerville Institute, titled "Assumptions for Innovation," gave me an important reference. It covered the content and process of innovation, the traits of people who innovate, and the conditions for innovating, managing innovation, and spreading innovations. In the report, the Institute observed that "Innovation is not readily institutionalized, given its origin in individuals who resist structural containment. Rather, it is the condition for encouraging and enabling employees to innovate that can be embedded in organizational fabrics."[15]

To work with Joe, I knew our organization would need to be able to "resist structural containment." With that in mind, it was important to create the conditions for encouraging and enabling people to innovate and embed that "in the organizational fabric." We would set out high expectations for managing quality, complexity, adaptability, and learning, all the time making sure it was balanced with those things that make people thrive — laughter, love, camaraderie, and fun.

Some people use recipes; they do what has been done before. They want evidence that something works. Proof that what they are seeking to do can be done.

Others dare; they throw out preconceived notions and create with all of life's ingredients. These people reorder the universe. Joe was one of these people.

Joe made us feel like the only thing standing in the way of change was — not policies, not procedures, not program designs, and not money — just the limits of our own imaginations.

"What if I strike out?" I asked. I would often kid Joe that if this didn't work he would have to agree to enroll me in the witness protection program.

"Strike out?" he would repeat and then laugh. "Swing anyway!"

3

OWNING OUR OWN CHANGE

"Courage starts with showing up and letting ourselves be seen."[16]

— Brené Brown, <u>Daring Greatly</u>

The Trouble with Money

"I don't understand why they don't call me!" Joe chirped in frustration. "They just treat me like a rich white man!"

Laughing I replied to Joe: "I hate to be the one to break it to you, but you ARE a rich white man! The trouble with philanthropy," I continued, "is money!"

Joe would always laugh. He was the first to understand. He was clear about the potentially corrosive nature of philanthropy. "We have had ample proof of the corruption caused by compassion," he would comment, grappling with the contradiction.

In expressing his frustration about his relationship with early grantees, he blurted out the comment about being treated "like a rich white man," and I blurted mine back about hating to be the one to break it to him. But after our laugh, I suggested that he go find out why they hadn't called.

He crossed town. He couldn't bridge the history of race and class embedded in the relationships staying in his international headquarters. But because he was a self-effacing man, comfortable in his own skin, and willing to engage in a personal relationship with these three directors, finding the solution to why they didn't call turned out an easy one.

"We would never dream of calling the chairman of a billion-dollar company!" noted one of the agency directors. It was a different world. Daunting. And in his corporate role, Joe personified the issues of have and have-nots that bring with them a history and the expectation of disrespect, condescension, and exclusion.

Like the agency directors, I had worked my entire philanthropic career in the hard position between people with wealth and those in need. It is heart work. Done with passion. But that very emotional investment is what makes you so vulnerable to its stress and the dramatic ups and downs of success and failure. You brace yourself.

I had taken on non-profit leadership roles with all the never-say-die determination my father had given me and the entrepreneurial spirit that small town life instills in people, and never missed a fundraising goal. But the longer I went in my career, the more I found myself shocked by all too frequent rudeness, back-biting, petty jealousies, disrespectful side-bar meetings, hidden agendas, feedback loops that were like playing a child's game of telephone, and condescending — even abusive — comments that would capture in a moment the very worst of money, class, and privilege. These are what leave people who have to raise money day in and day out for their causes and communities weak and enervated. Sometimes even heartbroken and defeated.

I started noticing that there were lots of us around. People who cared deeply; spent their long days willing things into being, encouraging everyone around them, standing up to complaints and put-downs; and rarely — if ever — experiencing any encouragement themselves. These are the folks for whom when everything is tallied and the goal achieved, there are no fans to applaud their achievement. They simply thank everyone else, stare at the overwhelming need, embrace the new goal, and start over.

The longer people are in the field, the deeper they experience this sense of the chasm between funders and those they serve. There is an emotional toll to keep crossing that divide.

So *Joe* crossed. And not just once, but over and over again, acknowledging that what caused the divide wasn't just unfortunate; it was unjust.

And *that's* what changed things.

Working in relationship with Joe helped me remember all the caring and courageous philanthropists over my career who committed time and hard-earned resources out of a deep passion for paying opportunity forward, who appreciated the teams on the ground for making the world a better place, and who accepted their own roles with grace and humility. These philanthropists were angels who, for a moment in time, touched my life and left a lasting mark.

With Joe, our goal became to cross over. To give and receive as a valued partner. To refill the room with energy. To have faith in people and their gifts and talents. To help them through those times they wanted to give up.

To do this work we needed to shed the discussions about how to "manage expectations" and ask people to put their biggest and boldest dreams on the table. And together, we would try to demystify the process, work in partnership, level or even tilt the playing field, and confront the inequality, hierarchy, and arrogance that is often experienced in the institution of philanthropy.

Joe was conflicted by being "rich," a word he reacted to negatively and with feelings of guilt. "Rich people were spoiled; rich people were greedy,"[17] he wrote in his autobiography describing his astonishment at being called rich. Our discussions about wealth — his own wealth — and philanthropy's potential for corroding relationships, were as much a part of the journey for Joe as the experience of giving. But in crossing over and courageously connecting in such a personal way with the people he invested in, he set a course for his own voyage toward understanding "rich" as a condition of the spirit.

Many years later, Joe would get a letter from a mom who wrote: "I feel rich because my kids will never have to feel what I felt. I will feel rich knowing they are growing up to be good-hearted human beings who are open to learning about other cultures and their minds are sensitive to other people's needs. This is my definition of rich."[18]

"I _am_ rich…" Joe said in one of our last conversations, "…in my relationships with others." He had made peace.

The Answers Lie Within

"Miss Anderson, there are no words."

The young man captured my exact feeling at the moment the ribbon was cut dedicating the new Elementary Institute of Science (EIS), one of our first and longest-term non-profit partners. We were all speechless.

Several years into our work together, we had incorporated a sister organization to give ourselves more flexibility in the roles we could play and the tools we could create — a private, operating foundation we named the Jacobs Center for NonProfit Innovation (later changed to Neighborhood Innovation). Through the Jacobs Center, we were able dive deeper into working on how to change our own charitable process, how to build relationships of give and take based on a commitment to shared learning, and how to be an active and committed stakeholder with shared ownership, shared decision-making, shared risk, and shared responsibility for change.

Doris Anderson, Executive Director of EIS, once said, "No one had ever asked us before what our plans were and how could they help. When you said you wanted to 'be at the table,' I didn't know what that meant. This idea of working side-by-side with a foundation wasn't something we understood."

We didn't either. We just had this idea that if we shared a common goal and put our teams together to achieve it, we might have a better shot at leaving truly sustaining capacity for community change.

We were "at the table" for the learning — about the pace of change, the catalysts for change, and the process of change. We worked on defining and clarifying our partnership roles and goals as the work evolved.

While capacity-building and unrestricted organizational strengthening grants are more common in foundations today, in the early 1990s, they weren't. We had left the shore of historical practice, and our early partners first cautiously, then wholeheartedly, came with us into this vast ocean, and we were pulled and buffeted by the powerful currents of possibility.

When I first met Doris Anderson — literally bumping into her in line at a reception following a training I had done — I thought the Jacobs family would love the Elementary Institute's program.

Joe had been supporting scholarships at his alma mater, Polytechnic University, in Brooklyn, New York, to help create access for African Americans, Latinos, and women into the science and technology fields, and the experience led the foundation to seek ways to invest earlier and earlier in young people's lives, knowing that by college it can be too late. I thought Joe would appreciate the EIS model of exposing young people to science at age seven, providing them an incredible jump start. EIS classes were fun, hands-on, and taught by college students who brought the very latest in biology, geology, physics, chemistry, and oceanography.

Joe, who had grown up in a struggling immigrant family, felt his life chances had been changed by a chemistry set given to him at age seven. He had gone on to get a Ph.D. in chemical engineering, putting him on a life path for founding and building one of the top engineering companies in the world. He connected with EIS's work and mission.

Doris told me later that when I asked her to apply for a grant from the foundation, she thought, "Right. I've heard that one before." Her small organization with its grassroots history had submitted many a proposal to no avail. "You just stop trying."

But she did it anyway. A test of sorts for us; a whisper of hope, I suppose, for her in thinking about what her children needed to succeed. She was gutsy, resourceful, set high standards, and ran an amazing program — you could feel it the moment you walked in.

Sitting where I sat, at the table of a family foundation, submitting a proposal for $10,000 in unrestricted funds could have seemed a bit like a lack of creativity and inspiration. But it was what they most needed.

"I couldn't believe my eyes when I opened the check!" Doris took a breath and slowly exhaled. "The foundation didn't make us structure a special program for kids that are green and live on the moon," she said. "They just gave us a vote of confidence that we knew best how to make a difference."

And so it began. Trust.

A year later, we stood out on the front dirt. "What do you want to do next?"

The Institute was on a hill. Doris looked out over the surrounding blocks — a landscape of blight, an old abandoned industrial dump, a deserted roofing company (we jokingly called the tar pits), vacant lots, barbed wire. She smiled and talked fondly about the "beloved community."[19]

"We are afraid to dream, but we know we need to," she said, "for our children."

This center had an amazing track-record of success, but the facility was substandard. The program had been in a 2,000-square-foot condemned house for its entire 30-year history. According to the kids there was a monster in the bathroom. A pipe-like snake that wound through the space, black and daunting.

"We owe it to the next generation to build a new facility, buy new equipment, give our children the very best opportunity to succeed," Doris said.

I had spent the first 20 years of my career doing large multi-million campaigns, so the Jacobs Family Foundation "loaned" me to the Elementary Institute of Science to help them plan a campaign. Because EIS had never raised more than $80,000 in its best year, when I did the campaign feasibility study, conventional wisdom indicated that even a $500,000 goal would be an incredible stretch. But seeing the excitement of the youth who loved the center, I couldn't bring myself to be the one to tell them a million-dollar building wasn't feasible.

Campaign theory would have called for seating a "who's who" board, a step I thought could be potentially damaging to the small organization, so this was one of those moments when you throw out conventional wisdom and move to Plan B — twelve of the youth agreed to be the lead campaign committee. It was from these youth (the youngest 10 years old), in a simple team-building exercise, that I learned one of my most important lessons about courage and the achievement of bold goals.

For the exercise, the youth were to divide into two groups, take a pile of straws, and construct the tallest free-standing structure they could build. They could talk during the planning but weren't allowed to speak during the construction. They decided to divide up by girls and boys.

As they started construction, both groups' first attempts failed. The girls sat and stared. The boys very carefully deconstructed and began again. At the end of the exercise, the girls' structure went four feet in the air and the boys never got their's off the ground.

As they debriefed about what had happened, the girls shared that when their first attempt failed, they decided not to plunge into rebuilding. And as they examined it, they realized that the way it had fallen provided a stable base to build on and took it up from there.

I watched in amazement as the young people put flip chart page after flip chart page on the wall about what they had learned.

There are times in your life when you know you have been changed forever. No going back. Like a charge of electricity just went through your body, you know that you are now in an altered state. There were no bands playing, no fireworks going off, no rapid heart-beating signaling that my life was changing.

Like the first great novel I ever read, these young people opened up a world I had never experienced. A world where people ponder with patience and perspective the things that don't appear to be working. Where it's OK to not know what you don't know. Where everyone around you jumps in with the excitement of the ah-ha moment. Where people share in an open and daring way, knowing that all ideas will be embraced.

All I could think about was all the initiatives we, as a field of philanthropy, have launched, struggled with, reported on, and closed out. If it doesn't work according to plan, our instinct is to step away, abandon it, tear it down, or let it fall apart. If we haven't solved something in a handful of years, we go away. Form a new theory and plan. Start over somewhere else. Then we are disappointed when what we invested in is not enduring in some way.

This new world was about stepping back, looking at what unfolded from all angles and all possibilities. It wasn't afraid of failure. This world was about looking for every lesson, challenging our view about what success, failure, and feasibility look like, building systematically on those lessons.

This world didn't let you walk away. It captured you with the simple idea that perhaps the answer is right in front of you — if you can see it.

Building on the lessons of anything and everything that went wrong, these young people at the Elementary Institute of Science went on to lead a campaign that by standard methodology was not feasible. They were hungry learners. Every decision they made was based on not what they already knew, but on what they wanted to learn.

The EIS board, inspired by the courage of their young leaders, planned and launched a campaign with a stretch goal of $4 million and raised over $6 million. A game-changing achievement. Today, a 15,000-square-foot state-of-the-art science institute serves the next generation of youth in their community and stands as a symbol of the power of learning.

It wasn't just that the answers were right in front of them all along; it was that the answers were in them all along.

The Courageous and Disruptive Voice for Change

"Don't call us poor. Don't call us disenfranchised. And how can you even think we need a $500 loan when you can't even buy a computer for that!"

As the facilitator of the planning retreat, I paused.

A board member speaking with great pride about replicating a micro-lending model of targeting "poor and disenfranchised people for $500 loans" was stopped in his tracks.

At this moment, I came to realize just how thoughtful and forward-thinking this board and staff were. Although it was (and is) common practice for strategic planning to be seen as a function of the board and top management team to be done behind closed doors, Accion New Mexico invited a group of micro-entrepreneurs — clients and potential clients — to participate in their planning.

As the field of micro-enterprise was spreading in the early 1990s, the Jacobs Family Foundation had supported micro-lending organizations in Mexico, Latin America, and northern Africa. We had worked with Accion International on its U.S. resource strategy and its launch of the U.S. Network and helped Accion New Mexico raise its start-up capital. About a year out, I agreed to facilitate the Accion New Mexico planning retreat. Anne Haines, the CEO of the organization, and I had an immediate and natural values alignment about inviting entrepreneurs into the process.

Anne and I never thought the invitation to clients to participate was a risk we were taking. We thought it was being inclusive of all voices that mattered and didn't hesitate. But in looking back on the experience two decades later — over which time I saw the hesitation and fear of innumerable CEO's about the idea of open, participatory planning that includes the voices of those to be served at the same table as their boards — I have come to see Anne's openness as courageous. The epitome of grace under pressure, with a quick wit and warm embracing style and smile, I grew to marvel at the risks she was willing to take. Undaunted by criticism and a hungry learner, she opened the door to many powerful learning moments for me and others around her.

On the day of the Accion retreat, the entrepreneur's bold reaction to being called poor and her questioning the appropriateness of a $500 loan helped us realize in a flash how easily these insights can be missed if stakeholders are not invited into central roles in organizational planning.

In response to this entrepreneur and the others in the room, Accion quickly launched a task force, including board, staff, and clients, to innovate on the Latin American model, making it relevant to the U.S. market.

"The entrepreneurs so enriched the process by creating a moment of insight and exchange," reflected Anne. By the time other micro-lending programs were realizing that solidarity groups weren't an easy fit in the United

States, Accion New Mexico was already expanding state-wide, innovating on not just the products but the entire delivery system.

This was innovation on steroids, triggered by bringing the people served into the middle of the room.

The message from this entrepreneur was loud and clear and changed how we thought and acted. We no longer talked about helping poor people or working in a poor community or used terms like "under-privileged" to describe the people we served or the residents with whom we partnered.

As we were challenged to change our language, we had to reframe our work. As we reframed our work, it opened new doors of learning.

That we were having a "moving" experience was not lost on any of us. We were all moved. We were moving along a path of shedding our view of grassroots stakeholders as people we needed to help to people whose help we needed. This moment was pivotal. And it began pushing us gradually away from a model of community change based primarily on professional problem-solving to one that honored and activated the wisdom, creativity, and experience of residents as central players in the change process.

The courage that groups like the Elementary Institute of Science and Accion New Mexico showed was a gift. And like the many other daring partners we had during our non-profit strengthening years, Doris and Anne taught us that we — as a foundation — also needed to take the risk of lifting up the voice of our stakeholders, that we needed to be careful about assumptions, that learning by doing was more powerful than putting people in a classroom, and that it's better to be an active partner than an expert.

They taught us to be clear about values and to be willing to change everything but these. They taught us that collaboration needs to unfold gradually and organically and that there is a pace to change that requires a sixth sense about people's cracking points and requires not just persistence, but patience.

From these partnership projects, we also learned that new approaches require new voices. That the disruptive voice can be the one you most need to hear. That listening needs to be intentional and takes practice and structure.

By "speaking the truth in love,"[20] they helped us till a fertile ground for learning. And they taught us — like all great relationships — communication is hard, getting and staying on the same page is difficult, keeping your heart open is essential, and in the best ones, both parties are changed forever.

By holding up a mirror, they taught us how to own our own change.

OPENING THE DOORS TO CHANGE

ASKING MATTERS

4

THE POWER OF LISTENING

"Courage is what it takes to stand up and speak;
courage is also what it takes to sit down and listen."

— Winston Churchill

Taking A Lesson from Village Goats

In 1992, LA burned. Following the trial of the police officers that were accused of beating Rodney King and the riots that erupted, Joe Jacobs remarked emphatically: "Business has a responsibility. Those of us who believe in the free market system need to open it up."

It was a catalytic moment. People began calling me, urging me to have Joe put his money where his mouth was — a point well taken — but Joe was willing to take it the next step. He wanted to put his mouth where his money was. He wanted to help people achieve ownership.

This led the Jacobs Family Foundation to fund a collaboration of non-profit agencies working on entrepreneurship. We led with money. Big money for us. And based on the gaps community leaders saw, we put legal help with a group of agencies to design a "lenders partnership" to get big business to guarantee loans at a consortium of banks to lend to the non-profits to lend on to small businesses. The program design, the legal work, and the financial structure were all groundbreaking.

But our decision to lead with money and predetermine the collaborating partners we thought should work together set the table for disappointment and left me agreeing with U.S. Surgeon General Joycelyn Elders' quote about collaboration being an "an unnatural act by non-consenting adults,"[21] vowing never to do it again.

But the lesson wasn't really about whether or not collaboration is a good thing. We had forced the collaboration of the three agencies by tying their funding together — whether they wanted it or not. What we had given was a good idea but based on bad assumptions. Sound logic and brilliant legal work, but bad assumptions. We determined for others what they wanted and needed based on our own frame-of-reference. We didn't ask.

It was a big lesson. We thought the money would change the level of cooperation and improve the coordination of services. But we were trying to coerce change, push success, put people in circumstances that they didn't own. Change was resisted.

This early collaboration was invaluable. Both because of the lessons about the corrosive nature of leading with money and pre-determining who gets a seat at the table, and because it got us into a deep conversation about ownership. You can't give people ownership. They have it or they don't.

We decided to stop channeling "best practice" and re-arranging people's furniture (as we began to call it) until we were invited in, sat a while, built a relationship and were asked by people if we thought the couch would look better switched with the chair.

Two years later I was on assignment teaching participatory planning methods to an NGO that would then train others throughout the middle east and northern Africa. In the villages, I noticed a number of economic projects that had been built and then abandoned. When I asked why, I got a similar answer in every village — "We never really wanted it. What we really wanted were goats." No one asked.

When we got back to the United States, we decided we were going to make a practice of asking. And not just non-profit leaders. We were going to open up to the voice and involvement of residents whose lives were impacted every day by disinvestment in that listening. Door-to-door. Block-by-block.

The people that lived there, worked there, worshipped there, grew up there, and went to school there. We were going to ask for their help in our becoming relevant to the change they wanted to see.

It was time to take a lesson from goats.

In 1997, familiar with international community development, one of Joe and Vi's daughters suggested the foundation focus on a disinvested neighborhood and work across all the issues with all the people, all the complexity, and all the conundrums (as I loved to call them); figure out what worked and didn't work; leave a set of lessons for the next folks coming along; and go out of business.

The guiding documents of the foundation had a sunset clause making it a single-generation operation. Going out of business was especially important to Joe, who believed as foundations get farther away from the person or people who made the money, the more potential there was for disconnecting from its original mission, guiding principles, and entrepreneurial spirit.

The board agreed wholeheartedly, and with Joe's go-figure-it-out attitude leading the charge, they were game to throw out the recipe for how foundations typically operated.

No leading with money. No initiatives. No RFPs. We were going to move into the community and work side by side with residents as neighbors. Ours would be a learning partnership with a community, drawing out the wisdom, creativity and problem-solving of everyone, built on the power of having different and disruptive voices in the deliberation about direction.

And as Peter Block put it — be with people who we weren't used to being with and have conversations we weren't used to having.[22]

Informed by the lessons of the early collaboration, our non-profit partnerships, and the people in the Cairo villages, the questions that would lead us as we began our journey into community change were: To be a truly relevant partner, what would it really take? And to stimulate large-scale ownership of change, what kind of process, approach, and guiding principles do we need?

For even the most courageous among us, the complexity of the issues faced by people in communities that have suffered disinvestment is overwhelming. It is impossible to have answers. But to let go of the instinctive need to have those answers can be even more unsettling than the complexity.

Its impact on me was immediate.

We rented a vacant building in the community that had been a grocery store 30 years earlier, so it was a large open space, perfect for community gatherings. At our first open house over 200 people turned out.

"What are you going to do about the gangs?" a man stood up in the back of the room and yelled. It stopped me in my tracks. What was I going to do? Would I recommend funding prevention programs? Juvenile diversion programs? Midnight basketball? Or on a more macro-level, take on economic distress, concentrated poverty, urban policy, prison reform, school reform, or go after the crime rate? In the seconds I had to respond to the man's question all I could think of was goats.

I looked up at the man in the audience and said: "I don't know. What do you want to do about the gangs?"

To have the answers is to disempower people, stay in control, take ownership of action. Dead on arrival.

Three years later, that man would come up to me. He had actively participated on a number of teams. "I used to think you didn't know anything about anything." He paused. "But now I know that was a strategy!" He smiled and hugged me.

I guess I felt vindicated — or at least relieved — that he no longer saw me as completely incapable of solving problems. That had to be some kind of success indicator, I thought, although the truth was, I didn't know.

Over the next decade and a half, I got good at saying "I don't know...but what do you think?"

We had to step out of what we knew so residents could step into what they knew and see their own ability to contribute in a really significant and important way, and that meant I would have to let go of everything I thought

I knew about leadership, accept the enormous complexity of opening up a foundation's decision-making to broad-scale resident voice, acknowledge that I didn't really know what to do, and be willing to learn my way. I would have to learn to ask.

"Most foundations are 'head leads the hand' — we research," commented Michael Bailin. At that time, he was President of the Edna McConnell Clark Foundation. They were just launching their strategy to partner with organizations around long-term capacity-building, and we were comparing notes over dinner.

"But yours," he commented, "is 'hand leads the head' — you are always asking what can be learned from trying to make things work."

Our work was like attending the college of experiential learning. Practical and applied. Train to a task. Learn by doing. Experiment our way into solutions.

I kept conjuring up a line from American journalist H. L. Mencken: "Penetrating so many secrets, we cease to believe in the unknowable; but there it sits nevertheless, calmly licking its chops."[23]

I had this image of "The Unknowable," as a person sitting beside me kind of tickled that I was actually trying this. It made me want "to run on and see what the end's gonna be," and I could almost hear Sweet Honey and the Rock singing the refrain of the old gospel hymn like it was our theme song.

Organizationally embracing "The Unknowable" was a compounded challenge. We not only had to shed the "expert consultant" dynamic, but we also had to confront the foundation paradigm of being used to calling the shots.

When you don't, who does? And then what? Everyone we worked with was initially and periodically confused. Our non-profit and philanthropic partners just wanted to know what we were going to do and the timeline for doing it.

All I knew was that we needed to stay the course.

At a family foundations conference, someone asked me: "How do you get so much buy-in? We developed a youth center and don't know why it isn't used." The answer was we were striving to stop figuring out how to get buy-in for <u>our</u> ideas; we wanted to flip it. Like the lessons about the goats in the villages surrounding Cairo, we were now the ones learning to listen and buy in.

And that would mean that I would have to — as Rilke so aptly phrased it in his 1908 <u>Letters to a Young Poet</u> — not just ask the questions, but "*live the questions,*"[24] hoping someday to live my way into the answers.

5

DON'T DO ABOUT ME WITHOUT ME

---

*"We know as individuals that destinations chosen for us by others
rarely lead to our success or meet their expectations.
The same can be said for peoples, communities,
and indeed the country as a whole."* [25]

— Peter Pennekamp, "Philanthropy and the Regeneration
of Community Democracy"

Respect and Scrappiness

"My grandmother used to tell us *'**don't do about me without me!**'* She didn't coin the phrase but used it."

The day that Marisa Aurora Quiroz was describing her abuela, from whom she takes her middle name, Aurora was off protesting an oil spill.

"She's amazing!" chuckled Marisa, with her bright smile and her gracious and graceful style. "She could always put herself in other people's shoes. She was not detached from the woman who could not feed her family or from the person who could not find a job. From an early age, she taught us about social movements, talked about our ancestors coming from all over the world, made us feel like global citizens."

When Marisa used her grandmother's mantra "don't do about me without me" in one of the meetings in the community, it turned heads. "It was an equity thing for my grandmother. You need to ask."

We have both wasted resources and done harm to residents and their communities by making decisions that they should have been involved in. In addition, we are ignoring the greatest tool we have at our disposal — the wisdom, experience, and creativity of people on the ground in their own neighborhoods.

"It is all about dignity, people's ability to make choices about their own lives, and the scrappiness of the community teams," Marisa reflected. "You need that scrappiness."

Early in my non-profit work, I was trained by the Institute of Cultural Affairs (ICA) in their "Technology of Participation" (ToP) ©, which is both a philosophy and a set of easy facilitation methods that can cull the wisdom in a room and organize it for action. ICA had used these ToP methods all over the world, working across languages, ages, cultures, and levels of education.

When we were starting our work, ICA International had just conducted a multi-site evaluation on the impact of participation on agriculture and health in rural Kenya. In the report, its author, Mary D'Souza, contended: "When the will and motivation of village people are invigorated through grassroots participation, villagers find the ways to feed their children, build their roads, educate their families, and save their land."[26]

What she experienced was the power of people to tackle critical issues when support is offered for them to come together and work on issues of common concern. The villagers, having a stake in solving one problem, solved many problems.

In her research on the impact of participation, D'Souza went on to write: "Too often it [citizen participation] is seen as a low priority, thus becoming a 'good idea' added to some major, 'hard' or macro project. Too often it is pushed to an afterthought, causing the local participation factor to be viewed as 'more trouble than it is worth'."[27]

Also informing our approach was Charles Ballard, the founder of the pioneering National Institute for Responsible Fatherhood and Family Revitalization, one of our early non-profit partners. Charles was a soft-spoken and humble man whose influence on our organization was immense.

Growing up without a father, then becoming a teenage unwed and uninvolved father himself, followed by time in prison, Charles' life was changed forever by his decision on his release from prison to return and parent his child. Transformed, Charles then went back to school, earned his GED, Bachelor's and Master's degrees, and used the power of his personal story to help men connect with and take responsibility for their children. Passionate about stemming the rising rate of children growing up without fathers, Charles was brilliant in turning men with children into active and involved parents and was instrumental in launching the national fatherhood movement.

When I first met Charles in the early 1990s and wanted to understand and experience his work, I expected a prescribed set of activities — drug treatment sessions, job training, parenting classes — but while his program included these, what was transformative in these fathers' ability to get work, hold a job, get off drugs, and live a life they were proud of, including respecting and supporting their child's mother, was Charles' ability to draw out through a set of questions an awakening that moved them to ownership of action. His favorite question was: What would it take?

Charles would go into a prison, sit with a group of men and begin engaging them. "How many children do you have? What do you hope your son or daughter will say about you? If you want them to say you were there for them, what would you need to do? What would it look like? What would it take?" He didn't say "you should" or "why don't you." Through questions, he empowered them to figure it out for themselves; look inside to find the answers; own the change.

In our search for "hard" community development outcomes — number of acres of blight removed, square feet of new construction, jobs created, houses rehabbed — we have failed to incorporate the most important factors in human resiliency: relationships and people's belief that they are capable. By pre-determining a program design we think will address an issue and working in silos that separate how people look at their lives, we have closed down the creativity of people to address the issues in front of them.

We are not only being disrespectful by doing "about me without me," we are undercutting the natural will, motivation, and expectations for change that are needed for change to occur. In addition, by predetermining the agenda for change, we are undermining the "scrappiness" of the people with staying power.

By simply asking people "What would you like to see and what would it take?" we are cultivating the answers from within and stimulating the power of ownership.

In response to these lessons, we answered the question that resonated from Joe's Lebanese heritage about what business we were in as "*the resident ownership of neighborhood change.*"

We believed if we trusted people, they would seize opportunity. If they were at the forefront of creating the opportunity, they would have ownership of it. If they had ownership, they would have pride. Pride raises expectations for change and higher expectations push the envelope. Most importantly, working together in relationship changes us all.

Transformational change does not happen through increased productivity or filling gaps in services; when the existing elements need to be reordered and people accept ownership of a new future, people can muster the courage to act across organizational, sectoral, generational, and cultural boundaries.

Putting ourselves continuously in situations where new insight can be gained, a new world view can be adopted, a culture of dreaming big and taking risks can be embraced, and courage to try new ways of being are the norm — this is what opens the door to change.

6

INCLUSION STARTS WITH US

"It is true that the work of every expert panel has
a step called 'citizen engagement.'
This usually means that the experts take 'input' from citizens and
formulate recommendations; then they position the recommendations
so that citizens will 'feel heard.'
'Getting input' is a form of lip service that keeps ownership
and control in system hands. [28]

— John McKnight and Peter Block, <u>The Abundant Community</u>

The Voice That's Missing

"When you are in an agency like that you are only going to be able to hear three voices."

At the 2014 National Conference on Dialogue and Deliberation, David Mathews spoke about his term as Secretary for the U.S. Department of Health, Education and Welfare, which was one department prior to 1979 — the "Godzilla of government organizations," as he called it.

"You can hear the voice of politicians, and you should; you can hear the voice of experts and skilled professionals, and you should; and you can hear the voice of those groups that represent special interests, and you should. But what you don't hear," he continued, "is a public voice — the voice of people struggling with the tensions inherent in every decision. The tone of that voice is different from the other voices. It's pragmatic, practical and not ideological."[29]

In foundations, the voices we hear are not unlike what Mathews expressed in his speech about government. A public voice is largely absent. We listen to service providers; we pay for arms-length research and aggregated surveys, and we listen to each other. Then behind the closed doors of a board room, a small elite determines what will best serve the public's interest without ever directly consulting the public.

In the world of philanthropy, we must stare in the face the conundrum of money, power and control, have and have nots, and propensity toward professional elitism that limits rather than expands the playing field, and determine if we have an obligation to hear what David Mathews now, President of the Kettering Foundation, calls "a public voice."

Dr. Mathews, whose 2014 remarks were later turned into a published report, *A Public Voice That's Missing*," notes: "The public voice that I am talking about, the voice that is often missing, doesn't really exist until it is formed by the interaction of people as they attempt to solve common problems or decide on policies...It is the sound of people engaging one another, not simply the unconnected aggregation of individual expressions. It is the voice of democracy in its most basic form."[30]

It is an unfortunate disconnect in the field of community change philanthropy that this voice is rarely at the table, both because "there are things that a public voice can convey that no other voice can," as Mathews noted in his address, but also because creating the conditions for a public voice to arise catapults understanding, grows our appreciation of differences, and mends a polarized citizenry — the fundamentals of an inclusive, empowered, and deliberative democracy.

Graciously hosting me for lunch one afternoon, Dr. Mathews, with his look of distinction and his charismatic Southern drawl that can hold you spellbound begging for each new word, remarked: "Our institutions are bound and determined to 'do unto others.' No one would argue that people don't need training and education or that there are no impediments," he continued, "but it sends a message that 'you are deficient.' Often, we want people to do the work in the way we do it. But how do people engage on their own terms? Power is the ability to act. Power has to be in yourself."

As we enter the next generation of community change philanthropy, we must define residents, not as consumers of services, but as citizens who are capable of taking charge of change in their own lives and in their communities. We must work with them to build an infrastructure to support and sustain civic action, not as a touchy-feely idea that just happens to be getting better results, but because we are bold enough to stand on principle.

Inclusion needs to be more than a grantmaking focus.

It is time to end the long-held practice of doing "about me without me" and acknowledge that inclusion starts with us; appreciating differences starts with us; being willing to have our own world-views challenged and changed starts with us.

What are we waiting for?

LEADING
CHANGE

COURAGE IN A COMPLEX WORLD

7

TALENT WITH THE GUTS TO FAIL

"Vision without guts is fantasy." [31]

— Toba Beta

Guts

"No one has an unbroken string of victories and no one knows this better than an entrepreneur," Joe would say. "It's about intuition, hard work, and guts."

I knew about hard work and guts. I had grown up living Thomas Edison's quote: "Opportunity is missed by most people because it is dressed in overalls and looks like work." I was from a small Ohio town where there were few jobs, so we learned to create our own opportunity. My mom never told me I couldn't travel the world, though there was no money to send me anywhere. Instead she would say, "if you want to do it, figure it out."

With a friend, I had spent a summer working on a farm in Kentucky. Before the mass distribution of produce year-round, farmers had a very short window to get their crops to market. Watching this, we took advantage of the opportunity. Because tomatoes ripened six weeks earlier in Kentucky than in Ohio, we rented a three-quarter-ton truck (I was barely old enough to have my driver's license), bought tomatoes out of the fields, and hauled them to Ohio to sell. Using this six-week window, we were not only able to help the farmers unload produce stuck in the pipelines for the big producers of canned tomatoes, but I earned the money I needed to feed my wanderlust and travel to England, France, Belgium, Switzerland, Austria, and across the U.S. By the second year, I was able to use this business income to get myself to college.

Often holding my breath on the backroads of Kentucky, this indelible experience taught me about the risks and rewards of entrepreneurial ventures. And it taught me about the realities of hard work and guts.

I was born in a time when it was possible to grow up never seeing a woman doctor, lawyer, pilot, police officer, professor, or politician, so my sense of risk-taking and guts took on a broader social and economic justice meaning. I was challenged and changed by the women's movement and the social justice landscape of my generation — Brown vs. The Board of Education, the Civil Rights Act, bus boycotts, freedom rides, grape boycotts, and Title IX.

At fifteen I joined this struggle, working one summer with the Eastern Shoshone and Northern Arapaho building schools on the Wind River Reservation and another with Cezar Chavez and the Mexican American Farmworker Union in their effort to organize boycotts for better working conditions in California. In college, I was one of a group of Ohio women who successfully advocated for the marriage tax as a sustaining resource for domestic violence programs and the initial battered women's shelters. For the next twenty years, I raised money for causes I believed in — higher education, healthcare, and abused children — connecting people with wealth to the chance to create change.

By the time I met Joe Jacobs, I felt well suited to an entrepreneurial approach and had significant leadership experience. But if 70 percent of what builds leadership are "stretch opportunities," the challenge of the work ahead of me was about to provide an opportunity to learn about leadership in a way that no mentor, training, workshop, seminar, or degree could have prepared me.

What would become known as the Market Creek experience had its roots in a community meeting called by city, state, and metropolitan planning area personnel funded on a short-term grant to convene a discussion about the intersection of the two main thoroughfares through the community. In the meeting I could see that residents where concerned about the abandoned factory at the intersection and the scale of the blight surrounding it.

Attending that meeting was Doris Anderson, the Executive Director of the Elementary Institute of Science, and she was willing to present at a foundation board meeting to share what took place and the significance of dealing with the old factory. At the board meeting Joe exclaimed, "Let's buy it!"

And so we did.

The area was considered high risk, stigmatized by violence, the site contaminated, and the project considered not feasible. My calls to developers were returned at the mention of 20 acres, but when they learned where the property was located, they never called back again.

"You do it," Joe said one day with a smile on his face. "You lead us home."

I looked at him stunned. This was the development of a toxic dump that had every conceivable barrier to success. "But I don't have any development experience," I said.

He put his hand on my shoulder and told me to figure it out, follow my instincts, and not to be afraid of failure. "If this site *could* have been developed by people who *know* development," he said, "it *would have been* developed already."

I agreed to take it on not fully knowing how much of a stretch experience it would be or what guts it would ultimately require.

Remembering the fun and fearlessness with which the young people from the Elementary Institute of Science ran their campaign, we formed a cross-disciplinary team of risk-takers — a community builder, a commercial developer, a team builder, and me, a resource developer — and went to work on the long, hard undertaking of learning each other's languages and developing a common understanding of the work.

Roque Barros, the community builder, was a brilliant organizer. He never asked "how do I get people engaged in my issue," but rather "how do I engage people in the issues they care most about." He was a whisperer. An attractor. A magnet for the flying fragments of community momentum. Prior to coming to work for the foundation, he had been working in Mexico, two border towns, helping women organize their communities and build schools. Then he linked them to women in the U.S. and Canada who were doing similar things. He was a microscope, able to drill down, and a telescope, able to see the movement of the galaxy, in the same package.

At Halloween that year, Roque gave residents access to the property for a haunted house and family festival, which began to connect people to the site. Hundreds of families turned out.

"I never knew anyone who knew anyone who ever worked here," a local resident said. There was a fascination to go on the property and see inside the old building. "It was kind of creepy," Roque noted, "the perfect place for Halloween!"

Right after the event, Roque urged us to take down the barbed wire that formed the periphery barrier to the site. "It sends the wrong message," he said. He was right. When the barbed wire came down, the site quickly became a beacon for change.

From Roque's early work — surveys, door-to-door outreach, living room meetings, and hundreds of gatherings with groups throughout the surrounding neighborhoods — it was clear that people wanted to work together on securing a major grocery, first and foremost. Beyond that, a drug store, coffee shop, restaurants, bank, and community jobs.

Chip Buttner, a veteran of over 120 commercial projects, volunteered to help us interview other developers for the project and was not surprised when we came up empty. "You couldn't run a development company with these conditions," he noted at the time. "Developers are risk-takers, but this is too big of a risk." But because Joe wanted the foundation to serve as the community's development partner, we were able to talk Chip into being the one. He was comfortable with the idea of working with residents and — like Joe — was an entrepreneur by nature. He was the perfect development teammate.

Chip understood Joe and his commitment to building ownership, blending economic and social bottom-lines, and leverage. "Joe knew that leverage was the way for residents to make money," Chip reflected. "A foundation model of paying for things with cash grants doesn't get you the kind of leverage communities need. Greater risk, greater return."

Ron Cummings was the team-builder, "the values guy" as people called him. "Are we holding ourselves accountable to our 4 R's," he would ask, "respect, responsibility, relationship, and risk?" Ron brought his background in teaching, management of large teams, and juvenile justice. People sought him out when tough decisions had to be made and there was no clear path. Residents and team members alike trusted him to do the right thing.

Along with my background in mobilizing resources for large capital projects, we became the small, but gutsy team that would guide the process toward the "resident ownership of neighborhood change." Fun became our signature, learning our purpose, and questions our agenda.

Could you do development in a open community process? Would retailers be willing to put businesses down the street from the Four Corners of Death? Would residents trust us enough to get involved? How would the commercial timelines sync with the community organizing timelines?

We sat around my dining room table, tossing candy at each other — leftover from the Halloween party — for every and any good idea. Facing a daunting unknown, we kept our spirits high with humor. We created a short-term action plan, and then, to have fun with Joe's self-acknowledged impatience, a plan to transform the world in 90 days; "Joe's Plan" we called it. We laughed. And then laughed more. As a testament to who Joe was, he laughed at the plan too, but then told us to get busy.

For 15 years, no one could make me laugh harder than this team. Like siblings, we fought and played. No team ever worked harder or played harder. Humor always broke the tension, got us through the tough moments, gave us energy for action. On each other's birthdays or on down days when our spirits had taken a beating, we drank tequila, played drums, sang at the top of our lungs — "No Woman No Cry" — and by Monday morning were ready to embrace the charge to come back and tackle the impossible.

Our goal was to assure residents had a voice in planning their vision of a centerpiece to a vibrant village and could use the development to build resumes, get access to jobs, and recruit the businesses they wanted in their neighborhood. And we would do it with the idea of leverage and community benefit at the forefront.

The entire undertaking — not surprisingly — was fraught with challenges, but Joe's advice to me was simply "Don't stop. Take any role that's needed to keep moving."

After years of thinking about and talking with Joe about risk, I would have my mind-changing moment of truth about the risk I was taking. It would occur at the end of a long day when a resident recruited to serve on the original outreach team sat down next to me to share some coconut bread she had baked. I asked her about her day.

"I was so scared to knock on the door of my neighbor I had to get down on my knees and pray," she shared with me. "I was shaking."

She had survived.

She had gone door to door on her block, afraid at every knock, her courage tested at every encounter. While I was going along all day thinking about our risk — the possibility of losing the foundation's money — she was thinking about her life.

I never uttered the words "we are taking all the risk" again. This was clearly about "shared risk" in every sense of the word. The risk residents took to step out of their homes and the courage they held in their hearts, daring to dream of a better place for their children and grandchildren — these were incredible risk-takers.

"Now that's guts," I thought.

The Willingness to Face Failure

"I have not failed," Thomas Edison was quoted as saying. "I've just found 10,000 ways that don't work."

There were days when I thought we must be approaching this number as well.

There are case studies documenting the process, the teamwork, the financing, and the structure of Market Creek's resident ownership strategy. But these descriptions of the work never explored the dynamic of organizational and team culture we built upon Joe's unwavering faith in people's ability to figure things out. To truly engage in social innovation, we needed an organizational culture that could both expand people's thinking and help them overcome their fear of failure. We also needed a core team that was seasoned enough to take big risks and entrepreneurial enough to stare failure in the face. We needed big talent.

We sought out people who were entrepreneurial and deeply experienced in a discipline, but who valued listening and learning over knowing. People who were open, responsive, and quick learners. Team members were expected to bring a point of view, but also understand other people's points of view. We sought out people who had a "get-er-done" attitude and orientation, but who valued process and working through teams. They had to be to pathfinders, facilitators, and attractors.

Team members had to be able to work with a great deal of uncertainty, be unfazed with controlling few of — and sometimes none of — the critical variables, and be able to push themselves out of their comfort zones. They had to be bold, resilient, positive, with both deep professional expertise and good relationship skills. They also had to be humble, have a sense of humor, and be open to learning.

We were very careful in our team recruitment and approached it as life-path hiring. We were often criticized for the depth and length of our hiring process, but over the years, we built a strong team that thrived in this challenging environment, deeply loved the work, and respected resident process.

When innovation poses the possibility of failure, most efforts have trouble attracting and retaining human resources. People don't want to be associated with projects that appear at times not to be working or are perceived as "too risky" or certain to fail.

To attract people to this field, Joe and the board were committed to paying people what they were worth in the field of their experience, even if this wasn't considered "average" within family foundations. "If average pay gets you average people, you had better pay for the talent you really need," Joe would say. This community had been disinvested for a long time and if we were going to take this big of a risk, we didn't need mediocre; we needed talent. Joe didn't see this as "overhead," he saw it as funding a valuable resource for a do-tank.

To build a culture that could support this kind of team — where there was an expectation that you would "risk failure" — we also had to be careful to make sure a "cover-your-ass" dynamic didn't develop. Staff working in unproven areas can spend enormous amounts of time justifying what they are trying. As Clayton Christensen framed it in *The Innovator's Dilemma:* "Every innovation is difficult. That difficulty is compounded immeasurably, however, when a project is embedded in an organization in which most people are continually questioning why the project is being done at all."[32]

What was challenged in the organization was inaction — hitting a wall and stopping — never failed attempts. People were expected to understand hitting barriers as "the work" and not a frustration to get through to get the work done. Barriers were to be identified, clarified, and named. Team members were expected to know where they were stuck and why they were stuck. Figure out if there was a way over, under, or through. And if they couldn't see where to go next, they needed to convene a team, which not only stimulated creativity, but took the pressure off.

In these creative jam sessions, it was often the person with the least applicable and transferable technical experience who could see the way through. Both in the community and in our internal teamwork, we moved toward mix-and-match teams to constantly change the voices and experience in the room.

Many philanthropic leaders I spoke with over the years about opening up the field to greater flexibility for teams to set agendas equated it with lack of accountability. As a person who has very high standards for the quality of work from the sharpness of the vision to the smallest details of implementation, I was also concerned about the risk of lowered standards. What I learned, however, was the power of teams as a strong and effective accountability structure. People rarely had to be addressed by a supervisor for poor performance or lack of follow-through. These showed up quickly and peer pressure pushed everyone to be accountable to the team. Action agendas were reviewed by every team at every meeting and they created a "no excuses" dynamic. If someone's part wasn't moving, everyone knew it.

My role involved the creation of what I called "containers" for our strategic direction which required that I experience the natural momentum of these teams. I was very aware how much people needed assurance that I would stand by them and be there if anything went wrong. When someone was uncertain about an approach or direction, people would come to my office for ideas, advice, but more importantly, my vote of confidence.

Our culture of risk relied on Joe and the board having my back, and for me to have the backs of the rest of the team. If something did go wrong or didn't work, people were always given the opportunity to it figure it out, find a new path, or correct a problem.

Praise was sincere, criticism freely sought, and whining not tolerated. "The first one to say this can't be done gets fired!" team members used to kid. Fun, laughter, jokes, rowdiness, close friendships, and our celebratory outlets for tension belied the high expectations that people held and the hard work they did day by day. It kept us mapping the open ocean of possibilities and willing to work in uncharted waters.

More than once I wanted to put my head down on the desk and cry. Failures hurt. We all took them hard. But in the culture we built, we all knew that what felt like failures were merely setbacks, and that all of them were just moments in time.

A Love of Learning

Our muscles have memories.

Growing up before Title IX, which opened the door to a range of options for female athletes, I had few visible choices in my small town, but somehow decided I was going to ski. Because skiing was one of those sports considered too expensive by my parents, I got a job at a local ski area in the rental department so I could learn to ski for free. I studied the ski school instructors from the sidelines and then worked to figure it out for myself. By 19, I was the first woman and youngest person to ever make the ski patrol at this resort. I became a really good skier.

Fast forward 40 years. I updated my 12-year-old skis without thinking about the change in the ski technology that had occurred and immediately found myself struggling on the mountain, taking one fall after another. I could count the times I'd fallen over those 40 years on one hand, so I was confused and shaken. I psyched myself out. I started having conversations in my head about being too old and being too much at risk because of a damaged knee and a hip replacement.

But a man in the lodge said, "Don't worry. I had the same problem. The rocker technology in skis today is so different that I crossed my tips over and over until I figured it out. You'll do it too and then you'll love them."

I assumed that I could go out and use the style of skiing I'd used for decades, let the muscle memory take over, find my natural rhythm. But I was wrong. I had to re-learn. I had to acknowledge I was in new circumstances. Even though the world looked the same, a subtle change had jarred my universe and created unstable ground.

I stopped going to the top and like all beginners, worked on my technique on a gentle slope, retraining myself to shift my weight and lean into the turn in a very different way in order to keep my balance. No longer on the automatic pilot of muscle memory, I slowly regained my confidence and courage to head back to the top, staying very much in a practice mode.

Our muscles are trained. When we have been doing what we do in the same way for a long time, changing any element can throw off our balance.

Our behaviors, like our muscles, are also trained. We are used to doing commercial development, grantmaking, organizing, resource development, and capacity building in a certain way. We know our individual disciplines well but are rarely faced with the challenges of having to make them all work as an integrated whole with a truly balanced bottom-line and with residents who require a balance of power.

When we brought all these elements together, it was as jarring as my shift to a set of skis with rocker technology. Each subtle shift in the landscape of the community or within our network of partners forced us back to the bottom of the hill to retrain ourselves. We were in constant practice mode, and we found that looking back was not always the best way to inform the future.

The one thing we had to be was good at learning.

We not only needed "real-time planning," as David LaPiana has coined it; we needed "real-time learning" with a commitment to rapid response so we could incorporate the myriad of subtle shifts in our environment and regain our balance.

Peter Senge's learning organization theory was highly influential and helped us think deeply about how, as an R&D operation, to shape our culture. We wanted the Jacobs Center to be a place "where new expansive patterns of thinking are nurtured, where collective aspiration is set free, and where people are continually learning how to learn together."[33]

Our team was generative, flexible, and adaptive, and those rare team members that weren't, generally didn't stay long. If a person wanted a position with a defined job description and a predictable set of tasks that wasn't going to require them to stretch, they were in the wrong place. You had to be comfortable with the Zen "beginners mind" — letting go of what you think you know.

"Explain it to me like I'm a six-year-old!"[34] I would say to Chip, using the famous line from the movie "Philadelphia." Chip would laugh, and then he would explain it in ways we all could understand. He was good at breaking things down. "Can you explain it again? Can you give me an illustration? Now how do you go about doing that exactly?" With all the curiosity of an actual six-year-old, I was a million questions every day and Chip would always chuckle, tolerating my barrage on all topics — from some percentage he used on a proforma to how real estate investment trusts worked.

I had five major multi-million capital campaigns under my belt, but I had never assembled resources for a double-bottom-line commercial project. Of the 120 commercial projects Chip had completed, he never planned one with community teams. Roque had been a successful community builder for many years but had never aimed those efforts at a major 20-acre industrial site that was contaminated. Ron had managed teams of over 200 people but had never organized those teams by strategy rather than program delivery. We were all in a different business.

In addition, our refrain with residents was: "what do you need to learn and how do you need to learn it?" This kept our leadership team in a constant state of learning as well. If a group of residents wanted to learn about land trusts, they looked for a conference they wanted to attend and presented on it afterwards. As we embraced resident learning, we expanded our own understanding.

The community itself was rich in expertise so learning agendas weren't always about bringing in teams or sending teams out. When the discussion of disparities became paramount for residents focused on health and education, they turned to their local experts, reaching out to Dorothy Smith, the first African American elected to the San Diego School Board, to talk about the state of education in their community. And on the issue of community health, residents invited Dr. Rodney Hood, cofounder of the MultiCultural Primary Physician Medical Group, located in the community, who had dedicated his career to working to end racist attitudes in the healthcare system and was a national resource on health disparities.

Learning opportunities could be fun, like turning a search for information across cultures into a neighborhood treasure hunt, and they could also be hard, harsh, and disconcerting — the disruptive in-your-face learning that leaves you exhausted or even remorseful. It was not always easy. It required that we stop thinking of ourselves as "experts" and go back down to the beginner slopes to retrain ourselves — over and over again.

To love learning is to survive in this environment.

And as important to survival was the ability to forgive ourselves fast for the things that didn't work and to not try to second guess ourselves from some place in time looking back. The landscape on the surface might have looked the same, but thousands of subtle elements had realigned by the time we were back at the top of the hill.

By leaning into and leading with learning, we constantly retrained our muscles. We balanced and rebalanced.

8

A NEW VIEW OF LEADERSHIP

---

*"We need to stop seeking after the universe of the seventeenth century
and begin to explore what became known to us
in the twentieth century."*[35]

— Margaret Wheatley, <u>Leadership and the New Science</u>

I Should be Institutionalized!

"We get used to the way things are even if it's bad because change is scary and uncomfortable. Sometimes you have to be the one brave enough to say it doesn't have to be that way."

I heard this often from residents who talked about how they had learned to live with the conditions in their community by trying not to notice. They made me acutely aware that I needed to shed my comfort with "the way things are" in institutional philanthropy, just as they were doing in their community, in order to change what wasn't working and be a more effective stimulator and supporter of community change.

As an organization committed to resident power, what clearly wasn't going to work was a hierarchical view of and approach to leadership.

As a one-generation foundation focused on the "how" and not just the "what" of community change, we needed to be continually adjusting as an organization, aligning roles, goals, and corporate structures to assure that: 1) commercial development decisions couldn't move without community building, 2) decisions couldn't move without residents, 3) our team stayed accountable to each other, our board, AND to the broader community, and 4) we honored the natural momentum of teams as strategies were unfolding.

With this kind of peer-level, cross-disciplinary decision-making and the need to assure strategies were emergent rather than prescriptive, I needed a new view of leadership. The organizational lifecycle model[36] didn't seem applicable in this context. The concept of the five stages of organizational development, containing predictable patterns of growth laid out with universal diagnostics and tasks that needed to be mastered before moving to the next developmental phase, just wasn't germane to our situation.

Then, in 1999, I read Margaret Wheatley's <u>Leadership and the New Science: Discovering Order in a Chaotic World</u>.[37] Feeling like I was navigating a featureless ocean without a compass, this book was like finding the north star. Before the concept of "working wikily" and "network organizations" were on the scene, Wheatley's book took me on a journey from seventeenth-century Newtonian mechanics to quantum physics.

She broke open for me a non-linear, non-agency-centric view of what organizational life could be. She shared the stories of twentieth-century physicists facing unnerving confusion when the early atomic experiments presented them with paradoxes and the more they tried to clarify, the sharper the paradoxes became. She highlighted the way in which systems fall apart so they can reorganize themselves and how invisible influences that permeate space, can affect change at a distance.

We are still working in organizations designed from Newtonian images of the universe, she boldly contends in the book. We manage by separating things into parts, by understanding it as a mechanical process, organizing people into roles, believing change occurs by one person exerting force on another, planning as though all is predictable, searching for better ways by objectively measuring, and when things don't work, calling someone in to replace the part. It is a world that is distinctly anti-human.

"But in quantum physics, *relationship* is the key determiner of everything... The unseen *connections* between what were previously thought to be separate entities are the fundamental ingredient of all creation."[38] Today's scientists, she describes, can no longer believe that studying the parts is the key to understanding the whole. In a world where systems reorganize themselves into greater order when confronted with changes in their environment, disturbances are not a signal of trouble, but are a critical element in life evolving.

Disturbances as a critical element of life evolving? Now this was the organization I was experiencing. This was a world of both/and, not either/or, that had to leave room for multiple realities and perspectives. Our organization was becoming an evolving container and not a finite structure, expanding and contracting in relationship to the outside world. Jobs were not a description of tasks; they were focused on what kind of support residents needed to build relationships, design process, and move action.

This was a world in which relationships were challenging, complex, and close. And we had to let go of thinking human behavior should be predictable.

"No kidding!" This was one of Joe's indelible lines, and the inflection in his voice, when told of some amazingly creative or foolish act that anyone of us were involved in, was one of charming surprise. He responded to all the unpredictable range of human behavior with intrigue and boyish-like curiosity and taught us to do the same.

Many of our funding colleagues were driven mad by not always being able to see all the elements laid out in a direct cause-and-effect logic model, neatly separated out to fit into their specific areas of interest.

In trying to see the world in its unbroken wholeness, our sense of ourselves as a player in the ecosystem became real. We could no longer see ourselves as outside looking in, asking what will occur in the community if we add this program or that service.

The world was no longer flat.

Our linear model of *Funder* ➡ *Non-Profit* ➡ *Client* was evolving into a large playing field of stakeholders, including the residents, federal, state and local governments, businesses, foundations, organizations, institutions, and others, operating on different planes and tied together with some gravitational force that was difficult to measure.

Over time, there were networks cutting across cultures, faiths, neighborhoods, and sectors, working on civic engagement, physical development, social infrastructure, and economic opportunity, held together by a commitment to shared learning. We were becoming a network organization that had to continue to expand its universe while gradually shrinking in resources.

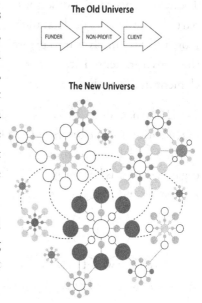

"Ten years into your organizational life-cycle you should be institutionalizing your programs," a foundation consultant advised.

My reaction was "Maybe what should be institutionalized is me!" I laughed. Designing a standardized and highly efficient grantmaking program sounded refreshing, almost therapeutic. But this clearly wasn't our mission.

My work was to figure out how to create and lead a one-generation organization that needed to be an expanding universe and could not afford to be agency-centric. We needed an organization that could adapt and change easily, morphing into what it needed to be. One where the sum was greater than the parts.

Margaret Wheatley's book made me think deeply about the creation of a different organizational worldview. Our mental model for the organization of the future couldn't be one focused on tasks, programs, efficiencies, and incremental growth. It had to hold and respect Joe's request to be an R&D organization, testing tools on the ground. To be about all-in-leveraged-change, this organization had to allow for elements in the ecosystem to be constantly reorganizing and for confusion to provide the seeds of innovation.

And perhaps most importantly, we had to learn how to generate the gravitational pull required for a large universe of players to accomplish change together.

Shifting Power, Safeguarding Process

"I've been following her around for five years trying to figure out what she has up her sleeve."

The man spoke up at the neighborhood meeting where I was updating folks and asking for their advice and feedback. He went on to say: "...and I can honestly tell you that there isn't anything!"

This kind of suspicion comes with the territory. When I started laughing — rolling up my sleeves as a symbol of transparency — the rest of the group started laughing as well. They appreciated the gesture and the break in the tension. I told the group how much I appreciated the man's honesty about the inherent mistrust that exists and that I understood.

In Collaborative Leadership[39] — a book I wish I'd had earlier in my community-based experience — Chrislip and Larson talk at length about the high level of mistrust and cynicism for all institutions that exist in communities.

Participants in any collaborative process, they note, are asking: "What is really going on here? Who is really behind this? What strings are being pulled? Have the decisions already been made? Whose interests are being served?"[40] They describe a world of frustration and anger over feeling that moneyed interests have more and more control over their lives. "Collaborative leadership," they contend, is critical to community change, and because of that, it requires a different kind of leader:

> "We usually think of leaders as those who articulate a vision, inspire people to act, and focus on concrete problems and results. Collaboration...needs leaders who can safeguard the process, facilitate interactions, and patiently deal with high levels of frustration."[41]

Our leadership team needed to understand our place in the ecosystem as peers, acknowledging we had little or no control over the elements that needed to move collectively. And in this role, we needed to be self-reflective and protect the openness and credibility of the process.

Social change is about people changing, power shifting, and systems restructuring. But most of us don't gravitate naturally to shared power and decision-making. As foundations, we want "systems change," but don't typically think of ourselves as one of the key players in the ecosystem that needs to change.

The issues we seek to address — whether substandard housing, under-performing schools, malnourished children, unsafe streets, blight, the loss of jobs, gangs that form families, or the deep divisions between black and white, rich and poor, privileged and excluded — are all intertwined. They can't be separated.

Yet those of us who work in foundations still fund in "areas of interest," launch programs that dissect communities, work at arms-length, and rather than safeguarding a process that shifts power, we safeguard control over resources and sustain the power to decide what strategies get tested and what policies will be the focal point of advocacy efforts.

Our team had witnessed how fast change occurs in the direct interaction of opposing forces, so we knew change wasn't going to happen if we were standing outside looking in. Resident-centered community change is fluid and organic, as well as disciplined and structured. It is pathfinding work, deeply rooted in process, not products.

The "secret sauce" is a mixture of a set of operationalized values, practices and principles, the ingredients of an entrepreneurial culture, and simple methods that move people quickly from vision and plan to implementation and celebration. True community building is at its core relationship building — asking people to reach for and risk change in relation to each other.

Being "change leaders" required us to live questions into the answers, work collaboratively in a context that was often ambiguous, be comfortable with complexity, and see ourselves as a critical part of what needed to change. Community change is human change and it is a journey that is deeply personal. As change leaders we needed to be highly self-reflective and collaborative and become facilitators, stimulators, and generators of the next sets of questions.

As the central player in a complex partnership whose goal was to unleash the creativity of people at the grassroots to take inspired and informed action with influence over and ownership of both the change process and the assets in their communities, my challenge as a leader was that I had to keep the questions coming. And I had to keep the questions coming even when everyone around me was asking for an answer. Even when what I most wanted *myself* was to believe that I had an answer.

But my primary role was to "safeguard the process."

9

FIVE LESSONS FOR LEADING AT THE HEART OF COMPLEXITY

"What do you think you were hired for?
You were hired to wrestle a paradox and pin it to the mat.
And not just once, but over and over again."[42]

Jack and Suzy Welch, "Eating and Dreaming"

Lesson #1: Keep It Simple

In the Search for Common Ground's manual titled: "Designing for Results: Integrating, Monitoring and Evaluation in Conflict Transformation Programs," a cartoon caption written by M. M. Rogers reads: "Dear Mr. Gandhi, we regret we cannot fund your proposal because the link between spinning cloth and the fall of the British Empire was not clear to us."[43]

Humorously illustrating how funders often want their implementing partners to conform to their frameworks, the caption speaks to the disconnect between what happens on the ground and institutional theories of change. As foundations, we have called for community change to come through non-profit organizations with a 510(c)3 tax status and a complex process map that gets people from cause to affect. In addition, we have created abstract, confusing language that separates us from the people in communities who are fighting to change conditions.

We gravitate toward funder-speak like "capacity to transform systems," which when "brought to scale" can create the kind of "social, economic, and political connections that lead to results."

Joe Jacobs' reaction: "I didn't understand a word you just said."

By the time I met Joe in 1991, I'd lived in the non-profit world for so long I didn't notice I was speaking a different language. Joe was quick to call it out. It reminded me of a family member, who when given some interesting new gadget for Christmas, would say, "Oh, that's really nice." Then there would be a pause. "What the hell is it?"

In our funders' world, we talk about how to achieve collective impact in a complex adaptive system, while addressing authentic demand, risk resiliency, and metro-level policy change in order to reach scale within a results-based accountability framework, but people on the ground are thinking: what the hell is it?

New terms and phrases help us think new thoughts and grapple with new ideas, but they can also separate people from each other. Across the country, residents trying to work with foundations indicate that they have great difficulty determining what funders are trying to accomplish.

I once asked a woman how she could tell if any of the work in her community was making a difference. She thought for a second and said: "Let me put it this way, honey — you wouldn't be sitting out here on my front porch if it was like the old days! You'd a been shot by now!" I couldn't draw a straight line between producing a grocery store and impacting all the issues of race, class, and public safety embedded in her comment, but to her, it made sense.

I believed that articulating a theory of change was important because it helped our team understand what we were trying to do together, but in the complex world of comprehensive community change, it had to be simple. I came to believe, with Joe's insistence that conversations and reports be in plain English, that language and concepts that are dense exacerbate the complexity and merely add to the confusion, particularly in cross-disciplinary work which borrows from so many field-specific languages.

In our community, we were working across so many languages — English, Spanish, Hmong, Lao, Tagalog, Samoan, Somali, Farsi, Arabic — and by the time you layered in community building, business, construction, and the public sector (each with its own language), communication became challenging and understanding hard to achieve. It became an important part of our organizational DNA to translate everything to its very core.

"Getting it plain and simple" became a guiding principle and primary role for our community work. Simplify everything — language, plans, concepts, and tools — to what would be most universally understood. Making things plain was hard work and often very time-consuming, but it was a critical choice we made to change.

We worked the framing of our approach for two years to get it simple and clear. Something our team could get their arms around. If we were in the business of the "resident ownership of neighborhood change," we saw three key components of ownership that we believed together provided the springboard for staying power:

- Owning the planning — so vision and hope could be built;
- Owning the implementation — so skills and capacity could be built; and
- Owning the assets — so wealth creation was a priority and tools for leveraging future change could be developed.

It was easy for people to understand. Everyone knew the proverb "Give a man a fish and he can eat today; teach a man to fish and he can eat for a lifetime." We just added that if you want people's children and their children's children to eat and thrive, they need to also buy the pond.

At the heart of it all was a very simple idea: look to people in their own communities for solutions. Ignite the spirit of people to work in relationship, give people a platform for seeing and experiencing their great gifts and talents, and build a mechanism for residents to control assets that can be leveraged for future change.

Lesson #2: Resist "Structural Containment"

"The processes by which a company would experimentally and intuitively feel its way into emerging markets would constitute suicide if employed in a well-defined existing business."[44]

In The Innovator's Dilemma, Clayton Christensen writes about how the abilities of large, highly-structured organizations, well-managed by accepted practice, are useful in refining current or "sustaining" technologies where analysis and planning are feasible. But the underlying values used by employees to make decisions, he contends, such as relying on a past body of work to predict cause and effect, can severely inhibit innovation. And because innovation is inherently unpredictable, it requires a high level of flexibility and a commitment to "discovery-based" learning.

From the outset of our work, we defined ourselves as an R&D company. Instead of trying to expand, extend, or refine the standard methodology of grantmaking, we wanted to move more toward the "disruptive" mode, experimenting our way into completely different roles, methods, and tools. Starting with our own team and then extending to our partners, our strategy for creating a culture of change became one of putting people together with different views in a fluid exchange in order to create new insight or new awareness. We had stopped being program developers and had become process designers and facilitators.

In foundations, this goes against all we have grown up with as a field. We have been structured for pre-determined and measurable outcomes, preservation of assets, narrow areas of interest, long lead-times, and evidence-based (i.e., already proven) strategies rather than the open, fluid, and disruptive exchange of ideas and strategies that stimulate innovation.

Looking from the outside in, this breaking from tradition made us suspect and invited detractors. When learning of our work, my colleagues would often say: "Foundations shouldn't be hands-on; if we are too close, we can't be objective." Or "putting a team on the ground will throw off foundation administrative cost ratios." The one we defied the most was: "You can't do that in a foundation; our lawyers say the corporate structure won't allow it."

With Joe, our manta became, "let no structure be a barrier to getting things done." If the current structure doesn't work, change it or create a new one. We had permission to "resist structural containment," as the Rensselaerville Institute's catalytic document "Assumptions for Innovation"[45] called it.

By breaking out of the very corporate structure of a charitable non-operating foundation — our first move — we were able to have the time and flexibility to put a cross-disciplinary team on the ground to grapple with the rest of the ecosystem of players, marshaling enough disruptive points of view to shake up our own beliefs, stimulate new knowledge, and seed innovation.

Over time, we would evolve into a network of corporate structures that gave us the range we needed to support teams, put expertise on the ground, match technical assistance where it was needed, and build — most importantly — ownership.

Lesson #3: Understand the Game Board

"What's your position with the foundation," a resident asked. "My title?" I laughed. "Dot Connector!"

It was true. To assume a leadership role in comprehensive community change, I needed to be able to connect dots. I had to trust the process and closely follow the natural momentum of the teamwork. I had to pay close attention to the opportunities team members were finding and moving with. And I had to assure we were all in the same room together talking through the direction each of the teams were taking so that one group's path didn't block another's.

From my position, I could see most of the field of movement. That said, I couldn't always see the pathway for connecting them. But that was my work — to build a pathfinding leadership agenda that would allow the work — as much as possible — to not get blocked; or when it was blocked, to figure out how best to back up and make room for taking a better path.

It was like a large game of Line Draw[46] that gets more and more complex as it moves along. At first with just four sets of different colored dots to connect, you can sometimes stare at it and see all the connections and the pathway between the dots; then the sets of dots increase to five, then six, and by the time you have to connect seven sets of dots, you have to deploy a different process.

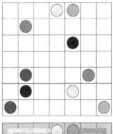

As the game progresses, it requires you to start the process of finding a route without really being sure if it will work. You learn quickly that you can't just take the most direct route between the dots, because if you do, you will block one or more of the dots from being connected. In some cases, you need to back up and start over. It is a game of take a step, start a line, and reflect. As you do this, routes become clearer and clearer. Then you move to the next level, face greater complexity, but practice the same process.

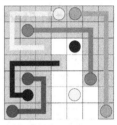

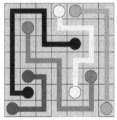

To create economic development in the most direct route can undercut people's need to keep their cost of living down and not be displaced. Higher rents for businesses in a commercial project help make projects more economically viable but push out local entrepreneur-owned businesses. Without considering social impact, physical development might move faster, but could end up cutting off the pathway for the health, education, and place-making agendas.

Balancing social, cultural, civic, economic, physical, and political development makes for more twists and turns, longer routes, more pauses, some backing up, but achieves comprehensive results.

There is the hope in community revitalization that all the elements will stay balanced and it will get easier over time, but that is not the case. The deeper we went, the more complex the dynamics became.

To work in this environment, "you have to trust in something — your gut, destiny, life, karma, whatever," as Steve Jobs framed it in his commencement address to Stanford University, because "you can't connect the dots looking forward; you can only connect them looking backwards."[47]

You have to enjoy mastering the connecting of the dots, which comes from studying the whole game board. And you have to be willing to start, back up, reflect, and try again in order to find the right path.

Lesson #4: Start with the End in Sight

"The proudest moment of my life is when you say to me, 'Joe, I don't need you anymore. Thanks for your help. I'm on my own and I'm on my way.'"

This 1992 line of Joe's was highlighted in one of the videos framing our work. Our team saw it so many times it became fodder for jokes. When we all got to point of frustration about a difficult person we had to deal with, someone would announce "I think he needs to be on his own and on his way!"

But it was a line we worked hard, and in all seriousness, to operationalize. How were we going to exit and leave something enduring behind that could go on without us?

It was important that we "begin with the end in mind,"[48] to quote Stephen Covey — the foundation's end.

At that time, it was common practice for foundations to have one-year grant periods and for community initiatives to be three to five years. For these initiatives, the ending was defined as a date.

As a one-generation foundation committed to leaving behind something that could go on without us, we knew that while we were spending down, we needed to be bringing up self-generating systems of wealth creation — assets and businesses owned and controlled in the neighborhood that could be leveraged by residents for future change.

The foundation literally had one lifetime to make a difference, with all the urgency that represents, and we made a pledge to not leave until sustaining capacity, infrastructure, and resources were in place, giving our team all the patience that means to figure things out.

As a small foundation, we would leverage the three things historically-disinvested communities have in abundance: 1) blight, 2) retail leakage, and 3) people with a pent-up desire to change things.

As an entrepreneur-driven foundation, we would take greater risk, accept failure as a natural dynamic, and experiment our way into roles, goals, tools, structures, and strategies.

And as a one-generation foundation, we would place a high value on learning and passing those lessons on to the next generation. Active learning agendas, ongoing reflective practice, and a commitment to sharing were critical to the legacy we wanted to leave.

In reflecting back on the 20 years, the value of defining the endgame as a clear sustainability mechanism for the momentum that has been built during an initiative's lifespan can't be underestimated. In the foundation world, we deliberate with each other over sustainability and are disturbed and discouraged by the lack of it. When the time period for the initiative we've launched is close to being up, we realize the population level impact we were seeking hasn't been achieved and that undoing the 200-plus-year history of disinvestment and structural racism is going to take more time, and then wonder why our community partners aren't set up for the work to continue.

The sustainability of philanthropy rides on assets. Long-term control of our portfolios. We actually know exactly what sustainability looks like, but think it is somehow different for our partner organizations. It is not only important to start where we are and leverage what we have, but it is also important to leave behind three things: 1) income-producing assets controlled by residents with the purpose of benefitting residents, 2) an infrastructure for ongoing citizen decision-making, and 3) a set of lessons for the next generation of community change leaders.

Documenting and distributing lessons is relatively easy. Creating community-controlled assets and sustaining infrastructures dauntingly hard.

Lesson #5: Know the Dragon

There are dragons in every room. There is no control over when and where they will arrive or what they will say.

But among them, it is important to know the Road-Blockers from the Difference-Makers.

There are the people that command attention, create fear, and deliver a fiery ball of feedback or advice in ways that shut down the conversation, causing people to want to either draw their swords or just run away.

They are the naysayers, skeptics, and non-believers that push against everything and try to kill people spirits. They meet every action with an equal and opposite reaction and push with gale-wind force to build a barrier to success.

Their can'ts can be unrelenting.

Some of these people will even up their game as change becomes visible — seeing any growing momentum as a threat to all their reasoning as to why things can't work. These are people who want change but don't want *to* change. They fight from the sidelines. These are the Road-Blockers.

But in Chinese folklore, dragons aren't fire-breathing, aggressive creatures; they are symbols of power, strength, prosperity, harmony, energy, and good luck. They represent a life-force.

In community-building work, you need the dragon.

Differences matter and the difference-makers are the people who in all their fierceness represent the life force. They are ones that make you look up and digest feedback whether you want to or not.

These people are the truth-tellers, as challengers of ingrained views and beliefs, and their disputes over the sense of direction and opposition to decisions, push everyone to a new place of understanding, help people see in their blind spots, advance change with their ability to re-see, re-think, and re-new the conversation. They push us out of our comfort zones.

These are the people whose passion and voice make a difference.

The culture of our organization was built on the value of all voices and that meant not just keeping the dragons in the room, but really knowing them and how to work with them.

With the Road-Blockers, we had to work with a spirit of exuberance, calculating the exponential factor needed to off-set the energy drain.

With the Difference-Makers, we had to learn to set aside our perspectives long enough to evaluate the merit, if any, of their challenging disagreement or dissension.

To build a culture of innovation, the work demanded that we make a place at the table for dissenting voices, disruptive voices, previously unheard voices, and work across differences of all kinds. We had to make time to understand them and create a culture that could withstand them.

We had to hear people, listen deeply, and evaluate their points of view. See if there was a bridge to be built. Invite everyone to come together and find a solution that worked for people. We had to look at the numbers, evaluate the information, and ask: Is it working? Are they right? Is there a better way? We had to let them teach us what we needed to know, and then we needed to make sure that teams moved forward in some way, anyway, and didn't stall out.

Our worlds are easier to manage when people think like us and act like us and when we don't have to work very hard at achieving understanding. But because social change requires new voices, new perspectives, and new conversations, we needed to make time and space for these differences so we could work as a fully integrated network of players, guided by a common mission and vision – a group of people and a set of organizations held accountable by the same plan, learning the same language, seeing each other's gifts, and most importantly, understanding our critical interdependence.

We learned to think of diversity very broadly. From the beginning, finding our philanthropic agenda at the intersection of the Jacobs family's conservative and liberal points of view mattered. The differences in world views kept the work from becoming politicized and polarized. Our internal and external teams brought for-profit experience balanced with non-profit perspective. Commercial development balanced with community development. Securities law with organizing. The teamwork also embodied the experience of young and old, privilege and exclusion, small town and big city. Enriching the experience were literal "world" views — African American, Latino, Laotian, Samoan, Sudanese, Somali, Filipino, Kumeyaay, Chamorro, Arab, European, Christian, Jewish, and Muslim.

People coming from different life-paths, belief systems, and histories helped everyone identify the issues, recognize the contradictions, pinpoint the opposing forces. They posed the questions that led to answers. They could see the underlying barriers that were standing in the way of change.

So many diverse voices at the same table could result in tension, conflict, and confusion, no doubt about it. But as teams learned to listen and honor each other's perspectives and points of view, it also helped us — as happened in innumerable moments in time — see in our blind spots.

"How about if we have a helicopter fly in the guest of honor," I once said in a community team meeting. The Laotian people squirmed. Some gasped. There was silence for a moment. Then a resident quietly shared: "We grew up in a war zone. Please don't bring in a helicopter." Then there was my moment of silence. I nodded to them with apology.

In these shared moments, our experience expands. We connect to each other's distinct histories. I didn't grow up in a war zone, but I could — in a flash — imaginatively identify with the wrenching past that brought the Laotian people to this time and place.

Blind spots can be deadly. We needed people who could see — some left, some right, some up, some down, some near, and some far. As trust deepened, we helped each other see, and as a team could envision together what none of us could see alone. Even if we didn't always want to hear it. Even though differences were hard to manage. Even though it took time. Even though it was hard to get agreement, gain consensus, and move in alignment, we needed to care about it anyway. It mattered.

When the door for change is open, it is clear that the inability to include, withstand, and survive criticism keeps us from making progress. Skepticism and negativity are fueled by the history of race and class in this country and further fueled by the political polarization of people. As a white leader, head of foundation that also represented power and privilege, my job was to assure that we do what another foundation representative in a Chapin Hall study once described: "You go in and you stay. You stay and humble yourself every day and you listen."[49]

I had to learn to set aside my reaction to how messages were delivered so I wouldn't miss the meaning. To do this, I needed to limit the distraction of the naysayers and keep my eye on, stay close to, and keep my heart open to the critics that were willing to:

1. Learn, speak the truth, move the work;
2. Have the hard conversations out of respect for giving the work its best opportunity for success;
3. Share and fight for their perspective, but listen and value other perspectives;
4. Dissent based on seeing and weighing information;
5. Define *consensus* as "what most people believe can work and everyone can live with;" and
6. Let go of blame.

Most importantly, I had to keep myself in a learning place. Listen. Humble myself. And stay.

MANAGING
CHANGE
━━━━━━━━━━━━━━━━ ■■

VOICE, VISION & INSPIRED ACTION

10

THE FOUR BUILDING BLOCKS FOR RESIDENT-OWNED CHANGE

"The fundamental Building Block for change is the ability of ordinary people to develop their skills and ability to work collectively."[50]

— Bill Traynor

The Conundrum of Where to Start

"Don't trust him."

Just an hour after a meeting in my office with four non-profit directors, each of them called me with the same message: don't trust the others.

While in the same meeting, they had all talked about how I needed them. They indicated that they knew "the way," but the private calls had the strong implication that if we had the other three non-profit leaders at the table, they would not want to participate. They should be the lead agency. They implied questionable ethics of the others. They all had histories.

"I don't want to go on other people's assumptions and histories," I replied. "I want to build my own relationships."

Later that day, another funder called and was frustrated that the initiative her foundation had launched was stalled by the lead agency losing its director. "It's taken more than nine months so far," she said, "to recruit a new one." In the meantime, they had consultants standing by, being paid, who weren't accomplishing anything. The foundation was putting pressure on the consultants who were putting pressure on the agency. The entire initiative, she indicated, was hung up on the capacity of the lead agency.

During this same timeframe in our own community, two community development corporations had three changes of leadership; the board of two coalitions changed two to three times, and between them, four directors were fired. In addition, agencies funded to play specific roles in a city-initiated "collaboration" stopped participating as soon as the money stopped.

Where to start was a conundrum.

By the time we moved our offices to the southeastern San Diego community, there was already a field of experience in managing comprehensive community initiatives (CCIs) to build on. While CCIs were relatively new, these ambitious, cross-cutting, place-based efforts were being launched in an attempt to address the complex and inter-related issues of disinvested neighborhoods by integrating service-delivery.

In the mid- to late-1990s, when we were starting out, the National Housing Institute, The Aspen Institute Roundtable on Community Change, and Chapin Hall Center for Children at the University of Chicago were engaged in documenting the lessons coming from the field and detailing the structures, strategies, tools, and processes being used in community change initiatives.

Emerging as "new partnerships for change"[51] based on the principles of comprehensiveness and community building, CCIs were charged with redefining how the players involved in community change interacted and innovating on the tools they used. In discussing the first round of CCIs, _Voices from the Field_, in the first volume published by the Aspen Institute in 1997, documented:

> "To a large extent, foundations still operate as grantmakers rather than partners in the change process; funding is still allocated in short-term intervals; technical assistance is still provided on a problem-specific, temporary basis; evaluation is still focused on measuring broad indicators that can

be unambiguously linked to particular interventions; and capacity building and community building are still considered secondary to putting programs on the ground."[52]

As the field's "best attempt" to modify rusty tools, CCIs put a spotlight on the tensions between product and process, the challenges of power and elitism, and the need for greater flexibility and respect.

The early CCIs were largely characterized by a relationship between a foundation and a community through a "lead" organization, capacity building to strengthen the lead organization, and collaborative funding as a way to structure cooperative non-profit work and minimize the conflicts that come with having multiple organizational players at the table. Most developed strategy around systems reform (defined as altering the way services are delivered to residents who need them), often led with a comprehensive neighborhood plan, and defined long-term funding as two to three years for planning and three to four years for implementation.

In the model for comprehensive community initiatives, partners launched their work with institutionally-established goals set within a framework established by a foundation. The need for well-defined outcomes, clearly-spelled-out work plans, and results-oriented contracting and resource allocation stood in the way of tilting any power toward residents to have a seat at the table. Resident capacity-building was largely training people in classrooms. Resident process was seen as something that would slow the work down — messy, risky, and uncontrollable.

But it was also clear that initiatives that shortcut resident participation upfront were much more likely to slow down — or even become blocked — from achieving change. In many communities, these initiatives had to back up and even start over in an attempt to overcome dissonance, resistance, and the disconnect with neighborhood residents and partners. In some cases, they were abandoned, reinforcing the distrust and frustration around the idea of doing community development at all.

Because the Jacobs Center's work was focused on how a community can organize across cultures to find its voice, link to needed resources, and disrupt the deeply entrenched impact of disinvestment — we decided to challenge ourselves to try to figure out how to achieve the full participation and ownership of all partners — starting with residents.

To do this, we had to move from seeing residents as clients and consumers to supporting them as citizens and central actors in community change. We had to go beyond asking residents to weigh in to asking them to dream, design, and implement work. We needed to move away from the mental model of exclusively supporting professional problem-solving to activating the wisdom, creativity, and experience of residents. We had to figure out how to change from inside-out organizational decision-making to outside-in decision-making. And we had to evolve from being a foundation located <u>in</u> the community to being a member <u>of</u> the community.

In short, we had to move from resident engagement to resident ownership.

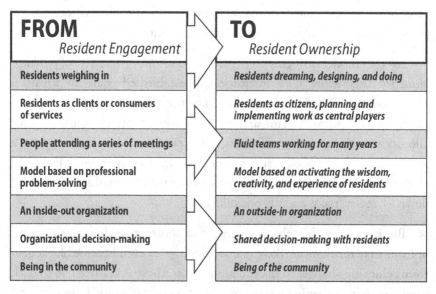

FROM *Resident Engagement*	TO *Resident Ownership*
Residents weighing in	Residents dreaming, designing, and doing
Residents as clients or consumers of services	Residents as citizens, planning and implementing work as central players
People attending a series of meetings	Fluid teams working for many years
Model based on professional problem-solving	Model based on activating the wisdom, creativity, and experience of residents
An inside-out organization	An outside-in organization
Organizational decision-making	Shared decision-making with residents
Being in the community	Being of the community

Today, I would define the work we were doing as *"resident-owned community change"* a comprehensive approach to neighborhood strengthening that is built on the direction, decision-making, and co-investment of people who live and work in the community. It is a process in which residents:

- Participate as full partners in the work;
- Guide the vision and planning;
- Share responsibility and decision-making;
- Build an ownership interest in the assets developed;
- Benefit from the profits generated and the growth in value of those assets;
- Build the collective know-how to maintain and sustain the revitalization of their community; and
- Build the community investment structures to leverage future change.

For years, studies had validated that human resiliency is based on a person having an important relationship, believing he or she has a unique gift or talent, having a vision of his or her future, and the opportunity to give back in some way. Our approach would reinforce these resiliency elements—facilitating people working in relationship; providing an opportunity for engaged citizens to discover untapped gifts and talents; creating a forum for igniting a shared vision of the future; and providing opportunities for people to give back so that future generations could live in a world better than the one we inherited.

At its core, this approach was based on four primary beliefs:

1. Residents have a living history in their community and understand its strengths, assets, and challenges better than anyone else;
2. Well-informed residents who are central in decision-making and work together to improve their community get a better result than models of revitalization that plan from the outside in;
3. Residents must own the change in their community for efforts to be sustained over time; and
4. Residents must be surrounded by resource networks that also own their own change.

In defining our market as residents and deciding that we would be in a direct and intentional relationship with them, our approach to resident-owned community change would build on the lessons from the field of CCIs but shift in fundamental ways. Most importantly, our work would give concentrated focus to what Prue Brown and Sunil Garg, in the 1997 Chapin

Hall report, called the "space" or "distance" between foundations and the players on the ground in communities. "As described by both funders and CCI representatives," they reported, "this space is too often characterized by lack of understanding and trust, dishonest communications, and struggles over power and accountability."[53]

Philosophically, we would approach our role, structure, strategy, tools, and process in this way, allowing our understanding to evolve over time.

Role and Structure

- We would not work through a "lead agency" or call our work an "initiative;" we would move into the community, work side-by-side with residents and stakeholders, and gradually discover what our right role should be and what non-profit partners were needed.
- We would create joint resident-foundation teams to plan and guide the work to shift the dynamic of residents needing to put pressure on decision-makers to becoming the decision-makers.
- We would not predetermine outcomes or a pathway but would use our operating foundation status to follow natural momentum of resident teams and use resources in a fast and flexible way to stimulate their ongoing resourcefulness and creativity.
- To address the community critics of start-and-stop philanthropy, we would let people know that the length of our commitment to this work was our "lifetime." Instead of holding on to our resources, we would use our assets aggressively to leverage change, and somewhere between 2020 and 2030, when the time was right for transition, we would close our doors, leaving valuable assets in community control.

Strategy

- Instead of targeting system reforms aimed at altering the way services were delivered to residents, we would activate citizen talent and leadership.
- Since residents had reported that they had been asked by another foundation to do a comprehensive plan and didn't know what that meant, we dropped the idea of leading with one and would engage

people where they were, around the topics that attracted them, and connect the teams as we went.

- We would radically depart from the theory that communities should spend two to three years planning before they started implementing. When plans got too big and the number of players needed to implement too large, community change efforts had stalled, so we would opt for a rapid rotation from planning to action. We wouldn't avoid tackling the big issues but would break them down so success could be understood, acted on, and celebrated.

Tools and Process

- Since we believed that who defined success mattered, resident teams would determine what success looked like and the benchmarks for measuring it.
- We would not use cash grants as a stand-alone tool nor work through intermediaries. Since we wanted comprehensive change, we would retool with a comprehensive perspective. We would use equity investments, loans, guarantees, project collateral, PRIs to lending partners, meeting facilitation and planning support, business development support, outreach, and organizing, along with cash grants, recoverable grants, and mini-grants.
- We would locate our offices in the community to serve as a hub for both large and small community meetings and as a way to anchor a project. We would build and field our own team, with the capability of working across civic, social, economic, and physical development.
- We would hire residents, as we did outside consultants, and see employment as a major component of the pathway to ownership of the work.
- In order to support action learning and further stimulate innovation, we would create ongoing learning exchanges with the residents of other communities along with their place-based funding partners.

We started door-to-door, block-by-block. We hosted living room meetings and attended all the community gatherings we could in order to meet people and listen to their concerns, hopes, and dreams. Then we started where residents wanted to start — securing a major grocery store and getting a 20-acre abandoned factory site into productive use.

The relationships that would be built, many residents noted later, were what would create the broader context of change.

People always ask me, "In comprehensive community change, where do you even start?" My answer is: "Wherever you are and with whatever you have."

Lessons that Shaped the Work

"As soon as you hear someone trying to warn you off your dream, as soon as anyone starts telling you to be 'realistic,'" noted John Eliot, in his work on cultivating exceptional performance, "X that person off your invitation list."[54]

Surrounded by so many big issues left in the wake of disinvestment, it was important that our approach was to not let ourselves be pushed by problems — to paraphrase Ralph Waldo Emerson — but rather to be led by dreams and to cross the skeptics off the invitation list.

We had to start where we were; approach the work as a learning adventure, try not to second guess ourselves, and try not let ourselves get scared off by the hard, messy, complex, or impossible. We had to stay hungry to make a difference, start and stay together, find the connecting points, and rekindle the belief that change is possible.

Our leadership agenda was pathfinding, and it was deeply rooted in a process of discovery-based learning. The guiding principles of that agenda were directly linked to our experience during the first 10 years of the foundation's work.

These lessons clustered around vision, teamwork, networks, and the need for supportive infrastructure.

VISION

- *With a big dream, ordinary people are capable of doing extraordinary things.*

The goal of focusing on a single issue or problem demands an immediate change. If the issue goes away, the people go away; or worse, when the issue doesn't go away, people wear out and go away without accomplishing anything. But when people have a shared vision so clear and so powerful that they can walk around in the future, they can commit themselves to finding ways to achieve it.

- *"Comprehensive change" doesn't mean doing everything.*

Focusing on everything meant we couldn't achieve anything. We needed to define "comprehensive" not as doing everything but aiming at a headpin and working in a comprehensive and integrated way.

TEAMWORK

- *Long-term learning relationships provide the most fertile ground for innovation and impact.*

Trust takes time and can only be built by working in direct relationship. In order to build a culture of learning, we needed to achieve shared risk, truthful communication, and equity in decision-making.

- *People don't like to serve on committees that don't have a clear purpose, go on forever, and don't produce results.*

Planning needs to be biased toward action with a clear beginning and end. We needed short-term results to build momentum and a sense of accomplishment, but plans had to be able to add up to a long-term collective vision of change.

- *Results raise expectations for change and those expectations seed ongoing innovation and transformation.*

Implementing in a way that is visionary, creative, and celebratory helps build an unwavering spirit and energy for action. By focusing on both long-term vision and rapid results, we could adapt as we went, push the vision out, and give it space to become more and more dynamic.

NETWORKS

- *Top-down funder-driven initiatives don't work and neither do bottom-up grassroots efforts without resource networks.*

  We had seen example after example of top-down approaches that never took hold because of power dynamics and bottom-up approaches that got stuck because of limited resources and technical expertise. We would opt for partnership — networks guided by resident voice, linked with the resources and expertise needed to move action forward.

- *If you want people to turn out, rely on natural networks.*

  In a multicultural, multi-faceted, inter-connected world, we knew we needed an intentional way to bridge cultures, generations, communities, art forms, disciplines, and faiths. To bring residents out with energetic efforts, we needed to harness the power of natural networks that could reach people and insure the work stayed culturally responsive.

INFRASTRUCTURE

- *Efforts need to be comprehensive, coordinated, and connected.*

  Because the issues within communities that have experienced long-term disinvestment are interconnected, they require strategies that are holistic and not broken down by issue. But this work requires an infrastructure — a center of gravity — that can connect the planning and coordinate action across social, economic, physical, and political development.

- *Civic action needs support.*

  Large groups of citizens working together need four elements to be effective: 1) space to convene that is central, welcoming, and free; 2) a team that can support community outreach and organizing; 3) mechanisms for "magnetizing" the work — food, fun, and a can-do spirit, along with encouraging entire families to participate; and 4) support for translating every document, message, process, meeting format, and structure into something that is culturally sensitive, language appropriate, and simple, clear, and understandable by everyone.

- *It's better to drive a hybrid.*

  To achieve a blend of social and economic impact, we would balance the best of the for-profit and non-profit worlds. Sustainability rides on an economic engine balanced with a strong, uncompromising commitment to equity, inclusion, and social justice.

These lessons about vision, teams, networks, and infrastructure would shape our four building blocks for managing change.

The Building Blocks — Dream Work, Team Work, Net Work, and Frame Work

"There's no there there."

Pete Ellsworth, a retired CEO and corporate attorney, was now leading a local charitable foundation. The foundation he led, the Legler Benbough Foundation, helped grow many of San Diego great arts institutions and research organizations, and Pete, I thought, would take a very traditional approach to funding in the neighborhoods. But he surprised me.

"What the Market Creek experience provided me was an opportunity to really learn," he reflected. "It was different; not like learning from other professionals and philanthropist, but with residents. We built personal relationships."

Pete had the courage to risk direct involvement. And because he did, he opened his heart and mind to a style of grantmaking that surprised even him. Mini-grants. Support for resident working teams. Graffiti as an art form. Eventually he even created a bridge from the mainstream arts institutions to the vibrant cultural arts of the community — not just to help the neighborhood, but to help the arts institutions become relevant to San Diego's changing demographics. He was a close partner in figuring out how to get resources to residents and follow their natural momentum.

"It was difficult at first. Both because I wasn't used to being personally taken on by people — it took a long time to understand the impact of disempowerment — but also because I didn't know how to fund a neighborhood." Pete was always commenting on one of the primary dilemmas foundations face in moving from funding tax exempt organizations to resident priorities — "there's no there there."

Funding a non-profit organization has a natural structure for strategic planning and oversight but working in a neighborhood was confusing. How do we know what to invest in? Who does the plan? Who oversees the work? Who provides stewardship and expenditure responsibility in reporting to the IRS?

Our work was to build a "there there" — create a container for action that would help residents plan, implement, and own change in their community and build a mechanism for funders and other resource partners to support work in this civic space.

Our guiding principles when we started the work were simple:

- Start wherever we are and build on whatever we have;
- Work in teams and carve out creative space for the natural problem-solving of people in their communities to emerge;
- Use tools and methods that engage people and are accessible, fast, participatory and fun;
- Focus on the skills and process for moving quickly from planning to action; and
- Build a "there there."

I kept my eye on whether we had a common language and understanding of our work, an evolving set of structures for inspired action, an open process, sustained participation, and a growing sense of hope and belief that change was possible.

The foundation's work clustered in four important areas that became our building blocks:

- *Dream Work* — supporting residents in envisioning a dynamic future for themselves, their families, their organizations, and their community;
- *Team Work* — forming and facilitating teams as a platform for building trust, focusing joint action, promoting learning, and creating a fun and magnetic environment;
- *Net Work* — seeing the collective work as the weaving of community-based, coordinated and comprehensive networks and partnerships that can bridge resources, create access to opportunity, deal with systemic barriers to change, and manage growth in civic action, and
- *Frame Work* — creating clear and flexible containers for action that help people see, name, frame, and do the work. This required building an infrastructure — a there there — to support resident mobilization, connect the work, push natural momentum toward short-term results and long-term vision, and provide a way for traditional funders to invest in neighborhood change.

Every year we documented challenges and the changes we made to overcome them, and while much changed, some things stayed constant. We never wavered from supporting people in dreaming big and re-imagining the future; breaking isolation by connecting to each other and working in relationship on teams; connecting to strong networks that would support change while honoring resident vision and voice as central; and creating an infrastructure for managing change.

11

DREAM WORK

*"If you want to build a ship, don't herd people together to collect wood
and don't assign them tasks and work, but rather
teach them to long for the endless immensity of the sea."*

— Antoine de Saint-Exupery, French Writer and Poet

Seeing and Believing

"Seeing is believing, but believing is also seeing," Doris Anderson observed.

In her role as Executive Director of the Elementary Institute of Science, she could see that as a vision materialized for a new state-of-the-art science center for the youth of the community, the non-believers began to change their thinking and wanted to become a part of making the dream a reality.

As the vision for Market Creek Plaza was taking shape across the street, Doris and her "mighty band" — as she called them — of youth, board, and volunteers were advancing their bold goal of achieving a new building. She realized at the outset that people needed to envision a new facility so clearly that they could walk around in it long before it was ever built. The vision needed to be so powerful that everyone involved was willing to stay at the table no matter how long it took, how many obstacles they encountered, or how many lessons they had to learn.

Their determination was not just a game-changer for the organization, it was transformative for all of us involved. It taught us that if we could see and believe in a bold vision of the future, we could create and experience it. If we decided to not define ourselves by what we already knew, but rather as eager students, the world's creative forces would take us to some new place.

The Institute's big dream taught us to take the vision of change as a dare. If we look beyond the dirt lots to the vision of a "beloved community" — a vision so clear we could see it and touch it — it can open up in front of our eyes.

The restoration of the vitality of a community is vision work.

Ten years after we started the community partnership that spawned Market Creek, Peter Block wrote a piece entitled *Civic Engagement and the Restoration of Community: Changing the Nature of the Conversation.* I didn't know Peter's work at the time, but it rings true to our experience:

> "The conventional view of community action and development address what we usually call problems; areas such as public safety, jobs and local economy, affordable housing, youth, universal health care and education. In the context of the restoration of community, these are really symptoms. The deeper cause is in the unreconciled and fragmented nature of our community. The fragmentation creates a context where trying to solve the symptoms only sustains them...The real intent of a restorative civic engagement is to shift the context within which traditional problem solving, investment and social and community action take place. The restorative context is one of relatedness, of possibility, and the affirmation that each of us has the capacity to transform, even create, the world we inhabit."[55]

As Peter Block discusses in his writing, people need to be invited to "co-create a future possibility." As leaders, we need to create the conditions, nurture the experiences, and invite the conversations that enable us to live out a desired future. Peter's work also frames a type of leadership that creates accountability by "confronting people with their freedom" — a key component of what ownership is all about.

If the work of co-creating a future possibility is vision work, the people who live in a community need to own that vision. When community-building practitioners inquired about our organizing strategy, they would ask: "Do you use issue organizing or consensus organizing?" We began to answer: "We use *vision organizing*."

Vision organizing, as we came to practice it, is rooted in people's need to define their own future and picture that future. It is a process of bringing people together, not around conflict, but around the dream of a better future and the power of possibility. Where other types of organizing are often a means to an end, we saw vision organizing as both a means and an end. It was the instrument that moved us toward inspired action and gave the teams the power to create change.

Vision organizing as a methodology:

- Moves people through a process of "see it, say it, do it" that is literally visual;
- Is open to all voices, inclusive, and focused on connectedness and relationship;
- Builds on the gifts of diversity, rooted in cultural awareness and large-scale cross-cultural sharing;
- Defines problems as opportunities;
- Is comfortable with change happening over time so it can expand and become increasingly dynamic;
- Instills a sense of responsibility for contributing, connecting, and acting;
- Uses rituals and symbols to celebrate traditions, ground people's sense of history, and magnetize involvement; and
- Demands shared leadership, shared decision-making, shared risk, and shared investment.

The issues our disinvested communities face are too interconnected to pick one — jobs, crime, blight, lack of access to fresh foods, failing schools, substandard housing, and hopelessness among youth. Vision organizing moves us away from isolating and targeting a single problem by aiming at the power of future possibility and daring to envision a different reality.

"I got a call from a neighbor and she said 'you should do this. It's fun, the learning style — it's different,'" Bevelynn Bravo, a long-time resident and community coordinator, reflected. "For me it was about being asked what we thought. Usually people wanted to train us saying 'you need to learn this,' but we were sharing about our experiences, our families, our values, and our vision of the future. Even when we disagreed, it was important," she continued.

As she talked, I remembered just how much I came to count on her to speak her mind. At first, I thought she was shy, but later realized how deeply she thought about things before she spoke.

Asking people to dream big and move collectively requires dialogue, debate, deliberation, and the ability of people to voice both agreement and disagreement so together they can arrive at a shared vision.

"In looking back on it," she reflected, "the only reason this worked over such a long period of time, is because the leadership around me was open to learning and that made it comfortable to disagree when we needed to."

"Through the process," she continued, "we started saying to each other 'why should we settle? Let's at least try.' Then we realized we were able to make things happen. We started seeing that anything was possible. This is our community and we don't have to put up with things. And we didn't have to wait for someone else."

We came to understand the power of focusing on a vision of the future. Community meetings went from 50 to 100 to 200 to 500 in a matter of years. Meetings were fun and energized. People were making a choice to be there and contribute. They brought their children. They brought their dreams. They brought their food and dance and song. They brought their smarts. And they restored each other's hope.

The Six Vision Elements

The work with Elementary Institute of Science helped the Market Creek teams clarify and define what was needed for vision organizing to work. Six elements surfaced: a catalytic target, so people can aim their change efforts; a galvanizing and unifying focus; a belief in the potential of people and the ability to build skills by doing; flexibility and freedom to explore how best to move projects from impossible to feasible; use of visual aids so people can literally see the future they are creating; and visible signs of change.

1) The "Catalyst"

Residents targeted a 20-acre industrial dump paired with the need for a full-service grocery as the *catalyst*. It was large enough to inspire action and attract people beyond its immediate borders, and was complex enough to connect across social, economic, and physical development goals.

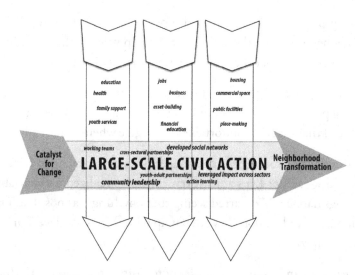

2) A Galvanizing and Unifying Focus

What started as a learning agenda to help teams break through the distrust and long-standing barriers among ethnic groups — arts and culture — became the *galvanizing and unifying focus* for building understanding, bridging differences, and uniting people; it became our primary outreach strategy and the foundation of the vision for a vibrant cultural village.

3) Belief in the Potential of People and Building Skills by Doing

By defining *community capacity* as the ability to dream big and move collectively toward a redefined future, we could learn by doing. To build specific skills, we put people — including ourselves — in situations we needed to learn our way through, and this revealed the largely untapped capacity for change that already existed.

4) Flexibility over Feasibility

As Joe Jacobs framed it when we first started thinking about developing a grocery: "If it were feasible, someone would have done it by now!"

With the Elementary Institute of Science, we learned that the right question wasn't "is it feasible?" It was "how do we make it feasible?" EIS successfully completed a $6 million campaign despite a feasibility study where expert methodology indicated it wasn't possible.

The discussion of feasibility prior to starting difficult work is discouraging and demoralizing. The key priority is to have the *flexibility and freedom* to figure out how to take a project that isn't seen as feasible, by any conventional standards, and get it investment-ready.

5) Use of Visuals so People Can Literally See the Future They Are Creating

Since many people are visual learners, the movement from vision to implementation is greatly enhanced through use of *visual aids.* We used storyboards, graphic illustrations, renderings, three-dimensional models, 3D architectural fly through animation, and any other supports that could make the work come alive for people.

Especially when working across languages, it was difficult to know if everyone was sharing the same vision when using just words. These aids provided people access to tools that could be shared more universally throughout the community than verbal descriptions. They helped residents understand the scale of the project to the neighborhood and its spatial orientation to the landmarks they cared about. They displayed how colors might or might not work together or architectural features might or might not reflect their cultures. Time taken to add illustrations to materials also helped people understand how debt and equity interact or how investment payouts would be made.

The investment in visuals was invaluable. Once people could see, they could do.

6) Visible Signs of Change

For vision to expand and become more dynamic, people need to achieve *visible signs of change* at regular intervals.

Residents envisioned a full-service grocery. Thirty years of attempts to recruit one had failed. People expressed that they were hesitant to believe, so we made a decision to start taking small steps before all the plans were complete, before the anchor was secured, before the financing was in place, and before contracts for tenants were drawn up.

When the barbed wire came down, excitement grew. When the demolition of the old factory was celebrated, more people wanted to participate. When the site was dedicated with a cross-cultural observance and blessing of the land being placed back into use, the number of people involved grew again.

Then the creek was restored. As CATS Excavating, a business run by two brothers who lived in the neighborhood, moved a crew on site to clear the land, people turned out to watch.

The work was incremental. The concrete channels that contained the creek came out, opening up the waterway. The grocery store contract was signed and celebrated with Food 4 Less. A team was initiated to work on community employment. The first building was completed in January 2001, and hundreds of residents gathered on site for the ribbon cutting. It was a monumental marker of how people had made way for change — one step at a time. And at each step, people celebrated.

For many, seeing was believing, and as more and more change became visible, belief grew. But for others — those who had served on teams from the very beginning, moving from task to task — there was a deepening of people's understanding of how believing was also seeing. Envision, act, see, celebrate, believe. Expand the vision and repeat the process.

The faster the rotation from vision to visible signs of change, no matter how small, the better.

The Art of Organizing

"When I told my dad that our meetings had all these ethnicities, he said 'that's impossible!' Then he came to a meeting. Now he's found his voice. It opened a door."

Macedonio Arteaga, a resident actively engaged in teaching youth about native cultures, often started a meeting by chanting to Father Sun and Mother Earth. He faced left, then right. The group would move with him. He might share his beadwork and ask others to share something that brought their history and heritage into the room.

Macedonio was born in Michoacan, Mexico, "land of the fish," he would tell you. His family moved to San Diego when he was five. He was bronze-skinned with beautiful black hair worn long, often braided down his back. The arch of his eyebrows and his gentle smile gave him a deep look, sensitive and probing. At first he was cynical and suspicious of "white people coming in to fix us." All he could think was "not again!" He didn't want to get involved.

What changed that for Macedonio was Roque. "For this guy to come here, it must be something." He had met Roque when he was Executive Director of Los Ninos, organizing in Mexico and found him "charismatic." He was an attractor — a person who had magnetic ability. And people trusted him. He was authentic and deeply experienced in how to reach people and get them involved.

So Macedonio started coming to meetings and "started seeing something that was revolutionary," he noted. "You were giving people a real voice. What sold me was that feeling you got when you walked in the room. Seeing so many people from different ethnic groups who felt they had a place."

"Dentenertulugar," he called it. "To have your place. We knew we would be listened to there, cared about there, respected — Somalis, Pacific Islanders, Sudanese, Mexicans, African Americans. Money can't build that. It was beautiful."

As the teams evolved, Roque would often ask Macedonio to facilitate the cross-cultural learning. "This kind of learning starts with the leaders," he shared. "If it's not in their hearts, this isn't going to work. There isn't any manual or book or training that can give you this kind of cultural know-how or proficiency. The elders could see it and feel it. I even majored in ethnic studies in college, but this opened my eyes! We all had a lot of stereotypes, false beliefs, and fears. They melted away."

"Perhaps you weren't even conscious of how you were building my leadership," he went on to say.

From where any one of us sat in the mix, it was hard to see all that was taking place at these gatherings, no doubt about it, but what I had become acutely aware of was my own relationship to residents as a peer leader. Roque was brilliant at finding ways to bring us together. Many residents described how Roque took their hands and would say "we believe in you."

"You believed in me until I believed in me!" Macedonio noted. "If you are Chicano, the messages don't stop; no matter who you are, you are less than. There isn't a day that you wake up and aren't conscious of your skin color. But when we were with you and your team, and our cultures were honored, we could learn about each other as humans. We felt free of the history of micro-aggression. You don't change a system to address this; grades don't measure this kind of growth. We didn't have to be defined by being poor. We were rich in culture. People could sing, dance, do beadwork — this was connecting us to our hearts."

The southeastern San Diego neighborhoods of the 1990's were both rich with diverse cultures, art, and traditions, and like many multi-cultural neighborhoods, also fraught with tension among ethnic groups and issues of isolation.

Working together to create a new future required us to be in new conversations with new people, to paraphrase Peter Block, and to do that we had to find a way to bridge ethnic divisions and create a platform for greater understanding. We put cultural appreciation and celebration at the heart of every meeting.

Early on, we held a series of **Ethnic Nights,** monthly events put on by residents from each of the major cultural groups. These evening events showcased and celebrated the history and heritage of people who lived in the community through art, displays, cultural song, dance, and traditional food. The series culminated in **Unity Day,** where all the cultures were celebrated together.

Resident-led tours throughout the neighborhoods provided a platform for people to tell us their histories through place — the parks where civil rights rallies were held, the hot spots where former jazz clubs attracted and energized people, the corridor once thriving with African-American businesses, and the site of the former Rancho Drive-In where stories of first kisses were shared.

These learning sessions helped deepen our understanding of histories and traditions, and they helped re-ignite the bond among people to place. This sharing was a source of pride for elders of the community, spurred learning among youth, and spawned ideas for the regeneration of their neighborhood.

Building on this momentum, vision and action planning workshops were held around every aspect of the project — art and design, business and leasing, construction, and ownership. These workshops were facilitated to also bring forward the indicators that would constitute success. It was in these large gatherings that Market Creek evolved from being a "neighborhood shopping center" into being a "center of commerce and culture."

Because the art and design team's work came first, it was fraught with challenges, but getting to the unique award-winning design that captured the beauty and spirit of the community's diverse backgrounds led to an important breakthrough in trust.

"It doesn't look like us," residents responded in reviewing the first architectural renderings of the project.

One-hundred-and-thirty-five people were present. Still early in our organizing, we were surprised by the turnout. We had hired an architectural team to create a site plan and design concept. We had asked the architects to do renderings that could be shown in resident meetings, but we were still new to how this type of participatory workshop process should be shifted in order to deepen the spirit of ownership of planning and placemaking.

Residents later said they expected that I would put the decision in the architects' hands, believing that they had the professional experience to know what was best. But when the architects couldn't translate what people envisioned, they were asked to try it again. The back and forth went on for months. The architects tried to capture what residents talked about but struggled to find the heartbeat and sense of place people wanted. All of us began to question whether or not design by committee was a good idea, including me.

But we all stayed committed to finding the ah-ha moment. Finally, with the process deteriorating, we asked the architectural firm to step aside so we could rebid the contract. Graciously the firm did that.

Residents were shocked. They had resigned themselves, thinking that out of frustration we would go with what was already on the table.

Four months later, when the Art & Design Team reflected on this moment, beaming with pride over their hard-won sense of place, a resident noted, "I learned we needed to stay at the table and keep at it when it's not right. We will discover what it is meant to be. We need to trust the struggle."

This resident bravely captured what we all felt — perhaps its most important learning. We needed to trust the struggle. Through this early process, trust was forming, and in this moment, residents realized we meant what we said about putting decisions in their hands. Residents would truly have a voice, and this voice went beyond giving input. To make this work, we would all have to stay at the table, stay in the struggle, stay and wrestle with the challenges until things felt instinctively right.

This process helped people see — in the most visual way possible — the impact of shared ownership of decisions. Organizing efforts leapt forward.

Form Follows Culture

"When the firm I worked for first started planning Market Creek, we thought our design direction was to do a shopping center. I remember presenting the master plan at the community meeting and a parent exclaiming, 'How dare you!'" noted Hector Reyes, the Plaza's architect.

"We had oriented the project to the main intersection, with a pathway cut diagonally through the trolley station from the corner to the site. She was upset that her children would be crossing the trolley tracks right where the trolley stops. She felt it was dangerous and was upset," he reflected. "So we came up with the idea of an underpass and integrated the trolley into the plaza with multiple walking paths. The idea came from the community."

This would be the first of many moments that upset or concerned residents would stop our team.

"Along with the safety of the walking paths, people were saying we shouldn't be doing something that can be seen anywhere and everywhere. They wanted it to reflect who they were. Everyone was having such a strong reaction the foundation wanted to try again," Hector reflected, remembering his disbelief. "What? New architects? What's going on? We were hurt and confounded that the foundation was stopping the process and doing a Request for Proposal for a design charrette with a group of architects."

"I went to my boss and said give me a week with free reign, and I can do it. Bravely, he said go for it. I wanted to kick ass. I wanted to re-win the contract."

In looking back on Market Creek, Hector notes that his biggest lesson was learning to "resolve a thousand voices into one communal voice." It was life-changing for this young architect who had grown up in Mexico.

"I learned how to dissect what the core pieces are and give them priority. I learned to listen and make decisions in that context. Everyone has something to say. Some people are more playful, some quiet, some not so quiet. You have to filter without something getting lost."

Since he was five years old, Hector wanted to be an architect. At age seven, he found a special leather trunk kept in a little cottage of his grandmother's.

"I grew up with my mamacita. She lived with us but kept her valuables in this cottage. When I opened it, it was filled with drawings, books, a protractor, and pencils. I was scolded for being where I wasn't supposed to be, but then she told me the story of my late Uncle Hector, who had studied to become an architect. He passed away after graduating from college in Mexico and my grandmother placed his drawings in this chest. "After that, I wholeheartedly knew I was going to be an architect."

Ready for college just as the Mexican peso was devalued, his father told him: "go to the United States and open your doors there." California Polytechnic State University, San Luis Obispo — top-ranked in architecture, followed by a year studying and working in Florence, Italy, Hector would land in San Diego with the firm that would take on Market Creek.

"I was young and at that moment in time had no business running that project," reflected Hector. "But I believe in serendipity. When moments come, what you do with them is up to you. This was my moment. My boss gave me a week to figure things out and that's what I did."

As part of the rebidding process, each of the competing architectural firms had to study the architectural character of the broad number of cultural backgrounds within the community and present their ideas to the group of 135 residents who served on the Art & Design Team.

Behind the scenes, architects shared how challenging it had been to find books in the local library — other than in the "primitive architecture" section — that reflected the range of cultures present in our community. Today with the internet, this dynamic may have played out much differently, given our ability to get beyond ethnocentric views of the world and search the beauty of the built environment from around the globe. But at that time, they had to stare in the face the racism inherent in architecture being defined by European models of cream-colored or grey square-box buildings and figure out how residents could see themselves in the character of the project.

To Hector, architecture without meaning becomes formulaic. "Form follows culture," he noted. "It became important to see the project as a whole, find its essence, and then to break it down into its component parts." As an architect, Hector had never worked on a project that was about "mutual authorship and responsibility by all who participated," but he was hungry to dig in and try it.

"I knew I was going against everything I was taught in school. I knew on this project the architect couldn't be the ego-centric carrier of the vision, so I decided to call all the artists that had been in the community meetings and ask them to come to my office for a working session on what they wanted to see. It was a wonderful blend."

Among the artists that came to Hector's office that day was Victor Ochoa. Roque had asked Victor to come to the table, knowing he was a respected and renowned muralist who had been part of the creation of Chicano Park. Many residents commented that San Diego's Barrio, the home of Chicano Park, was a place that spoke to them. Called the "East End" back in the 1800s, this area had transformed by the 1930's to one of the largest "Chicano Barrio communities" on the west coast.[56] In 1963, like many historically immigrant communities, Interstate 5 bisected the Barrio and by 1969, a new Coronado Bay Bridge opened with its huge pylons standing like monuments to the dislocation of families and the lack of community process.

In 1970, with 250 people occupying the land under the pylons prohibiting the bulldozers from moving on construction of a highway patrol station, Chicano Park was born, and its signature feature would become large colorful murals painted on the pylons by Chicano artists reflecting the Mexican-American culture. Among its muralists was Victor Ochoa.

Victor, who was strong, thoughtful, outspoken, and connected to a broad arts community, had played a pivotal role in helping Roque find a group of community artists that could participate on the resident team. "More sculptural, more playful, better integration of art with the buildings," were among the messages that came across loud and clear.

Three hours later, Hector quickly sketched the images he would present at the charrette.

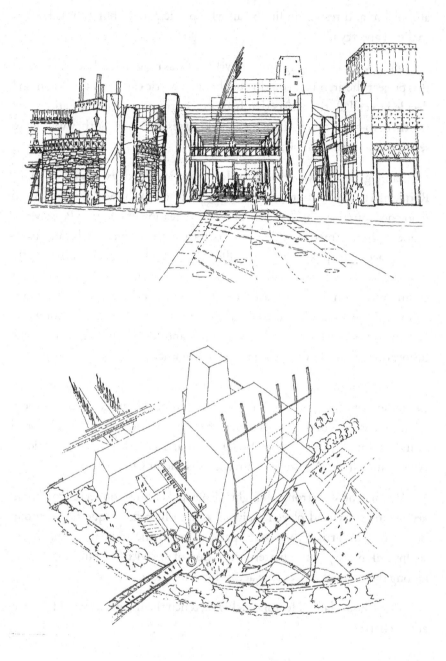

Illustrations by Architect Hector Reyes

"I thought I would be presenting, but at the last minute the format changed and everyone involved put their ideas in a big collage and residents were given stickers and told to put them on the ideas that best reflected who they were.

"My drawings got 80 percent of the stickers. We were back!"

Ironically, but not surprisingly, at the Art and Design Team's recommendation, we hired the same firm back, but this time with Hector Reyes in the lead and a team of artists working with him.

To support the undertaking, Hector and Victor asked residents from the various ethnic groups to bring the designs, textiles, tapestries, patterns, and architectural symbols that spoke to each of their cultures for a series of visioning workshops.

When residents shared their treasures, all of us could feel the commonality across cultures. "I came in the room feeling different and I left realizing that we all share a common human experience," one woman commented.

"Throughout both ancient and modern cultures, the carrier of the legacy and history of that culture has been its art. Because the southeastern San Diego neighborhoods are so diverse in cultures, ethnicity, and traditions, it seemed that Market Creek should share the story of the community through art," reflected Hector. "The search we went on together was to discover the architectural character of Market Creek, and it uncovered that strong, bold and colorful patters were the binding force."

Curves, domes, pyramid shapes, and totems were accented by terra-cotta, turquoise, blue, purple, orange, yellow, and olive-green colors.

In addition, a set of universal symbols were identified that crossed all cultures despite the vast distances, oceans, rivers, mountains, and other boundaries that separated them around the world. Three were selected.

Two — the sun and water, the elemental symbols of life in every culture — were selected because they seemed to capture San Diego's sun and the creek that cut through the property. The third symbol — the hand — in many of the cultures symbolized working together or unity. These three became the logo for Market Creek Plaza. Curved walls, pyramid shapes, cultural plazas and ceremonial grounds would become important design elements of planning Market Creek's sense of place. Time was also taken to master plan the site in a way to cultivate interaction. Rather than orienting the buildings to the street, buildings were oriented toward the amphitheater and creek with pathways connecting the trolley to the grocery and drawing people in toward the central plaza visually with bold tile tapestries and structural artwork and design.

Illustration by Architect Hector Reyes

Curved lines, iconographic cultural symbols and patterns, and bold colors captured the essence of multicultural unity and tradition. Hector, working in partnership with Victor and the other community artists, would win the American Institute of Architects, San Diego Chapter, Young Architect of the Year. The award — given for the application of architecture for community, social, cultural, and economic use, imaginative and powerful forward-looking ideas, and an understanding of materials and construction techniques — was a testament to the skill and bold ideas of a young man who valued listening and the co-creation of sense of place.

We all questioned whether taking the time was worth it. At the end of the day, we knew it had been. Hector had produced a dynamic and vibrant look and feel that was intended to provide the architectural character vision for all future buildings in the village, spreading the impact beyond the 10 acres to over 50. It created a beacon of cultural unity, bringing bright colors and unique forms to an area overwhelmed by grey deteriorating buildings and barbed wire.

"Many developers and architects are afraid of residents voicing what they want and need. They are afraid that people will ask for too much or that they will have unrealistic expectations. But for this project, we had to tap into the essence, the story, the history, and all the ideas that came forward and then put them all into the constraints that existed — and in a way that everyone could understand."

Hector, like the rest of us, had never done a project quite like this one. We were trusted, as Hector put it, "to figure it out in an unconventional way." He was a young and talented. "It was a success because of daring to do something nobody else was willing to do. It was for the future. It was about both physical and social change. Market Creek was a catalyst."

At the grand opening of the Food 4 Less grocery store, Hector remembers Joe asking him to sit down at a table with him. "You should go out on your own," Joe commented. "What are you afraid of?" To Hector, this moment was "so Joe."

"He was about risk. He was not going to give you anything you didn't earn," noted Hector. "My head was going a thousand miles an hour. Then he shared his own story. 'If you fail, you do it again,' Joe told me. Joe knew pressure. He thrived on it. He was a great mind. It was a wonderful moment with him."

Today, Hector has his own practice. "It challenges you to ask how flexible you are." He also teaches urban architecture and challenges his students to think about experiential space.

"I felt overwhelmed and privileged," he commented, thinking back the 16 years. "I learned that if people have passion, they do a good job. It was an emotional journey."

To See Yourself

"People need to see themselves... See themselves reflected back in the mainstream culture," said Jihmye Collins, one of the community artists working on the project. Jihmye was a poet and a painter. Some said he painted poems. Growing up in segregated Tennessee during Jim Crow, he had moved to San Diego in 1969 passionate about art and activism.

No one knew better than Jihmye, and all the artists who supported the art and design visioning process, about the importance of how we <u>see</u> ourselves and each other — literally and figuratively. These artists wanted art throughout the Plaza — art that reflected people back to themselves and was a part of everyday life. The art and design workshops were rich with ideas for visually making Market Creek come alive — ceiling murals, painted canvases honoring unsung heroes, cultural tapestries made in tile through the walkways, an opportunity for children to contribute hand-painted tiles for a retaining wall, and images of the sun, water, and hand imbedded in the concrete, adorning walkways and lights.

To begin implementing this goal of "reflecting back" everyday people in everyday art, the team began working on Market Creek's first major public art project, "Community Faces." Twenty-four panels, eight feet in scale, featured community members in portraits created by community artists and displayed on the sides of Food 4 Less. The city agreed to let us meet our "off-setting planes requirement" for the building (assuring it wasn't one big flat wall with no character) by constructing these panels. The project involved 12 community artists working in teams for the first time, 27 honorees, and 20 youth who were trained in videography, research, and interviewing and created an award-winning video on the lives of the honorees.

"It's like the Academy Awards!" one woman exclaimed.

The day of the unveiling the air was abuzz with red-carpet excitement. Traveling from all over the country, close friends and family of the honorees, the youth, and the artists — 500 people overall — packed into a tent to celebrate these community heroes.

To spotlight the individual cultures, we worked with the residents to find funding for cultural tapestries to be built into the Plaza's walkways. With resources in place for the first two, an African Batik and Laotian Tapestry were created, installed, and dedicated. A community artist and his son painted a ceiling mural on an expansive dome in the Mexican restaurant to commemorate the owner's family roots in Jalisco, Mexico. Later, as funding became available, a large sculpture of a Native American basket was dedicated along the creek near the Amphitheater.

A retaining wall was designated for neighborhood children to contribute a hand-painted tile to the Plaza. We had space for about 200 to 250 tiles, which became too small fast. When a thousand children turned out for the first workshops, we found a larger retaining wall. In the end, 1,700 children contributed their own signature art piece to a mosaic of a tree of life on a large wall overlooking Chollas Creek at the Amphitheater.

To bring added spirit to the green space graced by the **"Children's Wall,"** as it became known, additional funding was sought for Jean Cornwell Wheat, the community artist who had worked with the young people, to create a bronze statue for the green space near the wall. Her creative gift was of a young child in awe of a little dragon fly on his toe. The dragon fly, a symbol of change in ancient cultures, was for me Market Creek at its best.

I used to love to sit in that small grove near the Amphitheater and Children's Wall. One day, I overheard a child showing his mom his amazing artistic contribution to the tree of life.

"That's mine," the child said, pointing. He was beaming. So was his mom.

A Dedication to Placemaking

"Breaking new ground together" was the theme of the site dedication. It captured residents' sense of innovation and daring, as well as working together in unity.

Like everything else about Market Creek, the site dedication would not unfold in a way that was considered traditional for a groundbreaking — political leaders, foundation board members, other donors and a set of shovels. This would be a site dedication and groundbreaking that would push dream-making and spur residents to a greater platform for placemaking.

To dedicate and bless the site and future home for the community project, all the cultures joined together in celebrating, sharing, and learning. Each cultural group built a replica house from their native land or one that they thought represented their heritage. These temporary houses were placed in a circle, creating what the planning team called a "cultural village."

The dedication also included a series of large wood panels used to engage youth in reflecting a world village though graffiti art. The momentum that was generated by the young people grew, leading to reserving an adjacent lot for art panels and free spray paint. The **Graf Creek Team**, later changed to Writerz Blok, as the young people called themselves, was formed to oversee the art park and encourage youth to learn about graffiti as an art form.

A few years later, the cultural houses would be rebuilt with stronger materials and placed around a plaza that would become known as the **World Courtyard.** Attached to the 500-seat outdoor **Market Creek Plaza Amphitheater,** this plaza showcased both local and international talent and became a gathering place for community celebrations and cultural events.

These venues attracted thousands of residents to Market Creek each month, culminating in a major cross-cultural event. In 2010, the Arts and Culture Fest attracted more than 5,000 people from throughout the region to the site for a day-long celebration of cultural food, art, and entertainment.

This was powerful "dream work." The Village at Market Creek became more and more vibrant, colorful, and adorned with images that reflected back to people what they most treasured about themselves and their cultures. Blessed by Laotian monks, honored by the Native American ceremonial burning of tobacco, sprinkled with holy water by the Samoan priests, graced with a Samoan Kava Ceremony, and uplifted with African American spirituals, Somali poetry, and Mexican dance — this was land that each of us was given permission to inhabit, honor, care for, and pass on to the next generation.

And through each of these unifying threads of communication with the spirit world, we were all blessed in the process to see ourselves, each other, and our connectedness more clearly — a symbol of dynamic community placemaking.

Becoming the "Blok"

"I started hanging around at 16 years old," reflected Sergio Gonzalez, now in his thirties.

Sauntering into the local taco shop, Sergio would earn his street name — SergKat. "I came in like a cool cat," he shared, chuckling. "My role models were gang involved. I would study their arms when they came back from prison or jail. I loved the art, so I started tagging. I was 13 when I did my first tag. It was scary. All week that's all I could think about. Then I started teaming up. You could identify the ones you needed on your crew — they wore baggie pants, Pumas, hoodies, and hung out at break-dancing shows."

SergKat learned to "throw a bomb," meaning to hit a targeted mural wall quickly with paint. "You would scout out the walls during the day and then after the busses stop running, we would sneak out and throw up a piece. We looked for spots that would run the whole weekend. We knew if the business wasn't open it would stay up there. Later we added ropes and ladders — it was amazing risk-taking!"

Hanging out in Chicano Park, Sergio became familiar with and grew to admire Victor Ochoa, who was working on the Market Creek art and design, so he started coming around to see what was happening. "Supplies were getting tight," he remembered. "It was hard to get spray paint, and then someone said 'hey, there's a place where you can go on the second Wednesday.' I was riding the trolley and saw a bunch of taggers, so I just got out to see what was happening," which he did with caution. "There were these panels, and I thought: What am I walking into? Will I get jumped? Then I saw grown-ups! Yipes!"

The grown-ups were Victor and Roque. "Roque looked like a Peruvian drug lord handing out spray cans," Sergio laughed, remembering back. "He was clearly the bossman, the kingpin, and all I could think was 'this is not normal! I've seen enough of this kind of thing in the movies! I can figure this out! This is like the busts in the 1980s. I know what's going on!" Roque, Sergio contended, was trying to "lure" in the young people. And, in fact, that was exactly what he was doing.

With Victor and Roque passing out spray cans, the "Graff Creek" Graffiti Art Team grew its participation (once young people realized it wasn't a sting operation) from 30 to 40 to over 300 young people. With so much involvement, the Graffiti Art Park moved to a site across the street from Market Creek Plaza that could provide for over 13,000 square feet of outdoor art panels, and the team wanted to change its name.

"We got to paint the whole outside of the old Food-a-Rama building," Sergio shared. We were about to start demolition on the old corner lot grocery story, notorious for rats, beehives, and selling candy in the shape of drug paraphernalia, and the Graff Creek Team wanted to decorate the entire building for Halloween. "We turned it into a haunted house and called it Boo-a-Rama. While we were painting, one of the artists said I have writer's block, and we though that's it! Writerz is another name for tagging, and we are block of writerz, and so we changed our name to Writerz Blok."

The Writerz Blok team began expanding, going beyond just offering mural space, to teaching mural art. The San Diego Neighborhood Funders, a group of 14 foundations, banks, and individuals that formed a collaborative to support the community teams, provided funding to Writerz Blok for computers, silk screening equipment, and other business resources. Writerz Blok began to train youth in graphic design, silk screening, and poster print, and eventually added a range of income-producing activities, putting young people's gifts and talents to work.

Jose Venegas, who along with Sergio, would become the leadership team for Writerz Blok, noted that "the idea of graffiti wasn't talked about at school, but by third grade I was trying to copy the art. I was from Shelltown, right next to the Barrio. It was gang territory, and they put me in the class with all the bad kids. That's where I met Sergio!" he laughed. "We were on our way to commit a crime when this kept us out of trouble."

Many of the young people who would shape the agenda for Writerz Blok had "earned their marks by hitting all of the San Diego freeways," they would tell you. By the time they left high school, they were no longer taggers, but artists. And because Writerz Blok provided a safe place to do outdoor murals, world-renowned graffiti artists came to paint, providing mentorship to local muralists and leaving art for young people that was aspirational.

"We were scared and needed direction," Jose remembers. "Who's going to do all the hard stuff, like meet with the funders?" he remembers thinking. "We were afraid," added Sergio, "but we figured it out."

They divided up roles: Jose took production, graphic design, and screen printing. Another team member was a good speaker so he became program manager. When it was Sergio's turn, he remembered, "all the roles were taken except finance. What am I going to do? Then I thought 'Oh, fuck-it, I'll do that!'"

For me at the time, I thought if young people were going to accept serious roles and responsibilities, I needed to be sure that I took them seriously and got the tools they needed in their hands. I called the bank and asked if someone could come over and meet the new Vice President of Finance for one of our programs and help set up a bank account. It was a precious moment to see the bank manager's face when I introduced seventeen-year-old Sergio as the V.P. of Finance.

"There was kind of a shock both for the banker and for me," remembered Sergio. "I felt so out of place, like I didn't belong. I was afraid he would ask about my qualifications. Then you softened him up and put him at ease. 'He will be trained and will have support,' you said. The banker just went with it. I wasn't primary, but my name would be on that document. It was an awesome feeling. Now I belonged. I was no longer an outsider. I was part of a team and accepted."

Young people set the rules and because they owned them, they followed them, drawing youth from throughout the region and across gang affiliations. In 2000, Writerz Blok was honored with the San Diego Mediation Center's prestigious Peace Maker Award. Today, the work of Writerz Blok can be seen in venues from San Diego's Children's Museum and Contemporary Museum of Art to foundation lobbies and school walls.

Few people that have travelled to visit Market Creek from around the world have left without spending time at the amphitheater, on the World Courtyard, or taking a graffiti art lesson at Writerz Blok. These launched the tagline that Market Creek was a place "where the world meets." Whether it was the journey of people from around the globe to this place or the rise of the hip hop culture among young people — Market Creek's placemaking was shaped and celebrated by the community who envisioned it.

I know that Market Creek's accomplishments may be measured by square feet of construction, number of jobs, or value of contracts, but I think its most significant impact was the vision, spirit, and will of residents to create a place rooted in their heritage.

"It was a life-changer." Sergio gleamed. "To identify as a human being, a member of a community, to see change, to see life, my life, reflected in the youth that are there now and changing — it was an opportunity to envision something and bring it into being. Our moms are proud!"

A Vision Owned

For the 10 years following the first survey in 1997, the vision for the site of an abandoned industrial dump had grown from being a neighborhood shopping center to being a center of culture and commerce. Then, residents pushed the vision out even further to an entire village that would be a bustling residential, commercial, and cultural district built upon the multicultural strength of the surrounding neighborhoods.

As the dream of ownership took hold and the visioning process gave shape and form to an IPO through which ownership would become a reality, the vision expanded again into a global village that was community-planned, designed, built, managed, owned, and operated, providing residents a direct economic stake in neighborhood change. As work was implemented and became visible, so the vision grew and moved further out.

By 2011, it encompassed plans for eliminating the blight surrounding Market Creek Plaza and putting over 50 acres of land back into productive use — replacing substandard housing with nearly 1,000 quality affordable homes, restoring nearly 5,500 linear feet of wetlands, implementing over 1.6 million square feet of new construction with more than $300 million in community contracts, attracting over 250 new businesses, and creating over 2,000 jobs.

The village teams also focused on sustainability and challenged people to think about health, green buildings, solar energy generation, and water usage, side by side with the financial structures to sustain parks, support cultural venues, and build jobs. Over time, these teams found themselves working at the intersection of long-term community ownership and sustainable, equitable development.

Arts and culture became the unifying force for residents to work across neighborhoods, ethnicities, and generations; strengthen joint action and increase the ability to break down barriers; push through the issues of race and class; and engage in the creative exchange of ideas.

Long-term disinvestment isolates, causes a disconnect, disheartens people and traps them in their homes. But as engaged citizens of a global village, residents can connect with each other and their community. With dream work, residents can create a dynamic vision of a world built on the strength of cultural diversity, creative problem-solving, shared risk, and strong relationships — the foundation for long-term and enduring community change.

12
TEAM WORK

*"When I get together with other musicians for a jam session,
the group starts with a theme, plays with it, and passes it around.
Suddenly the music lifts off, flies. We all fly with it.
This is not formless self-indulgence or organizational anarchy.
The music follows an elegant grammar, a set of conventions that guide
and challenge our imagination. It is an explosion of inspiration
within the art's given universe. No matter how high we fly, we always
return with something new, something we've never heard before."* [57]

—- John Kao, Jamming

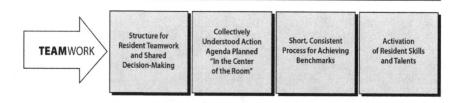

Structure for Shared Decision-Making

"I know how to stop things; I don't know how to build consensus to make things work."

Tambuzi had a long history of social justice organizing.

Named Bobby Dwayne Cunningham at birth, he was renamed Tambuzi in the late 1960's by civil rights activist, Vernon Sukumu, in honor of the African tradition of naming people for current circumstances or for the qualities the family hopes for the child. Tambuzi, which means clear-sighted or intelligent, was spot on. His range was extensive and he stood out — not because of his distinct Malcolm X-like look, chiseled chin, or West African orange and green cotton dashiki — but because he was formidable. Challenging. Smart. Experienced in social change movements and well-read when it came to the great leaders who fought injustice and changed the world.

"My mom had me at 15, and I am the oldest of six children," he shared about himself. "I have a restless spirit." And after 40 years of civil rights struggle, he can still get mad — about "black boys being killed by white police officers," about "being played," and about "funders who import programs from other places and don't care about social justice."

Southeast, as the community had become known, he noted, "started as a geography and then it became a designation given by the larger society, synonymous with 'that's where people of color live and where crime, prostitution, murder, and gang violence are.'" He had lost a child to gang violence and talked about wanting to use his hurt to heal his community.

Tambuzi's restlessness, formidable and disruptive style, and his ability to "stop things," as he put it, made him the kind of person I wished initially wouldn't show up to meetings. Later, I came to count on him as a truth-teller and difference-maker. He was not only clear-sighted and intelligent, he was a test for me about how serious I was about inclusion. He stood as a constant reminder that I'd better not "overlook the circumstances of economic injustice which makes philanthropy necessary" in the first place, as Martin Luther King, Jr. so eloquently framed it.

Having worked on the picket lines during the nationwide strike and boycott on grapes for Cesar Chavez, I understood the need for communities to "stop things" and exert pressure on decision-makers and found myself wondering if the rules that govern foundation support of groups with a 501(c)3 tax status and the proliferation of the non-profit world during my generation had been detrimental for movement-building. The rules and the model of funding program delivery seemed in the way of sustained efforts to achieve social justice.

Since our charge was not to stop things but try to "figure out how to make things work," we needed some way to shift the paradigm away from funding organizations that mobilize and train residents to put pressure on the decision-makers to directly asking everyday people — citizens — to step into decision-making roles. We needed to create the opportunity to build understanding, trust, and drive that comes from action based on their own decisions with their own capital at risk.

One of the conundrums in the early Community Change Initiatives (CCIs) was the issue of governance. By setting up highly-structured governing bodies early in the process, some of these efforts were not able to achieve broad inclusion because they became what residents described as "gatekeeper" groups of leaders, who were proprietary about information and couldn't build broad consensus.

Rather than moving immediately to governance, we opted for building the natural momentum by working together first, then asking for residents' help in figuring out how to achieve the design of an inclusive structure that would allow people in and out, wouldn't become a group of "gatekeepers" to decision-making and problem-solving, would value ongoing community listening, and could hold people accountable to a larger and larger network of residents. We would let governance evolve.

Our platform for shared decision-making became "working teams."

These teams were mobilized to build relationships and networks, lift up vision and voice, and keep the community good above self-interest in the planning. A working team was initiated by an open invitation to residents for a specific area of work. After all those interested set goals and established plans, a smaller team of residents volunteered to guide the work and make sure it stayed accountable to the larger group's goals. These teams were the platform for ongoing shared decision-making and trust-building. All project information, including the financial proforma, was made public so residents could grapple with the issues as they arose and gain a strong knowledge base about the project.

We were intentional about not labeling people "the leadership" of the project or creating a community board. Teams were facilitated, not chaired. In one exception, a team decided it wanted a chairman. Sadly, the meeting format drifted quickly away from group facilitation to Robert's Rules and became more of a traditional and hierarchical decision-making body. This team imploded within a year.

Creating an open process for shared decision-making requires a different way to manage teamwork. It is not about trying to get from point A to point B the fastest way possible; it is about getting at the underlying contradictions and barriers that keep disinvested communities stuck.

The Theory, Practice, and Power of Participation

"Lift every voice..." Ardelle Matthews would sing.

At the Martin Luther King, Jr. celebration, I could hear her voice above the rest. You could pick her out in a crowd. Her joyful spirit, like her reddish-brown hair with its distinctive flip at the ends, was uplifting. She was always looking after me. In the crowded room, she would move my direction and hand me the words to the Black National Anthem, smile, move back to her spot, and then continue. She approached "Lift Every Voice and Sing" as her charge, a cherished song, sung for a century. She was a link in the chain that had continued since James Weldon Johnson, who wrote the lyrics, and this was her watch.

Ardelle never held back — not singing and not in her commitment to participating in her community. She participated on multiple teams and would write me long letters, thanking me, encouraging me to continue, and sharing what else she thought her community might need that hadn't been discussed.

I had gotten to know Ardelle through her granddaughter, Breanna Zwart, who had served at age 10 on the Elementary Institute of Science youth board. I had the privilege of watching this bright young spirit grow up, and through Breanna, had fallen in love with her grandmother.

Like her granddaughter, Ardelle took ownership of change. She was not a side-liner. She accepted accountability for her watch. Her message to me wasn't just about "don't do about me without me," although she would never let me forget that. She intuitively knew that to go far we needed to go together and that inspired action road on the shoulders of her community's own creativity.

Ardelle, with sleeves rolled up, was not only prepared to be a voice in the crowd, she stood ready to make sure I lifted up and listened to every voice.

To do that, the theory, practice, and power of participatory planning became one of our first and most important tools.

In 1993, the economic development collaborative we were funding around small business development and economic opportunity in response to LA burning was falling apart. The group needed a time-out from the day-to-day stress and I recommended we spend a weekend together to get to hear each other's concerns and decide if there was enough commitment to continue. I hired two skilled facilitators from the Institute of Cultural Affairs (ICA-USA[58]), John Oyler from the ICA Phoenix office, and Teresa Lingafelter from Los Angeles.

Started in Chicago in the 1960s and growing to 34 autonomous offices around the world, ICA has been stimulating social change in communities for 50 years. ICA-USA, whose mission is to build a just and equitable society in harmony with Planet Earth (www.ica-usa.org), partners with a national network of licensed trainers who deliver facilitation courses to over 1,000 participants annually. Through practical experience and applied learning, ICA — with this network of trainers — has developed and refined a set of integrated facilitation methods that foster participation, enhance collaboration, and enable groups to think and plan together — across differences.

Experiencing these methods, called the *Technology of Participation (ToP)* ©, which I did for the first time at this retreat, was like being exposed to the awe-inspiring World Wide Web for the first time. I was speechless.

In his masterful book, Transformational Strategy: Facilitation of ToP Participatory Planning,[59] written 20 years after I first experienced the "happening" (as he calls it) of the power of participation, Bill Staples traces the history and evolution of the ToP process, from early theorists in social psychology and organizational development to more recent influences like Appreciative Inquiry.

In the book, he shares how early ToP founders were highly influenced by Victor Frankl's 1945 book, Man's Search for Meaning, noting that these methods weren't developed "merely as a way to increase productivity or efficiency, or even as a better way of getting things done, but rather as a way for people to take control of their lives and to transform the external situation in which they found themselves."[60]

The general theory of participation is based on the belief that people who are deeply engaged and contribute to a plan make a commitment to action and own the approach for moving forward. It is rooted in a philosophy of inclusion and empowerment. "Social change agents," Bill writes, "have always known that the best way to empower people is to have them participate in the decisions that affect them."[61]

Also influencing ToP were the existentialist philosophers and theologians of the early and mid-20th century who posited that every human being has unlimited power and potential and can make life-changing decisions at the local level that can alter both social and historical trends.

According to Bill, the single most powerful component of ToP comes from the Institute of Cultural Affairs' theory of "Imaginal Education," which was developed during the 1960s in ICA's community development work in Chicago's West Side. Imaginal Education links group-image, self-image, and messages with values and behaviors. By linking meaning with the development of a personal and group story and revitalizing the image of who people are and what they are capable of as a community, ToP gave practitioners in thousands of communities, organizations, and companies around the world the tool they needed to help people achieve a deep sense of purpose, commitment, motivation, ownership, and inspired action.

In the practice of participation, facilitators help large groups of stakeholders organize disparate ideas into consensus points by using half-sheets of paper to capture and cluster ideas. These are then organized on a large wall. To support the process, facilitators use questions to guide an open inquiry, surface diverse perspectives, pull forward unconscious feelings so they are not confused with facts, engage people in naming contradictions together so everyone has a common understanding of what needs to be addressed. Through this process, strategies are aimed at what is standing in the way of success in order to move rapidly to actionable plans.

The discovery of the Technology of Participation, and the underlying philosophy, placed in our hands a critical tool for lifting up the voice of residents and avoiding a group dynamic in which having differences engenders conflict. It gave us a straight-forward methodology for achieving understanding and having differences pave the way for a sense of connectedness with a common story, creative solutions, genuine commitment, and ownership of action.

This was exactly the kind of planning process and group learning theory we needed. These methods not only helped our team facilitate diverse groups of stakeholders create and implement a shared vision for their community, they were also methods that could be easily shared in the community.

John Oyler, the ICA facilitator who conducted the retreat that was my first exposure to ToP, and his wife Marilyn, another master ICA facilitator and one of the founders of the ToP Network, became early members of our team.

"The most powerful experience," John reflected, "was that as facilitators we didn't go in as outsiders, but rather came in as part of the team and worked together. To me, that is the best kind of facilitator. The conversation wasn't about 'what are you going to do' rather 'what are we going to do.' We were looking for the same thing from the group. What are we causing and holding in place, and what will we do together."

As a tool for community change, three things made these methods different, in both philosophy and process, and incredibly powerful for getting at the deeply entrenched issues disinvested communities face:

- the uncompromising commitment to being broadly inclusive,
- the fundamental focus on "contradictions," and
- ownership of action.

Over time, the various community teams modified, added to, and adapted these methods, but the fundamental philosophy of participation developed by ICA continued to guide our work for nearly two decades, and the tenets of inclusion, the naming of underlying contradictions, and a focus on ownership of action stayed fundamental and important parts of our work.

The Uncompromising Commitment to Inclusion

When Albert Einstein said "You can't solve a problem with the same consciousness that created it," he could have been pondering the conundrum of foundation "initiatives" in our historically disinvested communities.

To let go of old patterns and discover new ways of thinking, we needed – as funders — to embrace world views different from our own and that required a very broad definition of "stakeholder" and an uncompromising commitment to inclusion.

Participatory planning techniques provided an important tool for gaining agreement from and managing action with large numbers of people — teams ranging from 25 to 125 and town hall meetings with 400 to 500 community residents participating. Broad participation at this level of inclusion was essential for two critical reasons:

1. New ways of thinking

    All Market Creek stakeholders — each of us individually, not just institutionally — needed to have our perspectives confronted so we could see the world in a new way, open ourselves up to new risks, and think freely about new ways to do the work of community regeneration together. Working across disciplines, sectors, areas of interest, cultures, and age-groups built understanding, helped us see in our blind spots, and kept us constantly challenging old assumptions. Diversity was our greatest asset.

2. Modeling the future we hope to create

    If our goal was to achieve a society that is inclusive, embraces differences, is built on a foundation of dignity and respect for all, and can tap people's gifts and talents, we needed a process that was uncompromising in reflecting these values. All planning, deliberation, decision-making, and teamwork needed to model the future we wanted to create.

Dealing with Contradiction

"It's hard getting at the underlying contradictions, being able to call them out and have people embrace them and take them seriously," noted Marilyn Oyler. "People have generally noticed them but have written them off as just the way life is."

The Technology of Participation gave the Market Creek teams a process for getting at the unspoken barriers that were blocking success. Discussions about what was standing in the way of the future envisioned — particularly with diverse groups that have multiple interpretations of what those barriers are — could be challenging or even painful, but naming them provided the doorway to strategy, innovation, and change.

"It's important for groups to notice and name the contradiction, not to beat people up, but to trigger forgiveness and get people to say to each other 'This is a goal that is bigger than us, so it requires all of us.'" noted Marilyn. This conscious naming of the tension between the current situation and the vision has to be stared in the face, and this gave us a process for doing that.

To illustrate the concept of contradiction, Bill Staples in his book on transformational strategy notes: "Racism and slavery were not only unjust, they were genuine contradictions that attempted to hold back a new world of freedom and opportunity by maintaining an old world of class domination."[62] This contradiction impacted our country's bold vision of freedom so deeply that its impact is still being felt.

There is never one view in any group, but what do you do in groups where the table has been set with electrically-charged perspectives? In an ethnically diverse group, how do you assure that the dynamic articulated by the old Southern saying "if you are white you are right" doesn't take over how issues are defined before solutions get articulated? How do you surface everyone's reality and jointly name what's in the way?

The focus on contradictions or underlying barriers created the kind of action planning we needed. We didn't just pose the question about how to get to an outcome the fastest way possible. We needed to give people space and time to surface issues, bring them into view, and *agree* on what they were so joint action was possible.

This process helped teams get beyond emotional hurt, breakdown resistance to change, let go of blame, and embrace the opportunity to give strategic focus to achieving a new future with renewed energy so everyone could take action in a daunting and complex environment. This was particularly important in situations where everyone knew emotions were going to be high, hurt deeply rooted, and risk defined by lives that had been lost.

One of the most profound examples of how confronting the tension of opposing viewpoints can lead to break-through occurred when law enforcement and residents joined together on a team to create safe streets. In the gulf between how white people and black people view the police and in the crevices between how residents and law enforcement experience each other was the exact space where these conversations needed to occur.

The team created a series of conversations between residents and the police called "Safe Talk." At first, the exchanges were challenging, hard, and harsh.

For residents experiencing beyond-reasonable suspicion, stop and frisks, the denigration of forced curb-sitting, and a long history of excessive force — and who feel they have not been heard — the response has been either shut up or shout. For police, who live out their daily lives in uncertain and potential danger, there was another side to the story that also needed to be shared. But because they represented power — and the historical abuse of power — they first needed to listen.

When residents first and then police were given the space to share without being shut down, without being stopped, and without the reproach of an immediate defensive position, the dynamic in the room moved from shout to share and ultimately to embracing joint action. Out of these meetings, police ended the practice of curb-sitting and developed strategies for ending excessive force. Residents joined with police in midnight rounds to get children home safely and worked in a very personal way to get rid of unsafe areas of their community.

People were humanized. Residents became more than potential criminals and police more than badges.

This teamwork and the process that created a shared understanding of the barriers to public safety provided the platform for people to be heard, agree on and name the barriers, and then find the most catalytic direction together.

Ownership of Action

For change to take root, people need to be involved, valued, and voice what they really believe is standing in the way, so that all stakeholders' ideas can be combined in a way that achieve economy of effort and leverages action. And change isn't something one group tries to "do" to another; it is an agenda that needs to be widely embraced and owned across the community.

When people make plans, they care about them. When they care about them, they can implement them. Culture might eat strategy for lunch,[63] but when it comes to inspired action, participation feeds ownership and ownership feeds change.

Over time, all of us participating on the Market Creek teams began to discover new levels of collaboration, caring, and accountability. "We need to slow down," one resident said in a team meeting. I was struck by the comment, because it marked a shift in our work from the impatience and frustration that had been profound in the first six months of teamwork. This resident, who had been voicing constant criticism, had changed. "We have people here who don't speak English," he commented, "and we need to make sure they understand and their voices are heard."

The Institute of Cultural Affairs opened a window for us into the world of participation. They showed us that consensus doesn't have to be about majority rule or going with the popular position; it can be about the discovering the common sense of a group — conclusions achieved out of shared understanding. It doesn't have to be about drawing logical deductions based on past assumptions; it can be about uncovering new options and opportunities.

And they showed us that when working across differences, the goal doesn't have to be about achieving compromise. With a solid process it can be about coming to value each other's ideas through challenging conversations so new insights are unearthed and the group can move together on the actions it comes to see as necessary.

When existing elements need to be reordered and people accept ownership of that new future, teams can muster the courage to act across organizational, sectoral, generational, and cultural boundaries. Transformational change does not happen through increased productivity or filling gaps in services; it is created by putting ourselves continuously in situations where new insight can be gained, a new world view can be adopted, a culture of dreaming big and taking risk can be embraced, and permission to try new ways of being are the norm.

Because community change is deeply rooted in people's will, motivation, and expectations, the more inclusive the planning, the more personal the motivation, and the broader the ownership, the greater the impact.

When Motivation Gets Personal

"Market Creek gave my family a sense of connection to our homeland."

The first thing you notice when you meet Rahmo Abshir Abdi is her large, captivating eyes that sparkle when she smiles. She draws you in. Her head-scarf — her hijab — frames her face making her eyes all the more unforgettable. She describes herself as shy, and she might be, but I think she is incredibly courageous. Because she is a mother of six, who recently earned her associate's degree, I also think she is tireless.

When Rahmo talks about the Market Creek experience, she talks about how people "just kept coming because it was like getting a one-way ticket around the world, and you could go everywhere in one day!" From the creation of the cultural houses and tile tapestries to the formation of the International Outreach Team, on which Rahmo served, the Market Creek experience was grounded in the celebration, appreciation, and understanding of culture and the connection of people to place.

"Market Creek was the first place to welcome the Somali community. It was a village for us. Its diversity was beautiful," she reflected.

One of sixteen children, Rahmo was born in Mogadishu, Somalia, and made it out of her civil-war-torn country with her grandmother and three of her siblings to a refugee camp in Kenya at age 10. "We spent five years there waiting for the United Nations with no electricity, no private bathrooms, living in a tent, and we were lucky it was only five years."

When they got to the U.S., she was happy to be safe, but she would experience the shock of being different. "I didn't know the language and the kids were mean to me. I was in high school by then and students would pull my scarf," she remembered. "With 9/11, it got worse for us. My sister almost got run over crossing a street, and the driver yelled out his window 'Go back to your country!' My sister yelled back at him 'This is my country!' There was a lot of harassment."

For Rahmo, the work of building cultural understanding was close to her heart. "Islam is a religion of peace, but people assume you are a terrorist. When people think of Somalia, they think of pirates or the militant youth of al-Shabaab," Rahmo reflected, "or they think because you are a refugee that you are nothing and that you know nothing, so the work at Market Creek was very personal for me. It wasn't really work. It was something I loved. I couldn't wait to get up and go back the next day! I liked that our voice was being heard. We were recognized as human beings. We were sitting at the same table with non-Somalis and were being heard!"

Rahmo found Market Creek because she was invited to attend a training given by the Refugee Women's Network, after which she made a pledge to help others. "I understand what it's like to leave your country because of war. It's hard to fit in here. I don't want young girls to suffer the way I did. I needed to raise money, so I would go to the Jacobs Center and bother Roque a lot! I didn't get a grant, but I got to use the facility to do a fundraiser!" She raised the money she needed to take her 10 women leaders to Atlanta for a national convening of the network.

Rahmo was hired to join the International Outreach Team and later became a Community Coordinator. "I was passionate about the work. I cared deeply about sharing the uniqueness of my culture, history, traditions, and food. Not only did I get to reach people about my culture, I got to learn about all the other cultures. Where can you get that?"

Along with the power of cross-culture learning, when Rahmo thinks of the Market Creek experience, she thinks of three unforgettable moments. The first was the experience of taking her children to the cultural houses. "They showed who we are," she reflected, talking about how they created a connection for them to her homeland. The second was her ah-ha moment about asking for assistance. "There was a moment with one of my co-workers when I learned to not be shy about asking for help. Working as a team was the most important thing, and that meant I needed to be able to ask my teammates when I was unsure about something."

Her third moment — and by far the most amazing to her — was the grand opening of the Joe & Vi Jacobs Center, an event that many have described as a magical gathering of 2,000 people experiencing the beauty of our multicultural world. "It was incredible!" she exclaimed.

What was incredible to Rahmo is that Lisette Islas, our Director of Community Organizing, listened to her and responded. Lisette had asked her how the Somali community might want to be involved, and Rahmo thought of bringing in Sadia Elmi, a famous Somali poet, now living in Seattle, to participate. "Somali is a nation of poets. Without an official written language until 1972, our communication was through poetry. Everyone recites poetry. I tried to translate Sadia's work so Lisette could understand and she agreed."

That day, the Somali community turned out. "I was so proud," Rahmo shared. "In Islam, women are not supposed to dance in public, so we were given our own large room on the second floor to share poetry and the women danced. Men were invited to watch from the side of the room. It was beautiful!"

For Rahmo, the work was very personal and grounded people. "In Somalia," she shared, "once you've shared a meal, you are family. It was like a second home." And if the resident teams were a family, they were an expanding one, which meant that we were constantly challenged to find new ways to manage work that was growing in scope, scale, and complexity.

Rahmo was one of hundreds of people that were drawn to Market Creek for very intimate reasons: hers the shock of being different. What was so magnetic about the teamwork was that the motivation residents brought to the experience that propelled cross-cultural understanding and drove community change was personal.

The Evolution of Teams

Our journey in forming teams started with Roque, whose early office was his car and a cell phone, walking the streets, knocking on doors, asking people about their community, the old factory site, and what they liked and didn't like about their neighborhood. He engaged them in conversation, asking them if they would like to work on a project to get rid of the factory. He surfaced eight people who were willing to serve as this initial outreach team.

With this group of residents, our teamwork for Market Creek Plaza would be launched. Over time, outreach, team development, and cross-team coordination evolved through four distinct phases:

1. An Outreach Team, Planning Teams, and Open Houses;
2. Community Coordinators, Working Teams, and a Working Teams Council;
3. An International Outreach Team, Mix-and-Match Village Teams, and a Village Teams Council; and
4. Project VOCAL

Phase 1 — The Outreach Team, Planning Teams, and Open Houses

The Outreach Team, which helped design the first community listening project and survey process, also became our first teachers about the neighborhoods' cultures, foods and traditions, along with what they struggled with and what they valued. They also worked to expand the number of people who wanted to be involved, asking people to participate on planning teams in their interest areas — art and design, construction, business and leasing, and childcare. Each time a new phase of the work was launched, a new set of teams was created to address the planning. The teams were open to any and all people who wanted to participate and the Outreach Team recruited heavily.

These teams were set up as time-specific groups and each had a clear goal to be achieved. Food, always purchased from local community businesses, made it possible for whole families to easily participate. A window was cut through a wall that connected a small area ideal for childcare so parents could see their children during the meetings. With the opportunity to come together, bring their families, share food and meet neighbors, people looked forward to participating. They knew they were going to be asked to work but felt their time was being valued. Later, translation and transportation were also provided if needed. Food, fun, and meaningful agendas magnetized meetings and kept people coming back.

The Outreach Team also helped us organize quarterly open houses to provide a forum for any and all community residents, whether or not they served on a team, to ask questions, provide feedback, learn how they could get involved if they chose to, and stay connected to the work.

Phase 2 — Community Coordinators, Working Teams, and a Working Teams Council

As the need for deeper and broader community listening grew, we hired residents within neighborhoods to add "living room meetings" to the surveys, outreach, and open houses. We rented their homes for $100 and paid for food that they prepared. This process helped us identify residents for a

"Community Coordinators" training program. The Outreach Team, which had been a survey group, phased out, and these Community Coordinators assumed the role of organizers.

As the turn-out for the large resident teams and stakeholder meetings grew in stages from 30 to 50 to over 200, smaller working teams were formed by posing the question in the larger community meetings "who needs to be involved?" — both specific people and or skill-sets — and "who wants to be involved?" These working teams were charged with guiding the implementation and the achievement of the goals set in the community planning process.

Working Team Process

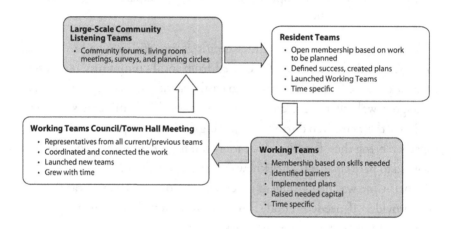

As the number of working teams multiplied, we needed some way to keep people connected. To assure that coordination, a *Working Teams Luncheon* was hosted with representatives from each of the teams, reporting on their work and planning open forums.

The open forum, named *The Working Teams Council,* was conducted as a town hall meeting to keep everyone updated about the broader work and promote individual team accountability to the larger community. Anyone who served on a team at any time was part of the Working Teams Council, so it was always expanding.

Often, the residents serving on working teams were hired as consultants to undertake the work set by the larger community team and then report back. Some people appreciated that we valued their time and paid them as we would all specialized consultants who worked on the project. They were thankful that they or their children could earn money working on improving their community. Others found it controversial and didn't take payment, not wanting to be seen as being "paid off" or their role as independent residents compromised. They wanted to remain volunteers.

Phase 3 — An International Outreach Team, Mix-and-Match Village Teams, and a Village Teams Council

To assure cultural diversity, our partners in the San Diego Neighborhood Funders collaborative helped fund an *"International Outreach Team"* made up of residents of each major cultural group. This group consisted of people who wanted to deepen or share their understanding of their own heritage (young people teamed with elders) and become the pathfinders for bringing more and more people together across cultures. They were Latino, African American, Samoan, Laotian, Somali, Sudanese, Filipino, Chamorro, and later Kumeyaay (the Native American tribe with historical connections to the land).

The International Outreach Team (IOT) provided a platform for cross-cultural learning. Trained as organizers and historians, they both showcased the rich cultural traditions of the community and were central in creating the vision for a cultural village.

Over time, the working teams evolved to achieve greater diversity — not just cultural diversity but more cross-fertilization of ideas. Residents had initially engaged on the teams that interested them, like childcare or housing, but as the vision of a large-scale cultural village took root, it was clear we would have to work at the intersection of issues, such as childcare and housing. To address this, we began to launch *"Mix-and-Match Village Teams,"* combining people from different teams to assure a range of perspectives and to balance social and economic goals.

As the work evolved from Market Creek Plaza to the Village at Market Creek, the Working Teams Council shifted to a *"Village Teams Council"* and continued as the town hall forum for large cross-team interaction.

Phase 4 — Project VOCAL

By 2008, we needed to find a way to build a larger and larger organizing capacity that could crisscross cultures, neighborhoods, and planning around specific components of the village. We also needed a larger network, external to the Jacobs Center, that could become the keeper, as people called it, of the village vision and values.

Rather than having an on-staff International Outreach Team (IOT), we moved to providing stipends to a network of community and cultural groups identified by the IOT, which then selected representatives to serve as a coordinating body. In addition to the nine cultural groups, representatives of other key networks were added to the mix — the Coalition of Neighborhood Councils, four of the individual neighborhood councils, the United African American Ministerial Action Council, the PTAs, the Diamond Business Improvement District board, the two ownership groups for Market Creek Plaza — Diamond Community Investors and the Neighborhood Unity Foundation — and a team known as the Youth Movement.

This network was called Project VOCAL (Voices of Community at All Levels). Since each of the groups selected their own participants, they now had a sense of ownership over the involvement of their individual network, as well as a commitment to the greater vision. In this way, we had moved toward being able to figure out what representative governance might look like.

Embedded in this larger network of organizers was the potential to become a platform for long-term ownership, sustainability, and governance of civic action within the village.

People often ask me "If you could start over, would you start with VOCAL?"

My answer is no. For this platform to succeed, it needed the work that preceded it — the track record, trust, and the rich history of the Outreach Team, the Community Coordinators, and the International Outreach Team.

And it needed the gradual growth of the working teams as the primary platform for shared decision-making.

This kind of teamwork was unheard of in commercial development. Typically, the planning goes on behind closed doors and is largely done with the developer, architect, and engineer. After plans are created, a community charrette takes place. Best case scenario, the role residents play is one of weighing in and providing feedback. Worst case scenario, their role becomes one of trying to put pressure on decision-makers to change what they don't like. Rarely, if ever, are they in situations where they are the decision-makers and have to weigh competing elements from this different lens.

Not only did residents have to get used to this kind of participation, but our internal team had to get used to working this way as well. We had to "do development" in open forums that involved residents at every phase from community listening and learning to implementation and ownership. The participatory planning process moved the working teams from the vision to defining the barriers that would stand in the way of success to an action agenda that would overcome those challenges and achieve their goals. It was through this process that a consensus was forged, and while that was underway, we had to be careful to not get in the way.

Whether it was the Construction Team figuring out a wraparound bonding strategy for community contractors — a solution worth $7.8 million — or the Employment Team figuring out how to get community residents into the grocery union, trained in Food 4 Less store, and then transferred back — a solution that achieved 91 percent of the opening day jobs — these community teams tackled the big issues by breaking them down so success could be understood, acted on, and celebrated. These teams, with their iterative process and hands-on learn-by-doing momentum, took ownership of identifying the key elements of the architectural character, developing the business and leasing strategy, creating the construction outreach process, and determining the place-making agenda.

Had we started with representative governance before these relationships had been forged, these open forums created, and the commitment to inclusion engrained through the working teams, we would have had a much different outcome. It was through these teams that accountability for achieving the greater community's goals solidified through listening, planning, doing, and reporting back.

Listen, Plan, Do

"We've been studied to death," more than one resident indicated when we started our community partnership. "We've had a lot of groundbreakings and no building dedications. How are you going to be different?"

When we moved into the community, two dynamics had converged to cause inaction:

- There had been many studies funded, but when the money ran out, the community was left with plans they had no way to implement, and
- People had been divided by fierce competition for funds. People not only distrusted us, they distrusted each other.

We had decided to partner with everyone — as many residents, organizations, funders, and businesses as we could. Our theme became "partnering for action" and we proactively used the tagline "breaking new ground together." We reinforced the idea that we couldn't "divide and conquer"; we all had to work on the project — together. And we had to hold ourselves and each other accountable to an action agenda.

Action is the core of capacity-building. Adult learning theory tells us that people learn best when they are involved in a process that is iterative, relevant, and urgent. We learn by doing. Time constraints push us.

Early on, we set a deadline of 90 days for the first surveys and organizing efforts. It was a timeline that worked well for the project, as well as the goal of having ongoing benchmarks of progress. It kept the momentum going and 90-day increments became the prototype for all future planning. Over time, the quick rotation between "**listen, plan, do**," gave us visible signs of success that could be celebrated. It became part of the DNA of the Market Creek experience.

To support residents in implementing a catalyst project the size of Market Creek required that we have:

- **A coordinated action agenda**, with all players working toward the same overarching goals across civic, social, economic and physical development;
- **A learn-by-doing approach,** with intentional and structured discovery-based analysis; and
- **A simple and consistent process,** for both action-planning and decision-making.

The coordinated action agenda and learn-by-doing approach had been part of our organizational culture since its inception, but the creation of the simple, clear, and consistent process for action planning and decision-making with residents in a central role evolved. If we wanted to assure that outcomes would be defined by the community and decisions made, having a consistent process was essential.

Over time, we developed a process that we all learned to trust. When we used it faithfully, good decisions were made, opportunities for course corrections were rapid, momentum grew, success was celebrated, and vision renewed and expanded.

LADDERing Action

We learned the art of partnership process with the Elementary Institute of Science (EIS).

"We were jumping off the cliff, and the odds against us doing what we did were enormous. Higher than enormous! It was the impossible dream!" reflected Joe Vasquez, a veteran board member of EIS.

Joe had gone to UC Berkeley in the 1970's where as a student he got involved with university-funded community groups and loved the work. He had a gift of bringing together the needed expertise in any situation — from legal and financial to local grassroots expertise. Joe was a person who liked knowing how things work and he was good at figuring them out, including how universities work, earning him a spot over time as Associate

Vice President of San Diego State University. As part of the San Diego State team, he would reach out to volunteer in the southeastern community by joining the Elementary Institute of Science board and would work on its campaign.

When Joe reflects on his years partnering with the Jacobs Team, he notes how people don't typically have the determination and focus to do something like this. "We had a hell of a good team, but the hardest part of something like this is staying the course. Being patient and persistent. We knew we were changing kids' lives and we couldn't quit."

To stay on course over a long period of time, we needed a partnership process that blended our commitment to participatory planning, a bias for action, and our need to achieve short-term benchmarks while working toward a dynamic long-term vision. We needed a way to track progress and move quickly in 90-day increments. We "LADDERed" action (Listen, Activate, Design, Do, Evaluate, and Refine) in order to keep a consistent pace and a clear process.

"It was important to see progress," reflected Joe Vasquez. "Just when I wasn't sure I could handle another meeting, we would look back and see how far we had come. I was well along in my career at that time, but I can honestly say that I never had to be that organized before. We accomplished our impossible dream."

In forging ahead with the vision for Market Creek Plaza, the same process was used. As an example, through community listening surveys residents ranked jobs near the top of the list behind the need for a grocery. A team was activated of committed community residents. Although the team's research showed that most redevelopment projects in California defined success as achieving 30 percent community hiring, it decided to set a goal of 65 percent. Further research showed that one of the key barriers to local hiring at the Food 4 Less Grocery, which would be Market Creek's largest employer, was potentially the union.

To design a strategy, the team asked the Food 4 Less District Manager and the head of the local union to participate in finding solutions for maximum local hiring. The design called for our team to do community outreach, a community church-based CDC to offer employment-readiness training, Food 4 Less to screen and hire at surrounding stores, train the residents, get them into the unions, and then offer them the first right to transfer back to the Market Creek store. The plan, implemented over the year leading up to the grand opening, worked. The District Management for Food 4 Less, the union leadership, and the new Market Creek store manager then held a set of meetings with the team to debrief and come up with a plan for ongoing evaluation.

In monitoring the store's operation, the team realized that the community hiring began to drop after the second year. Another working team was activated to understand what was happening and design a way to address the growing concern about not having an ongoing pipeline of people that were job-ready. To support the team's action plan, a resident who was an employment development professional was retained to work with the grocery to recruit qualified candidates.

By LADDERing action, residents could keep the work grounded in broad community listening, move quickly from planning to action, assure resident voice was driving each stage of the work, reinforce learning and ongoing application of that learning, and hold everyone accountable to the larger community at each stage of the work. And by repeating this process over and over, and expanding involvement as we went, we were also building the relationships, skills, strategies, and networks needed to create and sustain community change by the very act of tackling the key community challenges that stood in the way of success.

This process placed a high value on inclusion, community listening, participatory planning, and focused action. The vision a team created might be a marathon, but its work would be implemented in a series of sprints. The short action timelines made it easy for residents to:

- See both a beginning and an end;
- Commit to being involved, even with busy schedules;
- Keep from getting overwhelmed;
- Course correct quickly;
- Allow volunteers to enter and exit frequently;
- Keep the work accountable;

- Blend short-term planning with long-term vision; and
- Mobilize immediate action and achievable wins.

Over time, residents protected the process themselves, wanting to honor the need for community-wide input. "Wait!" I would hear. "We haven't done listening yet!" There were steps, and no step could be by-passed.

With a stair-step process and inclusive involvement, residents were extraordinary problem-solvers. They knew their community and knew when they needed to bring in outside expertise. Not only did their involvement through the working teams, matched with these tight timelines, make for a better plan, it also helped all of us be more creative, revealed what expertise was needed when, and made work that would have been otherwise long-term and grueling, fast and focused.

LADDERing Action
Listen Activate Design Do Evaluate Refine

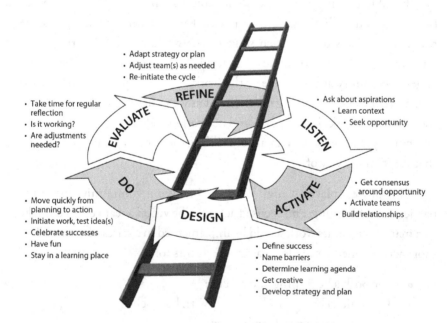

Planning in the Center of the Room

With the evolution of the external teamwork, our internal teamwork had to constantly evolve to mirror the inclusive, participatory culture we wanted to create in the world.

In doing that, we learned two big lessons:

- Getting on the same page is hard, and
- Staying on the same page is even harder.

Values, language, methods, approaches — these can be so different that even if the various players in community revitalization believe it's important to work together, actually doing it can be enormously complex and even frustrating.

In our work to become relevant to neighborhood change, we knew we needed an integrated, cross-disciplinary approach. All the variables impacted each other and solving one problem could cause a chain reaction somewhere else. As a growing staff, we needed to be able to see across issues, build an understanding of the neighborhood from the inside out and the outside in, and find the connecting point.

As fundamental as participatory planning was to our ability to plan with teams, it was equally critical to achieving comprehensive and integrated work. Rather than refining programs designs, as would be typical, we organized our internal teamwork by strategic directions to stimulate ongoing innovation and testing, and all strategies had to cross social, economic, physical, and political boundaries.

We called it *"planning in the center of the room."*

"When we plan in our individual offices — which are organized around the periphery of the Jacobs Center — our work gets compartmentalized," I noted in my journal in 2006. "Together we are greater than the sum of the parts. We must plan and work at the connecting point. Move away from the edge to the center of the room."

This work required us to get on the same page, speak the same language, develop a common understanding, stay on the same page, and learn to connect the dots. With rare exceptions, we never illustrated our departments in a linear chart. We always showed our organization and its work as a circle, each piece contributing to a whole. Each piece was altered in some fundamental way by being part of the whole.

Our team had to know each other, think about the work from different directions, look across disciplines, stay at the connecting point, and plan in the center of the room.

Every goal had benchmarks that were at the intersection of social infrastructure, economic opportunity, physical development, and civic engagement — the four "quads" — and at the center was the fifth important area — shared learning. Before decisions were made, we used what we called the "five-finger assessment" — a template of questions that covered the impact of those decisions in each of these five areas. Whether a team member worked in community building, physical development, economic and business development, or asset building, his or her work had to be planned as part of a united whole.

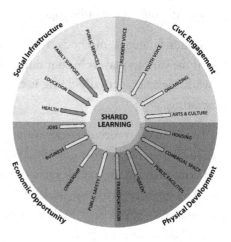

I was asked once why I didn't let my top team "go do housing," if that was their department, without having to meet with the whole team. "You might not get the house you envision, but it might be a more efficient way to get the house built."

I pondered the question for some time. The implication was that from the outside it looked like this centralized process was hampering the team from moving. But I understood that this person was taking a traditional view of how organizations should function.

"Yes," I said. "The house will get built, but that's not our goal. Our goal is to build a house in a way that empowers citizens, builds their resumes, creates unity and ownership. A Laotian volunteer told me that their community wouldn't live in homes that have people living above them. The Muslim residents want to work out a plan that doesn't require loans. The Somali residents are concerned that the artistic elements of the new housing don't reflect animals for religious reasons or they won't be able to live there. This puts housing development at the intersection of community building, capacity-building, cross-cultural understanding, and asset-building. That's our work, and it's work that no department head can do alone."

The power of Market Creek Plaza as a demonstration project was that it embodied the intersection of building vision and voice, strengthening skills, translating talent into economic power, removing blight, building individual and community assets, and recycling value back into the neighborhood under long-term neighborhood control. To make sure we didn't make irreversible or serious long-term mistakes, waiver in our focus on social change, or lose the opportunity for residents to have an authentic voice in the future of their community, we had to practice the African proverb: *"To go fast, go alone. To go far, go together."*

And that meant when we planned, it was with the full participation of our internal team across disciplines — in the "center of the room."

Inside-Out and Outside-In

"Who owns this?"

One of the most challenging parts of being in the business of the resident ownership of neighborhood change was integrating internal staff and external resident teams. In the early days, it caused confusion. Gradually, we hired residents to integrate internal and external planning teams and develop the pathway for resident ownership. We believed that by merging the teams, we would arrive at a sustaining structure, a plan for governance, an infrastructure for large-scale citizen action, and a solid process for teamwork that lifted up resident vision and voice.

Over time, JCNI's planning was first outside-in and then inside-out.

To support this kind of inside-out and outside-in planning, we had a cross-disciplinary **Management Team** to check-point process. The

Management Team played a critical role, and for me, it represented the very best of collaborative leadership and consensus management.

Each of us on the Management Team were committed to leading as peer problem-solvers, and it was our job to integrate and aim support. We were the glue that assured that organizing, grants or capital investments, physical development, and technical assistance or capacity-building were coordinated and worked in unison.

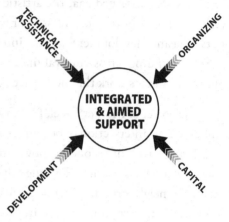

We depended on each other to challenge the way things were being done, articulate the priorities of our respective areas, understand everyone else's views, and believe deeply in the democratic process. We needed to know our specialty areas but also be open to learning from and coordinating our work with each other.

At first, we each pushed for our own areas, but as the work and our relationships evolved, we would argue each other's points, switch roles, and speak for each other if there hadn't been a strong enough case made for one of the points of view. Together, we grounded the work in values, principles, and practices that were agreed upon and operationalized in all of our work.

In planning, the Management Team received direction from the resident teams, discussed organizational priorities, guided internal decision-making, and shared accountability for achieving benchmarks. The Management Team then sought approval of the board on the overarching strategy and the financial framework. Joe was very outspoken about the board not micro-managing our team and was comfortable with a high level of flexibility in the use of resources once the framework was set.

A **Strategy Team** included all 30 members of our core staff, all of whom participated in strategy development. This team met monthly and for an annual retreat to do cross-organizational planning, discuss roles and action plans, and confirm organizational priorities based on the momentum of the resident working teams.

While the Strategy Team looked across the work, **Departmental Teams** looked down through the lens of individual departments in order to support each other in organizing, prioritizing, and implementing assigned work.

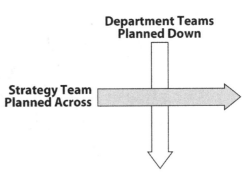

For this to work, everyone had to be informed about all teamwork, maximizing the ability of internal team members to address any resident on any issue in a completely transparent way, and it limited the opportunity for team members to be blind-sided. Monthly updates and a quarterly President's Report updated on all action across all teams and were also distributed to the board and to the entire team.

If the members of a combined internal and external team agreed, plans moved forward. If there was disagreement on a decision or strategic direction, the work was paused and the combined team would determine a process to reach consensus.

Over time, as more and more residents were hired, the lines blurred between what was out and what was in. By 2009, two-thirds of our staff were residents and it was not uncommon to hear questions like: "Is that our priority or the community's?" It was often hard to tell. Best case scenario, the only difference was what role people played in achieving it.

A clear, simple, and visual tool was critical to keeping this kind of outside-in and inside-out teamwork on target. This was our *Pyramid of Priorities*.

Building a Pyramid

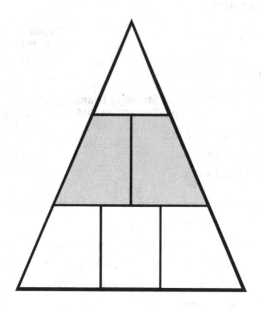

Pyramid of Priorities

As part of the ICA Technology of Participation (ToP)© facilitation methods, we had learned about the importance of having a motivating image that can help people quickly discern their key priorities.

ICA uses an "arrow into the future," although ToP methods encourage teams to design any shape that visually speaks to their key priorities. Adapted from ICA, we called ours the Pyramid of Priorities, so that people could quickly see the hierarchy of action and there would be no confusion about the overarching priority established by the teams. Since it is human nature to over plan what is possible in a short amount of time, everyone had to agree what was the most important action. The entire team had to pull together and target the greatest energy and resources from the top down.

The Pyramid focused the top benchmarks for the entire organization as well as individual teams for everyone to see. Internally, everyone knew that if workloads became overwhelming and something had to give, people were to focus on the top of the Pyramid. That benchmark would be achieved. People also knew that if their work was at the top, they could call on everyone they needed in the organization to move that mountain. Internally, every 90 days the Pyramid was reviewed and the process repeated.

"The Pyramid of Priorities helped change how I was thinking," noted Joe Vasquez from the board of the Elementary Institute of Science, which used the Pyramid during its $6 million campaign — a campaign thought to be infeasible and took years to complete. "It was the most important thing. It visually divided things up into enough chunks that we could aim. We still use it." As a board member throughout its campaign, Joe believed this tool kept them focused over a long period of time and gave them the focal point for aiming action. It was clear, simple, and agreed-upon.

Working Without Walls

'Wait a minute, wait a minute," I cut in. "We are all talking about this like the developer is the enemy, but we are the developer. The enemy is us!"

Working at the intersection of community building and commercial development took getting used to. It didn't come naturally.

For those of us who had worked to address social equity, environmental justice, strengthening democracy, and advancing human rights, becoming a developer wasn't easy. We knew the struggle over the legacy of unwanted land use, discriminatory urban planning, business decisions that widened health disparities, sub-standard construction, and poor tenant mixes that had impacted physical development in low-income communities of color.

We knew the stories of the "evil developer" — the person who comes in, controls decisions, ramrods them through community planning groups, has no commitment to local hiring or contracting, builds with outside labor, flips the property, and takes that value out. The developer is someone you organize to put pressure on, not someone you become.

For the team members from the physical development field, community meetings are something to be avoided and only the bare minimum that land-use policy requires should be held. Community residents slow down the process, rabble rousers are rude and try to control the meetings, and given that 'time is money,' getting through resident process drives up costs and impacts the viability of projects.

When the foundation decided to act as the developer of Market Creek Plaza, we had to challenge and change our disparate views and redefine what it meant to be a "community builder" in every way.

Peter Senge's masterful The Fifth Discipline guided us in building the ability of people "to look for the larger picture beyond individual perspectives."[64] Learning organization theory had to become ingrained in our organizational DNA. We had to learn how to learn together in a way that could unleash our ability to get the results we were after. In this complex environment, we would have to trust each other, as Senge poses, to be able to break out of silos.

Since the early 1990s and Senge's practice of "system-thinking," universities have created cross-disciplinary centers around social innovation, and yet for the most part they offer a class in real estate and a class in organizing, rather than a class that has people grapple with what happens in the interaction of these two fields when you put them together. The philanthropic world has also advanced the thinking about community change requiring holistic efforts, creating social innovation funds to move this agenda, and yet still largely operate grant programs in silo areas of interest separated from their program-related investments (PRIs). At the time we were developing Market Creek Plaza, the Heron Foundation was the only foundation we were aware of whose program officers did both PRIs and program grants.

Given the state of the field, it was unlikely that we would find talent already trained to think outside the silo. We knew we would have to develop this expertise. As Neil Smith pointed out in his article, "To Build Your Business, Smash Your Silos," this is just not how things naturally work:

> "Managers tend to look up and down only within their own silos — never looking around or across — so all they see, and tend to think about, is their own silo. They don't know what is happening elsewhere in the organization or

how their actions impact other areas. They act primarily in the interest of their own silo."[65]

We needed departments in order to align expertise and provide a structure for accountability. But at the same time, we needed internal strategies for looking across and not just down. For us to work across social, cultural, economic, physical, political and civic development, we had to get beyond organization charts that kept people departmentally focused and policies that incentivized people to only know their specialized area.

Our internal teamwork integrated a system for how information flowed (all key information shared with all personnel), how we planned (work aimed at a shared target and planned in the center of the room), how we drove deadlines (90-day benchmarks and pyramid of priorities), and how we coordinated decision-making across not just down (Management Team, Strategy Team, the activation of any cross-disciplinary teams).

But just as important as the teamwork structure and planning process was a deeply-held commitment of our core team to know each other, interact out of our roles, and value each other. We knew success rested on our ability to get outside our departmental walls and leverage knowledge, action, and learning and to do this required everyone to be willing to work without a musical arrangement. There was no score. Working without walls, as I called it, was working without sheet music. It would demand something of each of us personally that we had never experienced in our prior professional lives.

Without sheet music to go by, to follow John Kao's metaphor in Jamming, what we needed — to assure we made music and not noise — was a theme, a unifying beat, and a shared key. We needed a team process that allowed each person to bring their own sound, style and message in a way that we could build on each other, like in a great piece of jazz. We also needed to be at peace with paradox — taking tensions, contradictions, and differences and playing them for all they were worth.[66]

13

NET WORK

"Without active leaders who takes responsibility for building a network, spontaneous connections between groups emerge very slowly, or not at all. We call this active leader a network weaver. Instead of allowing these fragments to drift in the hope of making a lucky connection, network weavers actively create new interactions between them."[67]

— Valdis Krebs and June Holley,
"Building Smart Communities through Network Weaving"

NETWORK	Cross-cutting Resident Networks (by Culture, Faith, Age, Interests, Skills)	Funding Networks with Fast, Flexible Process across Types of Capital	Learning Networks	Coordinated Professional Networks to Support Neighborhood Strengthening

Building Bridges

It was a "random shooting" according to the police report.

On a Saturday night in the Gaslamp District, the streets were crowded. Now the heart of San Diego's nightlife, the Gaslamp's seven-block stretch of downtown was bustling with clubs and restaurants. For Lakeisha Mason's 21st birthday, there would have been no better place for her sister and friends to take her to celebrate.

"There were tons of people on every corner and this guy opens fire in the crowd," her father recounted. Keisha, as he calls her, was hit in the temple. Just a couple of hours after she turned 21, she was pronounced dead.

I have never lost a child. I have had hard times, but never this kind of tragedy, never this kind of loss. But your own heart stops when you hear the news that someone you know is experiencing this sudden horrifying and life-altering event. It could have been anyone in a crowd that size, and surprisingly not more were killed. But the one that was — was Keisha.

Sam Mason, Keisha's dad, a buoyant, gregarious man with a larger-than-life smile, was one I always loved to have on a team. He had come back to the community where he was born looking for business opportunities and was disappointed by what he saw. Wondering why there was so much blight and so few jobs, he responded to the invitation to come to a meeting at the Jacobs Center. During the day, Sam worked with troubled youth, a job most people would find exhausting enough to not want to come back out for an evening meeting, particularly one that is focused on what role you might play in improving your neighborhood. But Sam was all energy.

At first Sam was on the Ownership Design Team, and then it split into three sub-groups in order to implement its plan. "People kept coming and coming; then one group would create new branches and another 40 people would come," he noted. "When the Ownership Team split into subgroups, I chose the Financial Education Team."

He and some of his neighbors, planned and found people to run the sessions. In some cases, they ran the sessions themselves. Banking, credit, real estate, homeownership, and investment were all on the agenda. "Oh yes," Sam lit up, "the youth had their own series for financial education. My son, who was only eight or nine at the time, still talks about Daj'ahn!"

Daj'ahn Blevins, a committed community member who loves kids, ran the youth financial series.

"It didn't matter what the ages were. They were as young as three! If someone brought a child, they participated," remembered Daj'ahn. He was a kid magnet. Long, thick black dreadlocks with an engaging smile and a kid-like buoyancy about him. "I was a theater major so we just got the kids to volunteer for roles in the play. You are the banker and you are the investor and so on. The kids loved it."

Daj'ahn practiced and shared the values of Nguzo Saba, the seven principles of Kwanzaa, wherever he was. "The kids started their own company, made stock certificates, raised money, and put it in an account with Merrill Lynch. It was amazing. The name of the company was Kujichagulia, after the Saba principle of self-determination. To define, create, and speak for ourselves. It was our battle cry!"

Sam and his son will never forget Daj'ahn. "My son talks about investing all the time and now that he is older, he is evaluating what he'll need to start a business. The series really impacted him."

When Sam started working on Market Creek's ownership team, he thought change was right around the corner and he needed to make sure people were prepared, got a foothold, so they would benefit. "Little did I know that it would take so long," he now laughs.

"But what surprised me was how the group kept growing. Things in our community just appear or disappear and no one knows why. A group shows up and as the meetings go on, people fall away; by the end you are lucky if there are two people left." Sam continued, "As you can imagine, we were all skeptical that people's input would really be honored. But that did happen and more and more people showed up. We started to realize that there was strength in numbers. It put people's minds at ease. It was like a positive mob mentality! The work we were trying to get done magnified when a hundred people showed up."

After Sam put a year-and-a-half of teamwork on financial education, giving up his Saturdays to help conduct and promote the series, I asked if he would be willing to serve on the Resource Team. "It was the most mind-blowing piece of work I had ever been involved in," he commented. "Now to be meeting with Rockefeller — names you have only heard of in legend — at the same table, answering their questions... it changed everything."

Three people from the Resource Team accompanied me on each trip to meet with potential funders. "I thought we were there to pick their brains," Sam noted, "but they were asking us the questions! People valued our input and insight. We all started realizing how strong our community can be — how strong collectively. You think that if you take 20 people from other neighborhoods, they will get the job done, but you don't think you are capable of that in urban neighborhoods. We were changing our mindset about ourselves and about other people."

Then the unthinkable. The call at 2:00 a.m. Just when the Gaslamp clubs were closing and Keisha was getting ready to come home.

"You can't think." The words chocked in Sam's mouth as he described the loss of his daughter. "It's something you can never be emotionally ready to hear."

Sam went on to talk about the moment he got a different call. One from people he thought of as team members. People he had gotten to know through the Market Creek experience. "They were there for me. They wanted to see what they could do to help. Because of our teamwork, I trusted them. It was the most amazing thing."

The residents from the team asked Sam "do you need a minister, a church, a place to hold the services, a therapist or any other resources for the other kids in the family?" Sam reflected on the moment: "We were scrambling and didn't know what to do. No one ever plans for this and no one ever budgets for a child's funeral. They helped us think of things we couldn't have thought of. They said they would help raise money. They cooked for us and brought us food. It was all so comforting."

The team that Sam was describing called themselves "Project Compassion." It was a self-organizing team, spawned by a member of a different team, called Project Safeway. Tasha Williamson, in describing the genesis of Project Compassion, talked about two young Lincoln High School students, killed in a drive-by shooting. One had been helping Tasha mobilize students for Project Safeway. "We realized that the families needed help. After the police leave, what happens the next day? People needed a support team that goes out way beyond the homicide."

Tasha — with the help of two other co-founders, Lynn Sharpe-Underwood, director of the city's Commission on Gang Prevention and Intervention at the time, and Pastor Angela Ward, who along with her husband ran a church and a program called Inner City Youth, her teammates on Project Safeway, and Captain Tony McElroy, from the San Diego Police Department's southeaster division, now retired — went on to connect a large network of resource people from churches, the police department, the crime victim's fund, and the neighborhood, people who just wanted to help, some of them from families that had also lost loved ones. And because "what happens in court spills over into the neighborhood," as Tasha framed it, the team built bridges to the presiding judge and district attorney's office, trying to help families from being in harm's way of retaliatory acts or re-victimized by the legal process.

"It was an extended sense of community," Sam recounted. "They held a car wash to help pay for the expenses of burying Keisha, her outfit, food for the repast, photos of her enlarged for the funeral. Everyone turned out to wrap their arms around us. It was a family thing. It was so comforting to see the faces of people you knew and had been working with to better your community. And they linked us to people beyond our neighborhood that we would never have thought to reach out to."

Over the years, Sam has continued to look back on that moment. "This is work that goes unnoticed," he noted. "This is heart-wrenching work, and at the time, I thought it was just me they were helping, but then I realized they do this for every family in these moments of need." Over time, Tasha, linked to the San Diego Police Department, would know what happened and would be mobilizing resources from this network before most of us even got up and turned on the news. "You see so many examples where organizations will only hire people with degrees," Sam noted, "when there are these people out there who know how to get things done. They have a Ph.D. in the Streets!"

But for Sam, the story didn't end there.

On Keisha's next birthday — the first anniversary of her death — Sam's family huddled. They wanted to commemorate her life in some way. They discussed a whole list of ways they could do that, from planting a tree to creating a memorial fund somewhere.

I was in my office that day when I got a call asking me to attend a press conference. "Can you come down stairs to the lobby?" Sam asked me. "We are making a gift to the foundation."

On the way down the stairs I was trying to get my head around the idea of a resident and his family writing out a check to a charitable foundation. But that's what they had done. To celebrate Keisha's birthday, a large network of family and friends sold tickets to a local venue and booked youth entertainment. "Everyone danced, sang, and ate," Sam noted. "It was an all-day event. So many kids from so many neighborhoods coming together. It was beautiful."

During the press conference, Sam hugged Tasha and handed her $2,500. The family had decided to use this precious gift to help Tasha and the extended Project Compassion resource network buy "whatever is needed to continue this work," Sam noted. He was paying it forward. A piece of caring received passed on to the next family.

Sam had been a member of the Resource Team. This team had representatives from the other teams and Sam represented Ownership Design and Financial Education. This team was in a constant conversation about money. "You run the risk of believing that only wealthy people are philanthropists," we had shared. "There are many ways people give and pass on opportunity to others. Understand the gift you give first, then you can more easily ask others to invest also," we would repeat. This moment in Sam's life brought it full circle.

"When outside people looked in, I'm sure this all looked crazy. Our team meetings might sound loud or look out of control. It certainly didn't look traditional," Sam chuckled. "But what made the adults come alive was being empowered to bring ideas and be a part of the doing — not being assigned work — but taking our ideas and trying to make them work." Everyone brought their gift and the persistence paid off.

"You would always say," he commented, "if that's what you want, OK then, let's go do the hard work of getting it done." Sam continued, "I coach football and I know that you are going to lose some of the games, but there is always some success even in a loss, so long as you keep your will and spirit intact and keep going. Persistence made such a difference. You can look at that grocery now and have no clue what it was like before or what it took."

Will, spirit, and the ability to see and celebrate the successes — these things mattered. For Sam, teamwork created trust. A woman on one of those teams saw a pathway to get an extended resource network built to meet a need that was real in her community. She was able to mobilize and connect with people both inside and outside her community in order to get what was needed when it was needed to the person who needed it. No hoops to jump through. No permission to be sought. No proposals to be written. No barriers in her way.

A bridge was built. A network formed. It endures to this day.

A Network of Unlikely Actors Woven Together

"It changed my life. It felt so good; it made me aspire for more. Things got better for me, and I wanted life to be good for everyone else."

When Tasha Williamson looked back on her "Market Creek years," she remembers the meetings and retreats, leaving uplifted, empowered, together, caring about her community. She describes her work on the Project Safeway team as "a triumph," and it led her to branch out to build the Project Compassion network that Sam's family and over a hundred others benefitted from.

What started as a team of residents concerned about the level of youth violence in the community would become a network.

A few parents were volunteering to provide safe passage to and from their children's school so the Youth Violence Team decided to support and expand this effort. Project Safe Way (PSW) was born. Launched as a 10-week Safe Passage to School pilot on six strategic corners, PSW would grow into a comprehensive safe neighborhoods and street outreach strategy that covered 18 corners in six neighborhoods of southeastern San Diego, impacting a population of about 10,000 residents.

For Tasha, the laughter, hard work, and joy impacted so many people.

"I loved hearing how much people were being impacted by the teamwork. My team was provided two-way radios, and we were trained by law enforcement to observe and report incidents. I would listen to the conversations on the radio and smile. People were fearless. 'No,' Peaches [one of her teammates] would say, 'this is not going on in MY neighborhood! Not here. Not on my watch!' If an incident did occur, a call would go out, everyone would show up, the police would be dispatched. Afterwards, people would release with laughter and pride. The young people and the police grew to respect us."

Residents received intensive training in community outreach and action planning and organized a group of another 215 residents focused on positive relationships between residents and the police, educating residents about sexual predators, and creating a safer community, one block at a time. Youth who got involved held group discussions about non-violence, convened around their greatest challenges, and worked together to find solutions to overcome them. Although the Safe Passage Program was supported initially with paid coordinators, volunteer parents from the schools were recruited and trained to take it over.

As the number of potentially dangerous situations that were diffused rose, this growing citizen-police network expanded. And while impossible to draw a straight line between this network and the drop in violence, police efforts between 2006 and 2009 resulted in a 57 percent drop in gang-related homicides, a 24 percent drop in crimes by gang members, and the first year without a single youth homicide.

"We fail to see that there are leaders in every space until we get them involved," Tasha reflected. "It was like finding hope and restoring faith."

Before the term "network weaving" was coined, Market Creek Plaza was intended to serve as the catalyst for exactly this kind of bridge-building. Over time, the various teams merged and emerged as large networks.

These networks were formed with the goal of getting the right people to the table at the right time and with the right resource. For a family losing a loved one, it was food, counseling, and help raising money for the funeral. For newly-released prisoners re-entering the community, it was help getting the right health care resource and a network for getting people jobs.

As the broader resource networks formed, the working teams inside the community got better results. These networks formed sometimes from the outside in and sometimes from the inside out, but either way — and critically important to achieving results — was that resident voice was given front-and-center stage for how the work itself unfolded. Resource networks were asked to follow, not lead; support, not direct. Accountability for results grew out of people owning their own role and responsibility for the work.

Land planning improved because mothers who walked their children to school were in the center of the room when that planning was taking place, and the neighborhoods became safer because residents connected and built — not just safe pathways to school for their children — but relationships with law enforcement, which built relationships with OGs (old gangsters), who began to hold peace rallies and helped get young people into jobs.

"When you see a mom whose son has been killed by a police officer turn that hate around into action," noted Tasha, "when you see police officers stop their disrespectful practice of sitting people on curbs cuffed... when you see hundreds of residents turn out for the vigil honoring a police officer who has been killed in a probation check... when you see people stop their cars to break up an altercation... when you go to a community meeting on public safety and it feels like a reunion...you know that we have utilized our power to make a difference."

These were not just institutional partnerships; they were unlikely actors woven into a network of networks.

Each time a bridge was built, it took us to a new place — to a place we had never been before, to an expanded vision of the work, to a deeper understanding of what it takes to spark, support, escalate, and sustain efforts to reinvigorate and revitalize communities that have suffered long-term disinvestment.

We were joining together in the spirit of community. We were connecting to build a village.

To Build A Village

If it takes a village to raise a child, it takes a large number of people, linked together in an inextricable web of connections, to raise a village.

The development of the Village at Market Creek, up until 2011, was about building bridges. Literally. One that was a trolley underpass won four engineering awards. It was our construction team's pride and joy.

But these teams also built other kinds of bridges that went to the underlying purpose of Market Creek. These were bridges meant to connect people, organizations, and resources. These were meant to pull together a large universe of individual efforts by committed and dedicated people to serve their community in a way that could build hope, spirit, and a strong sense of purpose.

As Molly Clark, whose group of associates made Monument Community Partnership in Concord, California, a leading model in community-driven development at that time, framed it:

> "It is important to not only focus on building cross-sector professional networks; we must intentionally foster cross-audience personal relationships that form the underpinning of all other social transformation. By doing this, we unearth, mobilize and leverage community assets — most notably the previously disregarded expertise and ingenuity of the people who live or own businesses in our communities — toward common aims."

Network-building is strategic work. It gets intrinsically to the very heart of community building and its underlying goal of creating an inclusive society. It is work rooted in time, space, and opportunity for building deep relationships. These "cross-audience" relationships need to be fostered and people linked in a way that can set a table for everyone. They become the feeder systems for technical and financial resources to link effectively with action teams on the ground in real time that are up close to opportunity moments for change.

Without a commitment to weaving these networks, the work in communities fragments, and as Krebs and Holley put it, these fragments "drift in the hope of finding a lucky connection."

To give time and focus to building trust across boundaries and link people in communities that are highly fragmented into networks requires the intentional building of what Bill Traynor, after a career in organizing, framed as "connectivity infrastructure."

Before encountering Krebs and Holley or Bill Traynor, we were experiencing this fragmentation and needed to support efforts that created space for networks to form, first within the community where resident voice is strengthened and determination is built, and then to link them to external networks that honored that voice, bringing expertise and resources.

When we started our work in southeastern San Diego, there was a landscape peppered with groups serving people in need — 200 in a half-mile radius from the Market Creek intersection, the majority of which operated programs defining residents as clients and intervening with social services.

These groups were not only disconnected from each other, but they saw themselves as competing for a very small pool of resources. Most of these programs lived hand-to-mouth, expanding and disbanding depending on their ability to secure grants. And because the majority of grants were time-limited and weren't accompanied by the technical assistance needed to diversify resources, an unstable landscape of start-and-stop services and programs had been created.

Even when non-profit organizations do develop the infrastructure to secure on-going resources, their service-delivery mission keeps them focused — as Omowale Satterwhite, the founder of the National Community Development Institute, described it — on transactional rather than transformational work. In order to expand impact, they need to raise more money to operate. With more money, they tutor more children, mentor more young adults, feed more families. But however successful these organizations become in securing resources, they can't engage in work that connects social, economic, physical, and political development or requires large-scale citizen action. Even the Coalition of Neighborhood Councils in southeastern San

Diego, formed to link residents and lift up community political action, accepted program grants to run their organization that took them away from their network-building mission.

When collaborations do form to work cooperatively on a transformational goal, they are often stymied by how to address the complexity of the issues involved — the competition for and time-limited nature of resources; foundations' need to pre-determine partners, goals, activities, and outcomes; the professional arrogance of institutions that look down on the kind of inclusive process that gives everyone ownership and power in decision-making; and the histories of pettiness and politics that keep people from wanting to work together.

"This work requires really different practices and we keep slipping back," noted Bill Traynor. "The helping professions are really entrenched."

Raised on Sal Alinsky organizing before developing "consensus organizing," then growing the field of network management around the country, Bill both sighs and laughs when he describes his work with foundations and non-profits. "Teams get excited; ideas begin to flow; people feel liberated and begin to believe they can figure things out; and then I leave and the creativity gets crushed. If I don't come back for three weeks, they have slipped back! Letting people engage in the space that embraces 'I don't know' is frightening. The funders and large organizations already have a framework that they know and understand, so they go right back to it. But in reality, being effective in stimulating social change isn't about needing to <u>know</u>, it's about creating a process that allows us to figure out what we can <u>do</u> together."

Trust can only be grown as people work together on issues of common concern. That happens slowly and with steady commitment. For change to be enduring, it must be embedded in the history and wisdom of residents and emerge from their efforts. Once this has happened, the work can then be linked successfully to outside expertise and resources. It must have a significant target of action — an undertaking that ignites hope and creativity and has the scope and scale to connect people, programs, and resources in a coordinated strategy that allows multiple roles to be played and experience and skills to be deployed.

Most importantly, it must build bridges that result in ongoing networks with the capacity to expand and sustain the work it begins.

Opening Organizational Boundaries: Working "Wikily"

In looking for a metaphor that could describe our experience of managing an emerging network of networks, all we hit upon was the Olympics, in awe of the growing networks that were emerging and linking.

It felt like we were engaging as many "countries" as we could and supporting them in recruiting, training and sending teams to a world convening. To do this, we needed a strong group of sponsors and a well-run organizing committee. While the sponsors and organizing committee worked to stage the event, each country was working to train and send its best possible team.

Over time, our "world" had a very large set of stakeholders that needed to connect and stay connected to the vision of the Village at Market Creek for all the parts to work together.

On the up side, these interconnected networks that placed a high value on the central voice of residents helped weave a stronger community fabric — making the community a safer, more vibrant place to live.

On the challenging side, as momentum grew, our greatest strain was figuring out a way to effectively coordinate, connect, and communicate with this large and growing Olympic-sized network of networks. We had to figure out how to work "wikily."

In the summer of 2010, The Stanford Innovation Review published an article titled "Working Wikily."[68] The term, as the authors note in the article, is based on the word *wiki*, a website that allows groups of people to collectively create and edit information, such as Wikipedia. "Working wikily is characterized by greater openness, transparency, decentralized decision-making, and collective action," the article contended.

By the time this article came out, it was clear that our work was transitioning from its laser focus on teams to a focus on networks and network management and this metaphor resonated.

We had become fascinated by flash-mobbing and the growing scale of social media as a way to attract people to a place and time. We didn't believe that technology was the key to social change, but we did see its potential in getting people to turn out for accomplishing something by working in relationship. Coined from the Hawaiian word for quick[69] (wiki), Wikipedia had created a platform with free access and free content that everyone could participate in, contribute to, and benefit from. The analogy that the article drew in applying wiki to network weaving was intriguing.

Using the wiki metaphor, could we create some kind of platform on which everyone could weigh in, contribute to, and help advance the work? Not social media, but a network mindset. As we entered the next generation of our work, could we use this metaphor to begin the move away from organizational boundaries to an open community of practice that could maintain its emphasis on in-person deliberation and teamwork.

Roque and his teams of organizers were serving as "network weavers," deliberately connecting people. As Valdis Krebs and June Holley observed in their article "Building Smart Communities through Network Weaving," this helps surface "untapped opportunities for community members to produce better outcomes and encourage new relationships and collaborations. In some way, it's what community organizers have always done — only the new approaches emphasize a lack of hierarchy or traditional power structures, focusing instead on connectivity and social capital."[70]

We had learned how to team outside experts and residents and had developed working teams as the platform for shared decision-making. But as the inside and outside teams began connecting in larger and larger resource networks, our core team, which had provided the center of gravity to bring people to the table, including the hard to reach, was more and more challenged.

"It's hard for people to hear the unheard and engage the hard to reach," noted Roque, making it critically important "to never stop outreaching and never stop organizing." Given that, we needed to be constantly reinventing how we managed change.

Heading into 2011, we were excited to see if we could strengthen our network management and organize ourselves in a way to work wikily.

While we knew it would be an Olympic venture, we were poised to see what would happen.

The Challenge of Weaving Critical Connections

"Let's put it this way, you got $200 in gate money in your pocket when you get out of prison. You got a record, no driver's license, no one to pick you up — what do you do?"

Stacy Butler was low key, understated, on point. Exonerated on "cop-killing" charges after 12 years in prison, no one knew better than Stacy about the need for change, both in the system and on the streets. "I'll tell you what you do with $200 and no prospects. You get a bag of dope and go back in business!"

"Someone needed to help Stacy," and Rickey Laster would be one of those people. Rickey, who would go on to become a pastor and the Executive Director of the City of San Diego's Commission on Gang Prevention and Intervention, was part of the Market Creek Plaza team working on getting minority and women contractors on the construction site. "They thought that boy killed a police officer and once he was exonerated, who was going to give him a chance if we didn't? Because we did it for him, that's why he was inspired to do what he is doing now — marching for peace and helping to get jobs for young people."

Stacy knew the issues of the formerly incarcerated from the inside out and, along with others like him, would serve as a central voice in the design of a community network strategy for returning citizens.

Coming Home to Stay — as the community network strategy was named — didn't start with residents. It was spawned by linking a prisoner re-entry working group of our regional association of grantakers, the San

Diego Grantmakers, with the Market Creek process of resident-centered listening, program design, and network-building.

By the time this network was in formation, we had developed a strategy of planning from inside the community first and then linking to larger resource networks. We believed in planning initiated from outside the community but only if it assured residents were in the center of the room. Like the Cairo example, we needed to make sure we weren't creating macro-economic projects when what people intuitively knew would work were goats.

What Stacy knew was that people coming out of prison, most of whom had severed or severely damaged their family ties, needed someone to pick them up — a relationship — the ability to get a driver's license, get healthy, get a job. Pretty simple. Hard. But simple.

We had learned that our community (the Diamond) and the one next to ours (City Heights) had the highest number of returning citizens in San Diego. Research had shown that a driver's license, health care, and jobs were critical to returning citizens. But what we didn't know was how to connect resources and meet these needs in a way that could drop the 70 percent recidivism rate. So we put Stacy, and a group of others like him, in the middle of the room.

Town hall meetings were convened that included more than 70 parolees, service providers, and public agency staff to discuss what could be done to address the system's lack of success in keeping the formerly incarcerated from returning to prison. In addition, focus groups of former prisoners and providers explored how the town hall meeting input could be applied to create a coordinated and comprehensive approach.

Together 20 service providers, formerly incarcerated residents, representatives from the justice system, and community members began forming a coordinated peer-based approach surrounded by a resource network. The project was anchored in the creation of a "community of caring" network that went beyond being "case managed" to a process that could prepare, transition, and sustain residents who were coming home.

In addition, an Advisory Council included key decision-makers in the criminal justice field to inform the program on system resources and opportunities and advocate for changes in policy. One example was the data showing the number of parole violations for driving without a license which led to state legislation that enabled inmates to acquire a license prior to release.

The person at the center of the network was Jim Sanders. "He got me my first job," people would say about him. "Son, if your appointment is at 8:00, you show up at 7:45" or "Son, you dress appropriately — have some self-respect," they would recount. "He didn't just teach us to be successful in getting a job, he taught us how to be successful in life."

To many, Jim was big brother, the father that was missing, coach. He was a man of integrity that believed deeply that "you can't play games with people's lives." He could read hustlers and three-penny players, as he called them, didn't tolerate hypocrites, and knew the power of relationships — with the cadre of employers he had built up over the years and with the people returning. "What will it take to not go back?" would be his leading question. If he felt people weren't committed, he'd say "When you want to stop looking over your shoulder, you call me. Come back when you're ready." He had nuts-and-bolts street-smarts and was personal, never treating ex-offenders as a case to be managed.

For twenty-seven years, he had been a specialist at getting the unemployed jobs. "I started because there weren't quality services for African Americans and Latinos, and someone had to believe in them and tell them they could do it." He had grown up in Arkansas, raised by his grandmother, his early bed a chest of drawers. "I was so black I was blue," he would laugh and light up with his great smile. He had a caring spirit and a distinct style. "I was born in the era of Zoot suits and chains," he commented, and ever since had a love for sharp fashion — usually a crisp white shirt with cuff links and a pin-striped suit. "He was the only man I ever knew who would do yard work in a suit!" one of his protégés chuckled.

Jim's office was in the Jacobs Center. "At first, I thought I was coming into a cult because everyone was so fanatically devoted," he chuckled. "Then I realized this was a community of values that people cared about and wanted to a part of. I suddenly loved coming to work."

When it came to working with the formerly incarcerated, Jim could quickly gain the trust of these men and women whose lives had been filled with distrust, and he was able to get the program up and running. Once that happened, the program won a prestigious Robert Wood Johnson two-year grant that enabled it to become staffed by a small team of residents who had the relationships needed to navigate larger community and employment networks.

Because the funding that was provided was to network and link non-profits who were already providing services and create a community caring resident network, rather than funding the service delivery components, many of the network's non-profit partners resisted participation. A few stepped up, however, to coordinate with the network around issues of health care, dentistry, and other critical needs. In two years, the recidivism rate for the returning citizens in this project would drop to 10 percent — 60 percent lower than the statewide average.

But after the initial two years, the local start-up group of funders turned to other priorities and the resource network never had a chance to solidify. Its great potential to become a pilot for one of California's first social impact bonds faded away, and when the Robert Wood Johnson grant ran out with no sustaining mechanism in place, the team was disbanded and the dream of a large, well-coordinated community network also faded away.

This moment told a story — voiced all too often by communities' residents — of one more project initiated from the outside-in with short-term funding, not enough time for the broader resource network to solidify, and further challenged by service providers unwilling to work collaboratively without supplemental financial support.

"Although the individual grant is the typical unit of analysis for most foundations, the success of any grant or organization is rarely sufficient to move the needle on a complex problem. We have all felt the irony when successful programs are lauded while the system they aspire to change continues to fail. The most effective funders of the future will not be satisfied with the philanthropic equivalent of 'the operation was a success, but the patient died.' The only way a whole system can be changed is by engaging and connecting the parts."[71]

This Monitor Institute article titled, "What's Next for Philanthropy: Acting Bigger and Adapting Better in a Networked World," touched boldly on the need for the players in social change to connect and articulated the challenge of finding — "or being found by" — the right partners. These partners, the article contends, "don't necessarily need to make decisions together, but they need their efforts to add up." In today's environment, this means building networks across sectors that in the past have not worked together. And it also means giving these networks the time needed to form.

When we started the Market Creek journey, we knew that residents, businesses, non-profits, the public sector, and philanthropy all hold part of the solution, but these actors had limited experience working together to build on. Even our local funders at that time had never collaborated on anything other than single-issue projects involving non-profit services, not an open system of resident network-building.

Twenty years later, the concept of "collective impact"[72] has captured philanthropy's front page, and these large initiatives are grappling with how to build "backbone" organizations and develop a more unified approach to the communities or populations they want to serve. But while most place a high value on having an authentic stakeholder voice, these are largely institutions setting an agenda — from the outside — for change that targets a population to be served.

"We need to get honest about what nurtures aspirational people," Bill Traynor noted after a career of being directly engaged in organizing, community building, and providing technical assistance to foundations undertaking place-based work. "This requires different practices from those learned by the helping professions, foundations, and social services."

Reflecting on his work with other seasoned change agents across the country, Bill described the need to "build new networks of relationships across class, race, geographic, professional, and other boundaries that otherwise hamper effective progress and functionality in our towns, cities, and rural areas. These new networks," he noted, "need to be designed to unleash the kind of creative and optimistic energy required to tackle the tough challenges our struggling communities face."

Like Bill, those of us who worked on Market Creek believed that "aspirational energy and creativity" exist in abundance "in most people and most communities," but that for the most part "this power is locked up and unrealized," as Bill frames it, "because we haven't made the investment in revealing it and putting it to use."

For Bill's team at Lawrence Community Works, like ours at Market Creek, the effort was to move toward a more organic and open system of achieving community change. Over time, we became firm believers that in a changing world, network management had to be a critical priority, and agreed with Bill that "the future of movements will be driven not by any one person or organization," but rather "small groups tapping into high-capacity networks, where valuable resources can move quickly to meet the needs of the people in the network."

14

FRAME WORK

*"Even in so-called free jazz, musicians work within a structure.
They agree on who is to play when and on a loose
conception of key or total center.
And then they let a stable beat determine a solo's rhythmic shape."[73]*

— John Kao, <u>Jamming</u>

Joe's Pilot Plant

"It is difficult to predict the behavior of a process of any complexity... Designers use data from the pilot plant to refine their design of the production scale facility."[74] Joe thought in terms of chemical processing in his professional life and had learned through experience that his team needed to test a process first before building out a large-scale plant.

"If the process is flawed," he would say, "the pilot plant will never work." In chemical engineering, pilot plants are used to test the behavior of a system and work out the kinks. This was always easier said than done.

"I went to work for Jacobs in the early 1960's when we were developing a project in Vicksburg, Mississippi," noted Noel Watson, CEO of the Jacobs Engineering Group in a 2004 interview.[75] "It turned out to be a very difficult project. Joe, in his book The Anatomy of an Entrepreneur referred to it as the Second Battle of Vicksburg."

Noel, recounting a remarkable man's dedication, determination, and willpower, told the story of Joe coming to Vicksburg to work with his team of young engineers in the trenches to gradually bring a very difficult plant up to full production. "He worked with us many times 24, 36, 48 straight hours while we were trying to bring this plant on stream. He was going to will that plant to work, his name was on the door of the company, and it was absolutely essential that that plant work successfully or there may not be a Jacobs Engineering today."

Market Creek, to Joe, was a pilot plant for understanding process — process that enabled residents to have a voice, not just in planning and implementing, but also in naming and building the ultimate "frame" or structure around the work. To do this, our team needed to see the naming and framing of the work as part of how residents took ownership for action and built the sustaining structures that would ultimately carry the work into the future.

As a pilot plant, Market Creek Plaza provided the opportunity to test our ability to change as a philanthropic organization with teams of residents as our learning partners; it provided us a target for action to see if we were getting it right, and there was a clear expectation from Joe that we were to will that plant into being.

Communities are hard to define. The boundaries are usually blurred. There is no corporate structure that makes sense for planning with residents. There is no 501(c)3 around them. No LLC. No LC3. This alone makes comprehensive community development difficult. But it becomes even more complex by needing a set of unlikely partners that have to operate together without a natural framework to hold the separate pieces together. This conundrum required us to start the journey without a natural container for action. One had to be built. Named. Given identity. And this container had to be developed in a way that a defined process could be evaluated to see how it responded in a complex environment.

In addition to needing a container for refining process and aiming action, civic engagement, like any long-term largely volunteer effort, needs an infrastructure to support and sustain it, requiring the Jacobs Center itself to evolve as a flexible framework. To support community change, we needed the capacity to evolve over time from managing core support for teams to organizing and planning as a network-management organization. The operating foundation became an infrastructure for supporting and resourcing a vast volunteer network, giving this civic space a "there there."

There were days I thought Joe had put me in charge of the Third Battle of Vicksburg. The good news about Joe was that he believed strongly that people could "only measure success against the consequences of failure."[76] Courting failure, he trusted, could actually prompt or goad success. The bad news about Joe was that it seemed like he was always putting me in circumstances to goad success in the face of failure. I could always hear him over my shoulder saying: "If you can't find someone to do it, you do it. Do whatever it takes but bring the pilot plant out of the ground...Then, before you go home, will it into operation."

Framing and Naming the Work

"Why did you keep your maiden name?"

A young woman in her early twenties came up to me after a brown bag luncheon where I shared some of my personal story. She told me she had been curious for some time and was afraid to ask. She thought it might be sensitive. "No," I said, "not at all." She smiled. "I was given this name and grew up with it. I am connected to it. I also came of age during the women's movement and got married in a time when keeping your name was a symbol of not giving up your identity for your husband's. It mattered to me."

My response resonated with the young woman. She commented that her mother had not only given up her name but had lost her identity and had become subservient. She shared her mother's history of domestic violence and how she wanted a different future for herself.

"For me," I continued, "it tells the story of an age. Today, I understand how a family name is a wonderful thing, but for me it was a symbol of wanting to keep my identity. Besides," I smiled, "my husband's name is Cummings and his family members are all tall; I'm only 5 feet 2 inches so I was afraid of being known as Short Cummings!" She laughed and asked if we could take more time to talk.

Over the years, I thought a lot about names and the naming traditions that guide how we choose names for our children. We are given names and they become part of who we are. We carry with us the history of those naming traditions. They give us identity, as well as an identifiable legal status. Later in life, we might take or be given a street name — SergKat, Kutfather, Bucket, Baby Chunks, Zoid, Churro, and Chunky — or a name rooted in culture that speaks to who you are — Kokayi, Tambuzi, and Sukumu. The community was rich with naming traditions.

When we unite, we are a group; when that group takes on legal status, it becomes a corporation. Established for a wide range of purposes and housed in a wide variety of legal structures, this "container" for conducting commerce or achieving a social purpose provides a platform for naming, branding, attracting and servicing its intent, hiring and managing its affairs, upholding its rights and obligations, and distributing its benefits. It is a recognized distinct construct that can be created, organized, and dissolved under the law.

While work doesn't always need a legal entity, it still needs a container — a construct that can be named that provides a **framework for action**. You can't touch corporations, but you know they are there. You can do business with them, invest in them, own them, sue them, interact with them, believe in them.

A critical component of our work over time was helping people create, frame, name, and give shape to the containers they needed for action. Community surveys, resident polling, contests, and workshops were all used to support the naming process.

Some were legal entities, like Market Creek Partners, LLC. Some were tools, like the Community Development IPO, which referred to the process and documents used for community ownership of Market Creek Partners. Others were names used to give identity, shape, life, and glue to a new growing body of work, such as the Center for Community and Cultural Arts, which emerged from a partnership between the cultural teams and San Diego's arts institutions.

Some were housed under the JCNI operating foundation, as fiscal agent, while groups moved toward some for-profit, non-profit, or hybrid structure. Some stuck; some didn't. Some transformed, like the shift of the graffiti art team from Graf Creek to Writerz Blok, as they became more formalized.

As the work expanded into an interconnected set of places, spaces, programs, businesses, tools, and corporate structures, a pattern evolved. There was more and more effort to frame the work, figure out what structures were needed, and what identity those structures should have, if any. Then the teams would choose a name and develop a logo so that natural momentum evolved into something recognizable and definable. Once a container had been defined, action could be planned and support could be attracted to the work more easily.

These were rites of passage. A coming of age. A marker of changed identity and a naming of the hopes and aspirations people had for their dreams. The naming process created a new and empowering story and opened the door for a new narrative to be written. A team aimed, framed their work, and gave it a name — an encapsulation of vision and values.

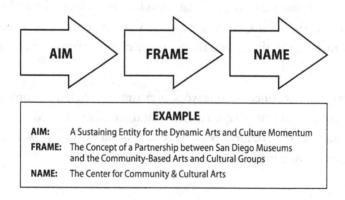

AIM > **FRAME** > **NAME**

EXAMPLE

AIM: A Sustaining Entity for the Dynamic Arts and Culture Momentum

FRAME: The Concept of a Partnership between San Diego Museums and the Community-Based Arts and Cultural Groups

NAME: The Center for Community & Cultural Arts

Structuring for Change

"As long as the risk on a scale of 1 to 10 is less than a nuclear power plant then I think we're OK!"

David Morgan was different. "Can't" wasn't in his vocabulary. He would puzzle and plan and then just figure it out. He would say "Well, I can't say that's been done before, but let me think about it.... Well, I'm sure the Department of Corporations has never seen this before, but let's try it... Well, that's maybe not the way it would normally be done, but we can make that work... Well, maybe that exact idea won't work, but there is probably another way to come at it."

In most foundations, you might need an attorney periodically to review your IRS compliance or resolve a legal action, but with our team, understanding the law was central to our work. David, our legal counsel, was a part of our design team, helping us find a way through any barrier and making sure no corporate structure stood in the way of what teams needed to accomplish.

With his white hair, Harvard credential, and sharp suits, David was the quintessential old school attorney. "He was the perfect personal lawyer for someone like Joe," noted Kurt Kicklighter, the attorney who teamed with David on our ownership structures. "He was in that last bastion of top quality people in small high-quality firms. Those, for the most part, have now all disappeared through mergers and acquisitions. He was good on the technical side, paying attention to the details, but he always tried not to over-lawyer things." A lover of history, classical music, and literature, he was also the quintessential gentleman, highly regarded as a person, as well as a professional.

David's practice emphasized securities and corporate matters. Quiet with a dry sense of humor, he became my strategic think-partner in making things work. If he thought we were way out in left field with some crazy idea, you would never hear him say the word "can't" — you would just see him rear back in his chair, light up like a bolt of lightning, and exclaim "HOLD THE PHONE!"

To plan with residents as the central players in decision-making and to keep the work comprehensive and connected, we had to find a different way to organize and structure our work, and David's role was helping us understand the benefits and limits of various corporate structures, non-profit and for-profit alike.

Over time, we became a fully integrated network – a set of organizations held accountable by the same plan, each one with advantages to be brought to the table and equally as many limitations, but guided by a common mission and vision, a common language, and close interdependence. These structures were put together in a way that the lines between organizations were only visible on paper, so we wouldn't lose sight of the whole and become the parts.

What started in 1988 as the Jacobs Family Foundation, a charitable non-operating foundation, created its first sister organization in 1995 — an operating foundation. The Jacobs Center gave us the ability to be in a direct relationship with residents and play a greater number of roles. But after ten years of building capacity for social change, the work had not only changed who we were, it had change what we were.

Non-Operating Foundation
Grants and Investment

Operating Foundation
Community-Building, Capacity-Building, Learning Exchanges, Strategic Support

S-Corporation
Subsidiary of the Operating Foundation
Triple-Bottom-Line Physical Development

Community-Owned LLC
Managed by the S-Corporation
Asset Building

Network of LLC Subsidiaries
Managed by the S-Corporation
Economic and Business Development

We had evolved into the **Jacobs Community Development Group**. Guided by a common mission, an entrepreneurial set of values, and an integrated set of strategies, the Jacobs Community Development Group was the name we gave our network of mission-related organizations that were trying to create a "there there"

— an infrastructure for supporting residents in owning the change in their neighborhoods.

Because foundations typically have a "non-operating" status, most can't do much directly. We have to implement our missions through indirect involvement. While this limits our ability to gain a first-hand working knowledge, foundations have attributes that make us essential partners. Our ability to use our assets for research, grants, below-market rate loans, guarantees, and early-stage investments can be pivotal. Risk is a choice. Without the burdensome regulation and oversight required of government and public charities, foundations can be daring and courageous — stimulating creativity, inspiring action, design and testing new ideas. As investment companies with a social purpose, foundations are needed.

If communities want more than a make-over, organizations that do community building are also essential partners. What do people hold in their hearts as important? What do they believe should change and how? How can they contribute? What skills will they need to implement their ideas? Who in the neighborhood has those skills and who might be needed from outside? These are questions communities must ask and answer for themselves. Foundations must be linked to community builders to engage residents in answering these questions.

Communities also need developers with a double-bottom-line purpose. In under-invested areas, blight represents opportunity. The process of developing unused, under-used, and blighted land is a powerful platform for creating vision and for recycling that value back into the neighborhood through jobs, contracts, and ownership of assets. The economic agenda makes the social agenda sustainable.

Projects must be planned with profits in mind or they can't be financed. When they are planned with *only* profits in mind, residents are either displaced or get unwanted land use. Developers must be able to afford the time and costs to work with community builders and train people on projects. From jobs and contracts to ownership, residents must be the primary beneficiaries. This makes developers' know-how, vision, risk-taking, and deal-making critical to reinventing the process.

To put the best of each of these worlds together — foundations, community-builders, and developers — we needed ways to connect for-profit structures, where investment and ownership are possible, with non-profit structures that have the social mission essential to getting opportunity to the very residents impacted by change.

"A lot of creativity flowed from the teamwork," noted Chip, who led the physical development work. "We were all in the trenches together. No one sat in their ivory towers. It taught us to walk in each other's shoes."

The Framing Structure of Ownership: The Theory of Thirds

"I've never owned anything," shared one resident. There was a pause. Then the next person enthusiastically blurted out: "Can we buy in early?"

In 2000, I facilitated a series of discussions with various neighborhood groups around the community: What does ownership mean to you?

There was a wide range of perspectives from people thinking of ownership as having participated in the planning of Market Creek and seeing their mark on the project. Others wanted literal ownership.

Joe had spoken at a dinner around the holidays of 1999 and explored the idea of ownership. I thought he was insane. Here was the head of a billion-dollar company seeing if people wanted to put "their hard-earned dollars," as he phased it, in the project we were doing together. What seemed crazy was the juxtaposition of a wealthy man suggesting co-investment from people who would perhaps struggle to assemble the smallest of investments.

I learned to pause when I thought Joe was crazy and think about it intensely. By doing what he was suggesting, we could create a mechanism to bring ownership full circle. We could innovate on an asset-building tool that had been used throughout history to grow wealth (from the early Romans to the New York Stock Exchange) and use it here.

When Joe asked if residents wanted to invest in Market Creek, we were still early in the process. Resident teams were just beginning to work on plans for harnessing local retail dollars, building an emerging market, developing ways to capture the benefits of an expanding economy, mostly through jobs and community contracting. But this raised the idea for the final piece of the puzzle.

As an anchor project for reinvigorating an urban marketplace, Market Creek Plaza's purpose was putting people's gifts and talents to work and figuring out how to build individual and community assets while rebuilding their neighborhood. Creating a platform for residents to have a financial stake in their own community was a way to give everyone skin in the game, recycle increasing value back into the neighborhood, and keep social responsibility at the forefront of business.

After the 1999 dinner, residents approached us. "Can we invest?" they wanted to know. I was surprised and grateful. The question they posed was a vote of confidence in the project. Groundbreaking had occurred, and the goal of bringing a Food 4 Less grocery in as the anchor tenant was achieved. The series of workshops I facilitated in early 2000 showed that residents would be willing to consider putting their own money "alongside of Joe," as people phrased it. Many were willing to volunteer to work on an Ownership Design Team.

David Morgan, our attorney, wanted a top securities lawyer to assist. That person would be Kurt Kicklighter.

"When David called me, he said you needed a securities lawyer for trying to do this kind of weird offering!" Kurt laughed. "Maybe I was the first person who didn't say no! It was certainly different," he reflected, "but I think I said that at least theoretically it could happen!"

Anyone who said "at least theoretically it could happen" was in.

David, Kurt, Chip, our developer, and I would be our starting team, and the four of us would work on figuring out the right structure and deal. After evaluating all the various options, we all thought the best idea was moving the land into an LLC and taking 35 partners in a private offering, which wouldn't require a lot of work — other than finding the 35 people.

This sounded good. We felt ready.

But the call for volunteers to serve on the Ownership Design Team prompted 125 people to show up for the meeting! The idea of the private offering was never going to work. I was surprised and concerned. People really liked the idea of owning the project and were afraid that only a small, highly-selective group of people would get in or there would have to be a lottery for the handful of slots.

"Look," someone explained, "a lot of us invested in our cousins' uncle's big idea and lost, so why not Joe? We are doing this together. He is successful. Of course people are going to want to get in on the deal."

Yipes! I thought. Now what? We are clearly going to need some other solution.

Kurt was a self-described Navy brat. A Berkeley undergrad, Columbia law school, University of San Diego post doc in tax law guy who was "doing the typical lawyer thing" when we met him. A project that was "certainly different" was about to be an understatement.

Initially we hoped that a co-op structure might work, but as a commercial center, it didn't meet the definition of an enterprise engaged in the production or distribution of goods and services by its members. Taking over 35 investors meant that the "private offering" wouldn't work and we would have to "go public." To go public, we would have to secure a permit from the State of California Department of Corporations (now called the California Department of Business Oversight), and we could take up to 500 investors before we would have to secure a permit from the Securities and Exchange Commission.

On almost every team there were polar positions, but our team had designed methods for finding the "both/and." Using half-sheets of paper, goals would be self-organized into thirds — each of the opposing forces and something in the middle. On the Business and Leasing Team, the opposing forces were anchor tenants that could provide living wages and pension plans side-by-side with "entrepreneurs who look like us," as residents framed it. In the middle were opportunities for franchise ownership and manage-to-own businesses.

On the Ownership Design Team, these opposing forces were self-interest and community benefit. People thought self-interest was important because it would incentivize people to care for the project. But there were others who were concerned that self-interest could also be taken to extremes — that people looking only for the financial bottom-line could easily lose sight of the project's roots as a social enterprise. These two elements needed to be balanced.

Chip, who had been working with a number of Native American tribes developing gaming operations, shared in a meeting how several were approaching their economic development using a "theory of thirds" — one third of profits to be distributed to tribal members, one third for education or other programs that could advance the tribal community, and one third for diversification of their financial investments for ongoing benefit of both the tribe and its members.

People latched on. It spoke to everyone, residents and staff alike. For those of us working on the project, it was a simple framing of the "both/and" approach we had been using to manage opposing forces. It was easy to remember and easy to structure around — the balancing elements of individual ownership, social responsibility and community impact, along with ongoing sustainable economic expansion.

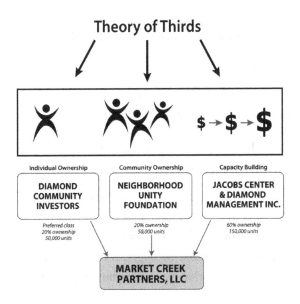

185

The framework for ownership contained three structures — one involving individual ownership, one involving a way to return profits for community benefit, and one involving the creation of a company that could continue to develop resident-owned projects based on this same process and structure.

Working with the legal team on the corporate structuring and with the community-building team on the naming of the entities, we determined that the best route was the creation of a limited liability company, to be called Market Creek Partners, LLC with its ownership structured along the lines of the "theory of thirds."

In a naming process for the "thirds," each of the components came alive — *Diamond Community Investors* (individual owners), the *Neighborhood Unity Foundation* (a community foundation pubic benefit owner), and *Diamond Management, Inc.* (the ongoing community-based development company and asset manager).

"It was a tripartite!" Elaine Kennedy, a resident who served on the original Ownership Design Team, exclaimed, referring to the theory of thirds. "We all loved the tradition it came out of."

In addition, the Ownership Design Team set goals to be achieved in the process:

- Broad access for residents of all income levels,
- Low minimums for cost per share,
- Caps on what any individual person could own,
- Ability to buy Jacobs out, but not too soon, and
- Training in the theory of investment along the way.

Once these preliminary goals were set, three sub-teams were created to work on each of the components.

The Investment Company Act would not allow us to set up the individual owners in a separate company, so Diamond Community Investors (DCI) was created as a class of members who would purchase and hold shares or "units" in the LLC. Units would be sold through an Initial Public Offering (IPO) and these units would have priority for distribution of profits. Since an LLC has a managing member and not a board, the DCI governance structure would be an Advisory Board, selected in a one-member-one-vote election with representation on the managing member's board of directors.

"As the lead attorney working on it, what was nice was being given leeway to make it work," noted Kurt Kicklighter. "The residents asked good questions. It was invigorating."

The community benefit structure would be formed as a community foundation 501(c)3 public benefit corporation. The small working team on the creation of the Neighborhood Unity Foundation (NUF) quickly expanded to over 250 people who volunteered for the NUF Design Team. NUF's governance, which the team struggled with over a nine-month design period, would become an eleven-member community board, voted in by the community of actively-engaged citizens — anyone and everyone involved in the design team's community listening, which was about a thousand people. This group's goal was to raise the capital to buy its shares, which would then serve as the endowment for the community foundation. Over time, plans called for diversifying its endowment, but as an act of pride and social responsibility, the Neighborhood Unity Foundation (NUF) would place priority on keeping its investments lined up with its community benefit purpose, unlike many community foundations they researched.

To get the development company — Diamond Management, Inc. (DMI) — up and running, JCNI would loan its development team and, because of the risk, set it up as a fully-owned subsidiary, until it was profitable, had a pipeline of projects that could keep it profitable, and had built a team of community residents to run the company, manage the Market Creek assets, and conduct ongoing development. Since a number of community-based CDC's had come and gone, residents were anxious that JCNI not back out of the project too soon, staying for the seven to eight projects it would take to make this a sustainable entity. Once sustainable, this company was planned to spin off as a independent community-owned enterprise.

The design called for DMI to be the managing member of the limited liability company, Market Creek Partners, so it needed to have a small ownership share. DMI, as a company initially owned by JCNI would come as part of a third ownership category along with JCNI. DMI and JCNI would be tasked with building the community capacity to diversify resident-owned assets and, through that work, build a community-owned development company. Once the concept of DMI was established, the third sub-team on ownership design transitioned its purpose to providing neighborhood residents with financial training, which people saw as an important capacity-building mission related to ownership.

Our attorney wanted JCNI to maintain the majority ownership until Jacobs and all of the program-related investment (PRI) partners were refinanced out so as to not impact the charitable purpose or tax status of these investments. The initial ownership design called for Diamond Community Investors (DCI) and the Neighborhood Unity Foundation (NUF) to each have a 20 percent ownership share for a total of 40 percent and for JCNI/DMI to have the remaining 60 percent until 2018 when residents would have the right to buy the Jacobs Center's ownership share.

The timeline for the transition to full community ownership was established based on the estimated increase in value of the lease of the project's anchor — Food 4 Less. Documented in a case study put together for the Rockefeller Foundation with Steve Godeke, entitled: *Financing Change: The Social and Economic Costs of Market Creek Plaza*,[77] in 2004 — the year the project was completed — projections showed 1) the estimated increase in Market Creek Plaza's value (using a 7% capitalization rate), 2) the increase in loan value above the original $15 million, and 3) the ability of the community investors to pay off the PRIs and replace Jacobs capital through a project refinance just after Year 10.

These numbers, which I've placed in the chart below, illustrate the growth of the loan value as the primary indicator that full community ownership was feasible without additional investment of community capital. Recognizing at that time that we were still a couple of years from running the IPO and that Market Creek Plaza needed time to stabilize financially, 2018 made sense as the target community buy-out year.

Market Creek Plaza Early Projections

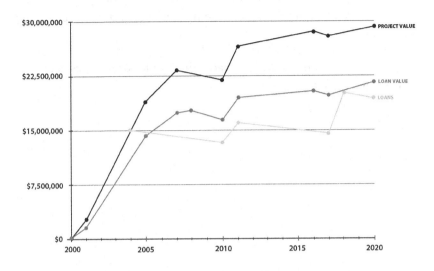

We were always in a search for sustaining structures — the platforms for planning, implementing, and owning change that could be linked together in a self-financing whole. This gave us the framework we needed to do some of our most pioneering work.

We had unearthed the mechanism for taking blighted land, turning it into value through a process that built skills and a strong sense of community, and harnessing that value to build individual and community assets. That mechanism would be found in:

- A 10-acre industrial dump and its surrounding blight;
- Inclusive and ongoing community listening;
- A large-scale vision organizing strategy in and across cultures;
- Resident working teams to plan, design, and build a commercial project;
- An infrastructure that could support civic action, promote shared learning, manage emerging networks, and integrate grantmaking, organizing, training, and development;
- A resident-led community foundation;
- A management and development company; and
- A Community Development IPO.

We had pushed the boundaries of what was familiar, rethinking all we thought we knew. And like the jazz musician, by taking the music to new places, we were stimulating change in ourselves and in the ecosystem around us.

Through this "frame work," we had built the platform for resident voice and investment in community change.

FINANCING
CHANGE

COMMUNITY & CAPITAL

15

THE MONEY MATRIX

*"We need to move away from silo approaches when we ask
'Where can I make meaningful loans?' or 'How
can I give away my grant money better?'
Instead, we must ask 'How do we work together to
solve the social challenges that matter."* [78]

— Antony Bugg-Levine, "Complete Capital,"
Stanford Social Innovation Review

It Takes Money to Make Money

"There are only three ways to get access to capital: a lot of discretionary income, an asset that can be leveraged, and crime."

Bob McNeely, senior vice president and head of corporate community development for Union Bank of California at that time, was on point. Short of crime, it takes money to make money.

In our under-invested neighborhoods, job creation and employment development are a start, but asset poverty is deep. "Working" and "poor" still go together, and many people have little or no cushion to survive a job loss. An illness can quickly deplete what they have. Many cannot afford to improve their education or job skills. They have no resources to invest in a home, a business, or higher education for their children. They cannot plan for retirement. They cannot pass assets on to future generations.

From the Homestead Act of 1863 to the GI Bill in World War II to the modern-day tax code, the United States has provided support for asset building throughout its history on the assumption that a job alone would not lead to prosperity and economic security. By 1998, it was being well-documented by foundations that these benefits had advantaged white Americans while racially-discriminating housing policies and red-lining by financial institutions had broadened the wealth gap.

Communities, like individuals, suffer from asset poverty — the kind of public infrastructure and land values that facilitate wealth-building — and in the area surrounding the site that would become Market Creek Plaza, blighted properties were largely owned by people outside the neighborhood who didn't care about getting jobs and homes on them, keeping those land values low.

"Gangs claim territory," noted Reverend Ikenna Kokayi, who at that time was the Chairman and CEO of the United African American Ministerial Action Council. "But the truth is, none of us own or control this land. We need to. We are occupiers — not owners."

In 1997, when we went into escrow on the old factory site, we began to explore how a community might own a major commercial project that could provide both individual income and create an appreciating community asset that could be used for leveraging future change.

At that time, terms like mission investing, impact investing, social innovation funds, and blended value weren't prevalent in the philanthropic culture. New Markets Tax Credits hadn't been created, and few foundations were using their assets as leverage for people and neighborhoods to gain control of assets. But fueled by the courageous philanthropy of the Ford Foundation, change was slowly taking root.

Stimulating the national discussion on individuals and asset building during the 1990s were Michael Sherraden's catalytic book Assets and the Poor,[79] the Center for Social Development, which he founded, and its collaboration with the Corporation for Enterprise Development (renamed Prosperity Now), which resulted in the The American Dream Demonstration. This launched a movement to pilot IDAs (Individual Development Accounts) to help people save for school, start a business, or buy a home, which grew into an important tool for impacting this critical indicator of family well-being — assets.

The Ford Foundation also began raising consciousness about the use of foundation assets — not just income disbursed in the form of cash grants — to build community assets. Even though the Tax Reform Act of 1969 established the term program-related investment (PRI), foundations were slow to follow the Ford Foundation's lead in responding to the turbulent 1960's and 1970's by using this tool as a way to expand their reach. But by the 1980's, demonstrations on college campuses demanding South African disinvestment began to explode the conversation about socially responsible investing and got the attention of philanthropy.

By the late 1990's when we started Market Creek, smaller foundations had begun taking pioneering roles, such as the F.B. Heron Foundation and the Jessie Smith Noyes Foundation, by exploring everything from mission investment and PRIs to corporate stockholder activism — changing the marketplace of tools and talent in philanthropy.

By 2000, Jed Emerson had become a national champion of "blended value," the concept of integrating social and economic impact rather than siloing down for-profit and non-profit lines and thinking narrowly about how to affect change.

But the skepticism about using the full power of a foundation's portfolio in a seamless and integrated approach was still wide-spread, and many foundations were still reluctant to take on the additional challenge of full alignment.

When Jed Emerson, who went on to co-author the book Impact Investing,[80] and I were asked to speak at Stanford University's Center for Social Innovation in 2003 as part of its social entrepreneurship series, our presentations focused on the theory and the practical application of foundations aligning their purpose and portfolios. Indelible for me was Paul Brest, President of the Hewlett Foundation, who in offering the closing remarks for the session said with his dry humor: "I don't understand why more people don't try it. It may be because it could be easier to send a man to the moon."

In reflecting on our brief six-year experience at that point and considering the challenge of moving from a single silo to an integrated approach, I thought he was probably right. It was daunting to think about achieving complete alignment between our philanthropic approach and how we invested our portfolio, and at the same time support the development of a vibrant local economy — bringing money in, keeping it in, and circulating it as much as possible before it goes out — factoring in the impact of the larger regional and even global economy. We at least understood the jet propulsion required to get a man to the moon.

That year, however, efforts were initiated with support from the Ford Foundation and the Charles and Helen Schwab Foundation to develop a long-term asset-building policy agenda, and by mid-2003, I was able to join a newly-formed task-force called the Asset Policy Initiative of California (APIC) and participate with people from across the state who were coming together to shine a spotlight on the growing crisis of concentrated wealth at the top and broaden the conversation about the state of asset poverty. These advocates began the process of raising awareness and gave me a touchstone.

Today, a robust coalition of more than 40 organizations — the California Asset Building Coalition (CABC) — has picked up where APIC left off, advancing statewide policies and programs that help families save money, build assets, expand ownership, and protect financial security; and a national Asset Funders Network has grown to include more than 120 philanthropic leaders. The work of these groups is more important than ever. In 2002, a CFED report card showed that 28.5 percent of California households would have insufficient net worth to sustain living at the federal poverty level for three months if their income were disrupted,[81] a statistic that has shamefully continued to climb in a state that now boasts 131 billionaires.[82]

In a world in which it takes money to make money, Market Creek was one effort to address this issue on the ground — leveraging philanthropic assets as courageously as we could to build sustaining resident-controlled assets by reclaiming blight. As a small foundation, we needed to start where we were and build on what we had, and key to that equation was a market study that showed the community had $60 million in retail leakage in a quarter-mile radius. If other resources were sparse, we would have to bank on making the dollar bounce. Organizing would have to be deep and broad. Everyone would be asked to think like an owner.

We knew that neighborhoods become safer when people create dense social networks, local jobs are created when entrepreneurship is encouraged and access to capital supported, and businesses thrive when retailers come together for mutual benefit. We also knew that land comes alive when it is not developed as isolated parcels but assembled for synergy and scale.

To accomplish its mission, Market Creek would need to be developed by finding ways to blend community building with business development, business development with physical development, and physical development with asset building — so that residents would no longer be "occupiers," as Reverend Kokayi put it; they would become the owners of valuable commercial assets giving them control over key decisions in their community.

The Blended Approach

"Meetings are a waste of time." If I heard this once, I heard it a million times.

When I heard it, I would always laugh and say: "If I had a dollar for every time someone said that to me, we would have our financing!"

This was always the view of people who weren't participating and who hadn't experienced the power of participatory planning. It was also the view of people who liked to pontificate on the benefits of command/control decision-making. These folks always reminded me that action and outcomes were what mattered and if people didn't show up for public forums, it was on them. This always led to the question: "Why do you need so much process or such a big organizing team?"

When criticized for how expensive it was to support a six-person organizing team capable of mobilizing civic action across nine-cultures, I loved using Geoffrey Canada's line, "Expensive? Compared to what? This guy," he continued, "is in front of the judge being sentenced to prison and no one stands up and asks 'now how exactly will we scale that?'"

The outreach and organizing was expensive compared to what? There are a lot of sophisticated theories of change and large numbers of organizations that are accountable and efficient, run well-designed programs, track and use data to measure success, and are successful by industry standards. But then we wonder: "So then why are our neighborhoods getting worse?"

"We've made a collection of great grants to great organizations in this one neighborhood," one grants officer in a large foundation described to me, "but after two decades, they still haven't added up to any kind of neighborhood-level impact."

It is easy to continue business as usual based on the hope that cash grants with carefully detailed benchmarks and low-interest loans with secure income streams will stimulate the breakthrough needed for social innovation; that if all goes well, the government will pick things up and leverage change at enormous scale; that financial institutions will just decide to provide greater access to capital so projects and businesses will flourish in our disinvested communities; and if we train people, they will get the jobs.

But this is clearly not the case.

We were in the business of the "resident ownership of neighborhood change," and that required we fund not just programs, as in our past grant making history, but the ability people to reach out to their neighbors, come together, meet, deliberate in whatever language they wanted to express themselves, and set action plans. This was not about asking residents to come together to weigh-in on plans other people were going to be implementing. At the heart of this had to be an experienced team of process-designers that could move from community listening to resident planning before projects were ready for implementation funding — the phase when most foundations want to engage.

So we had to address a set of challenges in developing the resource strategy for comprehensive resident-driven work. How were we going to fund the ongoing organizing, listening, deliberating, and planning infrastructure that preceded specific detailed action plans? Since the majority of the foundations locally and nationally still operated in silos, how were we going to get resources behind cross-disciplinary work? And what would we do when implementation plans were developed if they required different types of capital — such as loans and equity investments, along with grants?

Fourteen local foundations, banks, and individuals agreed to form the San Diego Neighborhood Funders to support the revitalization efforts. For all of us in the newly assembled resource collaboration, we had to learn to work differently.

Among our local funding partners, many had evolved from making independent grants as individual funders to making collaborative grants, but historically, these had been within a single area of interest, like children or AIDS. For the first time, we had to learn how to work across areas of interest in an interconnected and synergistic way.

At the outset of the neighborhood collaboration, the Legler Benbough Foundation paid for an attorney to draw up expenditure responsibility agreements so funds could be made available to teams that didn't have a 501(c)3 status. The Alliance Healthcare Foundation served as the fiscal agent for the mini-grants program and assembled and worked with a resident team. The Jacobs Center served as the fiscal agent for the larger strategic grants and took responsibility for the feeder system for getting what teams needed in front of the group and for writing the reports for the IRS. San Diego National Bank took the lead on coordination with the IRS on bringing an Earned Income Tax Credit VITA site to the community. All fourteen funders pitched in $5,000 each for mini-grants and made at least one collaborative grant toward the larger strategic effort. Most did much more.

Most of our funding partners wanted to fund down, in areas of interest — health, education, youth development, arts and culture — so the Jacobs Family Foundation provided the connective glue by funding across — the civic space — support for community organizing and working teams, building social networks, managing cross-sectoral partnerships, cross-cultural understanding, and action learning.

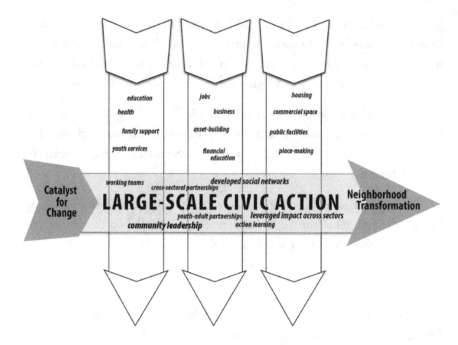

education
health
family support
youth services

jobs
business
asset-building
financial education

housing
commercial space
public facilities
place-making

Catalyst for Change

working teams
developed social networks
cross-sectoral partnerships
LARGE-SCALE CIVIC ACTION
youth-adult partnerships
leveraged impact across sectors
community leadership
action learning

Neighborhood Transformation

Aiming civic action at a catalyst project — planned and owned by residents — provided the platform for everything else.

To implement in this way, resources needed to be secured and assembled on a grid — a money matrix that went down and across — for a much broader range of strategic agendas than non-profit programs. Then as plans developed, we also created a process to mix-and-match resources using a much larger number of tools across types of capital. Resource partnerships expanded to include financial institutions and national foundations.

We had to move from one tool to many and learn to "work without walls" in blending them.

In order to bring Market Creek out of the ground, we would use cash grants, recoverable grants, equity PRIs, debt PRIs, loan guarantees, linked deposits, business investments, loan pools, tax increment financing, and work with a CDFI (Community Development Financial Institution) in the formation of CDEs (Community Development Entities) to leverage tax credits with for-profit investors.

The Evolution of the Resource Strategy

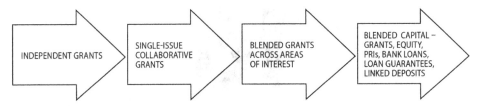

| INDEPENDENT GRANTS | SINGLE-ISSUE COLLABORATIVE GRANTS | BLENDED GRANTS ACROSS AREAS OF INTEREST | BLENDED CAPITAL – GRANTS, EQUITY, PRIs, BANK LOANS, LOAN GUARANTEES, LINKED DEPOSITS |

But as an up-close-and-personal study in answering the question "what does it really take?" — this was in no way easy and the complications were surprising at every turn.

The development of Market Creek was occurring before the explosion of program-related investing by foundations. It was also before the Department of the Treasury launched the New Markets Tax Credit Program, and while redevelopment agencies existed in California to leverage tax increment at that time, the one serving the southeastern San Diego community didn't have adequate bond capacity. Financing would be challenged at every turn. We encountered everything from the inadequacy of government tools to individual acts of resistance to just bad timing.

We had let go of the shore and could no longer function in the world of reading proposals and making independent decisions. We were in the new universe of grappling with how to make things work. With financing, like everything else, our options and choices were to: a) figure it out, b) figure it out, or c) figure it out.

16

CHANGE FINANCE

"This isn't rocket science; it's much more difficult."

— Angela Glover Blackwell

This Wasn't Rocket Science...

"We knew this wasn't going to be a cake walk," remembered Mike McCraw.

Mike, a self-described anomaly, was one of the first people with a wealth of knowledge in finance to reach out to help. "I used to go by the old Langley factory site when I lived in that area, and it was depressing seeing that abandoned facility adding blight to an already blighted area."

Mike grew up in Youngstown, Ohio — in those days a steel town. But just as he was graduating from high school, the mills were moving off-shore and the town was struggling. "I wanted to help my family," he reminisced. "I grew up in a single-parent home and decided to join the Navy to help out financially. Watching my community decline economically and socially was highly motivating."

Mike served four years in the Navy, concluding his tour with a sixteen-month deployment just as the Vietnam War was getting started. "I needed to remain employed, so I choose the Coast Guard for a second tour," he recalled. "That's how I ended up in San Diego."

"When I came here, the only housing you could get as an African American was in southeastern San Diego. We didn't have a choice. It was 1964 and Jim Crow was far from dead," he remembered. "But every major city had an African American business corridor. As a young person I wanted to be like the guy who owned the gas station. If you were a black business owner, that was big."

Mike had grown up in a mixed-race family and in the 1950s had the benefit of a good education and knew finance. When I met him, he was the President and CEO of the one of the 11 state-funded loan guarantee programs — the largest in San Diego — set up to assist small businesses that couldn't qualify for a loan without a guarantee. He knew how to package deals. But because of his African American roots, he also knew too well why the old factory site in southeastern San Diego wasn't financeable. "By this time, you could see the disadvantages starting to set in and the businesses were closing."

"I got a call from Murray Galinson, the President of San Diego National Bank, and he was the one who asked me to take a look and see what I could do. Murray said you had asked for his help, and because he asked me, I was willing to do it, but I was skeptical." Then he paused to back up, "No, not just skeptical; I thought this was pure insanity!"

Mike's first thought was that he would come over and give me a reality check. He didn't think anyone would invest in a retail center. "The area was becoming less and less attractive," he shared. "I knew financing would be really tough, and not just because it was an old factory with added clean-up costs, but because the stereotype of being in an African American community would make it impossible."

But when Mike stopped by to see me there was a community meeting underway. "That changed everything for me. Seeing so many residents involved made me realize that this would be different. This was a foundation that wasn't working in isolation like I expected. I had never seen this kind of inclusion. I suddenly wanted to help make it happen."

"Then I went up to Pasadena to meet with Joe, and he personally called me in from the lobby saying 'come on back, Mike!' Here was this guy with his name on the building being so personal. It was phenomenal."

Joe and Mike connected in a long conversation about entrepreneurship. Joe believed deeply in ownership and wanted local entrepreneurship to have center-stage in his philanthropy. He not only asked Mike to help secure financing for the retail center but wanted Mike to figure out how best to support local business ownership as part of the project.

Mike, who had lived in the community as a young person in the military, had a place in his heart for the community, and like the rest of us who participated in the Market Creek experience, he would be changed by it. "It forced us to all be together. To be in the room with all these people who didn't look like us. It was wonderful. And the work everyone contributed was making the community safe and desirable again."

Over the years, when asked why he wanted to work on financing for the project or why he took a risk and created a financing tool specifically for Market Creek's entrepreneurs, Mike would tell people, "It's simple. Because Joe asked me."

But while the reason Mike was willing to come to the table was simple, the actual process of getting Market Creek financed was anything but simple.

From the very beginning, Joe's success indicator for Market Creek Plaza was securing financing. He charged us with using everything that could be leveraged to get it to work, and to him, financing meant that the project's economic elements were aligned in a way that it could be sustaining.

The original plan called for developing the 20-acre site as one project at a total cost of $85 million. If we could put together a collaborative group of foundation partners, a consortium of banks, our local Community Development Financial Institution, and the redevelopment agency for covering infrastructure and public improvements, we believed it could work. The plan also provided the opportunity for residents to co-invest.

"I had 20 banks in my portfolio and I ran this by every one of them," Mike reflected. "I couldn't get one to take a serious look at it. They had to be willing to adjust their thinking about revenue projections. They also thought there wasn't enough strength in the demographic, so they wanted to charge higher rates. The rates they wanted to charge were prohibitive."

Mike's comment about knowing this wasn't going to be a "cake walk" would be an understatement. It would take six years to finance Market Creek Plaza and would be a roller coaster of ups and downs. Financial institutions, the public sector, and philanthropy all wanted to see community change, and intuitively understood the need for scale as a strategy to reduce risk over time but found it daunting. Too small was too risky and too big was too risky. No tool seemed to work

The community process required flexibility, which was difficult for the banks, and their standard risk-return formulas couldn't work with the added costs for clean-up and infrastructure associated with redevelopment. Until New Markets Tax Credits, public sector tools were designed primarily for municipal buildings, not commercial projects. Foundations, concerned about debt-financed real estate, feared being hit with unrelated business income tax. And all sources of capital wanted "shovel-ready" projects with guaranteed income streams — foundations, government, and banks alike.

Years after we started figuring out the financing, Angela Glover Blackwell, then CEO of PolicyLink, invited me to speak at a forum in Washington DC on the issue of community capital. When I returned to San Diego, I got a call from the Assistant Secretary of HUD, who said he had heard my speech and had a tool that could finance the project.

By this time, all I could think of to say was — "Is this a prank call?" I heard a big laugh on the other end of the phone.

Finance Phase 1 (1998 to 2001): Getting to the Grocery

The journey to finance Market Creek occurred on four fronts that needed to be blended: 1) financial institutions, 2) public sector, 3) philanthropy, and 4) community investment. These four sources of capital were challenging, but the need to blend them made them even more complicated. Often as we addressed issues for one, it created problems for the others.

- **Financial Institutions**

After months of work, Mike McCraw was able to get six banks to indicate they would consider joining a bank consortium when the plans were finance-ready.

But in the 1998 bank mergers and acquisitions era, the banking consortium became impossible. The individual banks were concerned that we had a letter-of-intent from Magic Johnson Theaters to place a 10-plex movie theater on the site. At that time, the movie theater industry's future was being questioned, and the volatility made the bankers nervous. We tried a number of approaches, none of which allayed concerns. Despite early excitement that the project eliminated 20 acres of blight in a CRA-target area, the banks were concerned about the fact that the project would still be surrounded by blight and determined it was too risky to touch right away.

Stalled without options, Joe moved personal stock to Wells Fargo to secure a working line of credit to keep the project moving until we could secure financing — a courageous and pivotal move.

- **Public Sector Resources**

At the very beginning when we moved our offices to the southeastern neighborhoods, the City Councilman verbally pledged Block Grant dollars to help advance the work to remove blight and create local jobs. He knew the community needed a major grocery store. But in the follow-up, it was clear that the majority of the Block Grant dollars were already pledged for municipal projects, leaving a very small amount for community non-profits that would have been damaged by the redirecting of funds.

In exploring tax increment financing (TIF), a tool of the redevelopment agency — a public subsidy for blight removal and infrastructure to be recovered through a boost in real estate tax revenue — we were informed that land had been removed from the redevelopment zone. Rather than targeting this property as a hot-spot to be cleaned up, the agency removed it because "it was bringing down the tax value of the area." Its removal created a donut hole right in the middle of the redevelopment zone.

Residents were clearly upset about the redevelopment agency, complaining that there hadn't been a project get off the ground in over 15 years. "No jobs means no tax increment and no tax increment means no jobs," residents noted. It had become a vicious cycle.

To secure the value of tax increment financing long-term, JCNI decided to take the risk rather than leave this value on the table. We paid for the property to be reinstated in the redevelopment area and for the legal team to draw up an Owner Participation Agreement (OPA) with the agency. We advanced the money for all the public improvements in exchange for 60 percent of the tax increment generated by the project, not to exceed what was spent. JCNI anticipated that it would begin to recoup this investment within three years.

We also researched every available public-sector financing tool. Most were too small to work. Even HUD, after the Assistant Secretary wanted to help, couldn't figure out how to make it work.

As we closed out the conversations with HUD, the Assistant Secretary told me to watch for the New Markets Tax Credit Program. It was under development and would be a better tool because it was intended for commercial projects like Market Creek.

- *Philanthropic Resources*

"Foundations are the venture capital of the non-profit world," I heard more than once, but nothing could have been farther from reality.

At that time, program-related investments (PRIs) were rare; even the Ford Foundation, the pioneer of PRIs, had put their investments on hold at that time to re-evaluate the future of the program. In addition, the Unrelated Business Income Tax laws related to debt-financed real estate caused many foundation staffs to think they needed to stay away from commercial projects. In San Diego, no foundation had ever done a PRI for any purpose — let alone to a commercial project.

It would take four years of discussions about risk, whether or not Jacobs had too much capital in the project or not enough, and the need for guarantees to solidify a strategy. The F. B. Heron Foundation, a leader in the field of job creation and asset-building, liked the project immediately. The Rockefeller Foundation had never done a PRI for a commercial real estate project in the U.S. but was interested; the Annie E. Casey Foundation didn't have a PRI program at all but was willing to create one; and the local Legler Benbough Foundation agreed to participate using one of the national foundation's contracts as a prototype. One of the requirements to secure the funding was a guarantee of capital from the Jacobs Family Foundation, reluctantly agreed to, and JCNI agreed to serve as the non-profit intermediary for the PRIs loaned forward to Market Creek Partners.

By 2002, the Heron and Rockefeller Foundations were in final document discussions when the worst possible news surfaced in prepping for an audit. Our Director of Finance had embezzled funds to feed a gambling addiction. It was a shock to all of us who knew him. All of our PRI agreements were put on hold while we reviewed all of the accounts, conducted a forensic audit, filed charges, put new controls in place, and recruited a new Finance Director.

Our operation would never be the same again, and neither would I. While I was proud of the teamwork that went into not just bringing us back up to speed, but in taking us to new levels of oversight, it was the most painful lesson of my professional career. Joe's line to me: "I remember when it happened to me. It hurt." He didn't want to fire me. He didn't want me to resign. He wanted me to dig in — as he did when anything went wrong — and clean it up.

Making the calls to the foundations we were working with was agony, but their understanding (some shared their own experiences) and their friendship meant more than could be imagined.

- *Community/Resident Investment*

By the end of 2000, the resident Ownership Design Team completed its work on a community investment strategy, and we were ready — or so we thought — to submit our application to the Department of Corporations for a permit to go public.

Finance Phase 2 (2001 to 2005): Completing the Project

In January 2001, the grocery opened. And at that time, there were still no banks, no foundation PRIs, no public-sector support, and the road to community investment was just starting.

JCNI had secured a contract with Food 4 Less to anchor the project, had purchased the land with its own equity investment, and had funded the demolition of the factory and the site preparation with a working line of credit. We had conducted extensive community listening, initiated community teams, planned the project, secured a General Plan Amendment, and produced a grocery on a former brownfield site in just three years. A milestone.

With the grocery opening, a new level of excitement permeated the community teams, the work to complete the remaining commercial buildings pushed forward, and the journey to finance Market Creek Plaza continued.

But the remaining months of 2001 would bring 9/11, a faltering economy, and a new set of challenges. The grappling didn't end.

• *Financial Institutions*

With a strong lease from Food 4 Less and the grocery open and operating, we thought the track-record would smooth the way for bank financing. But the back and forth continued and new issues surfaced.

The financial model for Market Creek Plaza called for the grocery lease to carry the debt service, allowing more flexibility for local community tenants in two small buildings along the creek. This was a critical component of the Resident Business and Leasing Team's plan, and to Joe, this was the most important part of the overall mission of Market Creek.

"We all liked Sister Pee Wee's," Mike McCraw noted, reflecting on the community leasing discussions. Sister Pee Wee's was the quintessential soul food lunch counter. I loved it, too. The menu changed every day based on what Sister Pee Wee felt like cooking. Her fried chicken or smothered pork chops came with cornbread and Kool-Aid. She would cook for anyone; even if you didn't have any money you were welcome.

"But we also wanted a full-service restaurant," Mike continued. "Something locally-owned that could be a catalyst for business meetings. When I first came to this community, Archie Moore owned a restaurant." The "Mongoose," as he was called, liked pinstriped suits, red silk ties, and fried chicken. As the world light heavyweight champion, he was a local hero. "After Archie's place closed down, this community didn't have anything but a couple of lunch counters and fast food," Mike remembered.

The small locally-owned business agenda made the banks uneasy. If Joe was committed to entrepreneurship, they wanted the foundation to take a master lease on the two small buildings that were intended for local businesses. But when we agreed to sign the master lease on the two buildings, they wanted to drop the value of the project based on the "quality" of the community leases. When we prepared ourselves for the drop in value, they then wanted one and a half years in full operation before loaning any funds.

In 2004, three years after the grocery was open and operating, we were still in never-ending discussions with banks when the New Markets Tax Credit Program, launched by the U.S. Department of the Treasury to spur revitalization of disinvested communities by creating greater access to capital for business development, looked like a viable option.

"I knew this guy who had gotten a large allocation," Mike remembered. "Doug Bystry headed the Clearinghouse CDFI and was looking for projects. I was in Joe's office talking about take-out financing when I picked up the phone to call him."

Receiving an allocation during the competitive first year of the New Markets Tax Credit Program was tough, and Clearinghouse CDFI had succeeded in its bid. With a mission to assist people and communities through innovative and affordable financing where conventional lending is unavailable, Clearinghouse was exactly the kind of partner we needed. Undaunted by challenging projects, they took time to work with us individually and appreciated the broad community input and impact the project represented.

And the rest is a story about how opportunity happens. People who ask people who know people. And timing. Joe asked Mike, Mike knew Doug, and Doug and Mike knew Bob Taylor, the President of the Community Development Bank at Wells Fargo Bank. Bob knew me and wanted to help, but now Doug had tax credits that could be brought to the table.

About the same moment in time, I got a call from a Wells Fargo team member responding to our request to consider putting a bank branch at Market Creek. They were interested but wanted a five-year lease. "That's fantastic," I said, "but I just got a call from another person at Wells Fargo who said they wanted to do our loan but told us any leases five years or less would not be considered bankable. That would make your lease unbankable by your own bank!" It started as a joke, but our request to have the team at Wells Fargo meet in the hallway and figure out what to do, accomplished just that. Wells agreed to do the bank branch and extend the branch lease.

Bob Taylor from Wells Fargo was the next person to call me. The Wells team, working alongside Clearinghouse CDFI, were also going to loan us the amount we needed at the cost of money we needed — $15 million at a fixed rate of 3 percent for seven years.

This time I didn't laugh. I cried.

- *Public Sector Resources*

Peter Senge, in one of his 11 laws of the Fifth Discipline, writes, "The harder you push, the harder the system pushes back."[83]

To phase the financing, we separated the land into two parcels, creating a lot line at the creek. A process that would typically take three months was extended to eighteen because of a change in the city review process triggered by the development of a downtown ballpark. The agreement with the redevelopment agency also had to be split along with the lot line. We were encouraged by the agency to move forward in good faith and told that when the planning was complete for both sides, the revisions to the agreement would move forward.

As the resident teams completed the plans, the redevelopment agency agreed to the terms of the agreement and directed their team to finalize the documents. But to Senge's law — we pushed, we met, we pushed, and we met and couldn't move the agreement. While these discussions dragged on, the agency director would be indicted and convicted on felony embezzlement charges, and we would start over with a new team.

Then hope surfaced on the horizon for public sector support.

The City of San Diego launched a pilot smart growth initiative in 2004 called the "City of Villages." The goal was to select a set of demonstration projects aimed at revitalization of existing neighborhoods while retaining their individual character. Incentives included infrastructure upgrades or replacements, deferral of fees, business and energy-efficiency incentives, funding for handicapped access, rebates on property taxes, and revolving loan funds. It included a "Village Overlay Zone," which offered an alternative permit process to accelerate development. A person in the City Planning Department would also be assigned to assist applicants in securing grants, remove obstacles, and expedite approvals.

We made a grant to the Coalition of Neighborhood Councils, headquartered across the street from Market Creek and long-time participant in the Village planning, to hire urban planners, form teams, identify the broader planning area of blighted properties, and work to secure the competitive bid. JCNI would be the development partner alongside of the Coalition.

The Village at Market Creek was selected as one of the four pilot projects.

But the City of Villages pilot program, which promised to boost San Diego's older neighborhoods' capacity to revitalize was anything but a catalyst for San Diego's smart growth. For the selected projects, incentives to speed up the revitalization back-fired. The mayor was recalled and a change in mayors caused a turn-over in staff. This along with a nearly bankrupt city and a disconnect among the various city departments that kept doing business as usual stood in the way of any implementation.

In order to apply for permits for a mixed-use project, we needed the promised Village zone, but in order to rezone, the zone had to be created; in order to get access to a Village zone, we needed an update to the community plan, which hadn't been updated since the Johnson Administration. Despite the promise of expedite status, a community plan update undertaken by the redevelopment agency itself took six years. The four projects that received the "honor and prestige of being selected as pilot villages" stalled or were stopped.

If anything got done, it was cited by all the "pilot" projects as being a coincidence.

- *Philanthropy Resources*

In September 2003, the Heron Foundation initiated the first PRI, followed by the Rockefeller Foundation in October. Within a year, our local-foundation partner — the Legler Benbough Foundation — became the third PRI investor for a total of $2 million. The Annie E. Casey Foundation, which had indicated the desire to invest, had started the formation of a PRI program, setting up its policies and documents, moving the possibility of a fourth PRI into the realm of feasibility.

The San Diego Neighborhood Funders, the newly-formed collaboration of foundations and financial institutions, was forging new ways to blend resources for resident teams and resident-guided projects. By 2004, its membership had grown to eleven foundations, three financial institutions, the United Way, and the director of our regional association of grantmakers.

Resident-centered philanthropy was a new idea and our learning curve was straight up hill. Learning from the history of East Bay Funders and LA Urban Funders, we continued to find new ways to balance the need to follow the natural momentum of resident teams within the grantmaking criteria and processes of each individual charitable organization. By this era of the work, we had agreed to a clear mission and were engaging in joint grantmaking for resident-centered action. The collaboration's potential was growing.

- *Community/Resident Investment*

In 2001, when we filed with the Department of Corporations (DOC) for a permit to go public, the DOC urged us to resubmit when the project was out of the high-risk stage of development and stabilized. In 2002, a second submission to the DOC also came back with questions and concerns about risk. Undaunted, the Ownership Design Team pushed forward on restructuring and refining the offering.

While this process was underway, JCNI made a challenge grant to the Neighborhood Unity Foundation (NUF) to help it raise its capital. NUF incorporated, began its community listening phase, and started fundraising to buy its $500,000 ownership share of Market Creek Partners.

In 2005, with completion and lease-up of all the remaining buildings at Market Creek Plaza, the public offering documents were ready for re-submittal to the Department of Corporations (the individual investor component) and NUF (the community investment component) purchased the first 20,000 of its 50,000 units — which began earning a 10 percent preferred return.

The Completion of Financing Market Creek Plaza

By mid-2004, the project was coming alive and becoming profitable. Gross sales for Food 4 Less were increasing by 10 percent per year for its three years of operation; two community businesses celebrated first anniversaries, two more opened; and the Wells Fargo Bank and Magic Johnson Starbucks were both under construction.

With the $15 million New Markets Tax Credit Loan made possible through Clearinghouse CDFI and Well Fargo Community Development Bank, we had hit Joe's personal success indicator. Market Creek Plaza's financing was complete.

Projected as a $23.5 million project in the original finance case study,[84] the final tally was $23.7 million all-in (see chart below). The Annie E. Casey Foundation finalized two program-related investments totaling $1,250,000 to complete the $5,250,000 PRI goal, the Jacobs Center and DMI's equity investment totaled $2,450,000, and Market Creek's crown jewel — community co-investment of $1 million — rounded out the financing.

Overview of the Financing of Market Creek Plaza

EQUITY	
Jacobs Center for Neighborhood Innovation	$2,350,000
Diamond Management, Inc.	$100,000
Diamond Community Investors	$500,000
Neighborhood Unity Foundation	$500,000
PROGRAM-RELATED INVESTMENTS	
Jacobs Family Foundation	$2,000,000
F.M. Heron Foundation	$500,000
The Rockefeller Foundation	$1,000,000
The Legler Benbough Foundation	$500,000
The Annie E. Casey Foundation	$1,250,000
DEBT	
New Markets Tax Credit Loan — Clearinghouse DCFI and Wells Fargo Bank	$15,000,000
TOTAL	**$23,700,000**

"Seeing the transformation of the corner into an economic catalyst was emotionally overwhelming for all of us," Mike McCraw reminisced. "It still is. For many of us, it was almost like a spiritual commitment. This could only happen because it was rooted in a culture of participation and inclusion and because we had Joe," Mike continued. "No one else had the vision and deep commitment to rebuild. It pulled everyone's commitment forward. Joe realized that mistakes would be made but was willing to step out with us. He encouraged everyone to take risks."

While we grappled with how to solve the financing challenges, the whole field began to change. New Markets Tax Credits, social investment funds, impact bonds, federal and state revitalization incentives were all advancing the field of social change finance. All of these tools were beginning to make a difference.

Still standing in the way of achieving the vision of vibrant village, however, was San Diego's system of infrastructure finance — a challenge that simply got bigger as we moved to scale Market Creek from 10 acres to 60.

And there would be another challenge — one that we didn't have when we developed Market Creek Plaza. This one more daunting. We lost Joe.

In October 2004, just as Market Creek Plaza was completed, tenants in, and financing secured, Joe passed away. Before he died, at a luncheon thanking Wells Fargo Bank and Clearinghouse DCFI, our tax credit partners, and the community teams that had worked on the financing of the project, we had the special honor of a champagne salute by Joe for this milestone success. In his salute, Joe thanked everyone from the bottom of his heart for making Market Creek Plaza possible.

17

THE PEOPLE'S IPO

*"We're allowed to buy Lotto tickets
and that's got to be a riskier way to make money
than land in our own neighborhood."*

— Resident on the Ownership Design Team

Old Tool, New Place

"Innovation often is based on a new combination or ordering of existing elements. It does not necessarily involve the creation of new elements themselves, but rather the transfer of a practice or a concept from one realm to another."[85]

In the mid-1990s, our early non-profit strengthening technical assistance team had carefully studied the Rensselaerville Institute report, "Assumptions for Innovation." This line stuck with me — not necessarily the creation of something new; sometimes just the transfer of practice.

Our tool, called the Community Development Initial Public Offering (CD-IPO), was just that — an old idea in a new place.

Taking the concept of an initial public offering, a stock market launch used widely to raise capital and establish broad ownership of an issuing corporation, was the old tool; using it as a community-building strategy in a disinvested neighborhood was the new place.

The opportunity to develop an abandoned factory site in a community partnership gave us a platform for the design of a pioneering mechanism for making residents direct and explicit beneficiaries of development in their community.

The IPO provided a platform for stimulating a discussion about asset-building and the power of collective investment. More importantly, it created a provocative discussion about resident ownership. People resonated with the idea of the community control of land and the idea that collective ownership could provide a vehicle for the rising tide to raise more ships.

Ownership changed the decision-making. Most community development practitioners say the biggest hurdle they face in spurring effective urban revitalization is the disconnect between the financial goals that come with capital investment and the social goals that come from the community. Market Creek's Community Development IPO brought these two worlds together. Because the source of capital _was_ the community, it brought clarity to the balance of social and economic goals and became an innovation in the formation of capital partners for community change.

To make an IPO a new tool with a fresh set of goals, we had to grapple with the old rules. Without the benefit of the current crowd-investing movement that exists today, this was long and patient work.

David Morgan and Kurt Kicklighter, our legal team, took the "theory of thirds" and turned it into a set of corporate structures as both containers for action and vehicles for ownership. It was time to go public.

Kurt, like David, was the consummate professional. "Dedicated and brilliant," one of his colleagues described him. We needed these qualities of Kurt's because he was going to be negotiating a permit for a hybrid tool through a government department that had never seen anything like it. But there were other qualities of Kurt's we needed as well. He would be working directly with residents. He was kind, patient, personable, comfortable in his own skin, and able to connect across difference. He could speak plain English.

With his thick black hair and his sleek stature, Kurt had a boyish charm. People were attracted to his spirit and his natural can-do attitude. "I'm a born optimist, which is unusual for a lawyer," he would say with a laugh. "Everything is possible, it's just a matter of working out the legal, financial, and people issues!" He brought a sense of humor into the room and made the meetings fun. He created an engaging atmosphere and made securities law something residents — of all educational levels — could grasp and were eager to learn.

His short-term gig, like mine, turned into a long-term undertaking. In making the CD-IPO work, there would be four distinct chapters he would guide us through: the first was focused on tackling scope and scale; the second was developing our risk response; the third was discovering the IPO's community development mission and soul; and the fourth was challenging what it meant to be "sophisticated" — the sophisticated investor criteria.

Tackling Scope and Scale

"You could tell the document was drafted by us lawyers," Kurt reflected chuckling. "Boy can we pack in the words!"

When we applied to the Department of Corporations (DOC) for the permit to conduct the offering in 2001, we had prepared the application the way they are traditionally done, privately and confidentially with a team that consisted of our senior counsel, our securities lawyer, our developer, and myself.

The application read like a traditional offering, except for language about the double-bottom-line purpose of the project and the fact that a foundation was applying for the permit on behalf of the LLC.

"The first guy at the DOC was a dyed-in-the-wool government employee with 40 years behind him," Kurt remembered. "He was brusque so the conversations were very brief. When we received his response, there were 115 comments!"

We had set a record for the number of issues highlighted and questions (and no doubt eyebrows) raised by the Department of Corporations.

The Department of Corporations (DOC) — now called the California Department of Business Oversight — is responsible for the qualification of the offer and sale of securities. When we first submitted for the permit, the main concern of the Securities Regulation Division was the scope and scale of the plan, which called for developing the entire original 20 acres at a cost of $85 million. The DOC was concerned about the risk of financing, given the project's size. Since our targeted audience was not a group of high net worth individuals, the DOC team wanted to safeguard investors.

When we split the land into two separate parcels in order to bring the financing goal down, we realized that one of the benefits was being able to carve out a higher percentage of community ownership. In 2002, we responded to all 115 of the DOC's comments and resubmitted our application.

Still no permit, but this time we were narrowing the field of questions and concerns. The DOC wanted us to further reduce the risk factors, pointing to two primary issues: 1) a master lease JCNI held on the two buildings with community tenants, and 2) the need to protect investors, given that residents were unlikely to meet California's criteria for investor qualification.

The Next Risk Response

"Today's problems are yesterday's solutions."[86] JCNI's master lease on the two buildings with community tenants was Peter Senge's first law of the Fifth Discipline.

This master lease was created to address the covenants the PRI investors and financial institutions wanted. Concerned about the quality of the leases held by local entrepreneurs, the master lease gave the lenders added assurances. JCNI under the master lease would be responsible to Market Creek Partners, LLC, and the small businesses would pay JCNI. With JCNI taking the risk on the entrepreneurs, rather than the LLC, the lenders were satisfied. It gave them protection.

But the Department of Corporations (DOC) didn't like it. In the review process, the DOC was concerned that the master lease increased the percentage of dependence the project had on JCNI. The tool that had solved the problem with the lenders had caused a problem with the ownership strategy.

To tackle the issue, we offered the lenders a "guarantee of rent payments" on the community tenants and removed the master lease on the buildings themselves. This addressed the problem to everyone's satisfaction.

With this risk factor resolved, the last remaining challenge was how residents would meet California's net worth and income qualifications — often referred to as the "sophisticated investor" criteria.

For risky or speculative investments, such as real estate, people have to meet a high standard for net worth and income to be considered "accredited" or "sophisticated" investors. The assumption that is made is that people of high net worth with high incomes 1) can hold their investments long-term without needing to liquidate them for cash, 2) can afford to lose their investment without personal damage, and 3) have financial advisors that can understand and evaluate the risks.

To be a qualified investor in California, a person must have $200,000 in income or as a couple $300,000 <u>AND</u> net worth of at least $1,000,000. These investor suitability standards were created by the State of California to "protect" people of modest economic means who might be unfamiliar with investing from getting involved in scams. But it also meant that people with the greatest community motivation and self-interest in the project would be excluded from investing in Market Creek Partners, LLC.

While most states conduct a "disclosure review," California and a few other states conduct a "fairness review" of securities offerings to determine whether they are "fair" to targeted investors. The rules related to real estate syndication offerings tend to be especially detailed and complex. What needed to be proven was not just whether we disclosed all the risks and all the information, but whether the project was viable and worthy of investment for the specific people to whom the investment would be marketed.

This would be our largest challenge in securing a permit from the State of California to go public.

But while this problem-solving around risk to investors was going on, a different kind of challenge was beginning to become critical in the community. The "quiet period" regulation was keeping us from being able to discuss the offering with the Ownership Design Team.

Residents as Insiders

"Joe Jacobs thought people were important, all people, no matter what your income level," noted a resident on the Ownership Design Team. "He thought all people could contribute. If he hadn't talked about risk, we wouldn't be here wanting to try these things."

We needed to create a place at the table for all people, no matter what their income, and people's excitement about participating in the ownership of Market Creek Plaza was palpable.

But the enthusiasm of residents working on the Ownership Design Team began to turn to confusion and in some cases suspicion as the "quiet phase" dragged on.

For companies filing for permits to conduct public offerings, securities law requires a "quiet period" to keep potential investors from making decisions based on pre-disclosed information or "gun-jumping." Because we were not allowed to discuss the offering in the community, we had put the Ownership Design Team on hold while we were going through the process.

Since all of our work had been to support working teams in an open and inclusive process, not sharing what was occurring on the public offering had gradually begun to damage the long-nurtured trust we had gained with residents.

By 2003, we had a history of inside-outside teams, meaning they were made up of both internal staff and community residents, and a solid process of shared decision-making, but when we started the application process with the DOC, we didn't realize it would take so long to complete. After a year of struggling with the "quiet period" ruling and concerned that the timeline was lengthening, we had to figure out a solution.

We talked about a range of ideas – some we thought might take too long and others created additional complications

Then Kurt hit on the simple idea to solve the problem.

We asked the Ownership Design Team if they would be willing to sign a non-disclosure document that made them "insiders" in the corporation's deliberations about the terms of the offering. As insiders, they were allowed to work on every aspect of the structure, language, and campaign planning so long as they agreed to hold that information confidential until we secured the permit.

The Design Team and extended network of residents felt this solution honored the community process and protected their interests. They became insiders.

This was when the magic happened.

What started as a legal construct done in the way a traditional offering would be put together — four people behind closed doors — would evolve into a pioneering community development tool. This team took each challenge in the design process head-on — from the issue of investor access to the exit strategy.

With legal expertise at their side, residents would develop the outreach and education strategy, study and weigh in on the operating agreements, and simplify the legal documents so they could be understood and embraced by a broad range of people.

This team would get us ready for round three.

Finding the IPO's Community Development Mission and Soul

Residents and staff involved in the IPO planning meetings during the quiet phase did not discuss the deliberations, but once the permit was secured to "go public," people shared their experience with exuberance.

"Remember waving people down every time there was a hundred-dollar word!" one resident exclaimed.

A typical offering memorandum is written in legalese. Because speculative real estate deals are complex, controlled by broker-dealers, and target high net worth individuals, everyday people rarely read them. An investor is going to call his or her attorney to review the documents. In our situation, we needed documents that everyday people could read.

In working on the documents, one of our guiding principles, we would say kiddingly, was that no words greater than "twenty-five cents" could be used. A hundred-dollar word — one that would require residents to have a glossary — had to be cut. In addition, we also set up a "no whereas, no thereby, and no-sentence-longer-than-two-lines" rule.

Residents would kid Kurt that instead of paying him by the hour, he needed to be paid by the word — every word he could <u>cut</u> from the document. "I became a cleaner-outerer of useless words!" Kurt chuckled. Simplifying the tax law descriptions alone saved 15 pages.

"I like to think of myself as persistent," Kurt reflected in thinking back on the process. "This stick-to-itiveness served me well going through 26 versions of the operating agreement and 18 versions of the offering circular! The thing I really liked about it was that so many people took ownership of it."

In April of 2005, Kurt was diagnosed with a brain tumor, and it would be a year before he would be fully back into his work load. His colleague, Elizabeth Foster, with her high energy, engaging style, had the mind of a great corporate lawyer and the look of a tennis player. She stepped in right away to guide the team and complete the drafting of the documents.

Lisette Islas, the member of our staff who supervised community outreach, moved over to take the helm for ownership. Like Elizabeth, she was bright, engaging, and an energetic learner with an unflinching commitment to social justice. An urban planner by training and an organizer by experience, she could learn anything and was tireless in the review of the documents and the design of the process. As the bridge between law and organizing, these two would make it happen.

In addition to putting two women together who were smart and effective, teaming Elizabeth with Lisette brought out the mischief in all of us and made the work fun.

By the time we finished, we had a simplified document, an executive summary we called "IPO Illustrated", and an excited community team. The campaign was called "Own a Piece of the Block," and IPO — in addition to meaning Initial Public Offering — meant Invest, Participate, Own.

"For me as a corporate lawyer," Elizabeth reflected, "it was really challenging and rewarding to explore how to expand the concept of an IPO, usually a legal process done by big corporations for already-wealthy investment banks and their equally wealthy clients. Our team had to figure out how to make the ownership concept available to ordinary folks."

As a collective investment, residents believed that participation was an important goal of the offering. Many residents had been influenced by Dr. Maulana Karenga's work on practicing the culture of Kwanzaa and its seven principles — the Nguzo Saba. "This is about building comm-unity," as one resident put it. "The principles of Ujamaa, cooperative economics, building businesses, and profiting together; Kuumba, of leaving our community more beautiful and beneficial than we inherited it; and Ujima, of solving problems together and taking collective responsibility for our community were all fundamental to the how this IPO fit into the cultural village."

Reverend Ikenna Arnyanwu Kokayi, the person who would be elected as the first chairman of the Investors Advisory Board, noted: "Malcolm X might not have been a world-renowned economist, but he taught us that wealth is in the dirt. We were ready to see what 'together-money' could do."

One of the youngest members of that Ownership Design Team, who was 15 at the time, noted: "You work so hard for so many years to build a dream. Being an investor is a physical connection to what you've worked for."

In 2005, the IPO had found its soul. We were ready to tackle the last issue — the sophisticated investor criteria.

Challenging the Concept of Who's Sophisticated

"You talk about offering us 'financial literacy', but for yourselves you talk about financial planning and money management!"

The woman had a point. She was insulted by the words "financial" and "literacy" being put together.

"It's not like we aren't literate," she said. "We just don't know about investing."

People living in disinvested neighborhoods know more about money than people outside assume. Some know every $100-dollar decision can be the difference between food on the table or keeping the lights on. Others know the underground — the barter systems, the cash economy, income patching, the regular wiring of money to younger siblings or their homelands. Some know from a deep place that they are not immune to hard times, so they reach out and put money under their neighbors' door mats if they know it's needed. They share what they have. Still others have backgrounds in banking, took or taught classes in finance, had long professional careers, or owned businesses. Many bought homes. The diversity on the team was broad.

What was clear from the teamwork was that no matter where people were in their understanding, the IPO would honor everyone's level of expertise and make room at the investment table. Classes would not be focused on "financial literacy," but on investment readiness and financial management.

Later, in reflecting on his work with residents, Kurt Kicklighter would say "I was clearly one of this project's unintended consequences." "How so?" I asked. "The experience I got learning about bringing together disparate points of view, starting and staying together, and managing in a participatory way — because of what I learned though this experience I was named managing partner of my law firm!"

In preparing for the third submission to the DOC for a permit to go public, Kurt was back on deck to work with Elizabeth and Lisette and would once again become the Ownership Design Team's bridge to conversations with the legal team at the DOC. We were now ready to tackle the final and most challenging issue — the investor qualifications.

Known as the "sophisticated investor" criteria, the use of the word "sophisticated" had a lot of the same reverberations that "literacy" did when put with the word financial. Being deemed sophisticated, while intended to connote sufficient investment experience, in practice means clearing a high bar for income and net worth. No one in our circle of stakeholders, despite the community's income diversity and breadth of working knowledge of finance, would meet these criteria.

The Ownership Design Team was excited to figure out a way to tackle this issue and the meetings were lively. Two really good ideas surfaced from the energized discussions.

One of the lessons from the earlier community teams was to not allow information to be taken on its face value without research. People wanted to make sure they had all the facts. In hearing the conversation, Kurt said, "Good point. We can figure out whether this is the actual regulation or departmental practice for implementing the regulation."

The second idea surfaced when a resident sarcastically commented: "Protecting us from risky investments? We're allowed to buy Lotto tickets and that's got to be a lot riskier way to make money than the land in our own neighborhood!"

Everyone laughed then got excited. This resident had made an important connection. The State of California not only sanctioned the buying of Lotto tickets — the most speculative investment on the planet with the highest risk-reward ratio imaginable — it actually ran the program. In addition, it was an income-producing strategy for the state that was disproportionately impacting low-wealth investors. "How about if we all buy Lotto tickets," others chimed in, "and go before a public hearing?"

The team took a two-track approach: 1) Kurt began legal research on whether or not the communicated income and asset requirements were actually written into the regulation or just departmental practice, and 2) the team started to prepare the Lotto strategy for public hearings.

Most of us really wanted to use the Lotto strategy, but it was the research on regulation versus departmental practice that was pivotal.

Kurt's research revealed the income and asset requirements were only guidelines set by the DOC for implementing the regulation governing sufficient investment experience, so the team then focused on how to meet the intent of the law in such a way as to not shut out our targeted investors.

We developed a strategy that would allow people to take a risk but protect them from losing significant assets that could be personally damaging. We called it our "10-10-10 Plan."

The caps on the level of investment were set as:

- 10 percent of a person's income (no matter how much that was);
- OR (instead of AND) 10 percent of a person's net worth, excluding their home and car (no matter how much that was);
- AND no investment greater than $10,000

The value of a "unit" — or ownership share — was set at $10 and a minimum purchase was set at 20 units. Payment plans could be set up to achieve the $200. Anyone with at least $2,000 in annual income OR $2,000 in assets could invest.

To further mitigate the risk the individual investors were taking, Diamond Community Investors (DCI) would be first on the profit distribution waterfall, meaning that if profits were generated, DCI would be paid first — up to a 10 percent preferred return. If there were additional profits, the Neighborhood Unity Foundation would be paid next up to a 10 percent preferred return. If there were any profits remaining, JCNI and Diamond Management, Inc, would be paid up to a 7 percent preferred return. After that, all profits would be split.

Since 500 investors was the dividing line between being required to work through the Securities and Exchange Commission rather than the State's Department of Corporations, the investment was capped at $500,000 or 450 investors, which ever came first. The 450-person limit was set so as units changed hands, we were less likely to pass the 500-member mark.

To meet the CD-IPO qualifications, investors needed to: 1) live or have lived in the Diamond, 2) own, operate or work in a business located in the Diamond Neighborhoods — the 10 neighborhoods that surrounded Market

Creek, <u>OR</u> 3) be a group or organization located in the Diamond or work for one, <u>AND</u> 4) volunteer in the community, in some way making it a better place to live. This commitment to involvement was important to the team as an illustration of caring for the broader community. The goal was to get as close to the 450 as we could when we hit the $500,000 mark.

A team of three would be hired from the community and trained to conduct the offering. This team would be made officers of the corporation so they didn't have to be licensed broker-dealers. We made sure at least one of the team members was bi-lingual in Spanish and an extended team of translators was brought on deck to support special meetings in any of the other languages requested.

The Department of Corporations wanted very detailed marketing and educational plans, knowing that we were targeting many people who would have never invested previously. Plans required every potential investor to attend a training and information session to review the specifics of the offering and the overall project. In addition, before signing any documents, every investor would have a one-on-one meeting to discuss the offering in a confidential setting, get help if they needed it in figuring out their net worth, ask any final questions, and develop a relationship with a member of the offering team. The plan also called for all investors to complete a survey that would be used in an evaluation.

As plans were made by the team, Kurt would run the ideas by the Gabriel Eckstein, Corporations Counsel for the DOC. "Gabriel was very thoughtful and really believed in it," reflected Kurt. He was receptive to talking things through. When we were down to the investor suitability criteria, David Morgan and I went to talk to him in person. When we left his office, David and I were confident that we were going to be able to move forward."

On January 6, 2006, we received a message with its importance marked as "High" and the subject noted as "STOCK PERMIT ISSUED!!!!" After six years and three tries, the Department of Corporations approved our permit. The Community Development Initial Public Offering (CD-IPO) was a go, making possible the opportunity for residents to invest their own dollars in the project they had planned, designed, and built together.

Once the permit was issued, campaign materials for "Own a Piece of the Block," which had been drafted and illustrated, were submitted to the DOC in English for approval and once approved, were translated and submitted in Spanish — Poseer una Parte de la Cadre.

On October 31, 2006 (Halloween), the offering closed with 415 investors having invested $500,000 with an average investment of $1,176. We had pulled together and pulled it off.

That night I left the office with tears in my eyes. We had lost Joe in 2004 just after celebrating the financing of Market Creek — Joe's big success indicator. But had he been with us that night in 2006, he would have been overwhelmed with joy.

"Residents might not have much money, but what they did have was a huge amount of appreciation for the opportunity and a lot of pride in their ability to participate," noted Elizabeth Foster, reflecting on her time with the legal team that brought it to fruition.

This tool — simplified by residents, illustrated by staff, translated from legalese to English and then English to Spanish, conducted by residents, and backed up by training — would mobilize our community and go on to inspire teams from around the country that visited to learn about it.

18

TRUST

"You see, you closed your eyes. That was the difference.
Sometimes you cannot believe what you see, you have to believe what you feel.
And if you are ever going to have other people trust you,
you must feel that you can trust them, too — even when you're in the dark.
Even when you're falling." [87]

— Mitch Albom, <u>Tuesdays with Morrie</u>

The Scavenger Hunt

Barbara Day was always open to learning. She had retired from a career in banking and volunteered to work on the Ownership Design Team. She wanted to serve on the team that was working on financial education. When the sales positions opened up for the IPO, she eagerly applied and was hired.

"The scavenger hunt was annoying yet humbling," Barbara remembered.

I had asked the members of the IPO Sales Team — the residents charged with conducting the public offering—to go on a scavenger hunt—a hunt for information we all needed to learn. Each team member was assigned a question that might arise during the offering and required them to search for the answer and report back. Barbara's assignment was a question about the asset limits put on investors who might currently be receiving public benefits. So no one would lose their benefits, the team needed to be able to address this issue for community residents who might be impacted.

Barbara embraced the hunt. She was determined and committed — determined to discover what she needed to know and committed to sharing it with her community.

"Until you have walked in another person's shoes," she reflected after the scavenger hunt, "you shouldn't judge why they are reluctant to participate in life-changing opportunities. Particularly after being subjected to the belittling attitudes of those who are serving them."

The scavenger hunt had taken her places neither she nor I expected.

"I remember going to the local office of the Department of Social Services on Market Street first, which was right near the Jacobs Center, to ask a simple question of whether a recipient of TANF [Temporary Assistance to Needy Families] could invest in shares of a company."

"I stood in line for at least 45 minutes just to get in the building. Once in, I was told since I did not have a social worker assigned I would have to wait until one became available. That took another two hours of waiting to get 'I don't know' as an answer." Barbara cannot recount her quest to find out what she needed to know without sadness and disbelief.

Not getting any help from the social worker, she took the suggestion of a Security Guard to visit the nearby Barrio office of the Social Services Department.

"I was imagining a larger, more spacious building with better parking and a more welcoming attitude," she remembered in arriving at the Barrio office of the Department of Social Services. "Well, I didn't get any of that." After waiting another two hours to speak to a person knowledgeable about what a recipient could and could not do when it came to investing, she finally received the answer she was seeking. "Yes, they could participate," she shared. "They would just have to report the interest or dividend each year at the TANF annual review during the time that they were receiving benefits."

This experience was indelible. The disrespect, the dishonoring, and lack of simple human courtesy would stick with her. "Each time I pass by the local Department of Social Services, I remember that experience," she recounted. "It is a feeling of not being worthy of answers to questions that may help lift me or my family someday out of poverty. Or give me hope for a more abundant future for generations to come. Or take advantage of the opportunity to pass on wealth through education and participation."

Following the IPO, she would come to my office to update me on stories about the owners. Standing in my doorway, Barbara was stunning. Her smile, her warmth, and her striking head wraps gave her a regal look. Often donning a mud cloth turban with symbols spelling out a story in shapes and color knotted at the side of the head, she always looked beautiful. Her creamy smooth brown skin, smiling eyes, and long earrings, gave her a look of royalty. She was poised and unflappable.

The investment of time she had given personally to prep her community for the IPO was extraordinary. For her it was like taking time for your family. Of the 415 resident-investors, she knew nearly everyone personally, and each one spoke afterwards about how much they appreciated her warmth, her inviting approach, her sensitivity in the discussions about their financial circumstances. One resident, when talking about how to keep people involved after the IPO, said what we needed was "something like a family gathering, like what we have here often...They will come to these gatherings."

Barbara had gone on a search for information to help her community and came back with a deeper sense of compassion and commitment. She used that compassion to build a family of investors. She was a good listener, and it had mattered to people. She had built trust.

The Responsibilities of Ownership

"It was hard to give up $200...but now I have something to leave my kids besides memories," Bevelynn Bravo noted in an interview with Anne Stuhldreher for a story in the Stanford Innovation Review.[88] In the article, Anne dubbed Market Creek Partners' Initial Public Offering as "The People's IPO."

People were proud of what had been accomplished. On Thursday, February 15, 2007, nearly all of the 415 investors packed in a tent on the site to celebrate.

"This is a miracle," Reverend Kokayi expressed from the stage. "You have made this happen!" The roar of applause and shout-outs brought everyone to their feet. "We trusted each other and together we have made this happen."

Reverend Ikenna Arnyanwu Kokayi, Chairman and CEO of the United African American Ministerial Action Committee at the time, had been elected, along with seven of his co-investors, to the Diamond Community Investors (DCI) Advisory Council. That day he was in a baseball shirt, but he was a person I mostly experienced in his West African crown-style Kofi, or hat — colorful, brimless — with long robes in purple and gold and detailed decorative brocade presiding over a church service, a funeral, or probably where I first met him, the Martin Luther King, Jr. Community Breakfast. He could preach. The Rev — as I lovingly referred to him — could get "revved up." He could bring it on. He could move an audience.

Born Robert Clarance Ard, he was given his African name in a naming ceremony of the Pan-African Association of America, which meant Father's power (Ikenna), dedicated to God (Arnyanwu), and call the people to hear (Kokayi). "I didn't choose or request it, but I proudly accepted it as my true name," he noted, reflecting on his life. "There hasn't been a day gone by that I haven't found myself inspired and challenged by its meaning."

Born in Bogalusa, a paper mill town in Louisiana — or Luziana, as he called it — he was part of the largest high school class ever to graduate — 49 — less than half of the starting freshman class of 105. His first act of protest was in his high school auditorium during a speech the head of the paper mill was giving, saying his company would hire anyone whether or not they graduated. After his one experience picking cotton and believing he deserved a life beyond either cotton or a paper mill, he walked out.

Reverend's life opportunities opened up through a series of events, miracles of his own making, starting with meeting his beautiful wife at a YWCA dance. "We liked it when the sailors came in," she would tell you blushing as she served you a piece of pie. "He was so handsome, but for a while I thought he had a crush on my best friend!"

After the Navy, Reverend would move from San Diego City College to LA City College to Pepperdine University, where he would complete his degree before taking a position with the Public Utilities Commission and then Bank of America as a loan officer. Over that time, Reverend's activism would increase from heading his college's black student association to being involved in the integration of San Diego's seventeen racially-isolated schools. After leaving Bank of America to start a church and run a youth services agency, things changed for him when a young man, Tyrone Thomas, was killed by a police officer. He created the preachers' patrol to walk the streets. "If we worked together as neighbors instead of turning our backs, we could change things."

"I first heard about the IPO in a parking lot, leaning on a dumpster," he remembered. "Tambuzi, who was on the Ownership Design Team, told me about it. I said on the spot that I had $5,000 and I'll put it down. This was exactly what I wanted to see happen. I realized this could give me evidence about my own theory. As African Americans working inside a capitalist structure, we never recovered after Tulsa's Black Wall Street was destroyed by the Klu Klux Klan. Within hours, our model of a major African American economic movement died. But it was time to revive it. I believed we needed to be more than consumers; we needed to become owners. This is how wealth is built, and this could bring people into a different conversation, new awareness."

What he liked most about it, he would say, was "I could come to the table with a contribution rather than a need. I could come, not to convince someone of the righteousness of my cause, but as an equal. I wanted to do it so others could replicate it. Once we had a model, it could continue. If a neighborhood council would get 200 people to put in $200, you have $40,000; but think about what would happen if each of the 26 councils pooled their money! You would have over $1,000,000."

Reverend would be elected to the Chairman position of the Diamond Community Investors Advisory Council. This Council coordinated the investors' annual meeting, where they reported to the larger group on the finances of the company and distributed dividends. They studied all the operating agreements making sure they knew what capacity would be needed for the buy-out of JCNI's shares in the company sometime after 2018. And they took ownership of the health of their investment. Committees of the

DCI Advisory Council published a business directory, hosted Market Creek business mixers and investor networking events, initiated the design of a website, and reviewed the organizational charter and proposed amendments to streamline operations.

Responding to resident complaints about the cleanliness of the grocery, DCI Advisory Council members met with the store management and realized the special challenges the grocery was experiencing. Store maintenance costs were double other Food 4 Less stores. In response, the investors determined they would: 1) create a "We Own the Block" campaign to make residents aware of their own responsibility for taking care of the site and store; and 2) create a Walk-About Team, which would make regular rounds, taking responsibility for reporting any issues that hadn't been handled by property maintenance.

In the spirit of teamwork that had been Market Creek's hallmark, these owners were always looking for ways to build trust with tenants and take responsibility for protecting their asset.

In my last meeting with them in June 2011, they were continuing to deepen the conversations about roles, rights, and responsibilities of owners. From understanding the charter to the balance sheet, the Council divided up to create sub-teams that would stay informed and current on what they needed to know.

Examples of the Questions Owners Thought They Should be Asking:

MISSION	Is the double-bottom-line mission being honored? Are project profits recycling back in the community? Is local entrepreneurship being nurtured?
MANAGEMENT/ REPRESENTATION	Are its fees and commissions within industry standards? Are residents represented on the management company's board and are Resident Working Teams engaged?
MAINTENANCE	Is the Plaza being maintained? Is it safe and well lit? Are maintenance costs in line with what small tenants can pay? Is there a strong resident feedback loop?
REVENUE & EXPENSE	Are rents and CAMs (common area maintenance fees) current? Are loan rates favorable and are they being paid down?
RETURN-ON-INVESTMENT	Is the Company profitable? Are there cash reserves? What is the R-O-I for each class of member on the waterfall? What is depreciation and how is the project benefiting from it?
TRENDS & COMPETITION	Is there synergy and compatibility in the tenant mix? Are the types of tenants current with trends?
COMMUNITY BENEFITS	What is the percentage of community employment? Are local contractors being used for any project improvements? Are NUF's grants benefiting the community and how?
STOCK TRANSFERS	Are the unit holders still community stakeholders? Who is monitoring the Repurchase Reserve? Is there a waiting list of people wanting to purchase stock?
BUY BACK (2012)	Do the majority of DCI members want to keep their units?
BUY OUT (2018)	Are the JCNI units earning at a high enough level for DCI and NUF to want to purchase them? Is there enough value in the Company to refinance JCNI out or is additional capital needed to be raised? Should it happen all at once or be phased?

A Different Kind of Offering

"Don't cash that check!" Reverend Kokayi exclaimed with all the passion and power that only a pastor can muster.

At the 2010 DCI annual meeting when investors convened, were briefed on the financial position of the company, and received their distribution of profits, Reverend Kokayi, talking about the significance of collective investment, unexpectedly "took up an offering," as people described the moment later.

"Not an initial public offering," someone commented, "but a 'pass the plate' offering!"

"Don't go out and spend that money," Reverend continued. "I want you to put that money in our next investment! We shouldn't stop with this. We need to continue. We need to build new assets. We need to grow our future ability to create change."

I watched in amazement from the back of the room.

By morning, 60 investors had turned in their checks and agreed to serve on a planning committee. This group was charged with figuring out how to hold this money in a collective investment account until a new ownership opportunity was available. What the team came up with was a simple trust account. Within two years, 193 had pooled their dividends.

"Before Market Creek started, it was hard to imagine a more disunited group," Kokayi noted. "When people took those checks they had received and never cashed them —and they were investing in a yet-to-be-determined project — I knew we had the potential to come together. Another minister," he continued, "Reverend Grandison Phelps, Jr. once said to me, 'Only those that own the forest can prune the trees; everyone else needs to ask permission.' We run around thinking 'we don't have,' but we can change our situation by changing how we react and respond to it."

Residents trusted each other and with that were willing to pool their money in a trust account. This trust would be named by the resident launch team the "Community Investment Fund (CIF)."

"Charles Johnson [the owner of one of the Market Creek businesses] once told me his mamma used to say 'keep your suitcase by the door.' When opportunity comes your way," Reverend reflected, "you need to be ready. We were packing our suitcase."

Literally and symbolically, they created a community "trust."

Expanding Collective Investment

"Can I talk to you, Miss Jennifer?

Marquis Snowden would respectfully stand by my door. He wanted to learn about fundraising, report to me on the money he had already assembled, and talk about becoming the CEO of a company someday.

He was 11.

Thirty-three youth participated in buying units in Market Creek Partners through custodial accounts, which were called Youth-Adult Investment Partnerships. Our youngest investor was Marquis, who was eight years old at the time. He brought in his piggybank and spread out his $200.

Marquis had an unforgettable smile with a distinguished look, even by age eight, and his maturity belied his young age. Money matters were the top of every conversation with Marquis. He launched a youth investment club and took a leadership role in a program called Mind Treasures. This program was created by a community-based non-profit to bring financial education to the youth teams at the Jacobs Center and in school classrooms. It included an introduction to finance and an in-depth seven-week class.

But like many residual impacts that are sometimes hard to quantify, Marquis didn't just think about finance as a tool to help himself. He understood it as a tool to help his friends, his community, and his school. When his elementary schoolmates wanted a climbing wall, he took the initiative to develop a lemonade stand and raised the $1,000 to build it. When the school had to cancel sixth-grade camp for financial reasons, he launched a campaign to raise the money privately — a goal he might very well have met if the school hadn't come back and said if one class went all the classes needed to go, raising the goal beyond his reach. Undaunted by disappointment, however, he kept going two years and used the money to bring down the cost so his classmates could take the eighth-grade field trip to Washington D.C.

He would come in my office sometimes after school and update me on his plans and get my advice. Like watching a plant grow on time-lapse video, you could see him sprout, branch out, and reach for the sky.

The youth-adult partnership custodial accounts that were a part of the IPO acted like trusts, with all the rights and responsibilities of ownership. We liked the idea of trust. Building trust. Holding land in trust. Creating investment trusts. The word spoke to every part of our mission and purpose.

In addition to the financial and investment management classes that preceded the IPO and the Community Investment Fund, resident teams continued to build the broader capacity of village stakeholders to achieve financial health and wealth, with hundreds of residents participating in workshops, forums, and activities focused on financial education and asset-building. Classes in the village, taught by a range of partners, included financial fitness, trusts and wills, types of insurance, organizing key financial documents, raising a financially astute child, and first-time home-buyer assistance.

Long term, we knew we would need another type of trust, one that could allow an unlimited number of community investors to participate and to diversify their holdings. Crowd-funding was just arriving on the scene and was exploding, but crowd-investing as a tool for democratizing real estate investing was still an idea being developed, and as it did enter the scene, had the same stringent requirements for qualifying investors as before.

What seemed promising was the idea of creating a "Community Development Real Estate Investment Trust" or CD-REIT. This company, once formed, could purchase, develop, manage and sell real estate assets. And it could provide a structure for an unlimited number of residents to take advantage of the benefits of being owners, without the liability or the obligation of day-to-day management of properties. This company could also "land bank" any undeveloped properties that still existed in the village at the time of JCNI's sunset.

The CD-REIT was envisioned as a publicly reporting company (an SEC filing), and like the IPO, it would have a mission of acting as a catalyst for community-owned developments, starting with the Village at Market Creek, and then eventually expanding to similar developments with geographic diversity. Also, like the IPO, ownership would be restricted to "stakeholders." Residents could conceivably have an ownership share of their local shopping center and have an ownership interest in the investment fund providing the primary source of capital.

The appeal of the CD-REIT was its scalability as an ownership mechanism. What the owners of Market Creek Partners might lose in leverage by reducing debt on the projects — the vehicle Joe knew was important to making money — they could gain by having an ownership share of a REIT.

When we first started considering this next ownership platform in 2008, however, we hadn't anticipated the economic storm that would soon hit. We were still years from stabilizing Market Creek when the economic downturn impacted everyone in the country. Because of the recession, we put conversations about a possible CD-REIT on hold.

And while we didn't know how long or deep this recession would be, what we did know was the power of ownership and the ability of people to rise up and protect what they had built.

In a luncheon address at a small 2010 convening focused on "Improving the Outcomes of Place-Based Initiatives," Janet Yellen, President of the Federal Reserve of San Francisco (prior to becoming Chairwoman of the Board of Governors of the Federal Reserve System), shared how she had become drawn to the field of economics, not "as a result of an early fascination for interest rates," but because she wanted to "understand how monetary policy and the economy affect the financial well-being of ordinary people."[89]

Yellen described how when she arrived at Yale in 1967, New Haven was at the end of one of the most massive and ambitious urban renewal projects in the country. After $27 million in federal grants and a vision of making New Haven the first "slumless city,"[90] the project had displaced 22,000 people,

2,000 small businesses, ripped through the urban fabric of the city, and fueled the exodus to the suburbs. She watched up-close-and-personal who and how people get left out and why, despite economic growth broadly, it is "not by itself sufficient to eliminate household and neighborhood poverty."

In posing the question of what happens when the market is not functioning for certain communities that now need to overcome long-term private sector disinvestment, she noted: "If anything has been learned from the past four decades of place-based initiatives, it is that investing in buildings without investing in local residents and institutions is too often a recipe for failure" — a lesson expressed by all of us who presented at this convening.

She closed by pointing to the need to pay attention to the "vital, but intangible social world" of community change, referencing the Harlem Children's Zone's success because of its focus on altering the expectations of neighborhood children and families. "Similarly," she noted, "in San Diego's Market Creek Plaza, setting up a community development limited liability company that gave residents an ownership stake in the project created a sense of participation and a feeling that they were not at the mercy of powerful economic forces beyond their control."[91]

There is a case to be made for nurturing the spirit of people, altering the expectations they have for change to occur, and building a bond among people that is so strong that when recession hits, labor markets weaken, and people are faced with the seemingly insurmountable force of an economic storm, they can figure out how to dust off, celebrate what they have that can be shared, and know that they have a stake in their community.

Market Creek's Community Development IPO was an innovative economic strategy that sought to expand collective impact through collective investment. These courageous and risk-taking residents had skin in the game and had built social capital through their sweat equity, then lifted it to the next level by creating financial capital through the investment of their hard-earned dollars.

19

SAILING IN HIGH WINDS

"We must free ourselves of the hope that the sea will ever rest.
We must learn to sail in high winds." [92]

— Aristotle Onassis

The Hard Middle

"You are approaching a hard middle," Doug Nelson observed.

At the time, Doug had been President of the Annie E. Casey Foundation for nearly 20 years. He had been courageous, I told him, for putting out "The Path of Most Resistance," a report documenting the painful mistakes of the Casey Foundation's first comprehensive community change initiative and questioning how to support community change in the future. It had been influential to many of us who were grappling with the same issues at the same time. Raw. Honest. And the best part — they were going to try it again.

Doug could light up a room. He had a great smile and a twinkle in his eye. He loved this work, you could tell. When he first visited Market Creek, I asked if he wanted to join a gathering of Somali women with their children that was happening in our building. He never hesitated. He was right at home talking to each one of the women who spoke English and asking for translation with the rest. Everywhere he went, he brought energy and passion.

In his office, he loved to grapple with the issues, find out what you were thinking, see where the challenges were, call a staff member and see if he could deploy help. "You are the only one I know who loves blight!" he exclaimed once, cheering me on. I did love blight. It represented untapped or hidden value. Somebody just needed to clean it up; love it back to beauty. I loved that Doug loved it as well.

Doug's support mattered, and not just because it came with a $1.25 million program-related investment (PRI), although that was an important vote of confidence, but because he was willing to put his team around us to help think through the challenges in what he had rightly framed as our "hard middle."

Doug was passionate about peeling away the layers of ways to help. He grew up in a development family and understood our situation and our financial dilemma. He coined the term "hard middle" because he could see how the development cycle for the land and the capacity-building cycle for village structures required greater capital upfront, with diverse funding sources reducing Jacobs' capital investment over time. He could also see that Joe's bequest in 2004 contained two venture capital partnerships valued over $80 million that, if not sold, would tie up a third of the Jacobs Center's asset until 2023 — just the opposite of when the money was needed since we were planning to sunset shortly after that.

Roughly a third of our assets were tied up when they were needed most and we would have a potential balloon in assets just as JCNI's involvement in the Village at Market Creek would be winding down. This was the dynamic that Doug Nelson coined as our "hard middle."

We had projected the hard middle for 2008-2013. This was the time when we would be half way through our sunset or "relay" plan, the foundations' assets would be largely invested in leveraging land and guaranteeing loans, and we would not yet be able to capture the value we were creating through refinance strategies. This hard middle would require that we have partners that could provide a bridge to the refinance.

But just as we hit 2008, the hard middle hit a bad economy, making it more challenging than any of us could have ever imagined.

The Memory of Pain

When the markets crashed in 2008, all I could think of were the challenging years following 9/11.

I was on my way to work that September morning in 2001 before I realized the towers had been struck. By the time I arrived and turned on the news, I knew the world had changed forever. I sat down and cried. It was hard to comprehend. The building collapsed over and over in my head. I kept thinking about our Heron Foundation colleagues. They were just blocks away. So close. Were they safe?

I didn't lose a loved one. All my family members were safe. But I was struck by one of the Community Coordinators saying once, "People think if you work in this business that you are immune to pain." The pain of this period was difficult to bear. Up to this time I had been good at handling hard times. But there is a memory of pain.

There is scar tissue on the back of my foot that tells the tale of a childhood mishap...a little red wagon run up the back of my leg. I don't remember how it happened, who pushed the wagon, or how I got home. But every time I go to buy a pair of shoes, I feel it. I remember its presence. I remember it wouldn't stop bleeding. I remember the weeks on crutches. This scar is not a symbol of some daring act or adventure. This one is right where the top of every pair of shoes I have ever tried on since then has hit, rubbing uncomfortably as a reminder that something way back went wrong and hurt deeply.

Even without remembering the actual feeling of pain, you can't forget the moments which hold the secret of a time of personal blood, sweat, and tears. You remember each high and each low. Each test of your endurance. You remember each moment you forced yourself to look past your own personal hurt to produce an impact.

I was supposed to be in Washington DC the week after 9/11. The folks from HUD called to see if I would be coming. I couldn't fly. They understood. I would fly a few weeks later and stop in New York to visit the Heron Foundation. They told stories of the heat through their windows. The evacuation. The smoke in the air.

Several residents came with me, and while we were there, I said I wanted to go to Ground Zero to take a moment to pay tribute to those who had died, and the others wanted to come. We were in disbelief. Rickey Laster, who served on the Construction Working Team as the head of the Multi-Cultural Contractors, was also a minister. He suggested we stand together in a circle while he offered a prayer. We grasped each other's hands.

"It was a very spiritual experience to be there," he reflected. "When we were standing there, I just remember that there were bits of clothes still hanging in trees. We were awestruck. Silent. None of us could speak. There was a eerie calm and quiet to it. That was the spiritual part of it."

Rickey bowed his head when he talked about it. "I also felt the American part of it, the patriotic part. They had attacked America, not just the World Trade Center. It was a stunning moment."

Our hearts were heavy. I kept remembering having dinner once in Windows on the World at the top of the World Trade Center in all its glory. "There but for fortune," I thought. We held hands and leaned into Rickey's prayer.

The years that followed 9/11 tested our hearts, our will, and our endurance. And along with the sadness that followed 9/11 would come literal pain.

In 2004, deteriorating vertebrae in my neck had caused a pinched nerve. The pain stretched down the right side of my back. It affected everything in my day-to-day life. I kept thinking of the Community Coordinator's line "People think if you work in this business that you are immune to pain." Truth is, no one is. Physical and emotional batterings can come from out of nowhere and set up camp. It was my job to carry on, rally the troops, show I was capable of the steep climbs and rugged rocks, but now what? Having nerve took on new meaning, and I would do just that — carry on.

"Can you come to Bellagio for a convening? It's kind of spur-of-the-moment, but I'd like you to present a case study on finance." Darren Walker, then our grants officer at the Rockefeller Foundation asked. "Sure," I said, "I can be there in an hour."

"No I'm talking about the real Bellagio in Italy, not Las Vegas!" Darren laughed.

I should have known to stay home. The pinched nerve by this time was severe and affected my thinking. The surgeon told me that I needed four vertebrae reconstructed and that I would likely lose my neck motion. On the flight to Italy, I had to stand at the back of the plane for the 17-hour trip to try to keep my neck from getting worse. When we arrived, I was grateful to Chip Buttner, another team member on the trip, when he suggested we go out on the town to explore grappa tasting, a uniquely Italian "firewater" that was like some horrible acquired taste, no doubt, but was sheer heaven for nerve pain.

When I returned, just short of reconstructive surgery on my neck, a pain management team tested injections considered experimental with low odds of working, targeting the exact nerve that was pinched. The injections solved the problem. They called it a miracle.

But with the memory of emotional pain of 9/11 and the physical pain of the pinched nerve still lingering, Joe would pass away, and with him, much of the magic. The bold heart-pumping fun that came with Joe's risk-taking — "crazy fun" as Chip described it — would begin to fade little by little, hardly noticeable at first except as a hole in my heart, then gaining speed as we headed into the "hard middle."

Trusting the Flow

"I found her crying in the stairwell," Lefaua noted with her eyes dancing. I wondered why she was excited by this. She would tell me in due time.

Lefaua Leilua, a resident who served as the first board chairperson of the Neighborhood Unity Foundation (NUF), was wondering about how this new concept they had been introduced to called "flow funding" might work.

"Flow Fund Circles" was a term coined by Marion Rockefeller Weber, when in 1991 she wrote her father saying that she was "overwhelmed and heavy with this money work...I know that having too much money to handle is unhealthy for myself and the world. Therefore I seek a better way."

The way she chose was more relational and built on her commitment to including the wisdom and creativity of others. "I began by inviting eight visionaries," she noted in a speech in 2006, "to each take $20,000 and give this money away spontaneously as they traveled." The funders were chosen for their generosity of spirit, and as people were engaged in the circle, Marion realized that she achieved more diversity in who was impacted by her money. After 17 years, she had touched people's lives in 23 countries through 89 new philanthropists, and the stories she described that resulted from this "foot-to-the-floor philanthropy" was "magical." [93]

The Neighborhood Unity Foundation board loved the idea and in considering how they might better address the impact of the recession on people in their community decided to each take responsibility for getting $5,000 out where it was most needed. They wanted to bypass proposals and see what happened.

Lefaua was both excited and nervous, leadership qualities that made her endearing. She loved telling groups she spoke with that before her work with the Neighborhood Unity Foundation she was a shy Catholic girl. "I'm still Catholic," she would follow. "But I had to get over being shy!"

She had gotten involved because Sister Margaret from her church had nominated her for a position on the NUF community board. Sister Margaret was a feisty and involved advocate for social justice and believed in the idea of community activism and ownership from the outset. "She gave me a push," Lefaua noted. "I was very active in my church — youth ministry, the choir, the bazaar, Bible studies — but I was afraid that no one knew me in the broader community."

Lisette Islas, who had helped launch the IPO and was then charged with helping to get the Neighborhood Unity Foundation's first board up and running, pulled Lefaua aside. "Don't worry; there will be a community meeting to get to know the candidates and your bio will be circulated." Lefaua was grateful that Lisette had encouraged her to think of herself as a great fit. She was one of the 13 residents who were elected for the board, and soon after she was elected as the chairperson.

"At first, I thought, no way! I can't present in front of groups! They are presidents of banks and foundations," she noted. "But the team kept pushing my limits. In our culture, the women are at the back, literally, and the men are at the front. They have titles. And my husband [a talking chief] was old school. I was out of my comfort zone."

For the wife of a "talking chief" in the Samoan community, seeing herself talk in front of groups was hard to imagine. "If it mattered enough for people to put me out there, I thought, I'll have to become modernized." She started changing. "It was an expectation that your typical Samoan chief [in this case her husband] never had to deal with. When I started changing, then he had to change as well. I could see it. He even started letting our daughter spread her wings."

For Lefaua, what surprised her even more than being brought out of her shell, as she would put it, was the high level of trust that was her experience with the Jacobs Team. "The leadership treated us like we were good people. I was used to being treated with suspicion — held back by rules and boundaries. Roque said he wanted me to do something to introduce myself to the staff and team, so I decided to do a luau. He trusted me with the money, and he trusted that I would get people to help and put on a good event. It was like family."

Lefaua had always been active in her cultural community, her church, and her children's school. Now she was active in the broader community. "When we came together, what kept us going was knowing we were building something that we could all be proud of — a community of caring people," she noted.

The day she saw the young woman crying in a stairwell, she was at Lincoln High School. She had been called by the school that day and asked to come in and help resolve a situation that had unfolded with young people. They knew she knew the youth and could translate for any of the parents or grandparents that might need support. While she was there she witnessed the young woman who had sat down on the stairs to cry.

For her senior project, the young African American high school senior had studied island culture and had planned a luau for her class. At the last minute, the corporate sponsor she had secured had called and indicated that with budget constraints the company couldn't do it after all. The young woman's high school graduation hung on completing this project. She was devastated.

There are moments of change that play out in simple acts of kindness. Whether you believe in fate, faith, or happenstance, the profound nature of these meetings and moments is never lost.

Lefaua said she noticed her because she had been grappling with the idea of "flow funding" and it made her pay attention to what was going on around her. It heightened her awareness of her own ability to make a difference. She quickly mobilized the Samoan community to assist, and with just a few hundred dollars to pay for food that was prepared by volunteers, the senior class experienced more than the event. They got to see and participate, alongside members of their own community, in a voyage to the islands and a deep dive into island culture. The young woman graduated.

A simple act of kindness. The response of a caring person helping a young woman in a stairwell. This generosity of spirit changed the trajectory of a life.

When the hard middle hit the worst recession since the Great Depression, it brought with it such large challenges, such high winds to navigate, we somehow took solace in the multiplication of these simple acts of kindness. They helped us lean into the wind.

Everywhere we turned, our most powerful lesson seemed to be about how the power of the human spirit emerges when times are hard, resources are limited, and the vision people have created together is challenged. Our team — from the residents to our community partners, from our investors to our learning partners, and from our staff to our board — were committed to digging deeper and holding tighter and letting these acts of kindness carry us safely forward.

The Hard Middle Harder

People who were sensitive enough to know about or remember the huge challenges of the period following 9/11 later asked: "What was the difference in your experience between those years and those that followed 2008?"

For the development of the village, the issues had become more complicated and interconnected as we reached for scale. But for my spirit, the big difference was <u>no Joe</u>.

With 2008, and no Joe talking about the kind of inspired and risk-taking leverage people can figure out during downturns, the already big barriers were just getting bigger, and we hit a wall of successive and converging challenges — one after another.

We continued to confront the large infrastructure deficits, the need for discretionary review by city staff, a creek requiring environmental clean-up, and poorly constructed interstate off-ramps holding up development, and if those weren't enough, the unprecedented recession forced businesses to cut jobs, community businesses to close, and banks to put lending on hold — just as our New Markets Tax Credit loans were coming due. With the recession, land values were dropping, which caused banks to push the cap rates up, causing project values to drop. At the same time, our portfolio assets not only weren't earning, but the values were dropping, and most of our upstream funding partners were pulling out or cutting support because of a drop in their own assets.

Any one of these would have been hard enough, but together, we had the perfect storm.

Over the years, we had taken our encouragement from Joe Jacobs' words: "All entrepreneurs face failure almost daily. There isn't one I know of who has had an unbroken string of victories. In the end, the success of an entrepreneur is the integrated sum of how he faces, handles, and finally overcomes the threat of failure."[94]

We knew and talked about how communities were organic; they change daily just like people. Demographics shift. Leaders come and go. Public policy is modified or amended. Resources swing from scarce to plentiful and back again. Earthquakes and fires happen. People build and then rebuild. And through all of this, we had to always ask: how do we best bolster a community of caring people who could weather any storm?

What was different about *this* storm, however, was its unprecedented and devastating impact on all sectors of the economy and its uncertainty.

No one could make predictions based on the past; no blueprint existed; no assumptions could provide guideposts. It was dramatically altering our landscape.

The last quarter of 2008 was a wake-up call. It was clear that the financial market meltdown, plummeting housing and stock wealth, escalating bankruptcies, growing unemployment, and overarching recession were going to be deeper and longer than anticipated. With our portfolio losses suddenly at 26 percent and many of our partners reporting 30 to 40 percent losses, we knew heading into year-end that we faced a unique challenge in achieving the promise of the Village at Market Creek.

I was still reeling from the memory of the painful and personal nature of the blows from earlier, and without Joe — the guy who would dust me off, hand me a Band-Aid, make me laugh, and put me back up to bat — my scar tissue was exposed and vulnerable. It made me want to put my head down on my desk and cry.

So I did what we all must do when we are tested in life — I dusted myself off, mustered what courage I could, grabbed a Band-Aid, laughed, and because we were in a confluence of dynamics that were creating a storm of enormous magnitude, got on deck and asked for everyone's help in adjusting the sails.

Adjusting the Sails

"We cannot direct the winds, but we can adjust the sails."

This simple quote credited to Dolly Parton, a person who grew up "dirt poor," as she called it, in the Smokey Mountains, one of twelve children, became our campaign theme for dealing with the hard middle and recession.

We had always faced challenges. Taking them head-on and adapting to the new reality is what we did best. In the early years, we didn't have any trust, we had no track-record, and we couldn't get financing, but we sustained our courage and kept going. When we finally opened the grocery in 2001, the victory was short-lived, as we fought our way through the economic storm of 9/11. Now we would have to do it again.

Without a safe harbor in site, we rigorously confronted questions about strategy, capital, budget cuts, if and where to invest, how to staff, what roles to take on, and with whom to partner in order to adjust to the new reality.

Nervous, but excited, our team rallied to brainstorm ways to achieve savings, realign the work, meet multiple goals with the same dollar, try new and untested ideas, leverage greater impact with less effort. We were squarely at the intersection of worst case scenarios and the possibility of untried solutions.

Like everyone, we scaled back the entire operation. Our goal was to preserve the staff — our family — and cut everything else possible. We cut our grants program, our operational budgets, and our Management Team salaries. We froze positions and raises, realigned our portfolio, and dropped out of escrow on properties not deemed to be essential to the village. We geared up to go after stimulus money and other public-sector resources that would allow us to initiate projects and generate fees.

At Market Creek Plaza, the locally-owned small businesses suffered declining gross sales and the lack of adequate working capital made them vulnerable. Aggressive turn-around plans included modification of loans and weekly cash flow forecasting and financial review.

At every turn, we tried to avoid complaining about what couldn't be controlled and address variables that could.

Changing market conditions brought sharp changes in the village development priorities and timelines. High foreclosure rates added growing pressure on the need for rental housing, and with declining business, we moved from planning office space to affordable housing. Tight financial markets turned the emphasis from New Markets Tax Credits to the stimulus package.

In order to be competitive for public resources for housing, such as the Affordable Housing Tax Credit and State Prop 1C Transit-Oriented Development Funds, our resident teams changed strategies from a small 52-unit housing complex, a project too small to be competitive regionally and nationally and bundled it with a larger housing development that was to be planned across the street. Richard Baron, who I had met at the Rockefeller summit in Bellagio, brought McCormack Baron Salazar (MBS) to the table to help us. The resident teams, which had been sensitive about bringing in large national developers, felt it was the right time to bring in a partner.

This new housing, which had become so important to the community, would give first priority to residents living in substandard and severely over-crowded conditions, giving them the opportunity to live in affordable, safe, and accessible child- and family- friendly housing. We also knew that multi-family housing across the street from Market Creek Plaza would increase foot traffic for the businesses.

The family feel to the teamwork brought everyone to the table invigorated and with their best ideas.

Barbara Day, who had served on the IPO Sales Team, reflected, "You touched so many lives during this period by helping us see that in any storm, if we just remember to 'adjust the sails', we will get to our destination just fine — and learn along the way."

We just kept adjusting.

With the two locally-owned restaurants at Market Creek under duress, teamwork was mobilized by internal and external teams alike. Increased catering, networking, and promotion were paired with improved customer service, the addition of new product lines, and a geared-up entertainment calendar aimed at generating traffic. Live jazz and zydeco, holiday pies, and new buffet formats turned out business and increased sales. Relationship marketing focused on residents making their dollar bounce in their own neighborhood whenever possible, saving a job at home.

During the worst year for business losses in U.S. history, Market Creek Plaza closed out December having achieved two major accomplishments: $41.8 million in economic activity — a 4 percent increase — and a 7 percent increase in the number of jobs.

But the impact of the recession in the neighborhood was too far-reaching and lasted too long. Six months into the next year the stress on people was mounting. Stories of residents losing their jobs and homes were escalating, bringing heartache. And as we headed into the fall, the revenues of the two big locally-owned restaurants took a dive. Despite everyone's best efforts, they closed.

Seeing these two community-owned businesses shut their doors was heartbreak. Joe Jacobs had cared deeply about local entrepreneurship, and our team, the investors, and other residents had done all we could to preserve this part of Market Creek's mission.

In March 2009, Angela Glover Blackwell, our unwavering advocate, met with our Diamond Community Investors, our elected officials, and the broader community. Her message: "As we move into this new era, let's not try to repair the damage by returning to what was, but rather, use it to find a more just and equitable society." Change forward, not back. Create a new economic direction.

We were inspired to rail against failure and seek what new potential was percolating just under the surface of this new reality. My role was to help people stay vigilant and focused, get creative, find the synergy, and unearth the opportunity of the moment. We knew we needed to chart a new course and remember the link between difficult challenges and innovation.

The Role of the Angel-Entrepreneur-Philanthropist

Mike McCraw was right. Financing community change is anything but a "cakewalk."

We financed Market Creek Plaza on will, persistence, determination, and the early blessing of Joe at our side. He had been no ordinary Joe. He had been a friend, a colleague, and a partner in big ideas. His years of experiencing the ups and downs, the gains and losses, the successes and failures of business gave him a steadiness and a calm. He took fire with challenges, loved learning, and always marveled in amazement at human behavior. He was smart, but more importantly, wise. And he taught us to believe in the power of trust, flexibility, risk-taking, and perseverance.

Joe occupied a rare niche in the social finance market-place — that catalytic role of angel-entrepreneur-philanthropist — a wildcat. He knew if most of what we tried was working, we weren't taking enough risk. He knew that social innovation rested on testing multiple paths to get the result the teams were seeking and not giving up. He gave us permission to not take the safe and easy way out. He saw that what was needed for social change were resources that came with an open field for people to really figure things out.

And most of all, he knew it took courage.

"I don't understand why foundations aren't the first and best to embrace these ideas," Jed Emerson noted in discussing the gap in venture philanthropy. "I think foundation trustees and staff may not appreciate the degree of flexibility they actually have as fiduciaries of philanthropic capital. If foundation leaders are scared of being the ones to provide risk capital when the money could be lost," he continued, "they don't get how money gets made."

Today, fourteen years after the Market Creek Plaza was financed, this need for risk capital to support community change is largely unmet. Conventional financing, governmental tools, community investment, and traditional philanthropy are all needed, and they each have a role. Standard risk-return formulas used by banks may not work in disinvested areas that need lower-cost capital, but banks are playing critical roles as they did in Market Creek by becoming the underlying investors in New Markets Tax Credits and the eventual take-out financing. Governmental tools are difficult to layer across local, state, and federal agencies, but New Markets is an essential program for commercial projects, and the public sector can be catalytic for projects in disinvested areas by providing extra points for social equity goals in competitive bids. Investment by local residents requires a high level of expertise and financial backing but is an important asset-building opportunity for the very people who care most about it and can sustain its vibrancy. Traditional philanthropy may have slow timelines, require guaranteed income streams, and need clearly-defined impact projections, which makes early funding for land acquisition and community planning difficult, but foundations can provide Program-Related Investments (PRIs) once the high-risk stage of development has been cleared and can provide the related funding necessary for leadership development, cross-cultural understanding, environmental justice, art, and placemaking.

While all these partners are critical, however, projects can't get from here to there without the indispensable role of the angle-entrepreneur-philanthropist — the person or organization willing to take the risk position and provide the patient, flexible resources needed to secure site control and get projects investment-ready or even partner-ready.

Look at the history of any foundation and there is an entrepreneur with a big dream, a tolerance for risk, a leverage-what-you-have approach, and a figure-it-out perspective. The field of community change is calling out for a reawakening of these deep roots and asking for a resurgence of this heritage to come forward. Financing community change requires that we move away from silo approaches and learn how to blend types of capital from grants and PRIs to recoverable grants, equity investments, bank loans, lines of credit, tax credits, public sector support, and — most importantly — community capital. As a field, we need to nurture a substantial affinity group of people who will take front-end risk, practice meeting the gaps that exist in the money matrix, and catapult the level of creativity and the number of tools available to community change.

Along with tolerance for risk, there was another part to Joe that is not to be missed. In financing change, our team's choices were simple — figure it out, figure it out, or figure it out — and to do that, Joe's exuberance and commitment kept us fired up and determined. But in order to keep ourselves steady and the work of meeting social and economic goals balanced, we also needed something else — his grace and understanding.

"Just remember," he once shared, "when confronted with tough choices, err on the side of generosity and carry on."

EVALUATING
CHANGE

WAYS OF KNOWING

20

EXPERIENCE, KNOWLEDGE, WISDOM

---

*"Our ancestors were very sensitive in their relationships with the land.
They systematically organized experiential information
about cycles, seasons, connections, and strategies in their cultures.
Experience was evolved into knowledge,
and knowledge was evolved into wisdom."*[95]

— Jhon Goes in Center, <u>Science and Native American Communities</u>

Day-ta, Dah-ta: "Let's Call the Whole Thing Off"

"Oh no! Not on my watch!" Doris Anderson did not hold back. "This shouldn't be a place with another barrier."

I was facilitating a strategic planning meeting with the board and staff of the Elementary Institute of Science, part of our early capacity-building partnership, and believed EIS should be evaluating the impact of its program. In posing the idea of adding a summative evaluation to the student surveys the organization was using, I said: "It would be good to know the percentage of kids that go to college or if the students' grades are going up. If you are going to increase your fundraising, people are going to want to have proof that this works."

In her position as Executive Director of EIS, Doris took her role seriously to protect and preserve the culture that Tom Watts, the founder, had cultivated. "From the very beginning he took a really strong stand that no parent would ever have to ask if their kids were smart enough to go here," she noted. "Mr. Watts believed that if you let a child explore things, be an engineer or a chemist or a geologist for a week, there is no way it's not going to have an impact. Sometimes it seems like people want tests so they can check that off the list. EIS is about learning that just because an experiment fails doesn't mean YOU fail."

Her response was rapid because she knew that if the evaluation started using college as a success indicator, funding would become tied to that percentage, and eventually that would prompt the staff to begin to target only the young people they knew had college potential in order to keep the number high. "Our kids are already being graded, scored, and tracked into failure. Students are tested enough. Young people come that don't appear to be college material and then they surprise themselves. This is a place for all kids to fall in love with learning without the pressure of someone else's assumptions about them."

While "po-tay-to, pa-tah-to" has come to reflect laughable trivial differences in pronunciation, initially, when the song was written for the 1937 movie, it was humorously describing the class differences embedded in speech and diction. While the pronunciation of the word 'data' (day-ta or dah-ta) is insignificant and situational, the wide-spread collection, control over, and interpretation of data is anything but trivial when it comes to the relationship between funders, grassroots non-profits, and communities.

In a community where you can still hear people discuss Tuskegee and feel the sting from the legacy of research where people of color were unethically made the subjects of medical research experiments, it should not have surprised me that any reference to needing data for funders was going to bring up long-standing class issues about how institutions of power and privilege control the agenda in communities from the outside through money, investigation, evaluation, and metrics.

Wrapped in the conversation at EIS were insights about the real purpose of inquiry and who does or doesn't benefit from it. It also highlighted how easy it is to derail the magic of something that's working by measuring impact based on someone else's assumptions and indicators.

At that time, the early-1990s, the concept of participatory evaluation was relatively new but was beginning to shine a spotlight on the issue of who initiates, undertakes, and benefits from evaluation. Teresa Lingafelter, one of the team members who had trained us in the Technology of Participation (ToP) ©, had been using it. Participatory Evaluation fit into EIS's mission of creating safe space for the love of learning and provided a framework for their students, board, and staff to be in the driver's seat, collectively setting indicators and maintaining responsibility for the data and analysis, rather than the model used in conventional evaluations with arms-length outside evaluators.

EIS's commitment to protecting space for learning and refusing to evaluate impact based on someone else's assumptions or metrics was the first of many lessons for me about evaluating change in communities. Another one, as indelible as EIS, would soon follow.

"Are you trying to put us out of business?" a woman yelled from the back of a crowded room.

I had just come from an earlier Construction Team meeting where I anticipated a rowdy, in-your-face dynamic. "It's how we do it," Rickey Laster had whispered to me in the meeting to plan the construction bid process. Rickey headed the Multicultural Contractors Group and was always looking out for me, orienting me to the "brothers," sensitive to race and gender differences. The passionate head-on conversations took some getting used to. But I hadn't expected the same strident dynamic in the team meeting that followed construction — which was women discussing childcare!

Our team was certain that the data from the initial Market Creek survey indicated a lack of childcare in the community. The assumption we had drawn, working with childcare experts, was that the community needed to build a childcare center. When we took the survey results to the community, there was an uproar.

"When the word circulated, we got 80 childcare workers at the next meeting," Roque remembered. "They felt we would drastically impact their ability to survive financially and referred to it as taking food out of their mouths."

At the heart of the disturbance was our interpretation. Were we sure? Had we asked deep enough questions? Who did we survey? How broadly had we surveyed? Were we prepared to put people out of business? Whose "truth" got to inform the action plan?

"If there is a lot of childcare in the community, why do you think people said they needed it?" Roque asked the group in the meeting.

Roque's brilliance as an organizer and as a facilitator lay in his ability to head into any conversation without being defensive. He used his great gift — humor — to engage people on hot topics, and his humor made him endearing. Because he never tried to deflect getting to the heart of people's concerns, they grew to trust him. They knew they would be heard. They knew there were no hard issues that would be designated as "off agenda" issues.

"If you don't stop and let people talk, give them space for their frustration, hurt, or anger, they will never hear another thing you say. Meeting over!" There was depth on the team in handling hard conversations, each of us in different ways.

And so, at the back of the room filled with frustrated childcare workers, I would get my next set of lessons:

- How data is collected matters.
- Who interprets the data matters.
- How that interpretation gets vetted matters.

A working team was formed to go to work on thoroughly understanding the data. There was clearly a need for parents to access childcare, but it turned out there was an adequate supply. At issue were 1) the disconnect between supply and demand, and 2) the standard of quality. The team shaped a training program for daycare workers to strengthen their knowledge of child development, promote their businesses, secure micro-loans to expand their play areas, and connect people across the neighborhoods with language-appropriate, culturally-sensitive quality childcare.

"They were passionate," Roque noted, "and we were able to find our way through it together. Their speaking up kept us from taking a wrong turn and opened up a new direction."

These two learning experiences challenged us to rethink who selects the success indicators that get tracked and who interprets the data.

The Pyramid of Knowledge

"Data meets the lived experience," I thought, amazed at what had unfolded in the meeting on retail data.

During our first year of work to secure a grocery, the City of San Diego and the San Diego Association of Governments (San Diego's metropolitan planning organization) thought they could help "market" the community. To provide that support, they hired a consultant from Portland, Oregon — an expert in retail marketing of districts. We convened a group of residents. During his first community meeting, he laid out his map of the area.

"Why would you want to build a grocery?" he asked. "According to the retail data, there is an over-supply of local groceries." He had used a business directory and marked the grocery outlets on his map.

The response from residents was rapid: "Have you ever **SEEN** Food-a-Rama!" exclaimed an animated resident, who was studying the dots on the map in detail. "These are all liquor stores!" The consultant clearly hadn't driven around.

Food-a-Rama was a 1,000-square-foot dark green tattered building that looked like it was about to fall down. It had rats and beehives. It was noted for selling candy to children in the shape of drug paraphernalia. You couldn't go inside without wondering where the health inspectors were.

"They were schooling us," Roque noted talking about the residents in that meeting. "We had been getting this same question over and over — this is what the data shows, so why a grocery?"

Before mission-oriented non-profit market research groups, such as Social Compact, were on the scene with drill down studies showing 20 percent to 30 percent higher aggregated incomes in disinvested communities than census projections, there were few choices for accessing market data. The data that existed was built around wrong assumptions about the buying power of people of color and was being translated inaccurately into retail demand assessments that served to support the case for abandonment of urban centers and communities of color by commercial services.

Residents across the table from the marketing consultant were adamant about the wrongly-assessed economic position of their underserved community. "We might be poor, but we still eat," a resident noted, "and we have big families." Technically, Food-a-Rama was classified as a grocery, as were a long list of small convenience stores and liquor stores, but residents' lived experience told them something different about the grocery demand and the state of their access to fresh foods.

That's what the data showed, but what were the underlying assumptions that that data was built on? We realized that these assumptions needed to be vetted carefully and that data or statistical analysis not be taken as truth.

Soon after the meeting with the city's consultant, Roque began working with an Outreach Team to create a questionnaire together, develop a strategy for reaching their neighbors, conduct the survey, and vet the findings. "We were really impressed with this early team of residents." Roque remembered. "They set the course for the rest of our work."

In his book The Ecology of Democracy, David Mathews, President of the Kettering Foundation, refers to the work of Elinor Ostrom, who won the Nobel Prize in Economic Science in 2009, noting that "Ostrom found that the knowledge citizens have of local conditions is sometimes superior to expert knowledge. Even though expert or scientific facts still sit atop the pyramid of knowledge, more arguments are being made that citizens have other equally valid ways of knowing."[96]

And this kind of knowledge is more than "information about local conditions," Mathews contends. This knowledge grows from the lived experience, and it is the space where common sense trumps scientific certainty. "Expert knowledge is specific and exclusive; public knowledge is multifaceted and inclusive, as is human experience. Expert knowledge puts a premium on excellence or accuracy; public knowledge puts a premium on applicability or relevance. Both kinds of knowledge are valuable, but they serve different purposes."[97]

Public knowledge is not information gleaned from a survey about "what residents want" — most commonly considered "community voice" in the non-profit and foundation sectors. It is not about what gets the most votes in a forum or on an app. And it's misguided to proceed to implementation based on this superficial information. To lift up and make use of true public knowledge requires a citizen-centered process for determining a course of action together.

For us, the working team was the platform for shared decision-making about the path that would be chosen, defining what success looked like, setting the indicators that would be tracked, and vetting the data that was important to learning.

"For the most part, people in foundations don't want to take the time for this, which is unfortunate," noted Roger Williams.

Roger, reflecting on his years working with a range of resource partners, noted: "In foundations, we think we know best," he reflected. "We seek out academic experts that have the evidence we need to back up our ideas. We invest in all of these studies that go nowhere because we get locked into a particular point of view that we are determined to pursue, and then we have trouble imposing these ideas on residents."

In addition to this "we know best" syndrome, staff in foundations also feel pressure to represent their board member's points of view and beliefs first and foremost, above residents. They become caught between a rock and a hard place. In a conversation with a staff member in charge of a foundation's major neighborhood transformation agenda, she said that the leadership accused her of "organizing residents of the neighborhoods against the foundation." Residents were just trying to vocalize their "discontent about how we were doing things," she reflected, "and yet I was pressured to get residents onboard with what the foundation felt was best practice."

"Regrettably, these differences in kinds of knowledge and ways of knowing can be seen as differences between superior and inferior knowledge,"[98]

David Mathews observes. "Those with expert knowledge are prone to try to 'educate' the public with facts alone without regard for what Pericles called the talk that teaches." Since public knowledge comes from deliberation and lifting up the things we hold dear, expert knowledge by itself, he contends, is "not sufficient to produce sound judgements."[99]

This inferior-superior hierarchy of knowledge is not new. It has been around for centuries. But it still has reverberations today — significant ones for today's foundation and social change professionals to consider in building knowledge systems.

No one doubts that residents need access to outside knowledge and expertise, but it is still debated whether or not foundations or non-profits serving the public good need access to citizen knowledge.

Ways of Knowing

"Western scientists can be unbelievably ignorant of animal behavior," Dennis Martinez, the chairman of the Indigenous People's Restoration Network, noted in the Journal of Sustainability Education.[100]

He cited this example of what happened when the Canadian government allowed the sport hunting of Arctic muskox who had passed reproductive age. Inuit hunters objected. They knew that elders were critical to the survival of the herd. They kept the younger muskox calm during sieges by wolves and were able to break through thick ice-encrusted snow, allowing smaller, younger animals to search for food underneath. It wasn't until the herds began to disappear years later that scientists recommended stopping the shooting of "over the hill" muskox.

The indigenous Intuit hunters felt the "mechanistic approach" of the scientists to animal management prevented them from recognizing the social ecology of these animals and from honoring the place-focused knowledge embedded in their societies' ancient wisdom.

"While western science and education tend to emphasize compartmentalized knowledge which is often de-contextualized and taught in the detached setting of a classroom or laboratory, indigenous people have traditionally acquired their knowledge through direct experience in the natural world. For them, the particulars come to be understood in relation to the whole, and the 'laws' are continually tested in the context of everyday survival."[101]

Because Native Americans welded values to knowledge systems, Cynthia-Lou Coleman and Douglas Herman wrote in their article for the Smithsonian Museum of the Native American,[102] indigenous "ways of knowing" landed in the category of "local science" or "little science," and was separated from "Big Science." Science was "big" if it was western and this relegated American Indians to the category of anti-science. Indigenous approaches to learning were condemned for being devoid of truth.

In a multicultural community where many heard "Big Data" with the same ideological reverberations that came with "Big Science" — used to demean and displace indigenous people as inferior, non-scientific, not capable of determining truth — we became very aware over time that we needed to learn from this history and embrace multiple "ways of knowing."

We had to be careful to protect residents' ability to decide what success looked like and we could not assume that our institutional frame of reference and the data we believed were important, by themselves, constituted truth, could build knowledge, or could deepen into the kind of wisdom real success stands on. We had to honor the knowledge and deep insight gleaned from the lived experience and rooted in long histories of inhabiting a place.

To do this, we had to lead with listening and back it up with learning. Each team that formed was initiated with the question: what do you want to learn and how do you want to learn it?

Over time, we established a standing Research Team of residents trained in survey techniques and broad-based community listening. This team not only implemented "listening projects" needed for Market Creek but shared its time with other funders and organizations that wanted specific community listening or focus groups organized around different components of their own work.

Teams researched the norms for success in their area of work (i.e., 30 percent community employment for California redevelopment projects, 2 percent minority contracting on San Diego public works projects), set their own targets (i.e., 65 percent community employment, 65 percent minority contracting), and defined the success indicators (i.e., What constituted a job? Did it need to be full-time, full-time equivalent, or just a person hired at Market Creek?).

As "wins" were crystallized by teams, the residents took ownership of not only achieving the goal, but for collecting and interpreting the data (i.e., did the number of community jobs drop because of a change in how the data was collected or was there really a drop?). Regular discussions took place about what was working and not working once data was collected to interpret what changed, if anything, and to decide if something wasn't working, what should be done about it.

As the work evolved, how we looked at data, research, and evaluation also evolved.

Several outside teams were hired to guide formal evaluations — faculty from one of our local universities provided counsel to five-year Quality of Life Surveys and PolicyLink guided the IPO evaluation — but in both cases, the evaluators were committed to participatory evaluation design with a community team shepherding the process and residents always the ones commissioned to conduct the surveys.

In every case, citizen knowledge was linked with outside expertise and we were careful to surface the underlying assumptions behind any and all research.

For information to be linked to the deeper human experience — which is shaped and lived in an interconnected way — we created multiple paths and approaches for success indicators to be experienced together, as a whole picture, rather than an isolated set of data points.

And along with surveys, data, research, reasoning, facts, and formal evaluations, we also learned to rely on observation, experience, sharing events, storytelling, intuition, and feelings.

The Evolution Toward a Citizen-Centered Learning Model

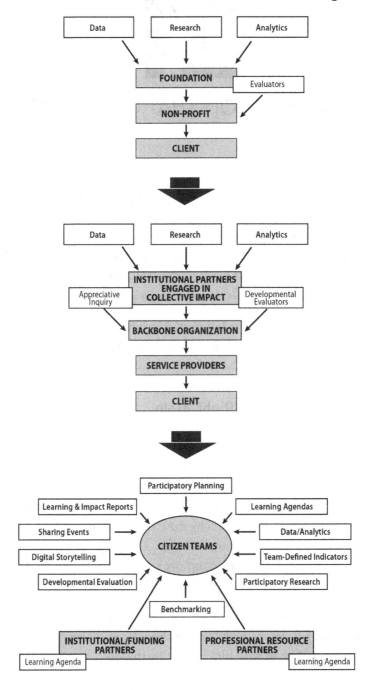

21

INFORMATION THAT CONNECTS

"Lest all this seem too light and fluffy, with stories
floating around in some ambiguous
ether populated by group hugs and tired parables, keep in mind the secret
is to integrate right-brain qualities of imagination and innovative thinking
with left-brain analytical thought.
The real goal is the whole-brain approach." [103]

— Sylvia L. Lovely, Introduction
to Lori Silverman's <u>Wake Me Up When the Data is Over</u>

Connecting Left-Brain/Right Brain

From an early age, I was highly influenced by working in my dad's business. He was a finance guy, an accountant by training and a plumbing contractor by trade. As soon as I was old enough to count, I worked in his business. By five, I was organizing all the pipes, handles, fixtures, washers, drain covers, sink heads, and replacement parts by size, the most fun part of my job, and counting each one when inventory was due. I was good at my job, carefully counting by 10s so I didn't mess up my tracking sheet and could report faithfully to my dad on the hundreds of parts I felt responsible for.

When he went out to a construction site, he would take me with him, give me a hard hat, let me look over his shoulder at the working drawings, and let me walk around with him inspecting the job.

I like numbers. And when I think of my dad, I am grateful. I am an unflinching perfectionist. I like things that add up. I like things that have a place and are in it. I like to know that things are going according to plan. I don't like messes.

Given that, I would not be the kind of person you might expect to thrive in community change — an environment where "good-enough" planning is critical and the ever-adapting and unpredictable circumstances require "being comfortable with the uncertainty and risk that come from operating in a context described as 'volatile, uncertain, complex, and ambiguous' in which the best strategy may not be obvious, results are not guaranteed, and past performance does not ensure future success."[104]

The perfectionist in me — the part of me that likes everything to add up in neat and tidy columns — struggled at every turn.

But what I didn't realize in beginning my work with Joe was how much my business life was also influenced by my mom — the real entrepreneur in the family — a woman who saw opportunity in everything and wasn't afraid of going after it. She was full of ideas and good at implementing them. When my dad ended up with a vacant warehouse, she turned it into a swap meet and rented out the space; when she noticed there was no food businesses nearby, she made big pots of pulled pork and sold sandwiches out of the office portion of the warehouse. When she wanted pink rose wallpaper in her kitchen and couldn't afford it, she painted roses on the walls, and talented artist that she was, no one could tell it wasn't really wallpaper.

With me, she was careful to never say I couldn't do something; instead she would say, "if you want to do it, go figure it out." Thanks to her, I was intrigued by doing just that.

As a teen, I "sang for my supper" in order to get from Ohio to California to work with Cesar Chavez. A catering business helped me raise the money to go to Europe. A tomato hauling business got me to college.

As a young woman I thought to be good in business I had to be like my dad — and I thought that meant to be decisive, analytical, systematic, good with the numbers. Over the years, however, what I learned was that I <u>also</u>

needed to be like my mom — creative, out of the box, unafraid to try things and to back it up with hard work.

I am a left-brain/right-brain person, a blend of both my parents, and I managed to escape childhood without too many damaging connections to the gender stereotyping of either.

I love proformas, capital strategies, and bottom lines. I like the numbers to work. I like big goals, raising the millions of dollars that are needed, and building buildings that work. And I equally love the creative part of working without a template, risking something new, working in entrepreneurial situations, stimulating the creativity of working teams, testing big ideas, and making people believe that anything is possible.

Engaging in comprehensive place-based community-building work means embracing both analytics and creative process. We need people who love numbers and can tolerate mess. It is right-brain/left-brain work. It is intuitive and intentional. It is process-driven and product-focused. It is rooted in history but must shoot forward to a new future. It is visionary and practical.

To maintain this balance for Market Creek, we needed to be ever vigilant in keeping the door open to learning and be able to see a whole and connected story.

We needed to be able to ask and answer:

- Is civic action increasing and are the teams diverse?
- Are the working teams achieving what they set out to achieve?
- Has there been an economic impact and how much?
- Are the projects completed profitable?

These questions were largely answered by counting things.

But we also had to ask and answer:

- What does this expansion in civic life mean and what is its impact?
- How are the teams and networks evolving?

- Are the teams strengthening the community and cultural ties of residents?
- Is there ownership of the work and how is that impacting expectations for change?

To ask and answer these questions, we blended workshops, conversations, and interviews with a focus on working at the intersection of fact and feeling, information and narrative.

"Facts inform, but stories...connect us in profound ways that go beyond mere intellect and get to the deeper currents that move us to reflection and inspiration."[105] Our job was to take a "whole-brain approach," as Lori Silverman framed it in her book, which was a blending of analytical thought and the power of story.

We supported digital storytelling, held regular convenings about what was working and not working, promoted sharing events and learning exchanges, and periodically did a "Wall of Wonder" — a workshop format created by the Institute of Cultural Affairs in which groups documented the stories, facts, people and moments that were important, where the turning points occurred, and what led to breakthrough. These were ways to document and honor the past. They helped us remember that none of us carries the entire story and reflect on the need to see a broader picture than any of us can paint by ourselves. They built understanding about what was changing, both intended and unintended. And they refined our practices and principles.

Most of all, they strengthened our "common" sense, our common story, our common belief in the benefit of moving forward together.

Indicators That Connect

"You had to check your silo at the door."

Rickey Laster served on a number of teams from construction to leasing to resources. At first proprietary about what was in "his silo," he came to see the value in connecting what everyone brought to the table. "Market Creek became a vision that wouldn't allow you to bring your silo," he commented. "You had to bring everything in your silo, but the silo wasn't allowed."

"If you show me yours, I'll show you mine," Rickey laughed, throwing himself back in his chair with a gleam in his eye. "At first, I thought if I put myself in a silo, I don't have to worry about being seen. But the teamwork was about seeing what was inside each other's silos. Then we were all exposed!" He laughed again. "We weren't allowed to protect information."

Like connecting dots in the game Line Draw, we needed ways to see information across the entire game board. Would one team be willing to drop its return on investment target because another team could get greater numbers of contractors on the job?

"What if you tried to live in a house without a kitchen? Or if you only had a front door? Or how about trying to get along with water but no electricity?" Roque loved to ask people to visualize what a united picture looked like. He was a master at analogy. "If you are going to build a home, you need a physical structure with a gathering place for eating and sharing, space for the family to connect, energy coming in from the outside, and the ability to pay bills."

People live their lives with a natural holistic view. It was easy for residents to connect. For funders, this was harder, given our propensity for working in isolation with a clear — sometimes legally-binding — mandate on our areas-of-interest which get linked to logic models that are often rigid. These silos and intractable logic models impact both process and outcomes.

"It's different sometimes from inside than outside especially if you are several steps removed," notes Elwood Hopkins, who led the Los Angeles Urban Funders for many years.

"Funders can fixate on their logic models and set an expectation that the work they fund will move logically from step 1 to step 10. But what if people on the ground can find ways to connect and leverage the work and create a shortcut to step 10? Instead of celebrating that unexpected victory, there has been a tendency sometimes among funders to insist in going back and doing every step that was skipped. That's when the logic model becomes more than a possible means to an end and becomes an end itself — and that's when it loses credibility with people doing the work and damages momentum."

"We know that challenges are all interconnected," noted Garland Yates. For over 30 years, Garland worked on issues of poverty, and racial, economic, and political inequality, and is a staunch believer in the power of community building. He has also spent years contemplating the role of philanthropy in community change, including involvement in two of the Annie E. Casey Foundation's major community change initiatives.

"Housing isn't separate from lack of youth programming, land planning, or schools. These things can't be attended to in isolation, but it requires this notion of foundations doing work that isn't in siloes. In my experience, there have been so many experiences where kids in certain areas have changed their attitudes and made their neighborhoods safer, but people's interest in a specific educational improvement or their preoccupation with a single specific indicator causes them to look past what's been accomplished. To see if the capacity for change has improved, you have to dig deep."

For resident-owned community change to work, each working team needed to set their own indicators. In addition, the wide variety of local and national investors — each with their own way of gaging success — all had to agree on both what was important to review and to review it all simultaneously so that no single indicator was taken in isolation.

The process of compiling data across these interconnected areas of social, economic, physical and political development occurred largely through the annual **"Social & Economic Impact Report."** This report combined civic engagement, community and cultural arts, the built environment, family and community networks, and community enterprise and ownership, along with partnerships and shared learning. Goals were set in a way that helped each area complement the others and questions were posed for tracking progress.

The Social & Economic Impact Report process focused on staying connected across working teams and blended left-brain data with right-brain narrative and discussions. We provided safe space for learning and provided multiple ways for information to be grasped, results interpreted, and learnings shared.

Since each Working Team developed its own outcome measures, this compiled report became an important document for reviewing the original benchmarks as points of comparison. Individual teams used the data to make adjustments to their strategies or to initiate new teams to deal with issues that were surfacing.

Over time, it became a running history of challenges and learnings across teams.

When We Learn Together

"P & L for $200," someone at Table #1 yelled out. I tore the sheet marked $200 off the board and under it was a piece of paper that read: "Gross revenues for Market Creek Partners, LLC in FY 2007."

"What is $20 million?" A resident from Table #1 shared as the team's guess.

"No. Your turn Table #2," I followed-up. They huddled for few minutes while I hummed the theme from the TV show Jeopardy![106] "What is $2 million?" they shouted out.

I asked the group who they thought was closer and everyone agreed Table #2. "Table #2, you get the $200!" I handed them the sheet with the $200 marked on it that I had taken off the wall.

There was a rambunctious spirit in the room, which filled up with laughter and applause.

We were always on a search for ways to get facts to people in a way that was fun, could be easily distilled and understood. Turning the "Social & Economic Impact Report" into a game made for a rowdy, energizing, and educational experience. Each answer and its related question provided a lively way to engage people in discussion of benchmarks, commercial values, and percentages of increases or decreases year to year.

During the game, we learned about the difference between gross revenues and assets. We discussed how Market Creek made its money in rents, how Food 4 Less was the biggest rent payer, and how the total of gross revenues also included CAMs, or common area maintenance costs, that were reimbursed by the tenants. Residents asked questions and other residents answered.

Each year, after all the data was collected for each of the success indicators set by the teams and compiled in the Social & Economic Impact Report, workshops were organized for people to review the information in both small and large groups. These, like all team meetings, were structured so people could share and learn — no matter how confusing or complicated the topic — in a way that all the information could be grasped by all people.

As a coordinating team, we were talented game-makers, fun-creators, and workshop facilitators. We used anything and everything to engage people in something that would get them in a creative space — such as drawing an illustration of their goals for the year on pieces of paper and assembling them in a quilt that would be hung on the wall. One resident built her vision of the village out of cardboard.

To ground people in the key dates that would impact the company finances — the refinance of the New Markets Tax Credit Loan, the "put and call" (their right to sell back their stock and their right to buy out the remaining stock), what year Market Creek would likely need a facelift, and when the PRIs needed to be paid — we created a parody of "The Dating Game."[107]

We structured our work on the belief that as we reconnect to our sense of playfulness and creativity, we become better problem-solvers. As we connect, share, and get to know each other, we break down fear. As adults, because we are afraid to talk about what we don't know, we need safe space to learn. And most importantly, learning improves when everyone is learning together.

Quarterly and annually, we "made fun" and provided a forum for questions to be asked, the interpretation of data to receive a check-point, and theories about the shifts in data to be discussed without fear, blame, or frustration.

In discussions about what was working and not working, we delved into what was standing in the way of achieving any of the benchmarks, recognizing that we couldn't control all the variables involved in hitting the mark. We sorted through what we could take responsibility for and those things were pulled to the forefront so responsibility could be distributed to new teams.

And what <u>was</u> achieved was whole-heartedly celebrated.

22

EVALUATING SKIN IN THE GAME

"Opportunity dances with those on the dance floor."

— Anonymous

Skin in the Game

Cooperative economics — Ujamaa, the Fourth Principle of Kwanzaa — was how some residents referred to the IPO. It was about building shared wealth and profiting together.

I had the memorable experience of sitting in on a focus group with owners shortly after the IPO closed. The comments shared were deep with emotion as people described what it meant to have skin in the game, sharing comments like: "Instead of talking about the problem, now we own part of the solution;" "I put my money behind it because I believe in it;" "You know generations with no hope and then this happens;" "Putting your money in something changes it, gives you a different perspective."

When people have "skin in the game," economic theorists argue, they are more likely to make prudent decisions because they share in the costs and benefits of those decisions — exposure to loss and the opportunity to gain. This goes beyond buy-in to a commitment that is now deeply personal. It is participation with risk. The IPO was rooted in shared risk, shared responsibility, and a shared economic destiny — Ujamaa.

What was at stake for investors was the value of the time they invested in planning, the value of their decision-making in creating a model that could be sustained, and the value of their money — all hard-earned. And all that had been built depended on assuring that the larger community's expectation that change would continue.

They had skin in the game.

Getting to Baseline

When PolicyLink's Victor Rubin and Lisa Robinson facilitated the Ownership Design Team in 2003 to begin designing the evaluation of Market Creek Plaza's ownership strategy, the goal was to explore the impact of the offering, but also to undertake a participatory evaluation that would draw upon the experience of residents.

Team members reflected on what ownership meant and what they hoped to achieve by having community members owning units in the project. Victor and Lisa then guided the team in sorting the outcomes into social and economic categories and describing changes at the individual and broader community levels that they hoped would come about from resident ownership of the Plaza.

Over the course of three workshops, the team discussed and refined the relationships among the immediate, intermediary, and longer-term outcomes. They also recognized the differences between the overall impacts of Market Creek Plaza and the specific impacts of resident ownership. At the very center of the diagram that was created was seeding the expectation and desire for change to continue.

In addition to establishing the evaluation framework, the design team set the goals for the evaluation, determined the approach, mapped out a process for recruiting the evaluators, reviewed proposals, and selected the team that PolicyLink would supervise for the evaluation. Dr. Zoe Clayson was retained as the lead evaluator.

Like the legal team, residents were comfortable with Zoe right away. Her warmth and smile engaged people. A strong advocate for public health over her career, she had grown to believe in the power of storytelling, the need for people to visualize research, and the power of community wisdom.

Abundantia, the name of her company, suited her, with its message of abundance and prosperity. In her self-effacing style, you might not know that she had travelled across the world, from Mexico to Egypt, to share her lessons; all you would know was that in the room with her, you felt special. Her eyes would draw you out.

With the resident team, Zoe mapped out the parameters of a baseline evaluation and clustered the "pathways" identified as essential to the model in three categories:

1. financial and regulatory mechanisms;
2. resident involvement/engagement; and
3. the institutional roles and responsibilities of the partners.

In the pathway analysis,[108] Zoe cited several factors that cut across the three pathways that were critical to the successful completion of the public offering:

- JCNI's vision of ownership and its capacity building and support;
- The willingness to guarantee substantial financial investment to reduce perceived project risk by financial institutions;
- The patience with the length of time required for plans to come to fruition;
- The continued receptiveness to the need for mid-course corrections;
- The Community Listening Process, which carried the CD-IPO strategy through difficult times;
- The inclusive, consensus-building approach that garnered respect among community members; and
- The skilled and dedicated legal team.

A baseline evaluation was conducted over the first 18 months, starting with an individual survey that was conducted with every investor, and a plan was put in place to measure the extent to which the outcomes defined were achieved. The team set a goal of conducting follow-up evaluations in five year increments.

Our team never knew Zoe was sick. She never complained. She continued to shine and was steadfast, seemingly indefatigable throughout the process. So we were struck with grief on June 25, 2010, just as the baseline was being completed when, sadly, Zoe Cardoza Clayson passed away from cancer. She was a loss — for the world, for the many communities she guided through learning, and for us.

She had brought us to our baseline, and we would have to go on without her.

The Impact of Ownership

"I'm just happy to see my son as proud as he is. I mean he has his own home now. You walk in his front door and you see his stock certificate up on the wall."

When the IPO closed, there were four hundred and nineteen investors, each with a story like this young man being described by his mother. Among the investors, 78 percent were African American, 11 percent Latino, and 5 percent white. The investor pool was made up of 66 percent individual investors, 33 percent married couples, and 1 percent came to the table in youth-adult partnerships. The ages ranged from 8 to 85, the majority were women, and the most powerful influence was involvement in church networks.

Residents cited many reasons for investing — they had helped build the buildings, worked on teams, were encouraged by their pastor, or just wanted an ownership opportunity in their community. In the final focus group that Zoe held, people shared the meaning of the IPO for them, their families, and their community. Trust, pride, and wanting to leave a legacy for their community and their children is what had mattered. I got to sit in and listen; their comments were indelible.

"I invested on behalf of my daughter," one mother shared. "My daughter had had savings accounts but would always spend the money. But now she owns a piece of the block... It's something that's still here, withstanding the test of time. And she's seeing money coming back to her."

It had been an "unconventional investment, an unconventional opportunity, using unconventional methods to reach people," as one resident put it, and it had required a risk. "Commercial property! That takes a pretty sophisticated person to do that, you know! It was a leap of faith."

We had ways to measure the increase in the number of local jobs. We could measure the percentage of community control over Market Creek's assets, the diversification of retail services, and the percentages of local hiring. But how could we measure the impact of this kind of inclusion, pride, participation, and cooperation?

"There are all kinds of ways of knowing. One way is counting," noted David Mathews, who has spent decades leading research on the work of democracy at the Kettering Foundation. "But there are other ways that can't be known by counting. What is really important? What is deeply valued? I can ask you how much you love your kids, and how do you know that?" He was almost gleeful in recounting the story of how a man once, when asked what results he achieved that year, indicated a 10 percent increase in hope. "In our pervasive metric-mania, we believe numbers more than we believe people."

The impact of ownership was deep and broad. "Did it matter? Hell-freakin'-yes it mattered. Look at me," Macedonio Arteaga recounted in discussing ownership and reflecting on the entire Market Creek experience. He had worked on teams from Arts and Culture to Project VOCAL.

"People felt validated. People felt worthy and well-prepared. There was experiential knowledge of growth. If a young person heals from his wounds and begins to believe in his culture as a brilliant history...If people fill the human hole left by the less-than dynamic — it seems elitist to just measure success by who goes to college or by dollars and cents. But then what? How do we measure this?" he questioned. "Measuring grades or return-on-investment doesn't measure human growth! It can be horrible to quantify things that aren't really a true measure of change."

Ardelle Matthews, when asked about the IPO, noted: "I came from Cotton Plant, Arkansas. I didn't see an indoor bathroom until I was five and here was a wonderful blessing that came to me. I felt gladly I will do this. I will be here and give something back. I can help others have opportunity."

In the early years of growing into what would become the Market Creek experience, the Annie E. Casey Foundation released a series of reports on social networks called *"Ties that Bind."* The Casey Team spent time conducting research and holding consultative sessions with residents, practitioners, scholars, and foundation staff. Since the timeframe was early 2004, the term "social network" wasn't referring to Facebook or LinkedIn, as it does today, but more of a theoretical construct for cooperative and interdependent relationships (social) woven together (net) in a sustained effort to overcome obstacles (work).

This report documented how people in neighborhoods experienced the "helping professional and people in positions of power over resources" noting the detachment that exists. The report pointed to the power of personal relationships and the networks which they operate within in communities when it comes to achieving results:

> "People are motivated and influenced by those with whom they are in personal relationships. These attachments give people more choices and encourage them to take risks and set goals they might not otherwise dream of or be able to achieve on their own. They enable them to connect to much more diverse networks of individuals and families providing access to new information and new opportunities."

Networks, noted the Casey Report, are critical in "addressing the issues that services cannot address, or in some instances, the issues that the service delivery system itself creates — isolation, powerlessness, and the loss of self-image and self-worth."

Diamond Community Investors and the large network formed by the Neighborhood Unity Foundation were beginning to play important roles. Even if you couldn't measure it, you knew it. People were beginning to tap into its power.

"Everybody's close together," I remember one Market Creek investor commenting in the focus group. "I see people now that I never would have known."

Would it achieve its goal as the Participatory Evaluation Design Team framed it? Would it "lead to more cooperation among neighbors and groups, greater pride in the neighborhood, and a widely shared sense of self-determination"? Would it provide a platform for residents to have "an increased voice in political, governmental and other issues and a generally higher level of civic engagement"? Would there be social improvements "brought about both by the **process** of creating resident ownership — and by the **results**—the tangible evidence of a successful development?"[109]

That is a story yet to be told.

23

MEASURING CIVIC EYESIGHT

"Public learning develops a citizenry's capacity
for seeing new possibilities in life.
You might say it improves civic eyesight."[110]

— David Mathews, The Ecology of Democracy

Evaluation at the Heart of Complexity

"For those with a high tolerance for ambiguity and a grand sense of adventure, this is an exciting world. For those with big control needs who prize predictability and strive for certainty, not so much."[111]

With his self-effacing humor, Michael Quinn Patton can reflect like no one else in the field can about jumping into the fire. Trained in a field that loves randomized control trials where there is absolute clarity about critical factors so rigorous testing can occur, Michael leapt onto the landscape of "ups and downs, roller-coaster rides along cascades of dynamic interactions, unexpected and unanticipated divergences, tipping points and critical mass momentum shifts. Indeed, things often get worse before they get better as systems change creates resistance to and pushback against the new."[112]

In his book Developmental Evaluation: Applying Complexity Concepts to Enhance Innovation and Use, Michael shares, when entering the daunting world of interconnected issues in communities — a world of "uncertain beginnings, muddled middles, and unpredictable endings that ripple on and on without end"[113] — traditional methods that require an explicit logic model showing clear goals — established prior to the engagement of stakeholders — aren't effective in the "great unexplored frontier" of evaluation "under conditions of complexity" and can actually undermine the work.

To deal with the need for people working inside community change to engage stakeholders first rather than after goals are set, he stepped out of the norm and developed a distinct approach to evaluation that embraces this need to declare peace in the "battle between funders, evaluators commissioned by funders, and social innovators."[114]

There is no doubt that this approach to evaluation, which came on the scene in 2011 just as I was leaving the field, would have been helpful in creating the language and broader perspective needed by our board and team. The developmental evaluation field, by using an adaptive approach, offers an alternative star in the universe of evaluation, which can accommodate the large-scale upfront mobilization of stakeholders, the crafting of strategies jointly in an ongoing process, and the stewarding of a long-term effort.

Mark Cabaj, who I met through the Aspen Institute's Roundtable on Community Change, had served as executive director of Vibrant Communities, a network of fifteen urban collaboratives focused on reducing poverty. He was a developmental evaluator by practice and by nature. He had the prerequisite sense of humor to be at peace with complexity, where issues are hard to define, their root causes are tangled up, and stakeholders are largely not in agreement.

Having the opportunity to work with Mark on a project spearheaded by the Roundtable on the topic of complexity theory and community change,[115] provided the perfect bookend to my early enthusiasm for Margaret Wheatley's Leadership and the New Science.

Wheatley's work had been influential in releasing me from the conventional hierarchical and mechanistic worldview that leads us to believe that running our organizations as well-oiled machines can be done merely by replaceable parts. Mark, along with his co-author Patricia Auspos, pointed out how this "machine model" still dominates the field, making us hold on to our need to control and predict. "Instead of perceiving adaptive practices that are systemic in their analysis, participatory in their processes, and experimental in their planning and implementation as 'second best' strategies," they noted, we should be acknowledging this "as the most robust way to make progress on the messy, complex issues in communities across America."[116]

This approach isn't about allowing things to be chaotic or unfold in a willy-nilly way. Adherence to values, clearly defined practices and principles, and a consistent process that puts discovery-based learning at the forefront — publicly articulated and publicly evaluated — are essential elements.

In community change, discovery-based learning needs to inform each round of action, and while we didn't have at our fingertips the methods and language of developmental evaluation at the time, we did practice its concept of "double-loop learning," which involves not just identifying and naming the problem as a collective group with diverse points of view, but questioning the "assumption, policies, practices, values, and system dynamics that led to the problem in the first place."[117]

"Tame" problems, contends Horst Rittel and Melvin Webber in their classic reference now cited widely by leaders in community change, "Dilemmas in a General Theory of Planning," are concrete and definable, making it feasible for them to be eradicated through professional expertise. But working to achieve change in the face of complexity renders conventional ways of responding to problems ill-suited to the job,[118] including evaluation. "Wicked" problems, those where the definition is unclear, the cause uncertain, and people are divided about what should be done about them, are "as tricky as they are aggressive and vicious."[119]

As David Mathews points out, "people are troubled by discrepancies between what is happening to them and what they think *should be* happening — yet don't agree on what the problems are, much less what *should* be done about them. Since the disputes aren't over questions of fact but over what is the *right* thing to do, citizens have to judge for themselves. The ability of citizens to exercise sound judgement in the face of disagreements and uncertainly is critical. There aren't any experts on what is right."[120]

It is difficult to work within a world where there is no "right" answer and no "expert." In the foundation world, we are on the search for best practices we can import or a set of easily-replicated steps we can follow. When citizens have to "judge for themselves," the game changes. That's when growing the capacity for civic learning — or improving "civic eyesight" as Mathews frames it — becomes crucial.

"Learning by and in a community is more than acquiring and disseminating information," David Mathews notes. "It is more than evaluating civic efforts. It is a mindset about change and progress, an attitude that is open to experimentation and reflective in the face of failure."[121]

This kind of public learning is the foundation of resilience.

Resilience rests in the ability to be open to trying again. To dust off and take roles. To engage in a sustained effort over a long period of time. To engage in your community with enthusiasm and endurance.

And because "wicked" problems are not technical, but human, and are embedded in the social fabric, we cannot afford to relegate citizens to the sidelines. "Civic eyesight" is impaired when we have no ability to see things from different points of view.

Appreciating each other's points of view, opening up new possibilities for people, and expanding insight about the connectedness of people as clear outcomes of Market Creek's ownership work was expressed to me in different ways by residents who participated and thought deeply about its impact:

> "So often, we miss each other's stories because we don't interact. We build up and start believing in the stereotypes. Breaking this down was the biggest work we all did together. It made us a community."

> "When things are predicated on the idea that someone here screwed up and we need to fix it, it's offensive. It keeps trust from forming. Why would I want to do something with people I don't trust? But with this, it was different. It seemed like everyone was around the table, so there were no scapegoats. We all had to learn about each other and just see that our actions really mattered."

"This was a conversation that unfolded over years. It put us in a situation where we had to get over our own prejudices about each other and get something done."

"People don't discuss things in the same way anymore. They say we can do this."

"At first I would ask 'what do you want me to do?' Then I realized this was a shift. Now I look at problems differently, see our potential, and ask 'what can we consider, what do we need to do differently, what if we partner?' Small changes can add up."

"There was no free lunch. We all brought our shovels to the table. We brought ourselves to the table. I never experienced such intense people work, talking about issues that maybe we had never thought about before."

"We learned to try and try again."

In a world of "wicked" problems and complex historical social dynamics, creating the platform for action-focused, citizen-centered, discovery-based learning opened up a whole world of sight for people who grew to appreciate each other's points of view, and by doing that, opened up new possibilities people never imagined.

Burden of Proof

"If we really care about innovation, we need to accept some failure."

Bill Traynor was right. Innovation and failure go hand-in-hand. But in the foundation world, perhaps in most fields, people don't take too well to failure.

"There is no denying effective learning is naturally about trial and error, do overs and resilience," Bob Giloth from the Annie E. Casey Foundation observed, but "overblown rhetoric about 'failing fast,' 'failing forward' and making only 'new mistakes' suggests we know more about the mistakes and success process than we actually do. And most mistakes are, unfortunately, about the daily grind of implementing what we already know."[122]

"People hired to steward money can't have honest conversations about that," noted Bill Traynor in discussing the dynamic that unfolds in foundations around discovery-based learning. "They are electric fence conversations. With the pressure on metrics, the space to maneuver can get limited," he noted.

In the field of philanthropy, we have an uncanny ability to require that grantees collect huge amounts of data at a rapid pace and produce evidence that what they are proposing will work. As Roger Williams so aptly put it: "You have to prove it before you can prove it. Nationally, the push for evidence has communicated to people that they can't be creative."

People without proof need not apply.

As the pendulum has swung from "democracy is messy, but worth it," to the need for "empirical evidence-based program designs," and "quantifiable return on investment," we have to be honest about how much social innovation we are really after.

"Evidence is for government, not philanthropy," noted Angela Blackwell from PolicyLink. "The use of our tax dollar should require evidence that it will work. But evidence-based requirements by foundations is locking out creativity. We need to use information to open up creativity."

Angela is clear about the importance of measuring impact. "We care about results," she noted. But she would agree with Ralph Smith, who said: "In this evidence-based environment, the price of failure has risen."

What is the price of failure?

To avoid failure, is there a cost to shutting down the natural creativity and problem-solving that exists in our communities? Is there a cost to turning inward to working only on those things our teams can control? And to accept the possibility of failure while working on the most entrenched or "wicked" issues of our day, at the heart of complexity, is part of the price paid the very real probability of losing your job?

A community-planned, designed, built, and owned commercial project was a risk. A big risk. And there was no best practice that could inform a logic model.

Joe Jacobs was fixated on operationalizing values, risking action, leveraging everything we had at our disposal, and continual learning, as opposed to hitting predetermined outcomes or preserving our foundation's control over capital long into the future. He wanted to see things work, as we all did, but he was as interested in the ups and downs, wins and losses, in determining whether or not the theory could be reduced to practice. He never expected that the work would be smooth sailing. He cared about duking it out — what Bob Giloth framed as the "daily grind" of implementing — where there is a fine line between success and failure and on a moment's notice, things can swing from one to the other. To require evidence upfront would have been antithetical to the process of innovation.

To maintain a team willing to take these kinds of risks over a long period of time, we needed to be evaluated on our response to hitting walls and not by whether or not the wall existed. Given that, Joe was careful to never blame his team for the barriers themselves.

If I had felt our team had to "fix" every issue that surfaced or that our organization was somehow "responsible" for everything that couldn't be fixed, my instinct would tell me to step away from the plate. Too much responsibility. Too many unpredictable variables. Too large of an historical disconnect between cause and effect. Too many national and international economic forces beyond our control.

Add to that the tension that comes with the expectations of literally dozens of partners, each defining success by their own standards and evaluating efforts by how far we "moved the needle," all assuming this should be done with efficiency and focus on a short timeline during the worst economy since the Great Depression? Who wants to carry that kind of burden?

"People are looking for simple solutions," Roger Williams noted, reflecting on his years at the Casey Foundation and talking about why the pendulum was swinging away from comprehensive community change back to silos that are narrow and more manageable.

Over the years, I came to appreciate that small changes could add up to big results. But from where I sat, people looking for simple solutions, without taking risks, the kind of risks that innovation demands — risking action, risking money, risking reputation, and risking failure — aren't really interested in community transformation.

The answers are not going to be upfront. The "proof" will be in the doing.

Embracing Discovery

"Their statements were the most authentic, grounded, and evidence-based data we possibly could have collected," commented Darren Walker about having the residents presenting on their project at the Rockefeller Foundation in New York.

Darren, now President of the Ford Foundation, was our grants officer during his time at Rockefeller. I first met him during his term as head of the Abyssinia CDC, when his team developed the groundbreaking commercial project that included a Pathmark grocery store in Harlem around 1999.

Born in Louisiana and raised in Goose Creek, Texas, Darren from an early age developed a belief in himself and our human responsibility to create opportunity for others. He relished challenging people's assumptions about race and class and working his way to the top of the philanthropic sector, he remained at ease trying things differently. Breaking from convention, he was open to our idea of bringing residents from southeastern San Diego to New York to present on their project and talk to the Rockefeller investment team about the idea of making a program-related investment in Market Creek.

Over the years, I have been told by many advisers to foundations that "residents aren't going to invest in something like this." It was a ridiculous idea, many believed. To this day, I still get this response to the idea of it happening somewhere else. Resident voice as "evidence," as Darren noted later, spoke volumes. And not just about the value of residents in the room, but about Darren himself, who embraced residents with an open heart and an open mind.

"When someone has an open heart, that person is respectful, sympathetic, supportive, tolerant, forgiving and compassionate toward other human beings," noted Omowale Satterwhite in the book he co-authored on building capacity for social change in communities of color. "When someone has an open mind, that person is willing to listen, observe, take advice, ask questions, suspend judgment, rethink assumptions and be exposed to new ideas."[123]

Ask any one of us who work in foundations if we have an open mind and the answer will be yes. But the idea of listening, being vulnerable, asking questions without knowing the answer, and rethinking assumptions is harder than it sounds. Omo, after 35 years in the field working on issues of community change and social justice, was unflinching in his commitment to being humble and vigilant in serving communities, not as an expert, but as a colleague. For him, keeping both an open heart and an open mind were essentials to do this work.

"The problem is, as foundations, we already have a framework," Bill Traynor reflected on his years of creating space that can feed aspirational people, "so this idea of 'I don't know,' which creates space for something new and dynamic, is antithetical to how we operate. We push people out, because inviting them in challenges the orthodoxy."

"If I'm right," David Mathews commented in a conversation, "then there is no reason for me to listen. You need a sense of uncertainly in order to listen. If I'm uncertain, I have to listen and deliberate." But the idea of "I don't know" causes a disruption in how we traditionally do things.

We had learned that innovation requires risk, and risk requires a certain level of comfort in not knowing the outcome upfront. Sustainability requires analysis and planning, but social innovation or transformation requires a radical re-examination of our assumptions, realignment of our resources, and a rethinking of our approach. We also learned, as Clayton Christensen discusses in The Innovator's Dilemma, that when faced with disruption, our abilities for running an efficient organization became our disabilities.

For us, this included the need for evidence-based quantifiable impact and guaranteed financial returns before investing.

When working inside complexity, methods must be continually adapted and can't be evaluated by the same metrics used for tackling issues with a known cause and effect. Quantitative analysis alone is not enough to know what is working and not working, and control groups cannot be separated from the historical race and class abuses that have occurred. That makes team learning, gleaned from real time experience, more important than evidence gleaned from past best practices.

For the process of evaluating change, we need to be careful about how success gets defined, who defines it, and how data gets vetted. Operating in the public interest comes with an obligation to hear the public voice and that starts with listening. Taking the risk to listen is how our assumptions get changed and as assumptions change, we are able to engage in an authentic process of joint learning.

When Darren Walker invited members of the resident teams to come to New York and present, he was willing to try something different. Step out of the Rockefeller Foundation's ingrained internal procedures. Keep an open mind. Listen to new voices. "Having the residents present disrupted standard procedure at the Rockefeller Foundation," Darren reflected. "They helped us see our own biases and made us better grantmakers and partners in an unprecedented project."

His courageous act of engagement put a spotlight on long-held and outdated assumptions in the room and changed them. A risk was taken on all sides of the room.

One that changed us all.

24

OWNERSHIP AND ACCOUNTABILITY

"There are all kinds of ways of knowing. One way is counting.
But there are other ways that can't be known by counting."

— David Mathews

COUNT-ability and ACCOUNT-ability

"While accountability is typically a matter of information to institutional leaders, it is very much a matter of relationship for citizens." Citizens, David Mathews contends, most often understand accountability, not as testing and data, but as being able to have "a frank, open, morally grounded exchange."[124]

By demanding more and more information from staff and pushing accountability through a strict adherence to rules rather than creating time and space for engaging in an exchange, Dr. Mathews shares, institutions deepen the distrust that exists with citizens, and it becomes a vicious cycle. Those of us in organizations who see ourselves as needing to be accountable for public benefit turn inward to the factors that are within our control so we can track and account for our direct impact.

We inadvertently create a greater gap in accountability by insulating ourselves from the public and their right to deliberate what is in the public good — particularly their own good.

In our journey to support community change, we were relentless in our quest to achieve results, hit benchmarks, and evaluate impact. But we were also aware that as we increased our capacity to "count," we needed to be sure we weren't under-cutting our capacity to "account."

As teams began to take collective responsibility and ownership of action, were we being careful enough to avoid imposing metrics from outside that would undermine the very thing we were trying to build — civic learning and the capacity to own and manage change?

As the number of team-initiated success indicators grew, we had to continually ask ourselves if we were avoiding the drive to turn inward to those things that could be controlled, undermining the efforts that were needed to link people, leverage action, and create a holistic approach to supporting change that citizens owned.

As we became better and better helping teams drive performance measures, we had to be asking if we were also becoming equally sophisticated in having "frank, open, morally-grounded exchanges" with the public.

"The checks and balances are often onerous, and all the metrics squish innovation," Bill Traynor noted, reflecting on the field of community change. They not only squish innovation, I thought; if you aren't careful, they can easily suffocate ownership.

Peter Block, in his book Community: The Structure of Belonging, notes that without careful deliberation and ownership of action, what gets lost is "chosen accountability." In discussing community transformation, he writes: "The essential work is to build social fabric, both for its own sake and to enable chosen accountability among citizens. When citizens care for each other, they become accountable to each other. Care and accountability create a healthy community."[125]

Challenging how we think about accountability, Peter notes in his work on civic engagement: "the existing public conversation claims to be tough on accountability, but it is unbearably soft on accountability. It keeps screaming for accountability, but in the scream, it exposes its weakness...The current conversation believes that retribution, incentives, legislation, new standards and tough talk will cause accountability."[126] Every time something goes wrong, we want someone or something to blame — leaders, laws, program designs, implementation, and oversight — while restoration, he notes, "comes from the choice to value possibility and relatedness."

Our willingness to connect to each other requires a change in the conversation away from fear and fault to creating something together.

If we want to be good at more than just counting, and be good at being jointly accountable for co-creating the new future we want to live in, that requires those of us in foundations to stop asking questions like how do we hold people accountable, how do we get people to be more responsible, how do we get others to buy-in, and how do we get "those people" to change?

"Questions that are designed to change other people are patriarchal and subtly colonial," Peter contends "and in this sense, always the wrong questions. Wrong, not because they don't matter or are based on ill intent, but wrong because they have no power to make a difference in the world. They are questions that are the cause of the very thing we are trying to shift: the fragmentation and retributive nature of our communities."[127]

To ask these kinds of questions, he contends, is to support "the dominant belief that an alternative future can be negotiated, mandated, led, engineered, and controlled into existence. These questions call us to try harder at what we have been doing. They urge us to raise standards, measure more closely and return to basics, purportedly to create accountability, but in reality to maintain dominance."[128]

Do I believe that boards and leadership of foundations should have expectations? Absolutely. And I am a stickler for high standards and for getting results. I am not advocating for moving away from these. I am advocating that we move away from predetermined, funder-set metrics that have no room for residents to define community "by its connectedness and its possibility."

I came to see how carefully this needs to be done — both in the community for residents to take ownership of action and internally to retain and grow talent that was willing to take risks and share decision-making and not turn inward to what can be controlled.

The grants officer, discussed earlier, who was accused by her leadership of "organizing residents against the foundation" and reprimanded for not "getting people on board" is an example of a philanthropic leader's lack of tolerance for real deliberation, placing value only on her own expertise and her foundation's theories of change. We, as a result, not only lose the value of resident voice, but we also lose talented people to the field, as we did with this young woman.

In philanthropy, lifting up citizen voices comes with risk, and the hardest of those risks can be that of being harshly criticized. But this is a risk we need to take if we want to build shared responsibility, accountability, and ownership. It is a risk we need to take in order to build a culture of experimentation that can hold up in the face of failure.

Success indicators are vitally important, but they need to be set and owned by the community teams. Evaluating this work is important, but we need to lead with discovery-based learning and team residents with a set of evaluators and advisors who understand complex community change and who believe that resident-centered participatory evaluation is important. Data is needed to inform action planning, but residents need to determine the data to be collected, collect it themselves, and vet the information, along with the data's underlying assumptions, to assure it honors and reflects their lived experience.

There is *count-ability* — and there was much at Market Creek we could count and did.

And then there is *account-ability* — and to evaluate that, we had to assess whether or not we had grown our ability to reflect on the many accounts of what was happening, the various interpretations of the story, the opportunity for people to share their account or narrative of the experience and contribute to a fuller picture of what had occurred and participate in a way that kept us all accountable to each other.

The story of Market Creek was a story about ownership — writ large. This was a story about what happens when people have shared ownership of what unfolds and, as Peter Block puts it, know from a deep place that they have "the capacity to transform, even create, the world we inhabit."[129]

We didn't set out with all of this in mind. Rather it emerged as the work developed and we were challenged and changed. As the teams brought new ideas forward about defining and measuring impact, we tried to add ways to honor perception, reason, emotion, language, intuition, imagination, faith, memory, practices, rituals, worldview, information, data, opinion, and story.

In looking back, I am grateful that I added to the list of ways we documented the writing of a quarterly perspective piece. Joe wanted to be a one-generation foundation, risking the discovery of an answer to the question, "What does it really take." Before going out of business, he wanted the learning shared. Anticipating that time, I pulled myself out of the work for one day, sometimes two, every 90 days to write. These pieces offer a 20-year real-time view on how our perspective of the work was changing, how our language was changing, and how teams were evolving.

In addition, I kept extensive personal notes of how I was changing. From the subtle shifts in understanding to the big ah-ha learning moments, these notes chronicled many moments of hurt and healing among the people participating, including myself, and tell a story of joy, celebration, connection and caring. These documents tell a story of personal change gleaned through deep and abiding friendships with people who graced my days. And they chronicle many of the surprising ways that we, as humans, stand in the way of change.

FLOURISHING
IN THE FACE OF
CHANGE

LEARNING TO LEAP SO THE NET WILL APPEAR

25

HOW TO ENJOY THE JOURNEY

"In the 21ˢᵗ century humanity faces some of its most daunting challenges.
Our best resource is to cultivate our singular abilities
of imagination, creativity and innovation."[130]

— Ken Robinson, <u>Out of Our Minds: Learning to Be Creative</u>

Ten Lessons

"Stay in the run," I would often chant.

When I was 28, never having run previously, I decided I was going to run a marathon. It was an endurance test. And not just on race day, but during the months of training that led up to it. I started slow. I set a goal of two miles, then five miles, then ten. I was living in Ohio at the time, so I learned to run the country roads in both heat and humidity, as well as the cold, snow, ice, and slush. Out on the road, I came to understand pace and the steady rhythm of my foot-fall, mile after mile, enjoying the contemplative time, the beauty of the corn fields, and the cloud formations in the sky.

I remember on race day my husband kept saying "stay in the run," meaning don't jump ahead, don't anticipate Mile 26 if you are only in Mile 5. Let each mile be its own experience. I also remember that he was with me at the end. He met up with me at Mile 20, the point where marathoners are expected to hit the wall, and encouraged me home. A runner himself, his steady pace provided a beat that kept me going. .

Pace, practice, persistence, the ability to enjoy each mile by itself, the corn fields, the cloud formations, and at the end a person by my side who believes I can do it — they all mattered.

"To stay the course, we need patience, compassion, and forgiveness. We should require this of one another,"[131] noted Margaret Wheatley in Leadership and the New Science. To endure change is to be willing to trust in our human ability for emerging solutions and inspired action. Have the grit to try something that has no guarantees. Engage with people in a way that brings purpose and meaning. Expose ourselves to the human experience. Find comfort in the reach and adapt when we fall short. Excel at patience, compassion, and forgiveness. And open ourselves up to our vulnerability.

Brené Brown, in her book Daring Greatly, notes humorously that we all want a "get out of vulnerability free card" but no such luck. We don't get the luxury of opting out. "Vulnerability is life's great dare," she notes. "It's life asking, 'Are you all in?'... It's courage beyond measure."[132] Taking her book title from Theodore Roosevelt's famous "Citizenship in a Republic" speech, Brené shares how "vulnerability is not knowing victory or defeat, its understanding the necessity of both."[133] It's about letting yourself be seen. Leaning into moments of discomfort. Noticing that you are not running the marathon alone. When we do that, she writes, our "courage is contagious."[134]

Over the 20 years I spent studying up-close-and-personal what community change really takes and what escalates that change, the lessons were broad and deep. And because the field of community change is fundamentally about human change, those lessons were largely, as Brené points out, both about risking our vulnerability and about being all-in. We needed to acknowledge that while "what we know matters...who we are matters more."[135] And because being matters more than knowing, we needed to show up, connect, engage in real relationships, humanize the work, stay true to our word, and take the dare, working with great care to not rob people of their faith and belief in their own ability to create the future they envision.

This is not always the case with institutional philanthropy.

Tonya Allen, who came up the ranks in philanthropy from associate program officer to CEO of the Skillman Foundation, noted: "Lots of people are drawn to this work because it's noble, but it is not easy. In fact, it is layered with difficulty," she shared. "The easy way to cop out is to use 'we don't have enough money' as an excuse, which people in philanthropy do all the time. When funders don't believe change can really happen, it zaps everyone's faith. It's critical for us to believe in the ingenuity of people."

"Philanthropy is potentially corrosive," Joe would say, reflecting on his desire to melt the walls between people of power and privilege and those who struggle or fight for social justice. He didn't romanticize philanthropy or need it to make him feel good. And like Tonya, he understood how large-scale change requires people to believe in and cultivate the ingenuity of others.

In dissecting the years with Joe, I asked myself why we were energized, ignited, and our most creative selves. What fed our endurance? What lessons were there from this experience that caused us to believe it was the hardest job we would ever love?

Here is my top ten list for thriving in the face of complex community change:

1. *Listen deeply* — Be willing to listen, free of all assumptions, and let go of trying to change who people are so you can begin to let yourself be changed by who they are. The answers always lie within.
2. *Choose to act; aim at a headpin* — Train yourself to see the whole and not just the parts, and then risk action at its most catalytic target.
3. *Make fun* — As Ken Robinson framed it, the creative organization values "the lively, the dynamic, the surprising and the playful." Fun is a highly under-rated strategy for long-term endurance that supports and sustains teams focused on the impossible, the improbable, and the impenetrable barriers that exist.
4. *Be personal* — Step out of roles and engage in real relationships. You can't think you are personally responsible for the whole turbulent history of race and class in America, but at the same time you can't think that you aren't — especially if you are white or work for an organization that represents power and privilege. It's up to each of us to model today the future we hope to create.

5. *Stay centered* — Plan openly in the "center of the room" and also stay true to your own optimism about and belief in the human capacity for change.

6. *Break it down* — Don't let complexity break apart the work or overwhelm those participating. Simplify everything to its common denominator so there is a common language and a common understanding.

7. *Look for the clearing* — Turbulence comes in waves and that's OK given that it is enormously rich space for innovation. The clearing will be up ahead.

8. *"Own" up* — Stay in a learning place and don't shy away from mistakes. Ownership isn't just about building assets. We must all "own" our own change.

9. *Refuse to be defeated* — The greatest innovations happen when we are stuck or when conventional ideas tank. Stay the course.

10. *Leap and the net will appear* — Don't wait for the answers. When in doubt, make a move and the path will reveal itself.

Practice these and you will love the work, keep your own faith, and avoid damaging the faith of others. Here is more on each:

1) Listen — Deeply

Gloria Steinem tells this story[136] about being in Ghana for a conference on sex trafficking, after which she found herself in a talking circle with 30 women from Zambia. Once the discomfort of being in a new place with new people was broken with song, the women opened up and described their situation — the painful reality of having to sell their bodies.

But when she asked what she could do to help, the women said: "An electric fence to keep out the elephants."

She thought she was going to be doing the "big things," like testifying before Congress, which she described as only too often having no impact at all. "Before I spoke to them [the women] if you'd asked me how to stop sex trafficking in this village, never would I have said, 'find a way to keep elephants out of their gardens.'"

Women were not allowed to be employed by the tourist lodges, so they had tried growing crops to support their families and pay for their children's schooling. But invariably elephants would eat through their fields, leaving them the only option of selling their bodies.

The money for fences was raised. A year later, the women had harvested a bumper crop, were able to feed their families, and could pay their children's school fees.

There was nothing about "best practice" — given Gloria Steinem's frame of reference — that could have informed the strategy to raise money for a fence. Fundamental to this moment was her courage to put herself in a new and uncomfortable situation, realize she had something to learn from the experience, and break the ice of differences by being willing to sing even though — as she describes it — she couldn't carry a tune. Then she had the courage to ask in an authentic way — "how can I help?"

Being truly helpful begins with listening. Listening deeply.

This is not like the "leading questions" of a courtroom. This is not about coaching or leading someone to a particular answer you want and believe is correct. This is not about questions asked in a way that tries to side-step our belief that we know better or already have the answer.

In the world of philanthropy, not listening is often the "elephant" in the room. We study and assess from arms-length. We convene among ourselves. We discuss and debate among ourselves. We miss the chance to see that a big problem might have a small solution. Or a different solution than what we first assume.

By asking questions, free of all assumptions, we let go of trying to change who people are and offer up our own willingness to be changed by who they are. When people are involved, valued, and voice what they really believe is standing in the way — including elephants — problems can be solved.

Transformation occurs when diverse teams of people are bringing their wisdom, creativity, and inspired energy for action to the table without boundaries and without the hierarchy of professional roles. When inclusion is valued and differences respected. When people listen, embrace learning, and accept ownership of the work ahead.

This is the pathway to change that endures.

2) Choose to Act; Aim at a Headpin

"If you try to write about everything, you'll end up writing about nothing," Ron would tell his writing students. "But if you focus on writing about one thing, you can very often write about everything."

Early in his career, Ron Cummings, the Jacobs Center's Chief Operating Officer and a master at team-building, had been a writing professor. To teach writing, he worked with students to overcome their fear of the creative process and risk exposing their most intimate feelings. Then he would show them how to focus, how to find the metaphor that could carry that emotion and articulate it in a broadly human way. To find the one thing that can speak to everything.

The connection of where a person lives to his or her opportunities in life is well documented. We know this is complex and interconnected work. We know social outcomes are connected to economic and economic to physical and physical to political. We know we must break out of our silos to keep the work holistic.

But two dilemmas challenge the effort to do holistic work: 1) the vast majority of the resources to power change in disinvested communities is still managed in silos, and 2) dealing with the interconnectedness of issues is completely overwhelming.

So what do you do?

First, you decide NOT to silo. Then you chose to act. Then you find the one focal point through which you can speak to all the universal issues, and you aim.

The idea of supporting the regeneration of a set of long-time disinvested neighborhoods — keeping the work connected across social, economic, physical and political development — is daunting. But our decision to aim at one primary focal point — residents wanting to get rid of a toxic dump and get a grocery in their neighborhood — changed how we viewed comprehensive work. Instead of thinking of comprehensive work as doing all things with all people around all issues, we came to see it as implementing visionary, targeted, and catalytic action in a comprehensive and interconnected way.

We trained ourselves to see the whole, not just the parts.

We didn't initiate a comprehensive plan for the future with a blueprint for tackling all the key community issues. We looked for a head pin, a target, through which interconnected work could get a foothold and push the vision out from there.

By aiming at the headpin, the other nine pins can fall without sending any more balls down the lane.

The development of a successful and vibrant cultural destination was an evolutionary and dynamic process. Having a concrete target for action, which served as a platform for vision-organizing, was catalytic. With Market Creek, that catalyst was a 10-acre industrial dump. Site control gave JCNI the ability to do planning in an open community forum and protect the integrity of the planning process. Once the listening, planning, and designing were underway and visible signs of change began to emerge, the vision could then be constantly reviewed and, more importantly, renewed and pushed out to a more and more dynamic place.

When brought into the planning, residents built a vision of their future and the belief that they can make a difference. When able to implement the change efforts, they built skills that could be used beyond the project. And by owning the underlying asset, they not only benefited from it financially but developed a deep sense of pride and responsibility for the success of community change efforts across the Diamond Neighborhoods.

Our headpin was a grocery. Through that grocery, community teams would work on job creation, access to fresh foods, local entrepreneurship, waterway restoration, brownfield clean-up, childcare enhancement, contracting skills development, arts and culture, public safety, land planning, asset-building, and leadership development.

3) Make Fun

"In many communities, civic life — from the city council chambers to the block club meeting room — can be a foreign, even hostile environment for the average person," wrote Bill Traynor, "ruled by cynicism and division, and dominated by entrenched habits of isolation and detachment."[137]

Anyone who has ever sat in on a public hearing, endured the outbursts, complaints, and disruptions, will break out in hives just thinking about civic voice.

Bill has been around many a block. He has been a voice for doing more than just reforming "the supply-side institutions to be more engaged and responsive to residents," contending that that won't solve much. "We need to address the "demand-side," he noted. "Fewer voices, fewer different voices," he writes, "sporadic action, and the inability to generate genuine representative samples of both, constitutes a market failure in the classic sense."

Part of removing the barriers to community change, he asserts in his article "Building Community in Place: Limitations and Promise," is finding ways "to entice people to step back into public life in a way that feels safe, fun and productive."

When I read his article back in 2007, the word "fun" popped out. I'd read a lot about safe and productive, but rarely heard anyone talk about fun. Fun, I had been contending, was highly under-rated as a critical tool for community change, which in the field of philanthropy is like trying to explain to the principal, who believes you deserve detention, that playing hooky had been a productive learning experience.

"Community building is not all business; it's not even mostly business. It is relationship building and the business flows from the strength and the patterns of relationships that are built," Bill wrote. It doesn't start in meetings; it starts with eating and talking.

In addition to the act of building community externally, our internal community also needed the power of fun. "Creative people run best on the high-octane fuels of play and freedom..." writes John Kao in Jamming.[138] To endure the process of change, people need to be given permission to create, to improvise, to fly, and to let their minds capture a million new connections.

We needed to be able to exist in an environment that kept us energized, attracted others to the work, and allowed us to enter toxic-free zones of celebration and fun. Building relationships helped us transcend roles. Dancing, breaking bread, and sharing music did more than just grow appreciation of history and heritage. They broke tension, released the day's defeats, built connection, and lifted spirits. This fun and connection was what kept people coming back. They were what made us want to wake up, dust off, start over, look forward.

Love, laughter, celebration, fun, joy — these are things that magnetize and drive us to inspired action over a long period of time.

Especially during periods of turbulence, confusion, or when we felt our backs were against the wall, we would find our North Star, our Polaris, in our teamwork and the fun we had as friends — what Chip called our "crazy fun." In these moments, our release came from laughter so loud we thought we would get kicked out of restaurants. When emotions were running high, it didn't take much — usually just Roque cracking a joke — to make me laugh until I cried.

4) Be Personal

"You were successful because you didn't take it personally, don't you think?"

Angela Glover Blackwell, CEO of PolicyLink at the time and a great mentor and role model, always seemed to stop me with her seemingly simple comments and questions. Then they would keep me up for nights trying to understand all the nuances and deeper messages tucked in my conversations with her.

"It sure felt personal," I responded quickly. But then I began my mulling.

It was true that I tried to see and understand hard moments about race or gender in the context of the history that brought us to these moments. Being white, I knew I represented the whole history of race in America when

I walked in a community meeting. Working for a charitable foundation, I knew I represented the whole history of class, power, and control.

On the flip side of power, as a woman, I knew I would be demeaned in subtle, and sometimes not so subtle, ways by men in banking, finance, and construction — both partners and community team members. In the community, people often assumed I was the CEO's secretary; outside the community, I was on the receiving end of comments like my not needing to "worry my little head about the financial structure for the loans."

These complicated moments about the history of racism, sexism, power and privilege that happened every day were both personal and not personal.

Many an article has been written about why you shouldn't take things personally, allowing someone to question what you feel or believe or who you are, giving up what you know is true about yourself. I understood this side of not wanting to take things personally, the emotional reactions that pull you away from who you are or suck you into other people's dramas, getting our buttons pushed, or being drawn into feeling insult, blame, and shame. My generation was trained to maintain professional, emotional, even social distance. But I also knew that those of in my generation who grew up in white privilege have been allowed to maintain emotional distance and have not had to own our racial history in America, from the mass genocide of Native Americans to the extreme brutality of slavery to the terrorism of Jim Crow.

Do we become complicit in genocide, brutality, and terrorism if we don't own the history and work to understand how it still plays out for people today? My journey with the Jacobs Family Foundation launched with the Rodney King acquittal, bringing the issue of police brutality into every living room in America, and two decades later, was bookended with the killing of an unarmed black teenager in Ferguson igniting right before our eyes.

Should we be taking this personally?

Between those bookends was the 2001 protest that disrupted at the New World of Welfare Conference. This convening included some of the biggest names in the welfare debate but didn't include a single welfare recipient; I should say not one that was formally invited.

"Were it not for the presence of Anderson [a single mom in the workfare program who came anyway] and about 100 other grassroots activists and welfare recipients," reported Z Magazine, "it would have been easy to envision the national dialogue about welfare reform as one of glowing agreement over the success of the 1996 measure that changed the nature of welfare as we knew it." As one conference attendee observed, "it is clear that many of their conclusions were reached by simply crunching data, without ever actually speaking to anyone on welfare."[139] Protesters wanted success defined by the reduction in poverty, not a drop in the welfare rolls.

In this position, I knew that in the hard or even harsh moments, people needed to be heard and they needed to know I was willing to be confronted, even if — no, especially if — it challenged my worldview.

Tamara Copeland, President of the Washington Regional Association of Grantmakers, in her powerful op-ed in the Chronicle of Philanthropy article "Philanthropy Must Understand Racism Is Not Dead" noted: "Philanthropists must recognize that no matter how laudable many of their grants, they will not reduce disparities in employment or wealth if they do not grapple with the unconscious, culturally ingrained, bias and racism that undergirds our society."[140]

We believed that racism needed to be acknowledged and discussed and that until that happened we would not be able to address the major contributor to the inequities in health, housing, jobs, pay, and assets.

For me both personally and professionally, I needed to deeply understand the impact of the history of racism and be willing to face it — in my own life as a white person experiencing white privilege, in the context of philanthropy as a structure of power and privilege, and as a citizen of a country that is racially polarized. In addition to me engaging in a way that I thought would improve race relations, we needed a team that could work across culture, have conversations about race, be willing to address racial and political polarization, and be comfortable bringing other funders and resource partners into the conversation.

"The secret to this issue of race is it can't be just the brown people talking it about," noted Doris Anderson, in reflecting on the Market Creek experience. "We have to broaden the conversation. That's what you brought into the room. You brought that voice into that room because you were willing to talk about it, and when you talk about it, you can begin to deal with it openly and honestly. It takes all of us doing that. You were trying to get a lot of people across San Diego having that discussion. That was unique for our community."

Over time, I came to see that the only way to address the "not-personal" part of the history that brings us to these moments is to make it all personal. Because we all work out of long-held beliefs, it is easy to target "the problem" as anyone other than ourselves. The very personal nature of the relationships on the teams made it difficult to dismiss that our own approach or belief system might actually be the problem, or at least part of the problem.

Easing the learning moments related to race, class, gender, and sector (there was also a deep disdain for "systems" and a belief that all "systems" are stacked against the people who live in disinvested communities) was by knowing people personally. We couldn't just disregard each other.

Being personal changed everything.

5) Stay "Centered"

Gus Newport, like Joe, was a man of messages. Our team called them "Gus-isms."

"To go fast, you have to go slow... No one of us can do what all of us can do... Don't discredit the resource that is right in front of you — find the beaver."

When we were struggling to figure out where to start, how to build resident teams, and how to blend so many perspectives, Gus was our soothsayer. Over time, it was these simple Gus-isms, most often captured in simple stories and vignettes, that became our guiding principles for community change.

"What do you mean 'find a beaver'?" I asked Gus, stumped. This had to be good, I thought.

"It came from a Tennessee backwoodsman," Gus shared. "He said 'find a beaver and see how they do it.' If you want to build a dam, there's your resource!"

Gus had been a part of the start-up of the Dudley Street Neighborhood Initiative in Roxbury, Massachusetts, serving as its second director, before working with other neighborhood strengthening collaboratives around the country. During a meeting in Florida on the fundamentals of community organizing and raising the voice of residents in revitalization efforts, an engineer who was moved by the discussion shared a story about working for the Tennessee River Authority when the first dam was being planned.

"We were surveying, testing, studying, and being challenged by the conditions in front of us when this backwoodsman came up to me," the engineer shared, "and said 'find a beaver! Just throw in a beaver! Beaver are experts at knowing how and where to build dams. They know how to work in teams to find the best and safest place, and they'll know the best way to protect the waterway.' He was right."

In sharing the beaver story with Gus, the engineer and the backwoodsman expanded the list of "Gus-isms" that would guide our work.

"We have a history of discrediting the resources that are right in our midst," noted Gus. His comment reminded me of the game I used to play with our children when they were young — "Look up, look down, look all around" — to help them become more observant, see more fully their surroundings, and expose hidden treasure.

We had to learn to keep our eyes open for the resource right in front of us and let go of our preconceived notions about what might or should work. To do that, we had to let go of any highly-charged meaning we wanted to pack into labels — conservative/liberal; for-profit/non-profit; rich/poor; educated/uneducated — the labels that pigeonhole and polarize people.

If we were going to become skilled at blending disparate world views, there wasn't a better set of teachers than Gus Newport in the same room with Joe Jacobs.

"My friends tell me they can't believe I'm hanging out with a communist!" Joe would laugh. He was a consummate conservative, a true believer in the free enterprise system. Gus's election as the mayor of Berkeley, California, was cited in the Encyclopedia of the American Left in 1992 as a victory for black candidates with ties to the Communist Party.

These two men would challenge each other in marvelous and meaty exchanges, valuing each other's ideas and enjoying the fun of the intellectual debate. Then they would embrace each other having arrived at some new place. I loved listening to their banter, the razzing, the jokes, along with the thoughtful, challenging, provocative discussions.

These conversations taught me that differences matter, and that when discourse is respectful and people are hungry to learn from each other, those differences hold the key to community change.

During the early days of working on Market Creek, I used to think it would be so much easier to intentionally polarize people. You can hold a strong point of view. It's clear. It's arguable. You can harness a set of principles, reports, examples, illustrations, and stories that back up your belief. No one really needs to listen to each other; you just need to be able to get your point of view out on the airwaves.

But listening is truly hard. You have to suspend your worldview long enough to hear what someone else is saying. You have to embrace it as a gift. Then you can open up the two-way back-and-forth of a meaningful conversation. And if the conversations that need to be had are hard and sensitive, you also have to suspend your reactions to how messages are being delivered so you don't miss the meaning. The hardest messages matter most.

We had to be acutely aware not to shut down a conversation or debate. Wait until folks arrived at a new place. Be patient with the process of getting on the same page, knowing that "to go fast you had to go slow," as Gus would have said. Tell critics or people with concerns to 'bring it on'. Keep our hearts open to hearing.

We needed to keep the work "centered," assuring that:

- The work stayed in the center of the for-profit and non-profit worlds — one focused on individual benefit and profit and one focused on democratic process, community benefit, and joint action;
- All decisions were made in the "center of the room," no decisions were made independently without residents, and everyone knew the decisions that were being made;
- All action planning was done at the center of social, economic, physical, and political development to keep these dynamics in balance; and
- Problem-solving was based on the both/and, not the either/or.

Working under a microscope of highly-charged dynamics around race, class, and gender made me increasingly self-aware. "What's a white girl like you doing in a place like this," I was asked more than once. Asked by residents, leaders of community organizations, and ministers. I'm also blonde (well, now white-haired), so I stood out. In addition, working around so many male-dominated disciplines — development, construction, banking, revitalization, politics — I was always aware of being a woman, as well as being a white person representing a white philanthropic family in a whole field that at that time was largely white and largely led by men.

In the face of these dynamics, I also had to stay "centered" in my leadership in every sense of the word:

- Taking feedback and criticism openly. Having to think about it deeply. Sort through it. Contextualize it. Understand it.
- Not deflecting the moments that trigger around race but seeing these as moments of personal learning.
- Waiting to be reflective before responding, except to say 'let me make sure I hear you.' Knowing that in the middle of a personal attack, in an emotional moment, I wasn't going to make good decisions.
- Staying focused on my belief and optimism that the world is capable of change, including me.

I used to kid Joe that I was going to produce a video called "Buns of Steel" and it wasn't going to be an exercise video. It would be the making of Market Creek Plaza and would show me getting my butt kicked from every direction. He would smile, tickled. "Good for you," he would say.

6) Break It Down

"We have an integration issue."

The residents in the room were aghast. We all thought we had done so well at creating diverse teams.

"No," said Kurt Kicklighter laughing. As the securities lawyer for the IPO, he was always check-pointing the team planning. "We need to be very careful that this offering doesn't look like it's being integrated with another!"

Kurt and the Ownership Design Team spent a year breaking down the offering documents into plain English. We all learned that what sounded like a reference to Jamaican music — Reggae — was really "Reg A," a regulation that governed the sale of securities — Regulation A. This world of "back-end pops" and "puts" became a hey-day for wisecracks that kept us laughing. We kept a glossary that read like a joke book.

By the end, our "IPO Illustrated" was simple and clear. Concepts were defined and literally illustrated. But much more importantly, we had taken a legal document and through this process had created a community development tool. It was a hybrid blend of the non-profit and for-profit worlds. It captured people's desires for a collective investment that could strengthen the community and benefit its residents. A capitalist structure of stockholders but governance of one member one vote. No one could have more power than anyone else.

Without this time taken, we would have had a document, not a deeply-cared-about structure. And it would have been a document few people could have read.

All materials were translated into different languages. But as or more important was the translation of all planning documents, proformas, policies, process outlines, and reports into simple, accessible, and rapidly-understood language. This process of breaking things down made the work doable and kept the work in alignment.

Like a big algebra problem, we kept reducing everything to its simplest form, to its ah-ha, to the clearest path through to accomplishment. Because all work was accessible to all people, it didn't have to become fragmented.

In the end, I came to believe breaking things down ultimately kept them from breaking apart.

7) Look for the Clearing

I was in a small plane, a puddle-jumper from Monterey. Storms were rolling in and 20 minutes into our flight, the turbulence was nerve-racking. I dug my nails into the armrest and practiced deep breathing. I have rarely been afraid on a flight, but this one was different. Our plane was being tossed around like a rickety roller coaster and it seemed unending. Were we safe? Would we land? Will we come through this storm? That's all I could think of as we made our way down the coast.

Then the clearing. We emerged from the clouds to the lights of Los Angeles below. It was the most beautiful sight — more brilliant than ever, sparkling in the dark.

Trying to secure the financing, finalize agreements with the redevelopment agency, get a mixed-use zone, gain approval for the IPO, or working with the business owners, it was often turbulent. Each major roadblock or shift in the economy was experienced with stressful impact. We were constantly hitting obstacles. We were up, then down. Then up again. And whether it was any one of the individual businesses getting stuck or the transitions experienced by the various teams as they completed a set of benchmarks and struggled to find the next agree-upon courses of action, we experienced the bumpy ride right alongside of them.

Sometimes four to six months at a time, we couldn't quite see where we were heading, we couldn't decide whether or not to push, and we didn't know how aggressively to move.

Would the natural momentum of the teams, blocked in one area, take off in another? Could we let discussions about barriers go on long enough that people would figure out how to go over or under what was standing in the way? If there were unfulfilled promises by partners, could we let the situation sit there long enough for another partner to take ownership of it? Where should we step in and where should we just hit the pause button and let things churn in order for a higher level of creativity to emerge?

And in these moments of turbulence, my role was to assure everyone that we would find the clearing.

Overtime, I learned to be OK with not seeing the shore, knowing that turbulence, disruption, and confusion were the nurturing ground for break-through. We knew that innovation was inspired by a culture of openness, vulnerability, humanness, and teamwork, where people had the time to get below the surface. And we came to understand that the very dynamic of turbulence and confusion were what was causing change to happen.

Coming to understand this cyclical and natural rotation of energy was important. One team member called it "the dance of chaos," and I came to appreciate "the dance" as periods of enormous creativity and to think of it, not as chaos, but as the "leap-phase." These periods were when confusion led us to a new land more amazing than the shore we left.

If we can, most of us would rather fly around a storm than through it. It's our human nature. Being able to fly in turbulence tests our ability to breathe deeply, stay relaxed, and keep our minds focused on the meaning of "now" and power of "destination." If we fly in turbulence enough, we come to appreciate all that we carry from our past to this moment in time and learn to have confidence that beyond the fog, wind, and rain, there will be a clearing.

And like the fog, wind, and rain, which can't be controlled and yet are important to our lives, the tension and confusion inherent in the interplay of diverse views are not challenges that need to be "fixed" in order to get work done. They actually cause the work to get done by providing the creative force for breakthrough.

At the heart of community change are the underlying and deep-seeded issues of race, class, power, gender, and bias of all kinds that lead to hurt, anger, and disrespect. If we don't engage, work together on shared goals, and stay at the table during the turbulence that arises from these deep-seeded issues, there will never be a clearing.

During turbulence — when I most wanted to give direction to go back to the last place we had refueled, to have a solution, to give an answer — I learned to convene the team, name the next set of contradictions and barriers together, and keep focused on articulating the next set of questions.

In understanding my role in this emotionally-charged ecosystem of change, I had to learn to take deep breaths, relax, forgive (myself and others), keep my mind focused on the meaning of "now" and the power of "destination," and assure people that this "leap-phase" is occurring specifically because we are ready to find the next shore.

"This was breakthrough work and there wasn't any manual. It felt scary — like we were trying to build a plane while flying in it," reflected Max Zaker, a Jacobs Team member. "But given where it started, the fact that at some point we could walk around a commercial center was nothing short of a miracle," he noted. "I left with more in my heart than when I came."

8) "Own" Up

When I shut my eyes and remember back...the scene opens with a board room. The room is dimmed to showcase the report on the screen. I know my stuff. I am the expert brought into the room and because of my position — being paid by the chairman of a billion-dollar company to be there—and I am wrapped in my own sense of professional privilege. I know exactly what's wrong and what will work.

Then the lights come up. And I am stopped in my tracks.

In the next scene, my being enamored of my own strategic thinking is jarred awake, and there is a young woman staring me in the face. In the hallway, I stumble to find words. "But...but..."

I am certain that I have just done exactly what people wanted me to do, and in that moment, I begin to reach for all of the excuses I can think of to justify myself. But from the look on her face, I had clearly missed the mark. I had unintentionally marginalized her in the meeting and just from the look on her face, she had mustered the courage to let that be known.

"I am so sorry," I said.

I was touched that she trusted me enough to share the truth. I had monopolized the presentation and removed her ability to have a voice and share the significant role she had had in uncovering the solution. This moment created an opening for us to sit down together and share our stories, drop our roles, expose our feelings, and dig for insights. Smart, open, talented, and willing to take a risk — this woman would become the symbol for me of how easy it is to diminish people as the recipients of our expert knowledge and what incredible gifts are lost in the process — lessons I would carry me throughout my career.

On some days I would laugh and think: "Courageous philanthropy means always having to say you are sorry!" This was only one of many apologies that would be a part of my journey to own my own change.

"Compassion becomes real when we recognize our shared humanity," notes Brené Brown in her book, The Gifts of Imperfection. "The fear of being perceived as unworthy is enough to force us to silence our stories." People want to share themselves, but there is an uncertainty that is caused when they think 'experts' won't understand. As Brené so beautifully writes, we need to share our stories to bring us courage, compassion, and connection. We need to share our own vulnerability to bring us closer to the truth about what and who needs to change and how that change should occur. And because we are slow to develop trust and quick to lose it, there is nothing more powerful than an apology. People who feel heard and respected are able to come back from hurt and re-engage.

When we believe we are the only ones to feel vulnerable, we are alone. For community work to be transformational, we must all show our vulnerability — because that changes everything.

"A good belly laugh, singing at the top of your lungs, and dancing like no one is looking are unquestionably good for the soul,"[141] Brené shares, and we created those opportunities for people. But "I'm sorry" can also create a release valve for whatever insecurity, hurt or harm people experience, and it had to be part of our practice.

When we think that ownership is about land and that change is about "those people out there," we are dead-on-arrival. We have already lost the opportunity to create enduring change.

Ownership is about each of us — and that started with me and my ability to listen and "own" up when I was off course, unclear, jumping to conclusions, or just plain wrong.

9) Refuse to be Defeated

"What <u>can</u> you build in a waterway?"

The Army Corps of Engineers would not give us a permit to build an amphitheater stage in the creek bed. Market Creek Plaza was built on a challenging site, long and narrow with a creek cutting it in half and the trolley cutting it off from one of the critical streets.

Joe Jacobs rarely drove his personal agenda, but he loved Chollas Creek. As part of the project development, the creek was taken out of its old concrete channels, opened up to become a 150-foot greenbelt, and restored with natural vegetation.

The community wanted a performance venue at the heart of their village and the only place to put the stage was in the creek, using the natural slope of the banks for seating, which the Army Corps policy prohibited.

"I'll send you to Washington to lobby the Army Corps," Joe offered.

There were many days that I'd find myself chuckling that if I hadn't heard that question "What <u>can</u> you put in a waterway" I might still be in Washington lobbying the Army Corps of Engineers! But in team meetings it was often the person that you least expected who would suddenly offer up the comment or question that would turn heads.

People started throwing out ideas: a barge, a dock, and before the next suggestion was put on the table, I could see Chip Buttner, our developer, light up. He could already see it. We decided to engineer the stage as a dock.

Over time, our team developed two mantras: 1) if you can't go over it, go under it; and 2) if it needs to float, build a dock. We did both — literally.

With Joe's directive to figure out how to keep moving, the culture of our teamwork was focused at all times on doing whatever it took to not get stuck. Name the barrier. Be clear about what is really in the way. We would always remind each other to remember that if "conventional wisdom" had the answer, our communities wouldn't be in this situation. We had to train ourselves to listen carefully to everyday people, not just experts, as they asked their questions.

Joe believed that greatness is only achieved by risking failure. His eyes lit up at every problem we encountered. His example inspired our team to believe we could will the impossible into being, and we embraced it as a labor of love. As more and more residents joined the working teams, a sense of resourcefulness and abundance began to overtake the sense of hopelessness and despair that had hung over the blight.

We stayed the course and refused to be defeated.

When construction companies wouldn't work with community contractors, we became the construction company, and in a city that shamefully let only 2 percent of its contracts to historically under-utilized business enterprises (HUBE), our community-building team's outreach and bidding process resulted in 74 percent of the contracts going to minority- and women-owned businesses.

When the Public Utilities Commission wouldn't give us access to the site over trolley tracks that blocked it, we decided to tunnel in under them. When the cost to reroute the trolley was prohibitive, we asked to shut down trolley for the weekend, and built a bridge in 19 hours, winning four engineering awards with our new method for bridge construction.

When the initial renderings of the commercial buildings weren't what people envisioned ("the off-white, square-box buildings looked too European," residents commented), the architect teamed with cultural artists and started over.

When the banks wouldn't finance the project, we studied every tool to come out of HUD and the Department of the Treasury. When there was still no tool that worked, Joe suggested using his stock as collateral so we didn't lose the grocery contract. When the New Markets Tax Credit program was launched, we were first in line to use the new tool and released Joe's stock.

When it was proposed by the Art and Design Team to put 16-foot-square frames on the side of the Food 4 Less grocery to hold portraits depicting unsung resident heroes, they immediately collapsed after being hung. We reconstructed them, making them stronger, and got them up just minutes before the unveiling ceremony, where 500 close friends and family of the honorees, artists, and youth storyteller/biographers gathered for a red carpet celebration.

When a community contractor accidentally striped the crosswalk prior to our securing the permit for the traffic light — leaving us vulnerable to a lawsuit — residents manned the site until the inspector arrived for final review.

When we wanted to "go public" and take ownership full circle, and the Department of Corporations regulations didn't allow us to sell shares of the project to residents, we drafted a permit application that addressed the regulations. When we didn't get approval, we waited until we were out of the high-risk stage of development and reapplied. When we still didn't get approved, we carefully researched the law and laid out a plan that showed that even if we didn't meet the current regulations, we met the intent of the law. Six years after the first application, preparing to be turned down again, we received the permit to go public.

By the time Market Creek Plaza was completed — a project we experienced as a million things going wrong — it had won 13 awards, including the EPA's Outstanding Brownfield Transformation, the ULI Social Equity Award, the International Economic Development Council's Excellence in Real Estate Development and Reuse, the International Association of Business Communicators Helios Award for the video documenting the "Community Faces" Art Project, the American Society of Civil Engineers Award of Merit for the gateway underpass, and the Council on Foundations' Critical Impact Award for innovative and bold solutions to enhance the public good.

Throughout this experience, when things went wrong, we redoubled our effort, called in reinforcements, and refused to be defeated. Many of these moments led to our greatest innovations.

10) Leap and the Net Will Appear

"We had a lot of stubborn people and you issued a challenge," reflected Joe Vasquez, who served on the board of the Elementary Institute of Science during its youth-driven multi-million-dollar campaign. "Working with you was like lining up along a cliff and being told to hold hands because we are going to jump!" he chuckled. "The odds against us doing what we did were enormous — higher than enormous."

"You can't be that kid standing at the top of the waterslide, overthinking it. You have to go down the chute," I chirped, using Tina Fey's line from Bossypants.[142]

In the Elementary Institute of Science campaign, the youth leadership was "magic," as Joe Vasquez noted. This team of young people wasn't afraid of the cliff. "The adults were busy saying 'this is going to be hard' and the youth didn't care about that. So often we lose that spirit of risk-taking and adventure. We had to risk a commitment."

Entrepreneurs risk action. They are able to live with uncertainty and tenaciously and passionately drive themselves. They respond quickly to market conditions or they create a market that doesn't currently exist. They are rule-breakers who defy conventional wisdom. If they fail, they start over.[143] Being a quintessential entrepreneur, Joe Jacobs created an organizational culture in which everyone was encouraged to risk commitment.

Within this culture, our team could aim at a new future and break free from an institutional construct created 100 years ago that keeps intact the power dynamics of wealth and control. We could value flexibility over feasibility, knowing that change wasn't going to happen in a straight line. Hardwiring only our values — respect, responsibility, relationship, and risk — we could look at every other aspect of the work with fresh eyes, from roles and responsibilities to structure and strategy to policies and resources.

We could create a solid infrastructure for civic action that was cross-disciplinary, stay open and transparent, and use participatory planning to achieve leveraged action. We could work in teams with a high level of diversity, supporting resident capacity-building in specialized areas, but mix up the composition of the teams for holistic planning.

We could work with groups to identify and call out the contradictions blocking the work by making sure these were named and informed by the participation and inclusion of stakeholders broadly defined. We could risk action, targeting the most catalytic opportunity to move teams toward their vision.

We could work like we were training for a marathon, even if we had to run in sprints, keeping our eye on the long term, but acting on short-term goals so visible signs of change fed momentum.

We could make peace with paradox, seeing opposing forces as necessary and complementary and going after the both/and rather than either/or.

Within this culture, we had to own it — in every sense of the word. We couldn't get caught thinking change was 'out there.' If we wanted to be part of this team whose purpose was change, we had to be willing to risk our own.

And lastly, we had to be willing to trust the process — "leap and the net will appear," as the Zen saying goes. If we had prepared and packed, at some point we just needed to part with the cliff.

The rest was all about trusting the leap.

26

EAT - STAY - LOVE

"And that is how change happens.
One gesture. One person. One moment at a time."[144]

— Libba Bray, <u>The Sweet Far Thing</u>

The Secret to Success

"In the end, maybe it's wiser to surrender before the miraculous scope of human generosity and to just keep saying thank you, forever and sincerely, for as long as we have voices."[145]

In 2010, I watched the movie <u>Eat Pray Love</u>. From Italy, to India, and ending in Indonesia, Elizabeth Gilbert's journey unfolded. It was the search for balance. Reigniting the surge of the memoir on screen, Elizabeth herself seemed genuinely surprised by the blockbuster response to her book and follow-on movie.

A year later, when someone asked me what the secret to success is in long-term community change, all I could think to say was "eat, stay, love." Not as a parody of <u>Eat Pray Love</u>, but as the underlying truth of enduring change, in every sense of the word enduring.

For 20 years in the Diamond Neighborhoods, I had journeyed around the world in a city block and experienced the "miraculous scope of human generosity," from rent parties to celebratory money trees to people bringing food to feed the spirit of people in need. In the search for what had staying power and for the energy and endurance to lift up inspired action in the face of all odds, it came down to these three things:

1. *Eat* — we must break out of roles by breaking bread together. To do this is to build a bond by coming together in the community kitchen. This allows us to:

   - express and celebrate culture and ground us in the strength of our heritage;
   - understand the healing nature of food and the act of giving that is the preparing and sharing of food;
   - see food as a symbol of equity and justice.

2. *Stay* — we must think about this work like we would our own journeys with all life's ups and downs, mustering the courage to dust off every day no matter what goes wrong. This allows us to:

   - discover the power of trust that rises up from real relationships;
   - build a platform for surfacing real barriers, testing ideas that may fail, and fail again — ultimately achieving breakthrough;
   - see failures and setbacks as moments in time that we can change, appreciating the journey as much as the destination.

3. *Love* — we must fall in love with the commitment, spirit, risk-taking, and courage of people to imagine their boldest dream of the future and realize we are in this together. This allows us to:

   - believe in and appreciate each other's gifts;
   - forgive and find value in human connections;
   - unearth a regenerating source of energy, strength, and courage.

This was the Market Creek experience.

Breaking Bread

"BBQ — always a favorite!" Lefaua Leilua, her wavy black hair held back from her face with a pink plumeria flower, was talking about the menu for the VOCAL convening. The room was full of amazing smells that night tempting us to the table of cultural foods.

I had never tasted roasted taro, the light purple potato-like tropical root vegetable with a sweet nutty flavor. "It's a staple in cooking back home," Lefaua noted, referring to her homeland, Samoa. I had never had many of the foods that residents would share at these gatherings. My favorites would become the long-grain sticky rice from the Laotian community, so sweet, and the Samoan Sapa Sui, the cellophane noodles stirred with soy sauce, chicken, cabbage, onions, and ginger.

"When the training kitchen opened, we taught the chef how to prepare the pineapple pie," Lefaua gleamed. Members of each of the cultural groups had shared a menu and taught the head chef to prepare their special foods.

For big occasions, like Unity Night, the annual Arts and Culture Fest, or the individual cultural celebrations, the groups took responsibility for preparing food themselves to share in celebration — Sudanese Kop, a ball of meat and vegetables with gravy; Chamorro Madoya, the sweet lightly battered and fried bananas; Somali spiced tea with its distinct cardamom, cinnamon and cloves; the Filipino lumpia, the fried spring-roll with sweet and spicy dipping sauce; and Champurrado, a thick hot Mexican chocolate drink. The Samoan team would roast a pig and serve it with their tangy pineapple pie.

There is a power in breaking bread together. We connect through food. Preparing food is an act of giving and a magnet for gathering. It is about hope and sustenance. The "comfort foods" of our childhood tell the story of a place, an age, a climate, our access to ingredients, our human creativity. As families and extended families, it is how we come together, how we celebrate, how we nurture our traditions. This is the family kitchen. It builds community.

"I knew everyone had different religions, cultures, world views, dressed differently, spoke differently, ate different foods, but it didn't matter. You just got this feeling of everyone's humanness," noted Macedonio Arteaga, who was a part of the VOCAL team. "We all have so many fears and stereotypes about people, and you can't get rid of them. This sharing just melted them away."

"It was special to meet so many different people," Sergio Gonzalez reflected in his introspective way about the Market Creek experience beyond his work at Writerz Blok. "When I was growing up, all I knew were Mexicans. But learning to embrace different people, open up and taste each other's food — I began to appreciate what it took for people to be here." Sergio shook his head thinking about what the Somali and Sudanese endured in their homelands with a sense of marvel that people were able to arrive together at this special place. "I call these people my family because we did this together."

In addition to food as tradition, culture, and connection, there is the sharing of food as an act of care and healing. And in a world scarred by long-term negative health impacts on children and families living in disinvested urban neighborhoods, there is also food as a symbol of human equity and justice.

Diane Moss, after years of working on the issues of teen pregnancy, began focusing her efforts on improving access to healthy food and now facilitates a community garden and farmers market. In sharing about the Market Creek experience, she reminded me of the many meetings that started with Macedonio Arteaga offering an acknowledgement to Mother Earth for giving us nourishment, moments like the Loa monks requesting permission to inhabit this land as a sacred place of giving, and the youth at the Elementary Institute of Science discovering the power of planting seeds. "You can tell the people who care about the seeds they sow and those that don't," Diane noted.

Today, she commits her days to fresh food activism and changing the delivery system from seed to table. "I grew up in Compton and wasn't exposed to the idea of food justice. I just thought you get what you get. But now I see abandoned lots as assets."

Having lived in communities where liquor stores substituted for groceries making wholesome foods difficult to find, Diane liked to talk about the symbolism of food in the Market Creek experience: "I related our work together as a community to food. The way your team chose to do things was different. There was no sugar coating things. You were open and consistent. It set a standard for things being resident-based and for placing value in the gifts and knowledge people brought to the table. There is food security and there is food sovereignty," she continued. "They are different. In one you get your needs met; in the other you are in control. This experience made me feel like I was part of an historical moment."

The Test of Time

"The hell with transparency! We want accountability! One means I can see you. The other means you are responsible in your work with us." Robert Tambuzi was a resident, an activist, and a philosopher. He wasn't going to be played, as he would put it. "That dog ain't going to hunt."

I had grown to love Tambuzi's special ability for insight meshed with shock value. With so much negative history between communities and philanthropy, someone needed the courage to call it out, and he could always be counted on. Being fully accountable to each other is deeply rooted in trust, and that, unfortunately, is something hard to come by in community development and philanthropy.

"A lot of people came before you," Doris Anderson, who led the Elementary Institute of Science (EIS), noted, reflecting on Tambuzi's expletive. "There is always this suspicion that is deeply rooted about anyone coming in." Her role at EIS had been powerful in clearing a space for us to start the process of developing trust. Many residents expressed how much our relationship with the Elementary Institute of Science had influenced them to give us a chance to earn their trust.

"In this world you don't get a chance to have a relationship with a funder; it's just not what happens," Doris remarked. "But I had a history of watching you engage the young people, being respectful of them, and building relationships. I tried to pose as a possibility that it might be different this time, hold some space for things to happen, judge on actions instead of perceptions."

In the history of community revitalization, there are countless examples of foundation initiatives — including a few of our own — where stakeholders, not invited into full participation, didn't have the chance to build trust, creating a dynamic where efforts were resisted or blocked. Change was never achieved. The only way to prove we would be responsible and accountable in our relationship with the community was to keep our promise: to work in partnership, to operationalize respect as the central value, to listen carefully, to do with not for, to keep our word, and to stay.

Residents know all too well that foundation and government initiatives start and stop, start and stop. People "go home." And the decisions to stop are generally made by a very small group who perceive things aren't working or just because the grant ends. Time's up.

But for the residents, this is home. To be embraced as neighbors on a platform of joint action, we needed to stay — no matter what went wrong.

Trust takes time and the lack of trust is one thing that can stop change in its tracks. To build it requires real relationships, not just institutional ties or professional position.

"Because God didn't give us the power of telepathy, we have to figure things out," Tambuzi commented. "What do they want from us?" He sat back in his chair and shook his head in his distinctive way of alerting me to prepare for a pronouncement.

"And because you represent a culture that has been traditionally oppressive, coming into communities and selling reverse mortgages and crap, distrust comes with the territory. We got white folks coming in here talking about the idea of a community-owned project! That was alien to people! In people's minds, a corporation that means profit means screwing with people. It means the armed and relentless pursuit of power and profit."

Then he sat back up to the table and paused for a moment of reflection. "Changing that was what the 20 years was about! The time it took for a bunch of cultures to get along. People can't pretend that would have just happened. That was relational. We had to figure each other out, see if we could even stand being in the same room with each other."

Tambuzi's "we had to figure each other out" was probably an understatement, but today, Tambuzi is proud that together we stood the test of time. "I can still remember our first meeting," he shared. "I was Special Assistant to then Deputy Major George Stevens, and we met at Kansas City Barbeque to talk about the idea of the IPO." Neither one of us knew then, as we were trying to "figure each other out" over barbecue how long it would take to bring the idea of the IPO to fruition, but he would become one of the original members of the Ownership Design Team and one of the IPO's biggest advocates, seeing it through the time it would take. By taking the time to incorporate the best thoughts, views and values of people working across cultures, we would transform a tool that was initially viewed as corrupt into an achievement for shared ownership and an inclusive economy.

And he was absolutely right — "that was relational."

As a community organizer, Roque Barros had spent the early years of our work in community change getting "jacked-up" by people focused only on the money. He had to use the power of his personality — his engaging and challenging mode of questioning people about who they were and what they cared about. "You can't just jump right into work if people haven't worked together before. You can't take on an issue, like dealing with the violence, before people even know each other, have personal relationships, and are comfortable. People want to know each other."

Whether or not we could measure the "realness" of a relationship, it mattered as a critical gauge of our ability to come together and tackle complex issues. To debate tough issues over what was valued, to figure out what needed to be changed or balanced, to sort out the either/or and the both/and, or to have to "own up" after hard moments, it mattered that our core team had these relationships. We were all good at "getting real." We were invited to people's anniversaries and birthday parties, participated in their cultural celebrations, sat in their living rooms, went to the funerals of those who were lost, knew the kids and grandkids, and danced together to Old School R&B on Friday nights.

As the Jacobs Center evolved into an outside-in organization with a high percentage of residents on the staff, the power of these relationships grew and deepened in interesting ways.

"Our street cred was strong," Jose Venegas noted in reflecting on the early work of forming Writerz Blok, the graffiti art park and social enterprise. "If something got tagged, we couldn't snitch, but we could say 'You need to stop this shit. You've been spotted and you're making us look bad.' People respected that. The Center could have approached the issue by hiring extra security guards, but you said 'let's get the kids and give them a place to paint.' Then it was up to us to get young people involved, keep them off the streets, and make our neighborhood safer."

Sandra Candler, who worked as one of ten residents on the Research Team that surveyed over 1,000 people about the formation of the Neighborhood Unity Foundation, took the work of trust-building personally. "I not only got to meet so many great people in my community, but when we got back to the office, we would think — our faces are out there! Folks are counting on us to put their comments in this report word for word. They were very sensitive about filtering information and about wanting us to get back to them. They told us they had had so many people come and research and never get back to them. When we did, it was heart-warming. People really appreciated it."

These relationships mattered. In a professionalized world where experience is often defined by college degrees and other credentials, this "street cred," as Jose framed it, was paramount and took priority.

"When Ms. Meschak, who was a fighter and had been in the community for 70 years, said to me 'What makes you think this will be any different than before,' all I could answer was 'because it's me and I'm going to keep my word.' That was our cornerstone," noted Sandra. "It didn't matter what bumps in the road we hit, we promised people and we had to keep our word."

Who are you had to come before *what can we do together.*

"We live in a world that is wishy washy," continued Sandra. "If you can't be trusted then everything else means nothing. All of us tried to stick to that."

For trust, taking time mattered.

It was important that we started slow, moved at a pace that respected community process, deepened and broadened organizing efforts over time, and pushed for the full participation and planning of residents. We pushed deadlines for agreed-upon action but tried not to set unnatural multi-year timelines for achieving big outcomes so teams would be more likely to take risks and have time to adjust and course-correct as barriers were encountered.

Even though we started slow and gave people time to get to know each other and build trust and experience together, the "taking of time" is not always intuitive. Allowing the time to build relationships and bring residents into the process didn't mean that timelines weren't essential. We were in constant conversations about the dollar value of time, the deadlines on contracts that were critical to meet, and the need for momentum to be constantly building.

Assuming that highly engaged citizens working to improve their communities would take too long, JCNI's own development team and early resource partners were highly skeptical. But over the entire time, a community process never slowed down the development process. When projects stalled, it was largely due to the cumbersome process of securing public sector approvals, permits, and cooperation.

Because time was invested in creating an open process and grounding people's understanding, residents respected timelines and deadlines and could push phases to completion, such as permits and other public-sector processes. In many cases, the working teams could figure out how to get things done without outside support. These teams were able to secure a General Plan Amendment (a municipal requirement) and plan, design, build, and open a grocery on a former brownfield in three years — the time allotted by most developers just for the General Plan Amendment.

After trust, stick-to-it-ness was paramount.

"The system is designed to make you give up," Tasha Williamson noted. Her team worked on public safety issues and building a strong police-community relationship. "The biggest thing we learned was not to give up. People came together across differences and were a part of retreats to help with communication across cultures, and it worked. We would leave empowered and together and ready to be focused. Things didn't always work, but we would always try again."

In talking about what it took for a team of youth and adults to build the new Elementary Institute of Science, Doris Anderson noted: "we learned you had to stay the course."

"The boldness of this idea — I don't know what we were thinking!" Doris recalled with a laugh. "We didn't know where to begin and how to begin, or what steps to take; we just knew we needed to do something. Those first steps were scary. To raise money in those days you had to be in places that weren't used to seeing black people. We learned that if barriers were going to be broken down, we had to step up and make things work."

When they started, Doris and the board at the Elementary Institute of Science now reflect, they didn't know it would take so long. "Not knowing can be good!" Doris joked. "But we were prepared for the long haul. We knew it was not going to be easy. No one in our community had ever raised that kind of money before. The question for us, though, was never **if** but **when**. You said 'we will be there when you cut that ribbon' and what was amazing is that you actually were! It was surreal! You never let us take our eyes off the ball."

Time is a gift.

And in most non-operating grantmaking foundations, where staff are considered overhead, it is largely a gift that cannot be or just isn't given.

To have the time to know people, how they think, what their lives are like, what concerns they have for their families, and what is most valued in the debate over choices and the decisions guiding the development of their neighborhood, it became important that people knew we would be at the table, acting as neighbors for our lifespan without unnatural pressure to complete "neighborhood transformation" or "systems-change" in the face of such high hurdles on a timeline of our own making.

At the time the Market Creek experience was launched, the average length of time for a grant cycle was one year. In rare foundations, like the Annie E. Casey Foundation that had initiated Comprehensive Community Initiatives (CCIs), timeframes were just beginning to push out in the three-to-five-year range. It would be many years before Casey and others like The California Endowment pushed out to unprecedented 10-year efforts.

"Foundations often ask residents 'what do you want?' because they feel they ought to and then that evaporates with deadlines," reflected Bill Traynor. "Typically, foundations would rather get buy-in for their own ideas, have passive recipients, and control things. But how do people develop an instinct to look for and reveal and hold space for people? The questions we should be asking are: How do we get honest about what nurtures aspirational people? How do we create room for that to have value and impact? Is there value in having the co-investment of residents even if co-investment isn't easy?"

In the ecosystem of social change, the players desperately want to be in real relationships, but that requires time for careful listening, trust, and truth. Traditions prevent us from taking what seems like precious time to really know each other, to step out of roles, to reach across differences, to be careful and thoughtful about how we see and honor each other.

When it comes to nurturing people's wisdom, creativity, and genuine caring for each other, time is a gift seldom considered in our search for impact. And getting breakthrough for the most complex and entrenched issues of our day will not happen without it.

A Heart for the Work

"You really love the Elementary Institute of Science, don't you?"

I was looking at each of the displays our partners set up for an open house and was meticulously adjusting anything out of place. I was intent on making sure the beauty of their messages came shining through. The resident commenting was standing next to me as I stood back and stared at the collage of pictures of children lit up by learning.

"I hadn't thought about it, but I guess so," I said and smiled. She was right.

I had fallen in love with the Institute's pioneering spirit, its visionary leader, its board and their tireless effort to create a new future, and their powerful commitment to honoring all those who had been important in their journey. I had fallen in love with the young people who had stepped forward to lead a campaign of a scope and scale beyond anyone's wildest dreams, their steadfast commitment, and their hunger to learn. I had come to love every adult associated with the Institute and their do-whatever-it-takes drive to create a pathway to success for each child who entered.

And most of all, I loved that the entire organization embodied its key message — everything around us presents a learning moment.

In <u>Eat Pray Love,</u> Elizabeth Gilbert chronicled her journey of letting go of all definitions of success, entering into the unknown, and shaking up her life in order to find what she was truly after. "We invent the characters of our partners, demanding they be what we need of them, and then feel devastated when they refuse to perform the role we created in the first place."[146]

In philanthropy, there is a dance. An order to who leads and who follows. Which steps go with what beats. Who sets the priorities and who is expected to perform.

But to achieve partnership, we must let go — let go of power and control, let go of how it's always been, and let go of trying to change others, instead of opening our hearts to being changed <u>by</u> them. This requires that we re-see our partners as they are and have the courage to put ourselves at risk — risk of getting in touch with our humanness, risk of achieving meaning, risk of facing partners who hold up a mirror, show us what is holding us back, and bring us to our "own attention" so we can change.[147]

Our whole team had a heart for the work and brought out the heart of others.

When asked about changes he experienced in his own life, Macedonio Arteaga, a man steeped in the rich traditions of his native culture, noted: "We learned from our elders that when the heart is open there is a vibration. Our elders could feel it and see it. During this experience, we started operating with our hearts. There was no manual, no book, no training to do this, but when it started to vibrate, we could hear it and then we could hear each other in a different way."

"We grew compassion for each other and understood when something hurt," noted Lefaua Leilua, after serving as a Community Coordinator.

To this day, the people who were involved over a long-period of time talk about the experience like they would a great love that comes around once in a lifetime.

"It felt like hope. If you had ever experienced hopelessness, you knew. We were not strangers; we were a family," noted Tasha Williamson, with her close cropped hair and beaming smile. By turning her childhood pain of abuse and fear growing up in Crips territory of South Los Angeles into "fierce advocacy for peace," as she called it, she would become one of many in this large family of change-makers.

"It took courage for everyone to work together," she continued. "If we don't get the human connection, if we think it's about the paper work or millions of dollars, and if we think this stuff doesn't work because we didn't ask the right people, we are wrong. I'm a single mother of four children, and I know we can do this. Some of us are not highly educated, some of us are self-educated, some of us are from the streets — but we all have hearts. I forgave those who mistreated me, who caused and created my pain, so now I can teach that to someone else."

Like so many, she brought her gift...and she brought her heart.

To flourish in the face of the constant challenges of change, we needed to break bread together and stay no matter what went wrong so that we left no room for question about commitment in the face of failure. We needed to be able to feel deeply. To fall in love. To relish every day and be inspired by the commitment, spirit, risk-taking, and courage of people to imagine our boldest dream of the future and to work in relationship, forgiving ourselves for our flaws.

"If you can't feel, you have no business doing this work," noted Tambuzi framed it. It is a business that starts with human connection.

In this time of increasing violence, hate speech, inequality, and political polarization, it is more important than ever that we act and interact from a place of appreciation for each other's gifts on a platform of respect and shared decision-making. When we do, we will find that "we are the possible...the true wonder of this world" as Maya Angelou wrote in her poem, "A Brave and Startling Truth."[148]

An inclusive, peaceful, and just society is ours for the making as soon as we can envision that future and walk around in it, knowing that each gesture, each person, each moment matters.

THE
BUSINESS OF
CHANGE

**BUILDING A MARKETPLACE
THAT WORKS FOR ALL**

27

TAKING CARE OF BUSINESS

"If the only tool is a grant,
then the world looks like a charity case.

— Jed Emerson

Market Strategies for Social Good

"What do you want to say in your first annual report, Joe?" I asked. "What do you want your key message to be?"

He didn't hesitate. "That I have been an activist in promoting the understanding and appreciation of capitalism and the free-market system as a dynamic wellspring of energy for human good."

In 1992, I had never heard business and human good in the same sentence.

Shaped by his heritage as the son of immigrants who took enormous risks to come to this country and his life as an entrepreneur, Joe would seed the foundation with a culture that welcomed innovation, sought untried solutions, and accepted the risk of failure. He believed that it was important to look beyond today's need to tomorrow's possibility, and he saw job creation as the most intrinsically socially-responsible act there was. He believed in exchange — pay in exchange for gifts and talents. It preserves dignity and builds self-worth.

From the beginning of the foundation, the focus was on economic opportunity — helping to expand organizations that created access to capital for businesses that were unbanked and providing direct capital investment in social enterprises — a concept just beginning to gain visibility and support in the early 1990s.

As a free market conservative, Joe wanted to see if market strategies could be more effective than social welfare policies. But because the foundation was a family business, he had to blend his beliefs with his liberal daughters. The foundation's agenda became a merger of his free market beliefs and their commitment to human rights and social justice. Micro-lending, which was rooted in trust and a sense of responsibility between the borrower and lender, along with investing in high-risk social entrepreneurs who combined market-based approaches with social equity goals, became the early focus of the foundation.

Joe talked incessantly about harnessing markets for social change and needing to accept the risk of failure. I talked incessantly about how the markets had failed our disinvested communities and why they needed to be reconnected to the economic mainstream. He talked about how markets operate and the levers that move them, and I talked about racism and the dynamics that keep some people from accessing capital — the major tool of a capitalist society. And together we asked: If we want to help kick-start a thriving business community in areas that had been abandoned by the markets and cut off from capital, what does it really take?

While other funders of that time period were making program grants, we began the process of stepping toward venture investing.

We would focus on taking care of business.

A Different Kind of Courage

There is a Chinese parable that is also the theme of many a children's story:

> *A Chinese farmer gets a horse, which soon runs away. A neighbor says, "That's bad news." The farmer replies, "Good*

news, bad news, who can say?" The horse comes back and brings another horse with him. Good news, you might say. The farmer gives the second horse to his son, who rides it, then is thrown and badly breaks his leg. "So sorry for your bad news," says the concerned neighbor. "Good news, bad news, who can say?" the farmer replies. In a week or so, the emperor's men come and take every able-bodied young man to fight in a war. The farmer's son is spared. Good news, of course.

This was the story of our work in economic development, business development, and social enterprise. Good news, bad news — it was sometimes impossible to know. On any given day, it looked one way and then swung back the other.

One of our first investments was a cooperative ownership venture, an artisan woodshop employing the homeless, a social enterprise in the heart of Los Angeles' Skid Row. We would provide support for business coaching, capital, and access to production space. Joe really wanted it to work.

After two years of coaching and start-up capital, the Skid Row team faced the most daunting challenge of its short history — a major order for 10,000 toys from a big retail company! Good news, of course.

We thought of it as a big break and never saw the end coming. When the enterprise tried to convert from an artisan collective to a manufacturing company, the team was not prepared. Toys were either rejected for poor quality or damaged in shipping. The organization took heavy losses and couldn't make it up with volume. The pricing couldn't absorb these kinds of losses. He — and we — couldn't learn fast enough. The Skid Row team was overwhelmed with growth, the complexity of reconciling social mission with business goals, and the reconciliation of heart and head. It imploded.

Joe wanted to continue. He thought the business could rally. Failures were a natural part of business. He wanted to stay at the table.

"Why?" we asked.

"Because I believe in the idea."

Every business is a dream; every risk is hope in action. Many more businesses fail than succeed, but when the dream is to change people's lives, it adds a layer to how people experience the losses. We came to understand that when a business closes, someone's dream dies, and with it, goes another little piece of your heart. [149]

Bob Giloth, Vice President at the Annie E. Casey Foundation's Center for Economic Opportunity, noted in his 2012 blog:

> "We in the nonprofit sector should become much better at recognizing more quickly tactical mistakes and taking corrective action or exiting. The challenge is with constructive mistakes, when we are pushing the envelope on what works to solve deep challenges. Failing fast may not be the right approach. We need to stick with promising ideas long enough to see if they are successes or failure. That's a different kind of courage." [150]

The hard part is we don't think we have enough time to fail; we don't feel we have permission to fail; it is incredibly difficult to decide if something is a success or failure; and it hurts. What feels like a failure might be just be a set-back — and there are many of them. It was constantly good news/bad news, who knows? And no doubt about it, it took a different kind of courage.

To the extent that I have any hair left, any hair that was not pulled out in frustration and disappointment, the businesses development work we did is not to thank. But we took inspiration and courage from a growing number of social enterprises and micro-lending organizations we admired from afar, like Pioneer Human Services, Greyston Bakery, the Grameen Bank, and later Evergreen Cooperatives, or invested in as partners, like Food from the 'Hood, Homeboy Industries, and Accion.

Harnessing Markets

Our journey to harness markets for the benefit of those who had not typically benefited from them — or who were historically excluded from benefiting — started with grants to micro-enterprise programs and developed over time into a large-scale effort to build community-owned enterprises that linked individual and community benefit. This set us on a path to create hybrid corporate structures that had the benefits of a for-profit, such as distribution of profits and ownership, and the social justice mission of a non-profit. We worked at the intersection of these two worlds.

As a neighborhood strengthening organization, two opportunities came to the forefront. One was the untapped value of land embedded in blight and one was the millions of dollars in retail leakage. Could this value be harnessed for the direct economic benefit of the community's current residents and organizations?

As we worked to answer that question, Market Creek became a container for creating community-owned ventures and recapturing economic leakage. Each project was an opportunity for nurturing new businesses.

What is so challenging about community economic development is that it requires a comprehensive approach. Strong social and financial networks, safe neighborhoods, good schools, quality housing, thoughtful land planning, and political will — these are inextricably linked to economic development. To get a foothold, we married community building, physical development, and asset-building, and we launched a set of social enterprises that were linked by their mission of resident ownership of neighborhood change. Some of these ventures held land for commercial, industrial and residential projects being planned, designed and built by community residents. Others were business ventures offering community residents opportunities for employment, management training, and ultimately business ownership.

By 2006, the economic activity created at Market Creek Plaza had surpassed its original benchmark of $34 million, a fact that fueled our optimism despite our struggle with both local conditions, like the lack of infrastructure, and the web of global and structural dynamics that were impacting business everywhere.

By 2008, that optimism expanded. Market Creek Partners, LLC had a strong foothold and had begun to achieve profitability. While its cash flow was still thin and collateral limited, it had strong brand identity, was able to manage debt, and had "gone public," with residents and the Neighborhood Unity Foundation having a 40 percent stake in the company.

Other ideas for community ventures continued to spring up, team by team.

In the "idea stage" was spinning off the Ambassadors as its own business. The Ambassadors, a paid team of residents who managed the security for Market Creek and the extended village properties, were well-trained and highly-skilled. Rather than contracting with an outside security company, this value was used to provide the jobs to local residents who had strong relationship skills, were welcoming to citizens across cultures, could engage young people in way that would encourage them to honor and respect the projects, and had the ability to deter problems rather than just handling them. Their plan was to form an employee-owned enterprise when there was enough scale in the village to sustain it.

In the "start-up stage" was Market Creek Events & Venues, a training business launched to recapture the local event revenue leakage, estimated at over $5 million, from quinceañeras to cultural holiday celebrations, keeping that value and those jobs in the community. As the major Market Creek Arts & Culture Fest gained regional notoriety and learning exchanges attracted people from all over the country, this business was envisioned as a complement to San Diego's larger tourism and convention business, positioning the community as the region's most culturally diverse setting.

Other community ventures were in the "pilot operations stage," trying to reach breakeven, such as WriterzShop, the social enterprise arm of the Writerz Blok graffiti art team. Graphic design, poster print, silk screen, skate-board designs, wall murals, and other income-earning endeavors were undertaken collectively and by individual artists.

The sunset plan for the foundation was deeply intertwined with these social ventures. They were the centerpiece of our ability to bring up self-generating systems of wealth creation that could go on without us. All structures needed to be designed to put profits back in the neighborhood — to build ongoing opportunity for collective investment, as well as to provide sustaining resources to the various teams, partners, and services within the village.

As these enterprises developed over time, each contributed to the vitality and double-bottom-line goals of Market Creek.

The First-Generation Nesting Dolls

Market Creek was like a Russian nesting doll.

Matryoshka or babushka dolls are Russian wooden folk-art creations with six to eight dolls of decreasing size hidden one inside of another. Just as I did, my grandchildren love the one I was given as a child and still have. As they open them, one after another, they become more and more fascinated by the dolls until they get to the tiniest — the best one of all.

Market Creek was a set of businesses inside a business — like a babushka. It was a double-bottom-line enterprise with layers of social enterprises within it. It was intended to make the dollar bounce, and that's what was happening as the strategy unfolded, each layer of business more fascinating, right down to the tiniest micro-enterprise inside a social enterprise — the businesses inside Where the World Meets, a store leasing to local entrepreneurs who were artisans and importers of cultural gifts — the best of all.

Market Creek Partners, LLC was a profit—generating project that would be community owned in a pioneering IPO, and for the enterprise within it, the original Market Creek Business and Leasing Team developed a three-part strategy of the enterprise: one third national tenants, one third local business ownership, and one third manage-to-own. This community team screened and selected the initial tenants against this criterion.

The first generation of local business owners received start-up planning grants and technical assistance on their tenant improvements, along with working capital borrowed from California Southern Small Business Development Corporation. California Southern secured a $1 million program-related investment to create this access to capital. Many of the tenants amortized their tenant improvements in their rents. The loans and leases required financial reporting on local employment and social impact.

In exchange for capital, businesses signed a "Spirit of Partnership Agreement" that defined our working relationship, community benefit goals, and reporting requirements. Two businesses were start-ups, one was a second location, and one was a local family business that had lost its lease on a previous site. JCNI's business development team provided marketing and business operations technical assistance, and the accounting department provided financial reporting support where needed.

The Food 4 Less grocery store anchored and provided financial stability to the project, a Wells Fargo Bank Branch and a Magic Johnson Starbucks framed the entryway, and the other two in-line buildings were dedicated to Joe's dream of entrepreneurship and the community team's goal to have local ownership.

Market Creek Plaza was the food and entertainment heart of the village. Among the selected businesses were restaurants, large and small; a manage-to-own box and shipping company, which successfully transitioned to resident ownership; and Where the World Meets, the micro-leasing storefront.

For many of on the Jacobs Team, our favorite business was Where the World Meets — made up of the smallest nesting dolls, community micro-entrepreneurs. Where the World Meets was a multicultural gift shop which opened up onto the World Courtyard outside to become a large international marketplace on selected Saturdays. It was central to the branding of Market Creek Plaza as San Diego's place-to-be for a multi-cultural experience. This store, with its collection of micro-entrepreneurs who imported from their homelands and community artisans with specialty gifts, brought life to the plaza.

In addition to these enterprises, the second largest nesting doll in the mix was Diamond Management, Inc. (DMI), the property management company. DMI hired local residents for the leasing, maintenance, and security and was on a path to become community owned after the completion of the eight projects it needed to be sustainable. Within this company, the residents who made up the security team, known as the Ambassadors, were already in the vision and design phase of also spinning off as an independent community enterprise.

The largest nesting doll was Market Creek Partners, LLC. This limited liability company held the land and buildings and following the IPO was 40 percent owned by the community. The year 2018 was targeted as its transition to full community ownership. Market Creek Partners provided the outer nesting doll to the layers of enterprise within it.

Going after the millions in event revenue and retail leakage, along with the economic value of developing land, the goal of Market Creek was to serve as a catalyst for building a marketplace that works for all.

28

AN INCLUSIVE ECONOMY —
ONE BIG MARKET TEST

"When you are at the end of your rope,
tie a knot and hold on."

— Theodore Roosevelt

Bringing the Markets to Market Creek

"Joe's refrain about Babe Ruth striking out 1330 times was so telling," noted Chip Buttner.

When the free market fails communities and they are left without commerce and work, the dynamic is difficult to turn around. You are going to strike out more times than you will produce a hit.

Chip had been in business for 35 years so he understood risk. But developing business synergy in an area known for blight and trying to figure out how to kick-start market forces that were working against us was challenging and we had to know we were in a long-term endeavor. "Are we harnessing a market? Or are we creating one?" Chip would ask. It was difficult to tell. In many ways we were trying to formalize the informal economy that already existed.

"Business was the hardest part," he reflected. "There was no comfort zone. It seemed like we were constantly between a rock and a hard place."

When we started the Market Creek experience, our goal was to create a network of commercially-financed businesses. And we would do it the way we believed was important — hands-on, engaged, embracing risk, working comprehensively, and sharing decisions with residents on any and all decisions impacting their community. Market Creek was a place to make Joe's dream of ownership and free market opportunity real, while meeting the community teams' goals of creating a vibrant center city. It was an arduous effort to blend economic development with community building, creating a platform for the exchange of people's gifts and talents — economic benefit — linked with people's great bandwidth for connection and compassion — social benefit.

As we began the work, we didn't know that bringing the markets to Market Creek and connecting residents to jobs in the village would be such a challenging long-term proposition. What we did know was that business requires safe neighborhoods, safe neighborhoods require scale in reclaiming blight, and reclaiming blight requires substantive business synergy. Efforts to improve conditions for small business and low-wage workers were further challenged by larger economic factors like rising energy costs, home foreclosures, and the loss of union jobs in industries, such as groceries.

To overcome these obstacles, we were in constant campaign mode to bring the markets to Market Creek, and to do that we led with arts and culture.

We strengthened the year-long cultural event series and the large popular Market Creek Arts & Culture Fest, which together were drawing nearly 25,000 people from throughout San Diego. We created a strong capacity-building plan for management of the major events venues in the village. We supported the expansion of the international marketplace concept through Where the World Meets, cultural houses, and kiosks. We brought in support for business planning and marketing for the businesses and for the plaza. In addition, Diamond Community Investors, the resident owners of Market Creek, took on key roles in promoting and strengthening the plaza.

We also conducted the next round of village business development planning around the concept of a cultural business district. We completed the next leg of the creek tributary restoration for a light industrial project. Because commercial development depends on "roof-tops," planning for the village's first 52 housing units was completed. And we secured the anchors needed for the next two commercial corners — a community clinic for one and at long last, after 10 years of negotiations, a drug store for the corner across from Market Creek Plaza. For every job that was created or recruited, including within our own organization, residents were given priority.

In tackling the ongoing work of creating a vibrant business environment with local job creation, we knew that we would continually encounter unexpected problems and challenges. But we were also becoming better risk-takers as we moved along and we knew if we kept the long view, we would discover new and unanticipated opportunities.

The Big Why

"We were in a community that hadn't seen investment for decades. It was also a community where residents wanted change but at the same time were apprehensive about change," Director of Business Development Max Zaker noted. "Our economic development plans made sense at 40,000 feet, but then when we tried to play things out on the ground, it would get confusing."

Max, whose birth name is Majid, left his homeland of Iran as a teenager, making his way alone to Germany and then on to England. He knew the meaning of hard work, his journey had made him comfortable with being uncomfortable, and he understood the power of entrepreneurship. Like many immigrants, learning the language and figuring out how to earn money were his priorities. He had extensive experience in building and selling businesses and knew multiple languages.

"What's your big why? What is your limiting belief?" Max liked asking. "Before someone can become an owner, there is often a mind shift. You have to be able to say 'I am responsible.' Have skin in the game. Not everyone is meant to be a entrepreneur."

With his distinct salt and pepper hair and neatly-trimmed goatee, Max was calm in a storm. And it was a good thing, because the work with the entrepreneurs at Market Creek could be maddening.

"It was easier to plan and talk about it than to implement it. The work changed all of us. For me, it changed how I measured success. I started asking how many lives I can change alongside of how much profit can be made. I understood companies needed to be profitable, but after my Market Creek experience, I started applying profit-sharing and ownership to my own company. Sharing the gift of profit with others makes good business sense. Why shouldn't I let go of a percentage of the profit to benefit those who helped build it? Then they have an ongoing stake in its success."

Max's question about "what's your big why" was one we had to ask the Market Creek tenants. We also had to continually ask it of ourselves. "We were saying to people that you shouldn't be measured by your past or your background check, but by what you are capable of doing," reflected Max on his business development work. "We could take those risks since it is synonymous with enterprise. But we also needed to have truthful conversations that were difficult to have." And because these conversations were difficult, we always had to be asking ourselves about our own why.

Our why was deeply rooted in a commitment to entrepreneurship, local business development, a belief that people are capable of creating their own success once historical barriers are removed.

"The fact that we were able to draw the level of attention we did, the attention the community deserved, and develop a commercial center was nothing short of a miracle given where it started," Max noted. Because of Joe's commitment to risk-taking and venture investing, we were able to provide the tools people said they needed to succeed.

We branded a cultural business district, supporting an arts and culture agenda riding on signature events. We piloted the international marketplace, tested business marketing strategies with mixed results, successfully transferred ownership of a manage-to-own business, hosted or sponsored business roundtable breakfasts, and supported the capacity-building of the Diamond Business Improvement District. We also developed a training kitchen so residents would have a place to test specialty food products and have access to a commercial kitchen and created a pathway for community contractors to secure 75 percent of the Market Creek Plaza construction, resulting in nearly $30 million in HUBE contracts (Historically Underserved Business Enterprises).

But despite these accomplishments, we also came to know all too well the reality behind the glamor of enterprise development. At a small convening hosted by Community Wealth Ventures (now Community Wealth Partners) that I participated in on the topic of "Achieving Impact and Sustainability through Market-Based Approaches" in 2007, George Gendron, Director of the Innovation and Entrepreneurship Program at Clark University and former editor of Inc. Magazine, noted:

> "In the retelling of these success stories we inadvertently create the impression that they are overnight sensations. Most of these success stories took enormous patience and decades of time to build... Remember, only a tiny fraction of successful companies ever scale. It requires an incredible confluence of the right idea, the right team, and at the right time. I would just be careful not to be too glib about scaling as if in fact it is an everyday occurrence."[151]

Despite the inherent challenges, Joe's belief in business as intrinsically socially responsible kept the double-bottom-line front and center in our work. His undaunted commitment to risk-taking as a practiced value informed our process. And the democratization and direct ownership of assets stayed unwaveringly our why.

Painful Lessons

"If you are going to be in this work, you have to get comfortable with the uncomfortable," noted Max Zaker. "You have to know that some businesses aren't going to make it."

Nobody knew about discomfort more than Max. "In Middle Eastern culture, you measure success by how many businesses you build," he commented. When Max was in business, his family understood. When he sold his businesses and joined the team of the Downtown San Diego Partnership, a business advocacy group supporting the business environment of San Diego's center city and then worked to set up Business Improvement Districts, his family — not quite understanding — kept asking: "Now what is it you do exactly?"

"I broke away from family tradition of owning businesses when I made a choice that my success was someone else's success," Max noted. "My work was helping people get what they wanted and that created opportunities, both big and small." But the hard part, Max would say, is that you can't make anyone successful. "You can have the right conversations and provide the right tools, but in the end, an entrepreneur needs to have the will — in addition to the desire — to succeed. Being in business isn't for everyone. Aside from raising children, it's probably the hardest thing to do."

To be in business, Max noted, "you need to have a really good horse. But you also need to be a really good jockey. It's about risk-taking, experience, liquidity, competition, and creating value for your brand. It's also about accountability, discipline, and being coachable. It makes many people feel vulnerable. Success is a jagged line, not a straight one, and most people aren't programmed for it."

And when your success depends on helping others become successful, you not only need to be comfortable with the uncomfortable, you need to acknowledge your own vulnerability. "It can get under your skin," noted Max, "I felt like I was failing because the businesses weren't making it. When I rewind the tape, I sometimes think I was too wrapped up in it. We took so much responsibility for business owner's success. The very essence that fuels business — that sense of responsibility and having skin in the game — shifted the risk of failure to us and opened up the opportunity for us to be blamed."

In reflecting on the lessons learned along the way, the list of learnings grew longer and longer as the work progressed and the larger national economy tanked. These are seven of the most impactful:

- The original Business and Leasing Team, which selected the first community businesses owners for Market Creek, placed relationships and business plans at the center of the decision-making and could have benefited from adding a clear, competitive component to the process.

- Market Creek Plaza, as the food and entertainment hub of a cultural village, didn't have enough individual spaces and enough variety in their sizes to spread our risk and the entrepreneurs' risk; as a result, some business owners jumped to a permanent commercial storefront unprepared or leased too large of a space; we needed a solid business development pipeline that enabled owners to graduate from temporary locations to appropriately-sized space, so they could grow at a pace that worked for their businesses.

- For the larger community businesses, which we had capitalized in the first round without enough of a financial commitment from the entrepreneurs, we needed owners to have more of their own skin in the game and have a financial plan for both best- and worst-case scenarios, demonstrating their ability to finance their operation and maintain adequate reserves.

- For the micro-businesses, the clustering of them in Where the World Meets in order to share overhead was complicated by uneven skills and product quality, so we realized we needed pop-ups and kiosks for high traffic locations where entrepreneurs could test products and services with very low upfront investment.

- Our "Spirit of Partnership Agreements," which we thought were of such great import, were unenforceable, so we moved to standardize and concretize requirements in the leases in a way that guaranteed ongoing commitment to community benefits and reporting on local hiring.

- By believing that we were giving entrepreneurs the very best opportunity for success by blending support with percentage rents, low-cost capital, and technical assistance, we caused role confusion with business owners by being the landlord, the investor behind the loan fund, and the business planning and marketing advisory team.

- And last but not least, tenants needed to take full responsibility for and ownership of their own businesses — with no excuses.

In short, we learned that overcoming historical disinvestment and market-flight is time-consuming and costly, requires multiple partners to spread the risk, demands a figure-it-out attitude, and most importantly — endurance.

Another Piece of Our Hearts

When the financial markets collapsed in 2008, followed by the worst years for business since the Great Depression, Market Creek would lose its major restaurants. Despite the ongoing struggles, these restaurants had been holding on — albeit by the fingernails — but the long and extended recession would mark the end of the first round of local businesses.

When the two largest restaurants failed, we started the process of rebuilding the pipeline for new community- or minority-owned businesses to locate at Market Creek, starting with the need for a seasoned (pun intended) entrepreneur.

Our baby, our tiniest nesting doll, Where the World Meets — which gave life to the World Courtyard and the international marketplace — was among the casualties. When Learning Exchanges brought groups from all over the country and when the amphitheater was in full bloom, the store did exceptionally well, but otherwise it was a challenge. The original model required entrepreneurs to rent space in the store and commit volunteer hours to its operation. When this proved unworkable, the store was fully staffed and entrepreneurs paid commissions on sales. The store provided an opportunity for a core group of entrepreneurs to become successful — the good news — but the store itself wasn't able to attract a large enough market to cover its operating costs — the bad news.

When the Village at Market Creek gained enough scale to generate ongoing foot-traffic to the area, we theorized confidently, the store would work. It brought life and spirit and energy to the plaza at a relatively small cost. As a social enterprise with a mission to provide retail space and business training for local micro-entrepreneurs who weren't yet ready for their own storefront, in one sense it was successful. As a stand-alone venture, it wasn't self-sustaining.

The question then became how long to subsidize it.

As the recession continued beyond anyone's prediction, we had to sustain a third round of downsizing and made a decision to close Where the World Meets. It was heartbreaking. When T-Mobile leased the space, we began to see the spirit of local entrepreneurship, which had been front and center at the Plaza — our why — begin to fade.

Afterwards, I regretted closing the store, even though T-Mobile paid higher rent to Market Creek Partners, because it seemed to back away from the heart of Joe's mission. I also regretted that I didn't practice what we had been doing all along — activate another community team to decide next steps. Would the creativity of people who loved it have figured out how to save it? I'll never know. For our team and for the resident teams that had worked so hard to transform Market Creek from a commercial strip to a center of culture and commerce, we gave up a little piece of our hearts.

There are moments when change comes hard. These are the moments when the changes that occur aren't what was envisioned, vigorously sought after, and worked for. These are the moments when the world seems too big, the discord too loud, and the barriers too great. In these moments, all we could do was grieve and then remind ourselves of what business we were in.

Keeping our eyes on the larger business of change, we would pull back and take in once again the vision of a vibrant village, built — despite the high hurdles of disinvestment and racism — through inspired civic action and owned by those who brought her into being.

A Day Off from the Business of Change

It would be a day like most in January — San Diego's January — clear, mild, temperatures rising into the 70's, no wind. But it would be a day like no other, as people poured into the new Joe & Vi Jacobs Center to find a seat.

The Joe & Vi Jacobs Center was a large conference and meeting space with a state-of-the-art training kitchen. The business plan for the center was based on harnessing the estimated $5 million in annual event leakage — money spent on community gatherings elsewhere because there were not enough local venues to support this level of activity. In its entryway were large cultural banners expressing welcome in nine languages.

On January 20, 2009, a thousand people were expected in the main hall of the center. As they arrived, most were wearing their Sunday best. An atmosphere of both reverence and exhilaration permeated the space as people tipped their hats in respect to each other and shook their heads in disbelief.

It was a time of struggle in the community. Friends and neighbors had been losing businesses, jobs, and homes. No one was untouched. But on that day, everyone would lay aside the challenge of community economic development to grasp what was occurring nationally.

Our team had arranged a live-feed of the presidential inauguration. The room quickly filled to capacity. "I never thought I would ever get the chance to see this," people would say to one another, offering each other Kleenex.

The sense of historical significance was visceral. Bone-deep. When Barack Obama placed his hand on Abraham Lincoln's bible to take the presidential oath at the U.S. Capitol, people were sobbing.

As Elizabeth Alexander's poem filled the room following the inaugural address...

"All about us is noise. All about us is noise and bramble, thorn and din, each one of our ancestors on our tongues."[152]

...you could still feel the stillness, see the heads shaking in disbelief, and detect the ancestors on people's tongues. Throughout the room, the I-can't-believe's would be spoken gently and then trail off into the atmosphere like a praise song being chanted as a collective reflection on the entering of a new era, profound and majestic.

I don't remember leaving that day. I just remember being transfixed, spellbound by the experience of joining the 37.8 million people who watched and the 1.8 million folks who assembled at the Capitol to see the 44th president sworn into office. Looking around the room that day, with so many people who had experienced the gut-punch of racism and disrespect personally, who had worried about the safety of their children and for themselves, who had been belittled, denigrated, and derided as less-than, and who had participated in countless conversations over a decade about how we might together achieve a fair, inclusive, equitable, and generous society, there was an expanded sense of promise and hope.

At that moment, nestled in a strong sense of community, so full of optimism, we believed as Obama would later phrase it at the 50th anniversary of civil rights march from Selma to Montgomery that "we do a disservice to the cause of justice by intimating that bias and discrimination are immutable, or that racial division is inherent to America."[153]

We believed in the promise of a multi-racial democracy, and for a moment in time, we took a break from the heartbreak and losses of the business of change to take a breath — not realizing that right around the corner the rise of racial slurs, overt hatred, and racially-motivated acts of violence were waiting to test our devotion to and endurance for achieving an economy and a democracy that works for all.

THE
POLITICS OF
CHANGE

POWER, PLACE & THE PUBLIC

29

POWER, VOICE, AND THE
POLITICS OF PHILANTHROPY

"The problem with America is that we don't live up to our creed...
Our task is to retrieve the language of liberty, and freedom, and equality,
to remove it from this idea of American exceptionalism and give it new life
in which every human being is accorded dignity
no matter their zip code or the color of their skin."[154]

—Eddie S. Glaude, Jr., "America's Racial 'Value Gap'"

Hoping No White Person Writes About Me

"Black Love is Black Wealth..."[155] Valerie Wright recited to me with the same vocal rhythm of Nikki Giovanni herself.

Giovanni's poem, "Nikki-Rosa," deeply impacted Valerie, and from years of reciting it over and over, she knew and felt every word, believing it described her own experience, like the line "though you are poor it isn't poverty that concerns you..."

She grew up in a small rural community along the Florida-Georgia border. She and I were two small town girls, one from the North and one from the South, who happened to link up to work together to figure out the right role for philanthropy in community change. "What are the chances of us doing this work together," we would marvel. When she first shared her personal story with me, what I heard was that she grew up poor, lost her mother young, and her father, who I assumed was deeply bitter, was wheelchair-bound, struggling to provide for his 10 children. I would learn to never assume.

"'I really hope no white person ever has cause to write about me because they never understand,'" Valerie smiled continuing to recite "Nikki-Rosa." When she ended — "all the while I was quite happy" — you could practically see the fun unfolding in front of your eyes — Valerie and her nine siblings, mischievous, playful, and close.

Valerie, like Nikki Giovanni, claimed the right to define herself, stay true to herself, and use her gifts of insight and grace to unfold learning moments for those around her. She had grown up in a tight-knit African American community surrounded by a loving and extended family she described as a web of protection, and true to her favorite poem, she challenged white assumptions about poverty being a "lack-of" issue.

Valerie didn't always have to say much for me to get her point.

Valerie went to her first integrated school in the fifth grade, the same year her mother died, and would step into a world of racism and hurt. "As a child I thought I would change the world," she reflected. "I had to stand up, but I stood up so fiercely my daddy was afraid of what could happen to me. This was the racist South. This was about encountering white people who could harm me or just as soon lynch me. 'You are going to be lynched with lighter knots,' my daddy would say to me. 'You can't say everything you think to white people.'"

I couldn't grasp why she wasn't bitter. "How do you ever learn to speak the truth of your experience with that hanging over every conversation with white people?"

"You can complain and talk about how things are but until you are willing to get down in the dirt and dig in, nothing will ever change," she would laugh a distinctive fill-the-room laugh, and her larger-than-life smile would draw me in. "My daddy challenged us to know our history, to see the big picture that brings us to this moment — this moment in time and all that happened to get us here. My anger wasn't resolving anything, so I had to learn to tell the truth in a way that it can be heard."

In a field of harsh critics and in the room with so many emotionally-charged conversations, I would watch Valerie and try to learn from her. Her lessons were about a different kind of risk-taking. If Valerie could find the courage to speak truth to white people, I could find the courage to listen, no matter how the messages got delivered, and if Valerie could graciously and gracefully tell someone "what you just said had an impact on me," then I could find the courage in tense moments to ask "can you tell me what just happened?"

It was important for us to talk about the context of power and privilege embedded in philanthropy — the cord of time, as Valerie called it — that brought us all together to change things. Her gift opened up a world of learning about race and class.

In hoping that no white person ever has reason to write about her, Nikki Giovanni could have been talking about the mile-high stack of reports foundations publish about "poor" communities. For the last 100 years, institutional philanthropy has had the power to create the framework, define the issues, research the causes, evaluate best practice, and write the narrative.

"People don't complain because it's the norm, but it's self-serving and feels like one more group exerting power and control," Valerie reflected on her career in philanthropy.

"My sister and I were working in the 'glades' in South Florida, and when we talked to people — from church leaders to everyday residents at grassroots gatherings — they wanted to work on HIV/AIDS. But the health foundation that hired us to help them get an initiative off the ground had chosen a different set of priorities. Without regard for resident concerns, the foundation staff had decided what was important and wasn't really open to changing that predetermined focus."

"If that wasn't enough," she continued, "this area had been colonized by the sugar companies and people had access to very few job opportunities outside of that. Even though the 40 percent unemployment rates were impacting people's health, the foundation only wanted to address health in a narrowly defined way and ignored the feedback that job creation was a critical factor. Because the work is not taken on comprehensively, nothing changes. No headway gets made."

Valerie, who has been a part of several major initiatives, led funder collaboratives focused on community change, and consulted with foundations wanting to address neighborhood conditions, saddens when she thinks about the power dynamic that occurs between foundations and communities, which leaves in its wake bitterness and distrust. "The non-profits get excited, fight over the money, and then get divided. But for the people who live there it's 'not another!' Residents are seen as 'apathetic' or 'agitators without action.' But if you understand the history of these communities, you have to understand you can't go in for five years, because it's going to take you that long to just get people to talk!"

"In my experience, people don't understand what it takes to do the work and don't really want to bring the people being impacted to the table; in fact, we avoid it at all cost," Valerie noted. "And so what we end up with is more research and a lot of great reports that aren't true."

The hurt runs deep for both residents and the staff representing foundations genuinely trying to bridge these worlds. In discussing the power dynamics in philanthropic institutions as someone who has represented foundations wanting to undertake community change, Audrey Jordan noted "for black and brown staff, it can be even worse."

Trained as an evaluator, Audrey supported community change teams throughout the country doing work that was initiated by foundations. "It can feel like we are missionaries used to go out and engage the people's faith and trust to do the foundation's bidding. Then when the people start voicing their frustration that they are being disrespected and their interests aren't being considered, the 'missionary' staff gets blamed. Respect by the foundation begins to dwindle, if it ever existed. Trustees then say 'we aren't getting what we were told we'd get,' and they are led to believe that this is because *those* people didn't cooperate or the staff members weren't carrying the right message."

Audrey sighs as she thinks about the dynamic set in motion. "Obviously it can't be that *those* people had a point or that the foundation was foolish in the first place to believe in the power of its little microcosm of accumulated wealth to make population-level impact. We go out there in good faith trying to do the under-appreciated hard work of building respectful relationships from broken trust, and for the trustees it's often just transactional. And then we get thrown under the bus."

Like Nikki Giovanni not wanting white people to write her story, there is more to the philanthropic community change story than the typical foundation report documents. "We need to talk truth," reflected Audrey. "But if we do tell the truth, it screws up the foundation narrative and we can't have that! So the story that gets told is the story that those who control the narrative want told."

"I felt like I was a part of the community because of my own life history and experience," noted Valerie Wright. "We promise to engage; then when it gets tough, the trustees say it's not working. They are just done. Now I've hurt people; now I've betrayed people. Many of these communities are already wounded by corrupt and oppressive political leaders and now it's coupled with foundations — one more power structure doing business as usual. People don't document that voice."

With political power held by white men, our country's founders could write the narrative of "the land of the free" while rationalizing slavery. And in control of the economic engine that the slave trade represented, it was easy to overlook this key contradiction. If women and people of color had been at the table with a real voice in the planning, how the barriers got defined and the actions needed to overcome them would have looked very different.

Every workplace and profession has its politics. The rating, ranking, and hierarchy of relationships. The use and sometimes abuse of power. In the foundation world, we seek "population-level change" by paying people to intervene in communities to change them, often overlooking or failing to target change in the "population" responsible for the wealth disparities, power imbalances, and control of the narrative. We see ourselves as stimulators of social innovation and power-building among marginalized populations yet are able to rationalize our control of what policy, what advocacy, and what activities are given priority. In the name of empowerment, we decide for others what is in their best interest.

In my years leading the Market Creek work, we tried to figure out a way to lift up the voice of residents broadly and share power through joint decision-making on teams. We tried to create a process that worked for resources to follow resident-driven dreams for their community and for a future of inclusion and civic participation. It was a step in the right direction.

But I became acutely aware during the Market Creek experience how we each hold a piece of the picture, not the whole picture.

At the end of the day, I am a white person, who worked within a structure of power and privilege, taking the risk to write a story, knowing there are many sides of this story to be told.

The Disconnect between Power-Building and Foundation Process

"'The political stakes go way up,' said one leader of convening people to deliberate," reported Rich Harwood and John Creighton in the Harwood Institute's piece entitled "The Organization-First Approach: How Programs Crowd Out Community."[156]

The work of public deliberation — "people coming together to consider issues and weigh choices and trade-offs"[157] — is inherently political and comes with risks. Because funding is almost exclusively tied to programs, the roles most organizations play are tied to providing services to targeted constituents.

As one leader quoted in the article explained: "We have a very specific goal. We work with communities that want to adopt our programs!'" Since leaders are largely evaluated by accomplishments and what the organization has gotten done, the report contends, community engagement is either not a priority at all or is thought of only as outreach to engage people in their organizations' agendas.

To lift up resident voice, build public knowledge and power, and provide an infrastructure that can support civic action is considered risky business. True deliberation, as the Harwood report reflects, is seen as something that can easily go awry and make their organizations look bad.

As we were launching the community partnership that became the Market Creek experience, the concepts of community-driven development (CDD) and asset-based community development (ABCD) were emerging worldwide. These approaches contended that the professional-client relationship was causing isolation and robbing people of their ability to see themselves as skilled. In addition, a wave of criticism of foundations and the NGOs they were funding was mounting for implicitly or explicitly colluding to propagate so-called First World interests in developing countries globally.

This got our attention in thinking about our own role and relationship with everyday residents and the dilemma of how we, as foundations, undertake power-building agendas.

In a 2007 Kettering Foundation report titled, "A Civil Investing Strategy for Putting Communities In Charge," Ramon E. Daubon discusses how development assistance institutions and foreign-assistance donors encountered challenges incorporating this idea of honoring the local community as the engine of change, even though they fundamentally believed it is important. This difficulty, he contends "arises not because the idea is too foreign to what these donors already do, but rather because it is so similar on the surface yet mandates a fundamental change in mindset and in the power relationship between donor and grantee."[158]

Daubon shares several international case studies from Ecuador, Peru, Argentina, and Brazil, arguing that "there can be no sustained social and economic advancement without a politics that gives ordinary people a sense of ownership and control over their circumstances."[159]

Philanthropy, he noted, seldom serves this purpose. By focusing "immediately and exclusively on the plan of action" and relying on "the opinions of experts or of community elites to define the problem on behalf of the public,"[160] it seldom encourages residents to try to change their communities through collective action. This work requires a "different philanthropy" — one that sees "that ordinary folks can exercise leadership on a day-to-day basis through their reshaped collective civic action." This requires that foundations help build "leaderful" communities rather than social entrepreneurs who are "lauded as heroic," which he believes, "has the pernicious consequence of cementing the existing dysfunctional relationships, justifying the need for endless philanthropy, and assigning its beneficiaries the roles of perpetual supplicants."[161]

The stories of international aid and the damage done by telling people what's wrong with them are many. In our own work, we had witnessed how people are given messages that they have failed rather than the message that things that go wrong are just moments in time. Paths can be rerouted and plans reassessed — the fundamentals of building resilience — but the conventional philanthropic process doesn't lend itself to this.

Over the years, much has been written about the socio-political consequences of foundations maintaining the power-elite through inherited control of concentrated wealth with self-perpetuating boards, but as Daubon contended in his report, it is difficult to internalize change.

Within the collaborative network supporting Market Creek, there were foundations that wanted to place a priority on power-building but could only fund specialized advocacy campaigns around specific policies. For these foundations, when their priorities conflicted with resident priorities, they found themselves encountering resistance.

In other initiatives around the country as well, we were observing, through both resident workshops in their home neighborhoods and in learning exchanges held at Market Creek, that collaboratives spearheaded by institutional partners often wanted to "shift power" to residents but only wanted residents to provide advocacy for policies the collaborative leadership believed important. Residents contended they had no power to set the agenda and saw this as tantamount to colonizing.

In describing a conversation with foundations about civil investing, David Mathews, President of the Kettering Foundation, wrote: "Their usual practice, these grantmakers said, was to select a problem, name it, get expert advice on how to solve it, and then criteria for getting grants and specifications for the outcomes to be achieved." He goes on to say that at some point in the conversation someone, in a moment of self-reflection on the irony of this, asked the group: "'Is what we are doing really promoting self-determination?'"[162]

Traditional foundation practices may actually undercut, he points out, "the practices that are essential to citizen-centered democracy" (i.e., practices that enable communities to solve their problems). A small elite with a large concentration of resources sets the table, controls the agenda, gets to call what success looks like. For 30 years in the field of comprehensive community change, we have been challenged by evaluating the impact of community building perhaps because, as Dr. Mathews goes on to say, this work requires looking into our own routines as grantmakers, not just the grants. "This kind of introspection challenges deeply ingrained institutional mindsets and protocols."[163]

We want to invest in areas of interest called civic capacity, civil society, social capital, and transformational change, but we are challenged to grasp that our own organizations, which are supposed to be operating in the public interest, have responsibility to engage and deliberate with the public. Assisting communities in achieving real ownership of the agenda remains a conundrum. It's much easier to grant a sole-source contract to remedy a need than it is to ponder our own role in generating the needs in the first place.

How Power Plays Out

"It would have taken a substantial amount of intentionality and hard work to wrestle the foundation/grantee relationship to the ground and re-ground it in co-investment," noted Bill Traynor, a long-time community change practitioner who has been a part of foundation place-based initiatives for over three decades.

"Foundation initiatives often follow a similar arc. Once the 'sites' are identified and notified, the initiatives feel like a horse race, with all the sites coming out the of the gate at the same time, all expected to round the first turn as a group and into the backstretch — paced too fast — and with wild overestimation about the capacity of each site to engage and execute whatever had been written into the proposal."

In the horse race, as Bill describes it, miscommunication and lack of trust take over.

"My sense is that neither 'side' has the ability to respond to what is, at some level, a genuine invitation from the other side to lean into a new kind of collaborative relationship with one another," Bill continues, "but neither side really knows how to be different in the relationship. The sites act like grantees. The foundations act like foundations. Despite the fact that the rhetoric is all about co-investment."

About six months into the effort, the hard part starts.

"The initial bright energy and euphoria gives way to a sense of confusion and anxiety on the part of the sites, once the full weight of a foundation's expectations and demands set in, including but not limited to the legions of 'technical assistance' help that is dispatched to each site, which is consciously or unconsciously a 'quality control' intervention on the part of the funders. This is, of course, consciously or unconsciously felt by the sites. Then there's the 'sobering up' period, where it all comes to a head, resulting in some rethinking and a re-set moment of one kind or another, such as re-framing the initiative or re-branding the first phase of the initiative in softer terms like 'planning'."

Bill's analogy of the horse race captures the intensely competitive, power-laden dynamics of the last 30 years of community change work.

"Eventually, there is détente and a settling into the grind. And I think grind is a pretty good word," Bill notes. "The dynamics repeat themselves in some form over again as the initiative advances. These issues, which had their seed at the onset, continue to haunt the initiative:

- Over-built, prescriptive and ever-changing frameworks. The 'framework' becomes king and the foundation culture becomes driven more by the point it was trying to make and its ability to shape and claim an elegance in its narrative, than by resourcing innovative and impactful work on the ground;
- Over-investment in technical assistance and evaluation resources, dispatched to the sites by the foundation, occupying too much time;
- Too much site staff time spent on foundation 'initiative management' and frustrations by the sites about never being able to get to the work;

- Jockeying for position as the lead horse in the race, and during the course of the initiative there will be a palpable and knowable sense of who is in the lead (i.e., the site with the best emerging story) and who is pulling up the rear. And like any horse race, the positions of these horses can change and do quite often. The sites know this, and it reinforces the traditional grantor/grantee dynamic; and

- Little investment is ever made in calling out and addressing the power dynamics between foundations and the sites, which happens only when there is a 'crisis' of trust or confidence — at the sobering up phase. But even then, addressing power is not seen as an important part of trying to forge genuine co-investment — the biggest failing."

Then, in what feels like the middle of the horse race, Bill shares with a sense of regret, "fatigue sets in and it just ends. We claim victory and move on."

"Collective impact is what people are talking about," noted another foundation staff member, who worked on community change initiatives for more than two decades. "But then when people on the ground are not talking about the same stuff as the foundations it becomes problematic. We believe in power, but...." her sentence trails off. "Behavior in foundations can be an abuse of power. What makes us think we know best what people need? We use evaluation as a weapon. Our program designs make people want to say back to us 'you fucking prove it!' It's insulting to think that people don't care deeply about results. Who gets listened to, who gets money, and who gets power is a dynamic that should be examined. Without a mechanism for accountability, we leave communities like road kill."

Another colleague and long-time foundation grants officer working on community initiatives, when asked if the foundation board he worked for thought and talked about sustainability, what would be enduring from their initiative, and what kind of help the community would need to transition smoothly as the foundation ended its commitment, replied "No, no, and no! They treated the community like a cash account. I was literally told by the leadership that place-based work was like putting money down a black hole!"

Stunned, I found myself pondering all the disrespect and deep-seated racial connotations implicit in that statement, trying to imagine how they thought a massive pit of need got created in the first place.

"How did you respond?" I asked.

"Do you mean a white hole?"

Who holds power and holds on to power and whose "public interest" is getting served? Is it fair to expect that communities change, systems change, but we — as institutions that represent the wealth inequity — don't need to change?

These were the questions the Market Creek team had to ask and answer. And we chose to seek answers for them through a lens of ownership and democracy.

Ownership and Democracy

"People believe you can't run a business as a democracy," Joe would say, "but the truth is, the greater the ownership employees have in the company, the more they invest in success."

Much of the business theory of this time was rigidly hierarchical to impose order and achieve efficiency. "Businesses are usually organized as dictatorships, not democracies," Joe would observe. But Joe, who not only believed deeply in the power of individual ownership, also believed in the power and promise of moral passion for the larger collective. He thought differently and challenged the conventional wisdom of his day.

He would share the story, which he also recounted in his second book, of how he decided during a period of rapid growth in his own business to reward people with bonuses based on the profits in their divisions, a tactic being touted widely in business schools as an incentive to boost profits. The program back-fired for Joe, creating conflict and competition throughout the company and undercutting the seamlessness of his workforce. To course-correct at this pivotal time in his business, he moved from profit centers to profit-sharing based on the total organization's performance and emphasized values — ethics, professionalism, honesty, cooperation and empowerment. More democracy and less structure in the workplace, he discovered, lifted up people's natural problem-solving and drive, and for his company, it paid off, as the Jacobs Engineering Group scaled to billions of dollars in annual revenues.

To Joe, democracy and ownership were closely linked.

"Joe taught us to practice the fundamentals," reflected Elaine Kennedy, a resident active on many of the working teams over time. "To Joe, teaching the fundamentals meant treating all people with dignity and encouraging people to have a voice in the success of their community."

To have a voice, to have ownership of the condition and success of your community, we came to believe working with Joe, was the best of what democracy is about.

In the Ecology of Democracy, David Mathews notes that "people practice a politics that is quite different from institutional politics — different in objectives, organization, and methods. That type of politics is what I've called citizen-centered because citizens are defined by their relationships with other citizens, not just their connection to the state. These civic relationships are based on reciprocity — receiving and giving in return."[164] At this level, he contends, their power "lies in the significance of the ideas they generate, the work they do by collective effort, the pervasiveness of their associations, and the hope they generate."[165] Unfortunately, he has observed, all too often institutions are "prone to act *on*" and "not in league *with*" citizens and the consequences of "well-intended efforts are often just the opposite" of what we set out to do.

Foundations are prone to define communities by their "lack-of" issues and don't fully connect. We want communities to do what we have predetermined needs to be done. We want "that population" to change without changing ourselves, undercutting the kind of democratic processes that can achieve a shift in the fundamental long-term control over decisions and assets.

In launching the Market Creek resident ownership work, we tried to figure out how to practice power-building through community-building — building public relationships and democratic civic participation on a platform that gave residents the power to name the issues and obstacles and to aim and frame action.

In the community, capacity-building focused on resident teams and their ability to bring their voice to the table, cultivate relationships, say what they cared deeply about, seek common purpose, and influence the public domain. Internally, we had to be careful not to take on community issues or address public policy that arose from the ideology of the board and staff, but rather from the working teams. We had our own self-directed capacity-building agenda, and this was focused on our ability to chip away at any of our own policies that undercut residents' ownership of change or their ability as citizens to act as the highest form of political authority.

As host to many learning exchanges with place-based teams over the years, we grew to believe in the power of connecting, not just foundation leaders, but most importantly, the resident community-builders participating in these revitalization efforts. At a convening in 2012, forty-one community builders and residents came together from fifteen cities to talk about lessons. Over the course of the gathering, the Aspen Institute Roundtable on Community Change documented what was shared and then worked with a smaller group to draft the final report, including a concluding message compiled by the group during the sessions. It was a message that — as residents and community-builders — they believed needed to be communicated as a manifesto to the field:

> "We welcome all who want to help our communities, but we don't want you to come in with your checkbooks, your professional credentials, your connection to power, and your jargon and impose your agenda on us. Respect us and our community. Don't do 'to' us but do 'with' us. Get to know us, learn about our community, and figure out how to work with us as people: as concerned citizens, neighbors, parents, brothers, and sisters, and sons and daughters. Don't patronize us. Tell us the truth about why you are in our neighborhoods, what you expect, and together we'll figure out the best ways to marry our strengths and assets with your knowledge, resources, connections, and good will.

We've seen too many of you come and go; meanwhile, we're still here. We really want to get it right this time, we think you do, too. Let's figure it out in genuine partnership."[166]

It was a plea for a different kind of relationship — one of partnership and respect. It was also a reminder that power-building starts with residents claiming their rights as citizens — "the most common way people give up their power is by thinking they don't have any,"[167] as Alice Walker noted — and as external change-agents, we — as foundations — need to be willing to give up our stranglehold over the agenda and narrative. This requires that we update our foundation policies, processes, rules and tools in a way that allows us to become co-authors of a world that genuinely honors inclusion, civic participation, shared power linked to the interests of communities, and shared prosperity rooted in our economic structures.

And because, as the Harwood Institute report contends, the work of public deliberation — "people coming together to consider issues and weigh choices and trade-offs" — is inherently political and comes with risks, we must be courageous enough to take the dare.

30

GOING UNDERGROUND: DIGGING UP THE HISTORIC INEQUITY IN PUBLIC RESOURCES

"All things start in poetry and end in real estate."

— Elwood Hopkins' Favorite Italian Proverb

Deconstructing Man-Made Barriers

"As a field, we pivot back and forth. At first, we want to measure obesity and then we want to talk about the more ethereal notion of resilience," noted Tony Iton at The California Endowment, reflecting on the state of place-based philanthropy after the first six years of the Endowment's Building Healthy Communities Initiative.

"The problem is we need to simultaneously drive both directions, away and toward. We need to figure out how to get people to doctors and help them get treatment and at the same time shift the conversation to health disparities and equity. Equity broadens the conversation to structural issues. Now we have to look beyond the healthcare delivery system to a whole ecosystem — food, parks, schools, the physical environment, and the fact there is no health without hope."

Tony was always interested in medicine. His mom, a nurse, contends that he wanted to be a doctor by age four and had picked Johns Hopkins for medical school by age twelve. Moved by famous doctors like Albert Schweitzer and being the precocious person, he is, he did just that. But growing up in

Canada under a system of universal health, he was taken aback by what he experienced in East Baltimore when he got to Johns Hopkins.

"What produced this situation?" he remembers thinking. "What drives us to tolerate this?"

After getting his medical degree, he would choose a different path "from seeing what could be achieved with pills and scalpels," as he describes it, "to seeing what could be done about reducing this demand." He would work on health policy on Capitol Hill, decide to get a law degree, and work to "deconstruct the man-made barriers" that stand in the way of health. A strong advocate for public health who has thought deeply about the social determinants of health, Tony notes "it's hard to ignore the correlation between health and lack of power. Democracy is the most important element in health."

The World Health Organization, in its 2008 report on "Closing the Gap in a Generation," noted that the "unequal distribution of health-damaging experiences is not in any sense a 'natural' phenomenon but is the result of a toxic combination of poor social policies, unfair economic arrangements, and bad politics."[168]

Tony is a staunch believer in "people power — what this democracy is supposed to be about," he says — in addressing voicelessness, and making sure that the "man-made barriers" are stared directly in the face. "We had a theory going into this work about voice and democracy, but now I have hardened in my belief that voice and power are critical," he reflects.

"Market Creek turned accountability on its head, breaking the pattern of miscommunication that comes with layers of intermediaries in place-based work by philanthropy being in a direct relationship with a community that owned the change agenda." Tony goes on to say how influential this was in the Endowment's decision to place program managers in each of their fourteen initiative sites and how they have tried, as much as possible, to give those communities a voice and "express their aspirations" in the direction of their work.

"Once you move from the idea of building social, economic, and political power to developing the concomitant practice, however, it upsets the status quo. People like the myth of democracy but don't really want to practice it." Tony describes himself as having x-ray vision for inequality. "This needs to be more than a grant here and a grant there. We need resources focused on knowing everything we can about power and politics. The root cause of inequity is about power and the legacy of racism and the other 'isms' — the things people are afraid to talk about in polite company."

Tony feels that the work of The California Endowment "got lucky" during this era of momentum around health policy in the state that was synergistic with their goals around building healthy communities but notes that that synergy isn't always there. "Policy advocacy matters," he reflected, "but when you move from talking about just services to talking about the big social justice issues that make the work tough and messy, Dr. Ross [President of the California Endowment] gives me cover."

For teams working on the ground, the political stakes go up as the work calls attention to the issues people don't want to talk about. Both inside foundations and in the public sector, Tony reflected, "The more difficult the work gets, the more skittish people can get, and they start feeling that dealing with ongoing inequality is too big and unchangeable."

In terms of being "in sync" with natural policy momentum, we were not as lucky. We were intentional about not pre-determining a policy agenda, but as the Market Creek teams took more and more ownership of what was standing in the way of change, the policy work immediately relevant to their lives and the revitalization of their community had to be addressed, even if it had no federal or statewide momentum to build on.

Alongside of residents, we advocated to reduce the disproportionately high and adverse human health and environmental effects that disinvested areas and communities of color have experienced through transportation planning, urging regional planning and infrastructure investment in poorly designed freeway off-ramps and access to bus rapid transit. To inform and enact this agenda, we formed a partnership between our metropolitan planning agency, the city, Caltrans, the federal Department of Transportation, and concerned families who previously had been told that "not enough people have died at their interchange to merit the work."

We advocated for HUD to consider expanding its primary emphasis on the highest-density neighborhoods to include areas that were historically single-family but were now suffering from infrastructure deterioration and severe over-crowding and desperately needed revitalization and affordable housing funds. Teams also advocated within the federal government for experts in the cross-departmental braiding of resources.

Teams lifted up the need for the EPA to consider waivers in the federal regulation covering brownfield clean-up so that not just non-profits, but fully-owned LLCs subsidiaries of non-profits could both reduce their risk in the clean-up process (through the separation of corporate structures) and still qualify for funds. We supported legislation related to the extension the New Markets Tax Credit Program and advocated for resident engagement language to be front-and-center in the federal Neighborhood Revitalization Initiative. We became proponents for stronger partnerships between federal agencies distributing funds to groups working on the ground and for the adoption of social equity principles in both state and federal policy.

The policy work spanned everything from land use, environmental sustainability, health and safety, and green energy to the state process for prisoner release and the police process for the handling of suspects in arrests — all policy agendas owned by the various teams involved in planning and implementing the Market Creek work. Where we could, we tried to pilot what federal and state personnel were trying to advance through their social equity and environmental sustainability principles. And locally, we provided transportation to City Hall for residents who wanted to participate as advocates for what they needed, like the passage of new zoning laws that had been delayed by the redevelopment agency for nearly six years and were impacting their community.

Elaine Kennedy, who would describe herself as someone who didn't speak very often, was one of the residents who chose to have her voice heard at City Hall. "That for me was exhilarating!" she exclaimed. Arriving on a bus filled with excited and determined residents focused on getting access to the same "mixed-use" zone that most other San Diego communities had, Elaine shared with City Council what she had observed about what her community needed, shared what steps people were prepared to take once this zone was in place, and requested that critical action move forward. With her red bandana pulling back her a long hair, she was an unflappable activist. She delivered her speech. The zoning amendment was passed unanimously with no further delays.

"Seeing the community step forward to do something we hadn't done or hadn't done in a long time — going to City Hall together — was really important," Elaine reflected. "A lot of people don't have the courage to do that alone, but when you have all your friends going with you, it was another lesson in civics."

But if public deliberation comes with risks, trying to scale impact in the world of place-based revitalization should come with more than a warning label for people to enter at their own risk. It should come with tenure. It not only made our board and foundation partners uneasy, it made the local elected officials, career special interest advocates, and government partners either grateful — if the issue-aligned with their agenda and where they needed community support — or uncomfortable — where issues were controversial and contentious, as it did around the large-scale inequities in the use of public resources.

Shining a light on equities was considered a "hot" issue because it began to shift the conversation from what changes the community needed to own to what changes the rest of the ecosystem needed to own.

"We doubt that anyone ever criticizes your character or your style when you're giving them good news or passing out big checks," write Ronald Heifetz and Marty Linsky in Leadership on the Line: Staying Alive through the Dangers of Leading. "For the most part, people criticize you when they don't like the message. But rather than focus on the content of your message, taking issue with its merits, they frequently find it more effective to discredit you...The point is not that you are blameless, but that the blame is largely misplaced in order to draw attention from the message itself."[169]

No one could argue with the message that it was wrong for some parts of town to be unduly harmed by disparities in the allocation of public resources that were impacting their health and creating barriers to economic opportunity. So as people tried to deflect these issues, we began to experience the emergence of a "discredit-the-messengers" dynamic.

"Making people grapple with unpopular tradeoffs can make you the target," Nina Smart said in discussing the rising tensions of this period. She was a long-time consultant to the foundation working on the issues of resource development and equity. She was right. To Heifetz and Linsky's thesis, there are risks working in complex, adaptive environments when the work surfaces long-held beliefs that need to be challenged and changed. People resist change because it demands new ways of thinking and being in the world. "You place yourself on the line when you tell people what they need to hear rather than what they want to hear."[170] And the resistance, they note, can come from places and people you don't expect.

As resident teams made their way toward the big "lessons in civics," the work went underground — literally under the streets, where the firmly entrenched and structural racism of public finance would be surfaced, and figuratively, where deep resistance to change lives.

With Scale the Public-Sector Barriers Just Get Bigger

A "$250,000 city-led analysis will result in a street design scheme and prioritize streets for improvement."

A local media outlet reported on a meeting being held in a neighboring community, which captured the history of neglected infrastructure in San Diego's older urban neighborhoods.[171] The meeting being held was to inform residents about the latest study being conducted in their neighborhood. This study, they were told, would be comprehensive and incorporate the work of 13 other studies.

The article went on to describe how there had actually been 27 studies since 1998, costing some $60 million. Money spent on planning was now feeding frustration because none of them ever resulted in any physical improvements.

This neighborhood was not alone. Pick a disinvested community and you'll hear the stories — how funding for substantive change feels to residents "like the rabbit in a dog race."

Lining up capital investment in development is more than a notion. It can feel like you finally made it to the gates at Oz only to hear the guard say: "Nobody gets in to see the wizard. Not nobody!"

When planning was launched in 1998 on the 10-acre factory site that would become Market Creek Plaza, there was one job, a security guard, and no economic activity. At the end of 2010, the total economic activity was $47.8 million and the total number of jobs at the Plaza stood at 215. Originally projected to create 166 jobs, the Plaza continued to exceed its benchmark. Of its employees, 65 percent were from the community and 84 percent people of color, surpassing those benchmarks. Of its $10 million in construction contracts, $7.8 million were to minority contractors, surpassing its benchmark through a "best bid" process and JCNI acting as owner-builder to control contracting. Once known for its gangs and drug deals, the community was now known for being home to fourteen major cultural events attracting nearly 25,000 people to participate.

With a track-record in hand and plans to scale impact, my expectation was that it would get easier. It felt like we had passed a test. We had figured out — through the working teams and a LADDERed approach to getting from planning to action — how to implement the change people wanted to see. People could come and kick the tires. They could see and touch the buildings that were being built, the jobs that were being created. Market Creek Plaza was profitable. And it was a place where cultural differences were celebrated instead of feared.

But this was clearly not enough.

By this time, Market Creek was envisioned as and becoming a cultural destination. But in order to successfully plan Market Creek as a "village" with connectivity, walkability, business synergy and a dynamic sense of place, we needed scale.

Scale was essential to sustainability for four reasons:

1. Reducing costs requires density and density cannot be achieved through spot development;
2. Isolated properties are difficult to develop because they are considered risky by banks and are not attractive to business;
3. Control of multiple commercial corners exponentially increases the ability to attract retailers, negotiate rents, and deliver community benefits; and
4. Greater efficiency can be achieved in management and operational costs long-term.

But achieving scale in any urban revitalization effort is up against a long history of disinvestment, neglect, and blight, and taking Market Creek to 50 acres would require every bit as much will, stamina and heavy lifting as developing the first 10 acres.

By the end of the third year (2001), when the opening of the grocery was being celebrated, Joe directed the team to buy as much of the blight as we could before any further phases came out of the ground and approved a land acquisition budget of $15 million. This budget would ultimately become a working line of credit with a local bank. A resident team walked the blocks surrounding Market Creek to assess the blighted, un-used, or under-utilized land to select those that should be purchased.

Contamination issues, family dynamics within trusts that controlled properties, and absentee land owners gambling on increasing values made land acquisition a long and difficult process. It took 10 years to assemble 52 acres.

"But it was brilliant of Joe," a resident noted, talking about how site control of this many contiguous properties made it possible for planning to occur in a completely open forum. Planning a transit-oriented village with the kind of connectivity could not have been possible doing it parcel by parcel.

In was time to confront the next barrier. The city's policy of tying infrastructure investment to area development had led San Diego to grow beautiful urban-sprawl communities with great schools, parks, and freeway access, all funded through the cost of high-priced housing and commercial space, but had left the older, urban neighborhoods without any infrastructure investment.

With infrastructure tied to infill development, the additional burden of financing projects in a disinvested community is too great to offset with a revenue stream. So when plans expanded from Market Creek Plaza to a 50-acre village, a scale we thought we needed to have a self-sustaining economic engine, development was destined to stall.

The perception by many at City Hall was that since we were developing in a disinvested community, it was cheaper to build. I found myself in countless meetings with public sector partners only to hear that they couldn't believe our costs. "You could develop a really nice project downtown for that!" was often the comment. 'No kidding," I would reply.

"Let's see," I would follow up, "building costs are what they are. Same labor. Same materials. Same building codes. What's different is that people assume land is cheap, but the fact is the impact of long-term economic decline makes it very expensive to redevelop when you add the cost of cleaning up that land and fixing the large-scale impact of neglected infrastructure."

Not only was development disproportionately more expensive, we couldn't pass these higher costs along to the end user — the retailers who would create jobs in the community or the residents themselves who needed lower-cost housing. I was invited into the home of a family, a small rental unit, who had six children in one bedroom. Residents reported that this was not uncommon, especially for the newer immigrant groups. San Diego's "smart growth" policies had priced them out of other communities and the high cost of development in the older communities had caused a severe housing shortage and over-crowding.

With a newly-formed Housing Team, we explored making up the higher costs through dramatic increases in densities but for housing to be affordable to our market, this only translated to a larger financial gap. In order to complete the commercial hub with higher densities, residents were concerned about abrupt and radical changes in scale in their historically single-family community. In addition to the infrastructure deficit, the land configuration and the creek and its tributary system made it very difficult and costly to plan projects.

Thinking the development process would get easier as we moved along proved disappointing. With scale, the barriers just got bigger.

Digging for Answers

"Probably the biggest accomplishment of the Market Creek experience was assembling and entitling the land," noted Charles Davis.

Charles grew up in the neighborhood. "We were the second African American family on the street," he would tell you. "It was a middle- and working-class community back then. We grew up with parks, schools, stores — the same amenities that other communities had."

But then in the 1960s that all began to change. "The blight crept up on us. The gangs, the drugs, the drive-by shootings, the factories closing and the loss of jobs," he reflected, "so by the 1980s it was all different."

Charles had building in his blood. His grandfather was a contractor, his dad an electrician. "It's all I ever wanted to do." By the time he joined the Jacobs Team as Director of Projects, he had nearly 30 years of experience in real estate development, construction, and project management, degrees in both engineering and business, and experience building his own company. Urban development was his passion, as was the southeastern San Diego community. "I never really left. I grew up here and I loved it. I loved the canyons and the hills, the creek, and the open space. It was home."

After decades of developing real estate, Charles knows what it takes. "With this kind of work, you have to take the long view," he noted. "When a community has experienced 40 years of decline, it will take 40 years to overcome the disinvestment." In helping to boost the economic development of his community, Charles believed the land assembly was critical. "It was perhaps the most important legacy for Joe. It set the foundation for large commercial impact that will be unfolding for decades to come."

Village plans called for putting 52 acres of blight back into productive use; replacing substandard housing with nearly 1,000 quality affordable homes; and restoring nearly 5,500 linear feet of wetlands. They included 1.6 million square feet of new construction, bringing more than $300 million in contracts to the community, attracting over 250 new businesses, and creating 2,000 jobs.

"When Market Creek Plaza went up, there was a big shift and everyone was excited by the village plans," Charles reflected, "but we knew it would take time to address the over-riding challenge we still faced in physical development."

In the early stages of our work, when our team talked about addressing community disinvestment, we were focused on the lack of private capital for new development, the blighted land, and the vacant, run-down buildings. This was the impact of capital flight that was visible. It was a picture we could paint.

But _what wasn't visible_ was the large impact of the disinvestment that was missing from the picture — the infrastructure.

"When an area is disinvested, it creates funding deficits so large," Charles Davis noted, "that certain projects can't afford to be there. After a while why would anyone invest in infrastructure if there is no development. It becomes a vicious cycle."

As in any market-depressed area, attracting private investment in residential, commercial, and industrial projects depends on infrastructure. Inadequate streets and sewer systems, missing sidewalks, poorly-constructed interstate on- and off-ramps, huge park deficits, too large of a service area for emergency first responders to meet their seven-and-half minute deadline — these are overwhelming barriers.

Our greatest challenge was that creating a major housing and job center that was affordable to the existing community was not possible if these multiple infrastructure deficiencies were placed on top of normal development costs.

This is exactly what happened.

Achilles Heel

"The only way to make progress is to have diverse perspectives in the room," Roger Williams commented. "When foundations only talk to foundations, city folk only talk to city folk, and developers only talk with developers, we miss the boat completely."

Roger, who was Senior Fellow and Director of Responsible Redevelopment at the Anne E. Casey Foundation, served as an advisor to our team when Casey confirmed its investment in Market Creek Plaza. He had joined the Casey team asking "why don't we put all the people together?"

Roger — Rogelio — was born in Panama and moved to New York with his mother and siblings. His father would join them a few years later after he paid off his family's passage. In these early years, he would call the couch his bed in their subsidized housing complex and grow to appreciate how important housing and economic development are for families trying to get a foothold. "For those of us who lived there, these things helped turn our lives around."

In law school at NYU during the late 1960s, Roger joined the protests, labeled "Gym Crow," in Harlem over the segregated gymnasium being planned on public land by Columbia University and worked on issues of urban distress in Brooklyn's black neighborhood of Bed-Stuy (Bedford-Stuyvesant). He would become, from that time forward, a passionate advocate of finance with a social mission. Serving as a Vice President with Freddie Mac, First Union National Bank, and Fannie Mae, Roger would focus his energies on minority lending and responsible initiatives aimed at assisting unserved markets.

Then he would join the Casey Foundation — and bring with him a different kind of expertise than foundations at that time had traditionally known. His background in finance upped the ante on neighborhood transformation, responsible redevelopment, and blended public and private capital strategies. He was a "gift" to us provided with our program-related investment from this national foundation, a resource who shared our commitment to having diverse voices in the room.

"People are afraid of projects that encourage local engagement. They see it as just adding to the cost. In some cases, it's just fear of dealing with people that aren't like them. I wanted to have developers see what you were doing with residents. They don't see the connection with how this involvement adds to the vitality of a community. Unquestionably your cross-cultural residents working teams," he shared when asked why he wanted to help us, "were perhaps the most important work being done. Folks were comfortable with each other."

In June 2009, he organized a learning exchange with The Urban Land Institute (ULI). "You had the power of resident engagement to share," Roger noted. "I had a long-term connection with the ULI to share."

We convened developers, foundation representatives, city personnel, and ULI members to explore the underlying issues of disinvestment in the Diamond Neighborhoods and the next community north, City Heights, and dissect how investors could get returns, how the community could benefit, and how inclusion and sustainability could come together.

ULI brought Dena Belzer from Strategic Economics in Berkeley, California, to talk about transit-oriented development (TOD) and provide examples of public and private financing mechanisms for the infrastructure and amenities that are needed to make it viable. Typically, she pointed out, when there is a TOD, the development process starts with the public sector funding the infrastructure and amenities and then the private sector takes it from there. "In disinvested communities, however, the projects typically don't generate sufficient revenues to cover the high infrastructure costs and so the process needs to reverse itself, which is very difficult to do."

It was at this summit that the head of the planning department for San Diego called the city's infrastructure financing policy its "Achilles Heel."

The group reviewed the specific details of Market Creek to advise on how to bring it to scale and concluded that the infrastructure costs needed to be shared across a much larger region, like a city-wide bond measure. The question then became how?

With the downturn in the economy, which caused a drop in the foundation and our partners' asset values, it was becoming imperative to move the pipeline of development any way we could.

To accelerate construction, JCNI's plan was to act as the master developer on the village to protect the resident team process, but partner with other developers. This proved challenging as well. The developers that were interested in "partnering" wanted us to provide all the advance pre-development financing. We were not large enough to do that and needed partners that could bring capital to the table.

We knew a bond measure for infrastructure could take years, just to build the political will, so we needed to find faster alternatives while this idea percolated. The issues that were in front of us that we needed to address were the timing for meeting the regulatory requirements, especially the restoration of the next segment of Chollas Creek, issues related to unfair cost burdening, and the log-jammed internal debate within the city about parking requirements.

Up a Creek Without a 'Dozer

"It was like riding on a Tonka Truck — a real one!" laughed Steve Groves, talking about growing up in his dad's business. Like Joe Jacobs, Steve's dad was an entrepreneur. His business venture, CATS Excavating, would evolve into a family business. "Dad not only made sure we had a work ethic," Steve reflected, "he took people in who needed help. He was a good man and a great role model. We learned a lot from him."

When you talk to Steve Groves and his brother Cliff Smith about bulldozers, you will hear a story about all children's love of trucks. You can just picture Christmas morning and two kids running downstairs to see what is under the tree and feel the sheer glee. The rugged steel loader, action levers, and big rubber treads — tires as big as dad — begging to be taken to the sand pile or mud pit. What you will also hear is a story about values, a love of people, and a commitment to learning.

Steve and Cliff took their childhood love of Tonka Trucks and family and turned it into a career on bulldozers moving dirt. "We grew up on tractors," described Steve. "We thought it was the most fun job there could be." Even their friends thought it was cool. "In high school, when our friends were out on a Friday night, they would go by us out on a construction site and wave. We had a kind of celebrity status!"

If Steve and Cliff had celebrity status as teenagers, they are now rock stars. Recognized a one of the top grading companies in San Diego, Steve and Cliff are now all about what they call "big dirt."

"We were working in our father's business doing single family homes and small subdivisions. Our niche was small lots — the places where no one wanted to go!" notes Steve, when their dad suddenly passed away. "When dad died, we lost our backbone. We were in mourning, our tractor broke down, and we didn't know what to do. Then Reese called."

Reese Jarrett, like Steve and Cliff, was born in the community, not far from where the lot that would become Market Creek Plaza, and he had a heart for building. After a four-year term as head of the area redevelopment agency in the 1980s, Reese returned to the private sector as a developer. "Reese came and got us and put us on a job. He was private about his generosity, but he gave us the money we needed to fix the tractor so we could keep going. You know how everyone talks about how it takes a village? Well, it took a village to nurture this company. A lot of people were there for us."

When the idea of developing the old Langley factory site — which would become Market Creek — was beginning to be planned, CATS had three employees. With the help of their community, they had come through the worst of times, armed with the work ethic their dad had instilled in them, and surrounded by people who were looking out for them, like Reese.

Cliff, who is eight years younger than Steve — "my baby brother," Steve is quick to say — first heard of the Jacobs Center through Rickey Laster, the head of the Multicultural Contractors Association, and wanted to be sure Steve and Cliff took advantage of the next opportunity. Steve, the skeptic, thought it was "some kind of hustle," he remembers. "Cliff dragged me to

Rickey's house to really listen. He wanted me to know what boat I was about to miss!"

"We were a mom and pop shop, but we knew dirt," notes Steve. "What we didn't know was bonding, business lines of credit, software for estimating, how to build a banking relationship, and managing change orders — these were all new to us."

The Construction Working Team had organized their planning around the things that they knew would stand in the way of community contractors getting on the job and created a program of "best bid" contracting and educational support in order to open the doors to the opportunity Market Creek represented, both in new construction and in creek remediation.

"We followed the program. We went to school, literally," Steve reflected. "It brought us into the new millennium to do business with the big boys."

Today, CATS Excavating, now CATS General Engineering, is an award-winning company of 20 people. "Armed with education and know-how, we went on to do a heck of a lot, including getting our contractor's license," Steve noted. On the tributary project, the second phase of the creek restoration, CATS was honored with both an Orchid Award and Project of the Year. "On that project, we had the opportunity to manage the subs ourselves."

Steve and Cliff remember Joe Jacobs vividly. "We met inside the construction office. Joe had on a baseball cap and it was an intimate moment with him for us," Steve noted. "He was very humble," Cliff added. "Here was this guy who had brought his company to the point of contracts all over the world...he was brilliant, but he was also just down to earth."

"What I'll never forget was that he was adamant that he wasn't there to give us anything but opportunity. That was his big message for us. It was on us to take advantage of what opportunity was being offered," Steve commented. "And because we did, it was like he was at our side. And his vote of confidence in us didn't end with Market Creek. He trusted us. He backed our construction bond for the first jobs following Market Creek, which gave us the capacity to participate on the demolition of buildings for the new baseball park downtown. He also backed an ongoing working line of credit that got us through the ups and downs of business."

As a foundation CEO, I was always in a conversation about the ratio of dollars invested and impact returned. With Joe, a risk-taker and a business man at my side, I began to see how small amounts of money could be leveraged into millions of dollars of capacity-building. By putting $50,000 in a certificate of deposit that would eventually be returned, CATS was able to open and manage a working line of credit that helped them compete with the big boys, as Steve framed it. "We were armed. We got paid on time because all of our paperwork was in and well done. Working on the types of big projects that historically were known as "sub-breakers," Steve and Cliff knew how to compete, manage money, grow loyal employees, and give back to their community.

When the IPO took place, they were all-in. "People invested in us, so we wanted to invest in our community. This is where we grew up. We felt proud. We still have the little statue we were given as one of Market Creek's contractors and investors of a symbol of a hand. It is in the middle of our conference table." The statue Steve referred to was a four-inch-high replica of a hand symbolizing the petroglyph carvings in rocks made by America's earliest artisans considered sacred testimony. The hand, a symbol of peace, strength, and friendship used in the Market Creek logo, sits on a rock platform and reads "I have made my mark and it will endure long after I am gone." From the grading of the initial 20 acres, to the restoration of the four segments of the creek, to the rip-rap that slows the force of the water, to the floating dock, Steve and Cliff made their mark.

"What was amazing is that the Jacobs Team never told us how to do the job; we had to figure it out," reflected Steve. "I'll never forget the time early on when we had to figure out a way to cross the site before the vehicular bridge was built and the trolley underpass connected both sides of the property. What we decided on was building an Arizona Crossing."

An Arizona Crossing is a type of bridge common in Arizona and other southwestern states where drainage infrastructure isn't seen as being necessary for dry riverbeds. These simple bridges allow small amounts of water to run through culverts, but overflow on the road in the rare times when there is heavy rainwater.

"We had the creek opened up, the permits had been pulled, and to get our tractors across we put six 48-inch pipes down and covered them with gravel so we could drive our tractors over them.

"One night we were on the job late, and it started to rain." Steve's eyes lit up in telling the story. "Then the water started to rise and we had all of our headlights focused on the channel wondering what was going to happen, crossing our fingers that it would hold up!"

"It was wild!" Steve and Cliff looked at each other and started laughing like people who had survived an exhilarating and hair-raising event. They had to take action. "If we hadn't pulled the 'dozer in front of our Arizona Crossing, all 48 pipes would have ended up down in the trailer park!"

"All we could think of was to pull a 'dozer in behind all the storm drains to hold them in place! The water came all the way up to the door of the truck's cab and we thought we were going to be washed away along with the pipes! We couldn't believe it! We knew we had ownership of this project; it was our project, and we had to figure it out!"

Steve and Cliff, along with everyone on the teams, were grateful that the pipes held, the trailer park was safe, and the bulldozers dried out. But what remained for everyone involved was an undying can-do spirit. For the people involved, ownership meant figure it out.

We would have to call on this can-do spirit throughout the project, one log jam after another. In facing the larger and larger challenges of infrastructure as the vision of the village grew in scale, we knew if we couldn't figure it out, we would be up a creek, only this time without a 'dozer!

In front of us this time were the problems of timing, cost burdening, and opposing forces over parking.

The Timing of Regulatory Requirements

We understood why in areas of long-term disinvestment the regulatory requirements would be greater than for projects in greenfields. The County Health Department was concerned, and rightly so, about the development of brownfields and wanted to assure they had been remediated. We knew this was critical.

We also understood why the State Water Resources Control Board, as well as other local and State agencies, cared about the area's natural resources, like Chollas Creek, which cut through the Market Creek Project Area. The waterway system clearly needed to be cleaned up and restored. To do that, a Creek Enhancement Program had been adopted by the city in 2002, a press conference held, and State commitments made to work with the city to assist in implementation. As a point of control for the city, all properties containing creek segments could not be financed and developed until the creek was restored. Despite the wonderful press conference held by the state and city at Market Creek, the $2 million allocated for restoration were used by the city for planning — and once again left nothing for implementation.

We didn't want to fight the regulation. The resident team just needed help with timing.

Through surveys and team meetings, the community had voiced the need for a major drug store as a priority after the grocery. After years of effort, JCNI had finally secured a Letter of Intent from Walgreens to anchor the next commercial phase of the village. This started the clock ticking, giving us 60 days to deliver a contract that could offer time-certainty for the business to operate.

Because of the property's proximity to the creek, the city required the project to include: 1) creek restoration, 2) development of a trail to make the creek accessible for public use, and 3) the requirement that we maintain and accept liability for the creek and trail under strict environmental laws in perpetuity as a condition of placing the drug store within a half-mile walking distance of the creek. At a cost of $3.2 million dollars, Walgreens could not adsorb this in its cost per square foot, requiring that we figure out how to raise the additional money

JCNI had already implemented, with a set of partners, the creek restoration on the south branch that cut through Market Creek Plaza and on its tributary to the east in preparation for development there. By this time, CATS General Engineering had considerable expertise in urban stream restoration so our applications for support from the California Department of Water Resources and the State Resources Agency for this northern piece of the creek enhancement — one for the trail system and one for the actual restoration — were well-received.

But the money for the trail system was awarded first and came with a tight timeline for implementation. The building of the trail wasn't possible until the restoration of the creek itself was completed and that grant decision hadn't been made yet. In the meantime, Walgreens needed to move forward.

These challenges were typical. When we started Market Creek, we thought lining up physical development timelines with community building was hard. Now it looked easy compared to lining up permitting, public sector fundraising timelines, and project development.

"That is what keeps developers from wanting to work here," Chip noted. He was the person responsible for bringing the project in on time and on budget.

Unfair Cost Burdening

The result of decades of disinvestment, the infrastructure deficits for the project area were evaluated to be $22 million, and the local redevelopment agency's estimated bonding capacity for funding infrastructure couldn't even reach the amount needed for one corner. Placing this expense on the first project to come out of the ground, we protested, was unfair cost burdening.

The city had held up permits for a small 52-unit housing development because of recreational park deficits in the community and would not let any additional commercial development move forward without fixing the off-ramps on the Martin Luther King Freeway. We contended that since the problem was created by CalTrans as far back in the 1960s and that money allocated to fix them was spent on other projects, CalTrans needed to address this as an environmental justice issue.

The park deficit requirement was later removed, but we had to apply for an environmental justice grant from CalTrans, which — once awarded — allowed the team to mobilize community planning around this issue.

Opposing Forces Around Parking

Along with timing, opposing forces within the city itself made development difficult. Parking requirements for housing was an example.

The city parking ratio requirement ran counter to the intent of the sustainable community development guidelines and California's targets for greenhouse gas emissions reductions. The goal of the city and state legislation was to provide people in smart-growth communities the option of choosing public transit, ride-sharing, or walking to workplaces.

The Village at Market Creek's first residential project was designed to provide 52 units of affordable housing located less than 50 feet from a multi-modal transportation hub. A smart growth infill project typically requires a parking structure because of land limitations, a cost estimated at approximately $30,000 per space. For this particular project — $3 million.

According to a study prepared for the San Diego Housing Commission and City of San Diego Planning Department in 2003, it was determined that parking requirements around transit centers with affordable housing should have lower parking requirements. The study showed that all the developments maintained empty spaces even during the at-home peak times. The city intended to amend the policy, so we worked with the city staff to get a variance to move ahead with the village residential project at the new proposed levels. Opposing forces within the city, however, stopped the variance, requiring us to wait until it completed the effort to vet the new policy citywide. The timeline — an estimated two years.

Should we wait and build a better project? Or should we push forward, waste money, and have vacant space?

Even before the number of foreclosures began to rise after 2008, people in our community were suffering from severe over-crowding. Now with the shift in housing needs, people were increasingly desperate for rental housing.

Large-scale infrastructure deficiencies, brownfield clean-up, the need to restore toxic waterways that cut across multiple properties involving multiple regulatory agencies, outdated community plans, unfair cost burdening — all

I kept thinking of was this line I heard once: "If it's hard, I'll get it for you right away; but if it's impossible, it might take a while."

The oppositional stances within the city over parking was minor compared to San Diego's public infrastructure policies. In digging down to the heart of these policies, we began to hit the bedrock of structural racism in public finance.

This was obviously going to take a while.

Underground Politics

"If you don't like the look out the window, change the landscape; don't shut the window."

Anne Haines, the CEO of Accion New Mexico and a partner from the very early days of our work, was reflecting on the partnership. "That's what you always used to say, and that's what I liked about working with your team. You have to have a mindset for change. You always have a choice."

The Jacobs Team had helped Anne launch one of the first six Accion micro-lending sites in the U.S. and she had been a pivotal partner in teaching us about taking risks, changing language, and practicing real partnership. Twenty years later, she had leveraged that early support into a five-state expansion and was always piloting new products to reach her market.

"It can be crazy-making for people who don't like change, however!" she laughed with her quick wit and mischievous smile.

As we hit 2011, I would think about the next round of challenges and choices and wonder laughingly if I could get the landscape to change before I had the window shut right on my head! I found myself thinking of Elizabeth Gilbert's line, "God never slams a door in your face without opening a box of Girl Scout cookies!"[172] I was hoping so. I could even imagine Elwood Hopkins, with that same mischievous smile that Anne has, chuckling, thinking about his favorite Italian proverb and saying to me: "I told you — All things start in poetry and end in real estate!"

To get the poetry back we had to face our next set of challenges and choices. To Anne's point, we needed to figure out what landscape needed to change since we weren't about to shut the window. That landscape turned out to be underground — physically and politically — making it difficult to shine a light on.

"Asking people to look at inequities across neighborhoods made many people angry, fearful, or defensive," Nina Smart noted. "The topic was considered politically dangerous. It required tradeoffs. At its heart was fear. People were wondering what would happen when these huge historical disparities in public investment were in the spotlight," she reflected.

Nina was probing by nature. You could see it in her face — as expressive as her clothing. She was a walking statement of wearable art. Eclectic. An angled mix of bias-cut multi-colored fabrics that would give her a sweeping flow — tiered and adventurous. If I didn't know her father was a hard-driving football coach, I would think she was born to troubadours or artists. Her soft and colorful style, along with her graceful, unassuming, and self-effacing way-of-being, belied her pragmatic, clear-thinking, and straightforward smarts. Members of the funders collaborative — on a journey to heightened awareness about how we all stereotyped each other — were often surprised by her Stanford education and her grasp of the most complex and interconnected issues.

In 2010, the team she was supporting called itself the "Commission on San Diego Regional Infrastructure and Equity."

Triggered by the Annie E. Casey Foundation's convening with The Urban Land Institute, the idea of an infrastructure task force had grown out of mutual interest on the part of several funders to learn more, including the Ford Foundation, The California Endowment, U.S. Bank, the Parker Foundation, and the Jacobs Family Foundation.

Following the convening, a 12-person "Commission" was put together to collectively represent a broad spectrum of the region and provide multiple perspectives on this issue. The seats were filled with representatives from San Diego's older urban neighborhoods, along with other south-of-Interstate 8 communities that also suffered disinvestment, an advocacy group called

Sustainable San Diego, the San Diego Chamber of Commerce, and the City Council President's office. It also included a representative from the San Diego Neighborhood Funders, along with ex-officio members from the San Diego's Association of Governments and another San Diego City Council office.

Two important partners were selected by the Commission to provide extensive experience in the issues of public infrastructure, equity, and public policy — PolicyLink, headquartered in Oakland, which conducted a review of community campaigns for infrastructure equity and synthesized four case studies; and locally, the Center for Policy Initiatives (CPI), which conducted a scan of infrastructure finance and equity issues related to public infrastructure investment in San Diego, Chula Vista, and National City.

Despite challenging delays in getting access to data, the Commission and its partners painstakingly pieced together how and why the infrastructure deficits began to grow exponentially, leaving behind a trail of blight. They tracked the brisk infill development during the period when development fees were waived and looked at the insensitively-designed, small multi-family housing projects that had been rapidly built to absorb San Diego's regional growth without any investment in new infrastructure. They also examined the long-term impacts of California's Prop 13, which capped property tax assessment increases and raised the threshold for approval of new fees and taxes, thereby seriously limiting cities' ability to raise revenue to pay for infrastructure.

The Commission also studied the consequences of Development Impact Fees as a mechanism for raising revenue. At first a model for capturing the cost of needed infrastructure, the strategy quickly began to unravel as development in lower-income older communities stopped and high-income, high-cost new housing was built in the suburban outer ring of the City of San Diego. Infrastructure (parks, schools, fire stations, and sidewalks) in the newer communities was built and paid for largely through developer fees, intentionally or unintentionally creating exclusive communities that were exacting a disproportionate share of the cities' budgets for ongoing maintenance and operation.

We thought the 2008 passage of California Senate Bill 375 — the climate action mandate to reduce greenhouse gas emissions through coordinated transportation and land use — would ratchet up the planning and financing of mixed-use, compact design, transit-oriented projects, only to have redevelopment agencies eliminated across the state. These agencies had the single — albeit completely inefficient and insufficient — funding mechanism that existed to advance the needed infrastructure for the older urban neighborhoods to participate with the rest of the region.

If a critical function of local government is to equitably distribute public services and facilities to its citizens, this Commission could quickly discern that for the regions' older urban areas, government was failing.

"This was historic discrimination," Nina described. "Anyone who had ever taken the trolley from downtown could see that there wasn't equitable investment along the route. Try to walk home from the transit station and the sidewalk runs out in 100 feet. Imagine you are a mom trying to walk your children to a park without a sidewalk or that you are driving your family somewhere and have to deal with the dangerous on- and off-ramps of the freeways."

"And what people don't see is even worse," she continued. "What about the slow response time for a medical emergency or a fire in your home because there's a shortage of four fire stations in your district? What about the fact that the 60-year-old clay sewer lines have been reabsorbed into the ground and sewage is just running through the dirt below the surface of your street, waiting to bubble up with the first rain?"

The Center for Policy Initiatives report cited two different San Diego studies evaluating response times to medical emergencies and structural fires, one undertaken in 2005 and one from 2011, indicating that District Four, where we were working, needed four additional fire stations to meet the standards.[173] The residents that served on the Commission were upset.

As residents delved into the information and worked with the larger team in drafting a report on their findings, they pushed to keep the language — in a field heavy with jargon — clear and understandable. They wanted the issue of infrastructure deficits defined more broadly to include access to fresh foods and services. And they didn't want to develop strategies divided between governmental jurisdictions — city, state, or federal. They just wanted their communities to work.

"From sidewalks to sewers to parks and libraries, infrastructure is the backbone of our neighborhoods. But far too often, cities cannot or choose not to provide adequate funding to build, operate, and maintain these community assets," the PolicyLink study reported, providing context to the history that led to the inequity across communities.

"The legacy of housing discrimination in this country along with decades of inadequate affordable housing options has pushed many low-income families and people of color into older neighborhoods, where infrastructure deficits are concentrated," the report highlighted. "Sparse revenue dollars cause city governments to push the cost of developing and maintaining infrastructure onto our neighborhoods directly, exacerbating existing inequalities as residents with higher incomes and greater home values have more resources to provide for their communities while leaving poorer neighborhoods behind."[174]

In the greater San Diego region, not only did older neighborhoods fail to keep pace, but the disparities between old and new communities had reached a magnitude of extraordinary scale. The disproportionate investment of public dollars was estimated at $2 billion.

And this disparity was being compounded daily by infrastructure investment decisions made through the capital improvements budget, which was not being guided by either community input or existing community plans.

Residents on the Commission had been questioning the why and the how. The question to follow was — what now? They believed the public officials they had voted for should be fighting for equity; elected officials argued back that without more community support and voter turnout, they were lacking the back-up they needed to tackle an issue of this scale. The prevailing thinking was a win for one neighborhood required a loss in another.

"Politicians feared that if residents really knew about the totality of the inequities, there would be an uprising — one which could wedge local politics into deeper rifts," Nina reflected.

Addressing the two-tiered area-wide system for allocating dollars to infrastructure required political will that was in its formative stage when the recession deepened, support was pulled in from the network of local funders, and competition among the participating non-profit partners for Ford Foundation funding escalated. Without adequate time needed to forge a process of accountability among the non-profit partners involved with the commission, the work began to fracture and fall apart. Capacity-building wasn't built in and the rivalry over funding created feelings of distrust among partners, adding to the challenge of political will.

On the search for what had caused this incredibly high level of historic discrimination, we had sent Nina — like Barbara Day's journey into the belly of the Department of Social Services — on a scavenger hunt, along with a resident team, but this time it was underground. Their charge was to go under the streets where the sewers, the water systems, and the utilities were telling a story. What surfaced was the giant gap between values and behavior that lives at the intersection of race and place — the perfect political storm.

The Perfect Political Storm

"It's wildfire," noted a local official. Calling infrastructure a "wedge issue." Political leaders were concerned about the public rising up to demand standards. It quickly became framed as "politically dangerous."

Members of the funders collaboration described it as "unsexy" — one posed the question, "Who wants to stand up and say: Oh, by the way, we need to spend millions of dollars on our sewer system?" It was becoming unclear about whether or not they would stand by the residents on the Commission with their personal political clout.

"Ask anyone if they believe that public resources, services, and benefits should be equally distributed among the pubic and they will say 'Yes, of course.' There is broad agreement that no matter your race, your income level, your community, public resources should be disbursed in a equitable way, and they have faith that the equitable distribution of public dollars is occurring. But what if it isn't? Since the issue was a costly one to address, the sentiment had been to delay, ignore and postpone," Nina noted. "But that's how the cycle of deepening the inequities got reinforced. Up to this time, it was easy for partners to blame the conditions on the community. People could see there was something unsafe. By keeping the focus on the gangs, it didn't require anyone outside the community to change. This did."

If residents stayed quiet, it was theorized, the issue could be ignored. But residents continued their effort to know the standards.

So to deflect the issue, the messengers were discredited.

Wrongly, we all under-estimated the role Joe played in our ability to keep things moving despite critics, confusion, fear, or political tension. In looking back on this moment, I didn't take the time to build a solid bridge of allies, including my board. Growing financial stress from the recession, the struggle heating up among the non-profit collaborators for Ford Foundation resources, and simultaneous hotly-debated board and community discussions over whether a Walmart could or couldn't lease in the village caused a chain reaction.

Within months I would be gone, and just two weeks shy of releasing the feared Commission report on infrastructure, which would have shed light on the disparities among neighborhoods and why the situation occurred, the team would be disbanded.

"I invested years of my life, paying attention, asking questions to understand the disparities among neighborhoods and why efforts to address those inequities continued to get stalled. We were uncovering the answer. We had raised the money to lift the issues up nationally and then it got dropped," Nina reflected.

The report would never be released, resulting in — as one team member framed it — "one big incomplete." Sadly, for me, for Nina, and the team that had given so much time and worked so hard digging through the facts and understanding the long history of disinvestment, we received an incomplete — an incomplete with the Ford Foundation, an incomplete with PolicyLink, an incomplete with our San Diego Neighborhood Funders, and — at least for this moment in time — an incomplete for the community.

Reflections on the "Incomplete"

In the search for truth, it can hurt — both personally and professionally — when you unearth it.

We were asking ourselves:

- If government has a responsibility to serve all people and equitably distribute resources for the benefit of the entire public, shouldn't there be an acknowledgement by the government of the economic distress caused by this not occurring?
- And shouldn't government then become an agent for economic development by rectifying the past politics of infrastructure resources that now keep certain areas economically distressed by addressing both the imbalance and the resulting impact?

We thought so.

"Infrastructure was considered a zero-sum game," noted Victor Rubin from PolicyLink, who was part of the team working on case studies of how other regions were addressing the issue. "Collectively, people weren't ready to tackle it, although you were clearly in sync with a growing national movement. The Commission just happened to be too early."

Today, the issue of infrastructure finance is a conversation that is in the public domain, but what I don't hear is the conversation about the scale of the historic disparities of public resources and what has resulted from it.

As so astutely pointed out in the USC monograph, "Place-Based Initiatives in the context of Public Policy and Markets: Moving to Higher Ground," today's community change work needs an integrated and dual framework.[175] I had long thought that infrastructure was an issue the large regional and national funders along with the big policy groups and think-tanks needed to take on rather than place-based foundations. I came to see that while local place-based efforts need to be teamed with regional and national movements to address issues of this scale, residents at the neighborhood-level play a critical role.

This experience reaffirmed my belief in three necessary components of community revitalization:

1. Policy work blended with place-based teams, which in this case caused the infrastructure issue to surface;
2. The central involvement of committed citizens, whose voices are needed to deliver with volume the message that historic disparities in the allocation of public resources is a primary root cause of ongoing disinvestment; and
3. The importance of the philanthropic community not working in silos, which dilutes the impact of inequity, making it difficult to see beyond single issues, like street lights, school facilities, bike lanes, transit, or the environment, to the totality of the equity issue.

"Our job at the Jacobs Center was to identify and remove barriers. Real ones. That's what we did. That was our very reason for being," Nina described. "And we had hit on what was keeping the community stuck. There is a case to be made nationally for community change efforts being targeted at the regional metro-level to break things loose. That was clearly needed. But without the place-based work that was unfolding, there is no doubt in my mind that this issue would not have been so clearly understood."

As the issue of failing infrastructure becomes part of the national dialogue, San Diego will be among those cities trying to figure out how to rethink public finance. Those deliberations are likely to be nested in discussions about job creation throughout the region and reducing greenhouse gas emissions regionally, not in the social and economic justice container it will need to be in to change the outcome of such major historical inequities.

But wherever the residents of San Diego's older urban areas find the right platform for these conversations, it is my hope that they are prepared, as a result of the Commission's work, and have the information they need to advance the social justice issues embedded in the conversation…before what happened in Flint, Michigan with the water supply happens with the Diamond Neighborhoods' dissolved clay sewer system.

ENDURING
CHANGE

DEEPLY INVESTED & CONNECTED:
RISK & REWARD

31

ENDURING TRANSITION

"Success can only be measured against the possibility of failure." [176]

— Joe Jacobs

All Change Must Be Endured

"This is a good sign, having a broken heart," writes Elizabeth Gilbert in her soul-searching novel about taking ownership of her own life, <u>Eat Pray Love</u>. "It means we have tried for something."[177]

I had my heart broken more than once — trying for something. Aiming at a new future, we had dared to dream big, worked together in teams, and laid a ground base for people to have ownership and control of critical assets in their community. We had invested and connected deeply.

I'm a resilient person by nature. In the face of failure, challenges, and setbacks, I dust off and try hard to bring energy, joy, and happiness into the world every day. But I also believe, to quote Teilhard de Chardin, whose line I read in Stephen Covey's <u>The Fifth Discipline</u>: "we are not human beings having a spiritual experience, we are spiritual beings having a human experience."[178] We not only need to <u>see</u> in the "human dimension," we need to acknowledge what it means to <u>feel</u> in that dimension as well.

But as we all know, it can be hard to keep our hearts open. To feel deeply can hurt.

For me, the journey toward the resident ownership of neighborhood change was two decades — extraordinary by all standards in the field of place-based philanthropy. It was long and precious.

But all things change, including families, and the foundation board, having added the next generation to its members, delivered my hardest heartbreak: "We've decided to go in a different direction."

It had been seven years since Joe Jacobs had passed away and the tone of the conversations about the vision and goals of the foundation had been slowly changing. Joe had thrived on risk and the blood-pumping stress that accompanies it. To do this work, it required us, as a friend once described it, to have the entrepreneurial spirit needed to "dive in the deep end."

In his book, The Ingenuity Gap, Thomas Homer-Dixon, commenting on today's work environment, could have been describing my life:

> "We demand that [leaders] solve, or at least manage, a multitude of interconnected problems that can develop into crises without warning; we require them to navigate an increasingly turbulent reality that is, in key aspects, literally incomprehensible to the human mind; we buffet them on every side with bolder, more powerful special interests that challenge every innovative policy idea; we submerge them in often unhelpful and distracting information; and we force them to decide and act at an even faster pace."[179]

"Well yes," I used to think, "but that's the job."

Market Creek had taken us away from how foundations typically function — a world of inside-out organizational planning and decision-making — to a place of enormous challenge and opportunity — an outside-in network of teams.

I had tried for something. I believed in Joe's dream of courageously leading with values, taking big risks, leveraging what we had, and going out of business. I believed in shared decision-making. I believed in the capacity of ordinary people to create a new future. I believed the idea of bringing up self-generating systems of wealth creation controlled by residents could work.

But with the entrepreneurial founder gone and the next set of challenges looming, the foundation board — redefined by new members and guided by new outside advisors — decided to make a change in how the work was undertaken.

And this is the risk any leader takes.

In the end, all change must be endured.

Stunned, all I could think to say to the board when they told me of their decision to change direction was — "It's been a privilege."

The Goal of Enduring Momentum

"Women have a different way of looking at things."

Tambuzi was always pontificating on some topic, and that day he had decided to school me on gender differences. We were having lunch at Market Creek, exchanging bites of catfish and barbecue ribs.

"No kidding!" I chuckled, imitating Joe.

"As a man, you get your testicles kicked, it hurts, but as soon as humanly possible, you just make sure they still work, and keep going." This was his way of making me feel better. He had a knack for getting me to laugh. "It's painful. You have to admit that! Don't get me wrong — they are going to be really sore!"

I guess it did make me feel better in an odd kind of way.

"I figured you must have been surprised, hurt, disappointed, maybe even angry, but if you didn't feel, you had no business doing this work. There were so many achievements. There was a new language taking place. Relationships got built. People now treat each other like old friends. Those things are endearing and enduring. That's what makes life worth living."

He went on to talk about how people picked up the gauntlet; how this work went further than any other attempts because we were clear, authentic, and genuine; how people just needed a centralizing force; how great it was that we didn't concede space for people to get to know each other; and how we all had to push through doubt.

But I was still thinking about his metaphor of getting kicked in the balls and his line about what makes life worth living. This had truly been an incredible 20 years of my life, but I now had this picture in my head of being doubled over in pain out on the basketball court unable to do the man-thing and get up and finish the game.

How you finish a game is important. I am married to an Indiana Hoosier — a basketball nut — and have three sons who all played sports, and I knew that success can come down to your strategy and will in the endgame. Can you maintain focus until the last seconds have ticked off the clock? Is it possible to sustain the courage to listen, hand things off in a way that honors all partners, and ensure precious momentum? This intense focus on the endgame had been a driving motivation for so long I wasn't sure what to do with this sudden picture in my head of now being carried off the court on a stretcher!

Joe wanted to sunset the foundation after one generation because he believed that after the entrepreneur who made the money passes away, the culture of risk-taking in an organization is difficult to sustain. Joe's love and appreciation for "railing against failure" and willing things into being had provided the electrical charge needed not just to endure, but to relish the challenging and disruptive nature of change in a large ecosystem of players trying to accomplish something in a complex environment.

Anticipating that that level of will would begin to wane over time was at the heart of planning the endgame for the foundation while he was still at the table.

In order to exit without harming momentum, there were three parts to the endgame strategy: relationships and rituals that can transcend any challenge, sustaining structures, and community ownership of leveraged assets.

And as in any major endeavor, after strategy there is "the why" — the driving motivation and the determination to pull it off.

1. Relationships and Rituals That Can Transcend Any Challenge

"My grandfather went to Kansas as part of the Union forces and wanted to stay because it was a free state," Dr. Robert Matthews shared.

With his twelve brothers and three sisters, Bob would grow up in Tonganoxie, Kansas, where his family would make up the majority of the total African America population, he would laugh, talking about this small town of 3,000 people. When he reminisces, he talks about the years he picked melons and potatoes as a migrant farmworker, and how he liked the potatoes "because they didn't leave anything on your skin that made you itch."

A talented student-athlete, Bob was offered a scholarship for track, but turned it down for a Parent Teachers Association (PTA) scholarship from the State of Kansas. "I wanted to be the world's best teacher," Bob reflected, "and sports took too much time." So he went to Kansas State Teachers College (later renamed Emporia State University) to become a teacher.

It would be there that he would meet Ardelle. They met on a bus and she took a risk and asked him on a date during Sadie Hawkins week. The two things she remembers from the experience was the movie they went to and the fact that Bob fell asleep. "I was the oldest of 16, so it was my job to send money back home," he reflected, which he earned waiting tables, icing soda fountains, and cleaning the YMCA in exchange for a room. "I slept anytime the lights went out," he laughed.

Bob might have been tired that night in the movies, but in college, he got fired up. In 1951, he went to a class taught by Bayard Rustin, the civil rights activist who had collaborated on the March on Washington and would become a trusted advisor to Martin Luther King, Jr. as a key strategist in the Civil Rights Movement. Bob has been unwavering in his dedication to service ever since.

That life of service started when he was recruited for a teaching position in San Diego and couldn't get housing. "In the 1950's, housing discrimination was everywhere." He called the Urban League immediately and would work to end it.

Bob became known in the neighborhood as "the educator." He had a Bachelor's degree in education, a Masters in childhood education, and Ph.D. in human behavior and leadership. He founded, along with his wife, Ardelle, the Association of African American Educators, and served for many years as the principal of an elementary school in the community before retiring.

But his so-called "retirement" didn't look much different when it came to working to advance his community. Whether it was the Jackie Robinson YMCA, the San Diego Human Relations Commission, the local community theater, the Elementary Institute of Science, organizing the Martin Luther King, Jr. parade and educators' breakfast, or the working teams for Market Creek Plaza, he never slowed down.

"We grew up with old ways. We would work together. Use rituals. That's what I found was so great about the Market Creek experience," he noted. "All these rituals helped us come together. They became real for everyone."

Macedonio Arteaga, who often opened large resident gatherings and Learning Exchanges with ceremonial blessings connecting us to our surroundings and each other, noted: "When I think of ritual I think of rites of passage, how important it is to acknowledge the critical parts of our development. We are going through passages all the time, our whole life, so ritual is a huge component of those rites. It's what keeps you grounded, thankful, and connected to your humanity."

Like rites of passage in our lives, we practiced them in our work. As another resident framed it, "For innovation in creating a cultural arts village where the world met, we needed CRC; we called it — Connect, Relate and Celebrate on every level."

There was also a ritualized pattern to the work, as Bob Matthews pointed out. It was standardized. Get to know each other, plan together, work together, reflect together, celebrate. Each phase incorporated time and space for people to tell their stories and for relationships to be nurtured and nourished. We devoted and protected time for relationship-building and the ability of people to work together in teams on the issues they cared about.

"Racism is in everything. It's there in every aspect of community development. The people I thought were racist thought I was racist, but we all had to pull together to discuss things and come up with solutions together," Bob reflected. "We had to take into account that there were viewpoints different from our own. But what made it work was that there was almost a formula for how we worked."

In describing that formula, Bob reflected on the power of rituals and relationships and having a pathway for how the work would unfold. "Before you start any venture, you should have a common interest. That's what happened. We needed to let people develop that common interest, develop common language, and create human understanding. Then you need a timeline, regular meetings in these diverse groups to discuss the issues, and work together to find solutions."

So often, we are drawn to jumping into creating timelines and plans before we've created "human understanding." To Bob's point, we needed to ritualize the work — both figuratively and literally.

Stories and rituals created a culture of community. Ceremonies were used or created in every aspect of the work, from cultural ceremonies that build understanding to celebrations at the start and finish of any major piece of work. When the building honoring Joe and Vi Jacobs opened, each cultural group determined how they wanted to be involved in the celebration. That day, 2,000 people packed in the new center to share in everything from Somali poetry to Samoan dancing.

"When you walked through the building, it was not just a conversation about culture. Things that represented cultural presence were everywhere. You could see the attention to cultural detail and know that this was a conversation that unfolded over years. We had a visual reflection of it," noted a resident.

In 2006, when the U.S. Treasurer Anna Escobedo Cabral and the Director of the Community Development Financial Institutions Fund at the U.S. Department of the Treasury Donna Gambrell came to Market Creek to recognize it "as one of the best examples of the effective use of New Markets Tax Credit funding in the nation," teams determined how to celebrate the moment. "Everyone contributed," noted Sergio Gonzalez from Writerz Blok. "I'll never forget that our team decided to paint a big $10.00 bill on a large canvas at the graffiti art park, 12 feet long and 10 feet high. We thought it would be fun to have the Treasurer sign it in person! She had to actually call the White House to find out if she could do it! What was nice," he recalls, "was that space was made for young people."

Making space for deep and abiding relationships across age, culture, economics, and education, along with a ritualized pattern to the work, were the keystones of the village, the central pieces locking the whole together, providing a pathway for the work to get done together.

This pattern of connection surfaced the great stores of human capacity for creating an equitable and inclusive future by modeling it every day.

2. Sustaining Structures

With our eyes on the endgame, we envisioned ongoing resident capacity-building and accountability occurring through working teams and Village Teams Council Meetings as vehicles for goal setting, planning, and guiding the work for village projects. The Village Teams Council, made up of the village owners and its diverse set of stakeholders, would provide a vehicle for resident voice and a platform for long-term planning and decision-making.

Village networks were becoming formalized and coordinated by 2011 as "Quad" Teams (the four quads being social, economic, physical, and political development) and were envisioned as a mechanism for connecting resources into and across the village.

Also being set in motion was a network of sustaining structures that promoted the community control of assets, starting with the Community Development Initial Public Offering (CD-IPO) and its central organizations. Market Creek Partners, LLC, the overarching community development limited liability company, had a clear mission to unite diverse communities in creating social and economic strength through innovative resident-owned developments, starting with Market Creek Plaza. This company and its three ownership groups — Diamond Community Investors, the Neighborhood Unity Foundation, and Diamond Management, Inc., had launched and were in the stabilization phase of their organizational development.

The Diamond Community Investors Advisory Council, the elected body of owners that had oversight of the operating agreements, management, and distribution of profits from Market Creek Partners, LLC, would serve a central role in ongoing governance and in protecting residents' investment in the village.

The Neighborhood Unity Foundation Board of Directors, the resident-elected governing body for the community foundation, with ownership of half the village commercial developments over time, would become sustainable through the profits generated by the projects and would be phasing up its funding for community-benefit projects as the Jacobs Family Foundation was phasing out, leaving a resident-built enduring structure with control over neighborhood grant decisions and investments.

Diamond Management, Inc. (DMI), the management and development company for the village, was envisioned long-term as a community-owned enterprise and was projected to be fully sustaining by the end of eight projects. With its operating income being covered by its ownership share of completed projects, this company would become the sustaining structure for reclaiming blighted properties and building value in the Diamond Neighborhoods – skills, jobs, businesses, and assets – by developing and managing projects that were planned, designed, built, owned, and serviced by the community.

A Community Investment Trust provided a platform for ongoing ownership and investment planning by residents, and the vision for a CD-REIT (Community Development Real Estate Investment Trust) could stimulate and link other wealth-generating structures.

These structures, along with a Center for Community & Cultural Arts — newly established in 2010 with ownership of the village arts and culture agenda and the community's partnership with San Diego's Balboa Park arts organizations — and other established and growing community networks and organizations, like a Family Enhancement Network and a Village Schools Principals' Collaborative, were all following a rotation informed by community listening from pilot operations to implementation, and resource mobilization to sustainability.

3. Community Ownership of Leveraged Assets

"Two mechanisms move the world: sex and plusvalías (surplus value)!"

This quote from Cuban author Alejo Carpentier, provided a central theme to a conversation at a USC convening on value capture as a tool to finance urban development. No one could argue with sex being a motivator, but what value belongs to private individuals and what belongs to the public are still topics for debate.

During the Market Creek experience, the teams were in a constant discussion about how residents could capture the value being generated by their actions and how their ownership and control of assets could be leveraged.

This was the 20/20 vision. With the anticipated buy-out of the Jacobs Center's stock in Market Creek Partners after 2018 by the Diamond Community Investors, the first phase of leveraging that value would be complete, coming full circle by approximately 2020.

In 2011, we were in the "hard middle" on a roughly 30-year timeline (roughly 1995 to 2025) that called for ramping up the mobilization of citizen action and assembling land, implementing intense community- and capacity-building agendas based on a learn-by-doing approach, and then gradually refinancing and phasing out — carefully and strategically managing the endgame.

Economist and head of the doctoral program in public and urban policy at The New School in New York Darrick Hamilton noted, "Capitalism without capital locks in inequality, so if we're going to have a capitalist system, let's arm people with the capital to be able to participate in it. The problem of inequality is bold, so our solutions must be bold and they must build wealth and assets."[180]

The bold vision of the Village at Market Creek was of community projects planned, designed, built, managed and owned by residents capable of generating ongoing income and assets, so that succeeding generations would have access to and control over the basic tool of our capitalist system — capital.

Aggressively building on the Market Creek Partners ownership structures in the years following 2020, plans for the 50-acre village, at full build-out, were projected to generate over $150 million in appreciated value in the land. If controlled by Diamond Community Investors, the Neighborhood Unity Foundation, and Diamond Management, Inc., this "value capture" would provide equity to leverage projects far into the future.

The value calculated in scaling to 50 acres was projected on a timeline synchronizing the foundation phasing out of its primary resource role with the development of a network of successful, double-bottom-line enterprises that were community-owned and a fully-capitalized Neighborhood Unity Foundation. Together, these enterprises would create a dynamic cultural destination, generate profits that community residents controlled, and build value that could be leveraged — the tools of ongoing economic growth and vitality.

As part of that plan, we would document our own learnings, discover the paths for dealing with the contradiction of foundations as structures of power and privilege, understand how the organization needed to change over time in relationship to the community, and work systematically toward going out of business.

Along this journey, we continued Joe's refrain: "The proudest moment of my life is when you say to me, 'Joe, I don't need you anymore. Thanks for your help. I'm on my own and I'm on my way.'"

Ending Well: The Driving Motivation

It is impossible to write the last chapter of your life because our experiences continually shape us and the path we take. But in the world of institutional philanthropy, there is a price to be paid for not spending enough time on thinking through and writing about the endgame and how sustaining momentum gets built.

As a field, we vigorously track and document our "initiatives" while they are taking place, but rarely study what happened when those initiatives end or when foundation or collaborations of institutional resource partners close out initiatives or shift direction in their goals and approach.

I was fortunate to be able to participate in a nearly two-decade-long community-building experience. This was extraordinary by any standards in the field. By comparison, one veteran of documenting the relationship of community change practitioners and philanthropy noted:

> "Inside foundations, 'initiative fatigue' typically starts setting in after about three to four years. In part, this is because it takes that long to really pivot on any one of the many challenges these communities are facing and because inside foundations people come and go."

Another colleague noted that "the hard part is that philanthropy has a short attention span."

Over the two decades, we had heard residents criticize how foundations start, stop, and change their relationships with communities. But residents are not alone in this criticism. Some of the most outspoken critics of this start-and-stop dynamic are foundation staff members themselves — those who have invested themselves on the ground in communities — because they feel responsible to their relationships with residents and responsible for the commitments made.

Long-time activist and foundation officer Garland Yates noted: "We assume that if we invest in a magic bullet for 10 years that that is a huge amount of time and enough to have systems impact. If there was a deep look, everyone would realize in the scale of the issues, the resources invested were a pittance and the time too short to have a catalytic impact. It's an iterative process, always evolving and dynamic. Not understanding this leads foundations to do more harm than good. They set up expectations and then walk away. It undermines potential."

In the field of community-building, where close personal relationships are so central to the work, practitioners from around the country urge careful planning of the endgame, noting it is critically important to make any transition as smooth and seamless as possible. But in asking colleagues from other foundations to reflect on what planning is typically undertaken in philanthropy, they noted:

"We make 'tie-off' grants so it looks good at the end. It's our way of trying not to leave too bad a taste in people's mouths."

"Any trust that was built evaporates. These changes set us back tens of years. People don't forget and you can't backpedal."

"Sometimes we transition initiatives to a local entity, perhaps providing a transition grant. More likely, there is a shift with no warning at all."

"Boards or new staff leadership have the right to walk away or change direction — and they have the lack of perspective that allows it to happen."

Some spoke about foundations' propensity to want community change in a way that adds up to their original theory without reality checks about what it really takes:

"Most foundations don't really have an appreciation for what it takes. To work the problems, you have to have a desperate determination to do it. But most people want a more effortless life."

"People thought that just dealing with the vacant lots would solve the problems. The foundation locked into a particular point of view that they wanted to pursue, but no one wanted to really tackle the racism, the need for housing, the need for jobs and economic development, and so it's not sustaining."

"The 'theory' says it will take years, but more than three years and people get frustrated. Then the conversation changes. The trustees start talking about why the needle isn't moving, start saying that money is being wasted on things that aren't getting hard outcomes, and then there comes the pivotal moment when they want change in the management of the effort. They say they are not abandoning the idea. They just believe the staff should impose on people what they think is best and start blaming the staff for 'those people' not cooperating. There is a pattern."

"It always starts better than it ends. We come in saying 'we are here for the long haul.' There's good learning, good relationships, and a certain level of respect that is created. But when it's time to act, suddenly it's taking too long."

Many talked of the institutional power dynamic and the personal sadness these transitions cause for foundation staff on the ground who feel they have made promises to the community to work together:

"Foundations don't really want the power dynamic to change. They have the privilege of walking away. This element of disconnect inside foundations is baffling. When foundations engage a community, there should be an agreement about how this will end and that it will end well. There should be a prenup!"

"Foundations are scared about giving up power. You try to convince people that it's going to be different this time, transparent and authentic, but then your own institution becomes the roadblock. In the community this is challenging and real. The staff can then be thought of as disloyal. These things collide on the personal side."

"It's not uncommon that the people who live it love it once they have stepped into the experience. But once a board member or advisor starts rolling their eyes, the board suddenly feels driven off-course. They begin to discredit the idea and the direction. The enemy is us."

In discussing hope, researcher Dr. Brené Brown points out that "hope is not an emotion; it's a way of thinking or a cognitive process," and notes that "if we want to cultivate hopefulness, we have to be willing to be flexible and demonstrate perseverance. Not every goal will look and feel the same.

Tolerance for disappointment, determination, and a belief in self are at the heart of hope."[181]

Like the need to model inclusion, those of us in foundations also need to model an approach of determination, perseverance, and regrouping after disappointment, along with joy, fun, and inspiration, and realize how many ways we communicate, unintentionally, that this is supposed to be easy, undercutting the work. This goes to the heart of hope. As two staff members whose foundations are engaged in community change noted:

> "These are places where hope is badly needed. When foundations change direction, shift funding priorities, or end initiatives, it leaves such damage in its wake that it crushes people who have been galvanized."

> "In our situation, people felt like we had been leading them on. Foundations can change their minds at the drop of a hat. It can be irrational. I've found that it's usually about new people wanting to put their mark on things."

As harbingers that perhaps the next generation of community change leaders might address the slow, safe, short-term philanthropy of the past are a growing number of examples like The San Francisco Foundation's rapid response fund, the W. K. Kellogg Foundation's explicit focus on racial healing, and the shift in thinking at The California Endowment about the timeline for the Building Healthy Communities Initiative. Describing the evolution at the Endowment, Tony Iton noted:

> "We came in with rigid dates, but that is becoming less and less of a concern for us. We are now asking how we build on the infrastructure in these communities to enhance health improvement across others. Rather than asking the question about how to end it [with a hard stop after 10 years] or how we 'replicate this model,' we are now asking how these sites use their work to accelerate change broadly."

Elwood Hopkins, who has launched, led, researched, and reflected on place-based foundation collaborations and initiatives over the years, noted:

"People like Joe Jacobs can't be under-estimated. These folks were tenderized by the hardness of their lives. They work and are patient to try again. This is not some ephemeral thought about leadership or the need for a strong ego. It's a conviction about the need to keep going when your reaction is to leave. Over time you lose whatever assumptions you came in with and that can be exhausting for funders. Having been the staff person living between these two worlds, I can tell you that it is easy to give up and it's easy to leave people feeling blamed and blindsided."

Joe liked to live at bat and took boyish joy in standing in there for the hundred-mile-an-hour pitch when most people's reaction would be to back away. This is clearly not for everyone. To Elwood's point, Joe's entrepreneurial experience was truly not to be under-estimated.

People have asked me if the decision in the Jacobs Center to change course was about the major challenge every foundation was having at the time — a deep recession resulting in a plunge in asset values and causing the need for major retrenchment. I was never told why the change was occurring or what the new direction was going to be. When the markets crashed, financing froze, property values dropped, development stalled, political pressure was mounting, and our funding partners all cut their support because of their own drop in assets, it had certainly gotten hard.

But it had always been hard. And one of the things I learned from Joe is that the money can always be figured out.

We were at the "hard middle," and it was being made harder by a recession of extraordinary impact and length. There were important choices to be made in reordering our universe. From where I sat, all the variables we had in our control, including every aspect of the more than $150 million in assets on the balance sheet, needed to be intensely debated.

Should we sell all or part of the venture capital company Joe left to the Jacobs Center in his estate plan seven years earlier and put those assets into charitable play? Could we reduce the amount of our loan guarantees with partners? Should we bring more partners to the table? Should we keep the land intact or talk to the community about selling certain parcels? Could we cut budgets a fourth time without harming the team? Should we mix and match?

During this period, budget cuts had been deep, but we had garnered the commitment and inspiring ideas of the entire team to do whatever was needed. Innovation, as we knew only too well, always surfaced in tough times, when our backs were against the wall. We had a long track-record of fighting our way out.

We believed we could find the right solution and opportunities were emerging. Walgreens, after years of negotiations, signed a contract to locate a store in the village. A community clinic that wanted one of the village sites received Recovery Act dollars to move forward. New leadership at the redevelopment agency broke lose the payment of $2.5 million. Creek restoration dollars of $2.4 million had been approved by the State of California along with another $1.2 million for housing and $600,000 for parkland infrastructure.

In the world of philanthropy, no matter how big or small your foundation, there is a sense that what you have is not enough to deal with the overwhelming need your organization witnesses day in and day out. But in the community change world of practitioners on the ground, to have so much at your fingertips is considered an incredible blessing. The only obstacles standing in the way of creatively re-arranging how foundation assets are used are largely rules of our own making and the will to rewrite these rules in order to envision something radically different.

The foundation and our philanthropic partners had a choice to make — to see the drop in the financial markets as a hardship or as an opportunity to further ignite the spirit of resourcefulness that we had always had. To see our situation as a "lack of" problem or maintain a spirit of abundance and sharing that is not tied to dollars and cents.

I had pictured myself bringing the sunset plan full circle. Sadly, that didn't happen. I may never know why the shift happened or why it was handled so abruptly, but what I do know is that new members of a family on the board, the shifting culture after the death of an entrepreneurial founder, the commonplace change of direction in foundations — these are storylines that are as old as grantmaking itself. But with so much attention on and rigorous planning around sustaining momentum during times of transition, it was a storyline I didn't expect.

When the change occurred, I found myself thinking back to an earlier conversation with Ralph Smith from the Casey Foundation: "Only the wealth-makers themselves can be in the genre of wildcat philanthropy. Anyone else would be labeled as foolhardy taking this kind of risk. After the wealth-makers leave the scene, the rest of us feel bound by our fiduciary obligation to take a less risky approach."

Without Joe, did the strategy of being "all-in" and "leverage-what-you-have" seem too uncertain, too stressful, and too risky? While I was at the plate waiting for the next pitch to be fired in the wake of an economic and political storm, was it already too late to continue Joe's swing-for-the-fences approach? I thought I could continue it without him. I couldn't.

But there would be another lesson learned from this, and like so many — learned the hard way.

We were a risk-taking, R&D, community-building, and network organization, and the relationships with the community and with partners were deep and broad. While the foundation wasn't departing the neighborhood, just changing direction, the sudden decision had widespread impact on the momentum that had been generated through the working teams, sustaining structures — many of which were still quite fragile — and the large-scale community building effort. San Diego Neighborhood Funders disbanded. And the entire staff turned over — a team inextricably connected for over 15 years to each other and this community — marking the end of the staff who knew Joe.

If sustainability, which had been the driving motivation in our work, rides on the power of long-term relationships and taking care to not damage precious momentum that has been galvanized, it hurt to see an entire team of people — talented, kind, and humble change-makers — leave or get taken out of the game. The transition of the staff, two-thirds of whom were residents who had put their own reputations on the line, caused what people described as going through a long period of grieving. There had been a deep sense of fellowship among people, the kind that happens when teams do something hard together.

I also experienced the grief. And my understanding of it changed and deepened over time. It personalized what I knew professionally but hadn't seen so clearly — the deeper meaning of building community, creating connectedness, and being intimately linked to each other by our sense of common purpose and caring. Until I was disconnected, I didn't realize how deeply rooted I was, how it had become "my" community, how I had become a part of something so much bigger than the work, and how that bigger something fed my own need for belonging and meaning. Our participatory culture, our deep respect for differences, our rituals and rites of passage, our almost spiritual connection to place, and our faithfulness to real relationships had grounded my own spirit, and I experienced the sense of loss as one who is suddenly uprooted from friends and family.

It was a risk I took by not staying at arms-length and it is a risk I would take again but with a much deeper respect for the meaning of community — which rides on the fragile and precious pillars of partnership, trust, respect, and responsibility — making _how_ decisions are made more important than _what_ those decisions are. Being unwavering in our values, committed to open communication no matter how hard, and uncompromising in our need for inclusion, transparency, and participatory decision-making that puts residents first in deciding what is in their own best interest — these all need to be part of a carefully thought-out set of vows we make both individually and institutionally.

We know community building — weaving the web of connectedness and cohesion — goes to the soul of neighborhood revitalization and social change. But as a field that has traditionally operated as a closed circle separated from the action teams on the ground, philanthropy that wants to be transformational must also go to the deeper meaning of building community and invest where transformational change occurs — working "_in relationship._"

32

WHAT WILL ENDURE?

*"Action and reaction, ebb and flow, trial and error, change —
this is the rhythm of living. Out of our over-confidence, fear;
out of our fear, clearer vision, fresh hope.
And out of hope, progress."*[182]

— Bruce Fairchild Barton, American Author

What's in Place?

Change in Philanthropic Practice

"We had more freedom to stretch our boundaries," reflected Steve Eldred, who represented the California Endowment in the neighborhood funders collaborative. "We led with equity and social justice. We hadn't ever talked like that before."

Steve had been highly influenced early in his career working with a Native American tribe involved in grassroots economic development. "The Market Creek experience got me back in touch with my love and connected my work to my passion," he reflected. "The traditional response to grantmaking didn't get to my core because it often makes you feel like you are in the middle of a top-down dynamic. With this, we had to focus on learning to let go of control."

Like many of us, Steve was influenced by his relationships with residents, his relationship with the other resource partners, and with the ability to bring forward his passion for social justice and the belief that power starts with people taking charge of change. This was a fundamental shift away from diagnosing what people needed and giving it to them to instead building a platform for people to lift up their own voices and determine, design, and coordinate action.

Many of the fourteen foundations that participated in the San Diego Neighborhood Funders collaborative described it like someone would who is on a twelve-step program — including me. Constantly challenged to change how we had traditionally done business made it easy to slip back to our comfort zones. These changes, which confronted long-held power dynamics, were being internalized by each of us in different ways, making it difficult to assess the project's enduring impact on philanthropic practice.

Those involved confirmed that important changes occurred. In reflecting on his own the professional changes, Steve Eldred reflected:

> "The California Endowment didn't have a place-based strategy at the time. It wasn't even on the radar screen and this helped shift our understanding of the importance of giving primary focus to place. In our work prior to this, we could impact individual families, but the conditions that were affecting them remained. By doing this together we got a greater whole. We learned how to leverage each other's support as grantmakers through deep strategy discussions about coordinating that support. And we learned how to leverage the broad experience residents have from living there every day."

Pete Ellsworth, who headed the Legler Benbough Foundation, expressed the change in this way:

> "Over time, it changed the way we looked at philanthropy. When you don't listen to someone, you can't possibly help them, so you have to pay attention. The hallmark of our foundation became our willingness to work directly with

people instead of creating our own programs. It made me very aware of the benefit of working together, and those associations continue to this day. Everyone contributed a lot of learning along the way."

And people were changed not just professionally; they were changed personally. In reflecting on the profound impact on his life, Pete noted:

"A lot of people don't usually get that kind of honesty. One person told me 'you are just the kind of person I don't like,' saying how he had been taken advantage of by people like me. People confronted us in ways I'd never heard before. It was hard at first, but it was helpful to me personally. In fact, I've been in the funding world for many years, and in looking back on it, it was the most instructional and enjoyable period of my years in philanthropy. Listening to residents — it wasn't what we were used to hearing — but it was important to understand what people felt and needed and to realize the tremendous contribution they can bring to the table. Only after that can you really work together to make things happen."

Poignantly Pete continued:

"For me, coming to work in the Diamond right after my role as CEO of a billion-dollar corporation with 10,000 employees, the journey was moving from a structure in which I was expected to know the answers and manage others to the goals that I and the board had created to an environment in which I was expected to gain guidance and direction from others who I thought were not as 'educated' or 'established' or 'experienced' as I was. In making this journey I came to appreciate that residents had far better ideas than I did when it came to the work we were doing and I began to understand and appreciate the circumstances and lives of people who were not as fortunate. Having this experience has, I believe, made me a better person. For that, I am thankful."

As a pilot plant to test the staying power of a resident-ownership approach to community change, nested in a direct relationship between residents and resource partners, the enduring impact Market Creek Plaza had on the power dynamics within philanthropic practice might take decades to truly know and dissect.

Whether or not I will ever know the extent of the personal and professional changes encountered along the way, during the 10-year track-record of the $5.7 million neighborhood funders collaboration supporting the work, this project provided valuable experience for San Diego's small philanthropic community in working across all kinds of differences — race, class, age, geography, and sectors. It also provided experience working across areas of interest and blending different types of capital, like bank loans and tax credits, with grants and program-related investments.

Most significantly, however, the tremendous value each of us placed on resident voice, involvement, and investment undeniably changed us all.

A Place of Beauty that Endures

Market Creek Plaza, with its award-winning architecture, vibrant colors, and public amphitheater, transformed a brownfield into a vibrant place of culture and connection. A community-designed, built- and owned-commercial and cultural center, at an intersection formerly known for its proximity to "the four corners of death," now provides goods and services to residents, including the first major grocery store to serve the 88,000 residents of southeastern San Diego's Diamond Neighborhoods in more than 30 years — noteworthy and important all by itself.

Thirty-two acres of blight were cleaned up, including over 2,000 linear feet of Chollas Creek. Once a toxic waterway that was hazardous, the creek was re-channelized and restored as a natural greenbelt.

The Elementary Institute of Science, once squeezed into a 2,000-square-foot condemned and deteriorating house, now resides in an architectural masterpiece with large science beakers and mammoth pencils adorning its position on the hill — a testament to the power of youth and adults working together.

The health center next door to Market Creek qualified for financing once the factory blight was removed, and its doctors were able to renovate their aging building and construct a second one, both expanding services and beautifying the neighborhood, picking up on some of the architectural characteristics of Market Creek.

Instead of gang-member tags, the community is now home to murals, portraits, sculptures, and tapestries and a provocative, bold, and vibrant graffiti art park.

Before I transitioned from leadership, contracts were signed, financing secured, and "village" architectural characteristics were incorporated into the plans for another community clinic to be built on village land. Contracts were also signed for a new Walgreen's drug store, the first resident-planned housing project was planned and on the docket for financing, and the money had been raised to restore the next section of the Chollas Creek waterway with significant partners like Groundworks and the California Water Resources Board.

All of these projects moved forward and will endure.

An Economy that is Growing

At an intersection once known for its methamphetamine industry, Market Creek became an anchor for the development of business in the surrounding area. Not only was Market Creek Plaza a profitable commercial center itself, but the work its teams did to assemble, clear, and entitle land, will allow it to grow as a major hub of commercial activity.

Originally projected to hit $31 million in gross sales, in 2010 (the last year a Social & Economic Impact Report was published) Market Creek Plaza had generated $47.8 million in annual economic activity and attracted an additional $46.7 million to the surrounding community. It had spawned a little over 200 new jobs and lifted the number of neighborhood jobs from the surrounding properties, from a starting number of seven to nearly 600.

A Community-Owned Asset that Endures

Market Creek has two sustaining resident ownership structures — the Diamond Community Investors and the Neighborhood Unity Foundation, whose $500,000 in shares are now growing in value.

This was spawned by the creation of the Community Development Initial Public Offering (CD-IPO), which can be used as a model for both other Diamond Neighborhood projects and other communities nationally. The sweat equity and R&D financial investment it took to develop this tool and get it approved was intended to be leveraged by its use beyond the first public offering and will only be fully realized when the tool is adopted and adapted by others.

As part of planning and implementing the IPO, over 500 adults and 200 youth were involved in financial education workshops focused on building their net worth. Carried forward by a program called Mind Treasures, the youth financial education continues to this day.

Last, but not least, resident investors created their own Community Investment Fund, continuing to pool funds for future projects — like Market Creek Place — that can be collective investments.

Civic Capacity that Endures

Over 150 residents participated as regular group leaders, trainers, and presenters, and using the expertise gained in planning Market Creek Plaza, and 570 people worked to develop the urban design, connectivity, and cultural branding of an expanded 50-acre village plan. This expertise and interest in civic involvement exists. Over 400 people participated regularly in Village Center meetings, ratcheting up their expectations for change, and creating a civic capacity that can be mobilized quickly around any issue or undertaking.

Market Creek's community working team process spawned other resident-led projects which significantly impacted public safety and dropped the recidivism rate of formerly incarcerated returning citizens, cleaned up unsafe areas of the community, created a network of residents volunteering for the safe passages to school programs, and built the leadership needed to link mothers with a message to end violence.

The work has provided a community listening template, a participatory planning and decision-making process, and a resident working team structure. These are all components of the process that are being used by other foundations, organizations and community groups, both in San Diego and nationally, building ongoing civic capacity.

Most significantly, Market Creek was about "ordinary folks" exercising leadership, as Ramon Daubon advocated in his Kettering Foundation report,[183] and those ordinary people are now taking that extraordinary talent to other jobs and other communities — organizing, planning, training, encouraging other people that believe that change is possible.

I will let the residents themselves articulate the enduring nature of change they experienced in their relationships, their civic life, and their personal and family lives.

What Endures — From the People Who Call It Home

"They wanted to bury it so it would grow." Daj'ahn Blevins was referring to the Nguzo Saba.

Daj'ahn talked at length about the time capsule for the building that the community wanted to name The Joe & Vi Jacobs Center. This building was to be office space with a training kitchen and event venue for cultural celebrations.

"This time capsule was huge. We all had to select something that we wanted the future to see and understand about us — those of us who worked to make Market Creek happen. The youth selected the Nguzo Saba, the Seven Principles of Kwanzaa.[184] This is what they wanted to speak into history," Daj'ahn continued. "The power of community."

Daj'ahn had been a part of the Arts and Culture Team from the very beginning. He remembered back to a time when young people could gather in the park to hear great jazz. He had been a strong advocate for engaging youth in an artistic renaissance, and at the same time, use the resurgence to ground youth in the rich history of African thought and culture and share life skills.

"When the kids put the document in the capsule, they had tears in their eyes. 'In the ground, it will grow,' they said. The youth were trying to get their heads around the idea of 50 or 60 years into the future having someone see how connected we all were. This whole thing blew my mind!"

The young people that Daj'ahn was talking about had been introduced to the values of the African heritage while they were working on the summer amphitheater series. He would talk to them in the green room about the values of the Nguzo Saba — unity (Umoja), self-determination (Kujichagulia), working together (Ujima), supporting each other (Ujamaa), purpose (Nia), creativity (Kuumba), and faith, especially faith in themselves (Imani).

Every weekend during the summer, the youth worked with adults to organize what they called "Party at the Amp." It included everything from Friday night movies to church-sponsored Sunday gospel.

"Our work was about connection and community. And it was about respect," Daj'ahn shared, reflecting on the impact of Market Creek. "I remember personally going to raise the summer employment money so the youth could be paid," he continued. "The businesses at Market Creek bought the kids t-shirts. And then there was the green room." Daj'ahn paused for a moment, choked with emotion. "That really communicated to the young people that we were respected!"

"People came together to build a legacy," noted Daj'ahn. "That's what those kids will remember. People wanted to come together on Saturday to share their cultures or be there after church on Sunday to show what unity really looked like. These were Crips and Bloods not warring but coming together with senior citizen grandmother clubs to demonstrate this!" He laughed. Daj'ahn had children and grandchildren himself, but with his long dreadlocks and youthful spirit, he didn't look much older than the members of youth team.

"Some of these kids came out of three generations of poverty and thought they would be dead by 18. What they most needed was to be respected. Little homeboys," Daj'ahn continued, "could come in and see a Latino boss of a restaurant or an African American business owner or participate in the storytelling events with the artisans showcasing their work at Where the World Meets [the store made up of local micro-entrepreneurs]. Some of those young people who had never been to Old Town or to a museum prior to this were being encouraged to become artists and entrepreneurs. One young Sudanese girl who was having identity issues with her dark skin ended up becoming a professional model at Vogue. It mattered."

In conversations with residents about what will endure from their points of view, common themes arose. Some of what was shared was about visible signs of change, but the majority of it was about people's sense of connectedness and pride.

"The physical change did occur," one resident noted. "When Market Creek Plaza went up, there was a big shift inside the community. It also began to shift the perceptions of southeastern San Diego. The perceptual change was as important as changing the physical environment."

"Now when we drive by, we see our hard work, the blood, sweat, and tears. We know what it took," noted another resident. "The fact that the grocery is there, given that all we had were small markets without quality meat or produce, is amazing."

Spoken about differently by each person, the comments about what will endure cluster around 10 important themes:

1. greater community connectedness
2. embracing differences
3. greater youth-adult respect and partnership
4. control, clean-up, assembly, and entitlement of land
5. a safer, less toxic environment
6. greater commitment to collaborative leadership as a way of working
7. a strong sense of pride
8. a sense of belonging and personal validation
9. a more resilient spirit
10. life-long relationships

Connectedness:

"Those of us who were a part of it are taking it wherever we go. We were part of a family and now we are taking what we learned and impacting other families as we continue this work in other places."

"We knew the people running the venues. We saw their kids' pictures by their desks. We knew their families. We knew their motivation and that gave us a sense of security."

"I was like a transient, going back and forth between where my mom lived and my dad, not feeling a part of either place. This connected me. The camaraderie really impacted me personally."

"It absolutely mattered. It built my character and my confidence. I learned so much. I have a better relationship with my husband, my family, and am now a trusted leader in my community."

"It was a triumph to bring people together."

Embracing differences:

"The interaction of the cultures, eating each other's foods, appreciating each other's histories... the stories humanized all of us. Anyone who came into those interactions knows that people no longer focused on the differences; they weren't strangers anymore and that will continue."

"You just got this sense of everyone feeling their humanness...so many fears, stereotypes, phobias about people...they just melted away."

"You were coaching and helping the funders to think differently about us, and that made it possible for me to be with them. I never would have imagined being with these folks. I realized I should and could be in relationship."

Control, clean-up, assembly, and entitlement of land:

"We had a challenge with zoning; most of the people didn't know what happened. We all thought it was just some 'powers that be.' Then when you think about people getting on the bus to go downtown to City Hall for the hearing, challenging the powers that be, getting that changed — that's permanent."

"The challenge was so huge to acquire and permit that land so it could be developed for jobs and homes. That is still in place."

"When a community degrades over decades, you have to take a long-term view and we did. When a building comes out of the ground, that is just the last part of what it takes. People can't always see what it takes to assemble, entitle, and plan that land. That was one of the biggest accomplishments."

"Over time, assembling and entitling the land will become a critical and an important legacy for those of us who worked on it because it created a foundation for the future."

"On what was a toxic dump now sits a Starbucks. Think about that!"

A safer, less toxic community:

"Before you were afraid of getting your car jacked or walking down the street. It was not a place you went. Then seeing all the ethnic groups...and not just seeing people but seeing that everyone felt they had a place to connect, to be cared about. Whether you were from the Pacific Islands or from Somalia, we each had a place and respected each other's place. It was beautiful."

"People had a chance to make changes — like getting the gun billboards down, changing the renter's rights ordinance. That is never going to go away."

"There is now a good relationship with the San Diego Police Department, the presiding judge, the supervising district attorney — people feel like they are not being re-victimized."

Greater commitment to collaborative leadership:

"This experience took the idea of what leadership is all about from being one seat at the head of the table to many people in a place of service."

"People now see the link between why it's important to have great organizations like the Jackie Robinson YMCA or an Elementary Institute of Science. They know why it's important to be involved with the schools and principals. And they know why it's important to have a global picture about what advocacy and organizing is all about."

Pride in themselves and their accomplishments:

"When you saw your children perform or any of the cultural groups perform, you knew it was the very best we could be. We were all proud."

"Then there was this amazing moment. My father-in-law walked into the Jacobs Center and saw himself — he saw the tapestry that had the Samoan greeting 'Telofa.' He felt represented, our culture represented, and then I felt proud."

"Now when I see the vibrant colors, the curves of the walls, the furniture, the niches, or the tiles, I feel incredibly proud. I can point to things and say that tile, that piece of material is from my culture."

"It's easy not to care. I didn't see myself as a leader, but it was a life-changer. To identify as a human being, a member of a community, to see change, to see life — my life — reflected in the youth that are there now and changing — this is no longer a ghetto."

"Today, a group came over from Palm Springs for a graffiti art workshop. They found us in a text book! People are always amazed!"

"We were young, but we were making a difference. You laid your head on the bed at night and realized you had taken on the challenges and you just felt so good."

"Everyone left their mark."

Sense of belonging and personal validation:

"It changed my life when I look back on it. It was the first experience that showed me I was really good at something, good at being a leader — I didn't know I could be."

"Sometimes you don't understand what is in you. This experience provided many of us the ability to discover our God-given gifts that we didn't know we had. It gave us the opportunity to learn what was there and hone that gift."

"I felt very validated for the gifts I have. I don't know what you saw in me, but it took me a long time to realize you thought I was smart. My self-esteem went up, and I felt important."

"I belonged. I was no longer an outsider. I was part of the team. Accepted."

Youth/adult respect and partnership:

"When you are young, it's easy not to care. It's so hard for young people to trust adults. But we were put in so many different situations with them the trust got built."

"Our opinions weren't belittled or cast aside. You gave us our own stationery and business cards and that gave us a level of professionalism that most people won't give youth."

"I was only 10 and a nerd. I was teased. In this effort there was no name calling. We were all working toward the same goal. There were no politics. No tension."

"Now I had my own meetings to go to, in a leadership role. I was asked my opinion and had my work to do. I no longer had to sit at the back of the room while my grandparents were meeting. I thought this was so cool."

"I think it will be known for its innovation. When I see buses pulling in over at Writerz Blok to do a tour of a graffiti art park, I feel it. You see our young people, how proud they are, and it's so powerful. This is in our community."

A more resilient spirit:

"The things didn't always work, but we tried, and learned to go back to the table and try again."

"We were timid. Now we take the initiative."

"I went through a metamorphosis. I morphed into a better person thinking about how my community affects me and how I affect my community."

"This helped me later in high school when I wanted to go Paris to study theater. I knew it was too expensive for my parents, so I thought: I'll raise it! If this is what I want to do, then I can figure out how to get there. I learned that if you have a dream, you have to fight for it."

"For the thousands of people that visited MCP over the years, we left a new sense of hope."

Lifelong relationships:

"The kindness and caring, the willingness to hear someone's story, becoming better listeners, learning together, realizing how important everyone's special gifts were — these things will endure in some form."

"We still have the connections we made and continue to interact — whether they are Sudanese, Somali, or Samoan...we became friends. They will be lifelong connections."

"It was a very human, gut-level experience that built a lot of relationships — that's the crux of the work and that will endure."

Foundation for the Future

If and how the hope that Market Creek generated will endure and the broader vision fulfilled remains to be seen. But if it is to be, new teams must build on the hard-learned lessons the Market Creek experience taught the original teams about staying power:

- Resident ownership, with intentional strategies and structures for broad inclusion, participation, and co-investment, must be designed for endurance.
- Understanding starts with listening.
- Shared decision-making requires skilled facilitators and working teams with diverse views.

- Decisions must be grounded in the social, economic, political and cultural needs and context of the community.
- Sustainability of the work rides on catalytic, profit-generating projects with a balanced social and economic bottom-line.
- The cultural richness of the community must be embraced, showcased, supported as a galvanizing force, and stamp the identity of place.
- Resource networks must be developed from the inside out — built on and sustained through a process that honors resident voices first and foremost.
- Partners must commit long-term, have skin in the game, and stay no matter what goes wrong or how badly they are criticized.
- A culture of risk must be created and sustained.

Achieving a new future requires more than projects and programs. It requires a "transformational" process of vision, inclusion, and ownership in which we lead together, honor all the gifts and talents at the table, and learn by doing. Most importantly, it requires a new kind of philanthropy that is willing to change, endure critics, tackle barriers, stay the course, and muster the courage to work in relationship and risk action

If anything endures, it's because we did this together. Despite insurmountable deficits in infrastructure, high crime rates, and toxic dumps that had kept economic development stuck for decades, we managed together to transform blight into a place of beauty. Despite deep-seeded fear that kept people disconnected because of differences, we managed to build bridges across cultures, ages, economic status, and parts of town in order to create pathways to opportunity. And despite securities laws that require people to have money to make money, we delivered an IPO that created real and tangible community ownership of an asset that is growing in value.

33

REFLECTIONS ON MARKET CREEK'S ENDURING IMPACT ON THE FIELD

"The real source of wealth and capital in this new era is not material things...
it is the human mind, the human spirit, the human imagination,
and our faith in the future."[185]

— Steve Forbes

Reflections from the Field

"It's so liberating to people. There is more energy. The room will be popping with ideas," reflected Bill Traynor, discussing the power of large-scale participation in communities.

"And then it gets crushed and pushed aside by institutional behaviors which play on fears and not aspiration. The idea of 'I don't know' opens up space for something new and dynamic. The problem is foundations already have a framework and the ideology evaporates with the onslaught of deadlines, metrics, reports, data, and the need-to-know."

People working to strengthen communities want "transformational" change. Thousands of foundation and organizational staff members visited Market Creek to learn about and discover ways to adapt or apply its strategies of shared decision-making, broad stakeholder voice, cross-disciplinary teamwork, and resident ownership. The challenge for them and for all of us who seek enduring change is that it is easy to revert back to simple "transactional" moves when the hard work starts, when the critics get loud, when the systems resist, and when people get confused by something new.

Unrealistic timelines, short-term funding, the polarization of the political landscape, and fear of failure shut down the necessary risk-taking, impede steady and patient effort, and deplete the energy, creativity, and ambition of people to achieve change.

We want breakthrough — we just want it without critics, risk, and discomfort, and we want it in a straight line and on a schedule. We want everything predetermined, predictable, and guaranteed. And from our position of power and privilege, we want everything to change without changing ourselves.

During the time I was part of the Market Creek experience, nearly 4,000 people from 31 states and 17 countries visited for learning exchanges with the resident teams. From policymakers to community builders to foundations working on social justice, economic development, and place-based revitalization, several themes emerged about why Market Creek mattered to them and to the field. For those who visited, particularly those who came with teams of residents seeking a new paradigm for difficult power dynamics, Market Creek provided a living example of:

- *Everyday heroes* with a *why-not* attitude;
- A *comprehensive* and *up-close-and-personal* approach to community change;
- *Shared decision-making with residents* as a foundation for going far; and
- A core belief in *community ownership* with *organizational values* in the pole position.

And these learning exchanges provided a platform for Market Creek's most far-reaching impact:

- Fostering *confidence, hope, and courage.*

While the measuring of impact in hard outcomes (blight removed, jobs created, waterways restored, and aggregated economic activity) is important, the impact of the experiential component of Market Creek is not to be under-estimated. Teams from Denver to Detroit, San Francisco to San Diego share that what they most often struggle against in this work is loss of faith, erosion of confidence, and discouragement. As a resident from Tacoma phrased it, people involved in community change need to "take time to re-energize because the work is daunting" and need space to "work through discouragement and sadness, validate those feelings, and get new inspiration."

For many, these resident-centered learning exchanges — where funders, community-builders, and grassroots leaders shared their common struggles, strategies, and beliefs — played that role, giving people the space to work through discouragement, experience the support of people across the country, and take heart and hope from each other's ideas and accomplishments.

"If you are not in the kitchen, you're on the menu," noted a Minneapolis resident at a learning exchange. Discussions about how residents stay central and avoid the syndrome of being "done unto" were spirited and lessons, conclusions, and suggestions for future work crystalized and documented.

People returned to their communities, as we did, with renewed hope and a sense of common purpose about the critical nature of resident-centered community change.

Everyday Heroes with a Why-Not Attitude

"Our culture gravitates to the heroic story of working against all odds to succeed. It is deep within the American psyche," reflected Salin Geevarghese. "I find that the more "heroic" the story, the less accessible it feels. We create distance from that story immediately. We easily explain the exceptionalism of people and organizations, and as soon as we do that, we make it seem like it can't be replicated. What was clear about Market Creek was that it was different when it came to the heroic."

Salin, who is "unapologetically an economy and equity guy," grew up in Chattanooga, Tennessee. "My family was among the first Asian Indians to immigrate to the city. My dad was a college professor and my mom was a high school teacher; they were both committed to service and inculcated that in me. I knew from an early age that issues of advocacy, law, and policy would be in my future." And that's exactly what happened. After law school,

Salin would enter the world of policy and social change working on the determinants that impact the lives of children and families and would find his way to the Annie E. Casey Foundation, where he would first learn about and visit Market Creek.

"Market Creek was intoxicating. I came four or five times. That you were able to integrate the key disciplines and create a platform for getting things done — the number of ripples must have been vast. What I liked," he recalled, "is that the residents drove the visit. All the stories were everyday hero stories. It was accessible."

In 2009, Salin's position at Casey led him to work on the Recovery Act innovations and strategies, and he was recruited to the Obama Administration at HUD, collaborating with other agencies, to create the flagship place-based initiatives for broader economic inclusion and prosperity through the Partnership for Sustainable Communities and the Office of Sustainable Housing and Communities/Office of Economic Resilience. By April 2014, Salin was appointed HUD's Deputy Assistant Secretary for International and Philanthropic Innovation.

"What struck me about Market Creek, from letting resident-vetted data-driven decision-making on tenants to the community public offering, is you reframed how people thought about expertise. There was appreciation for the lived experience and shared control. You gave new meaning to heroes as everyday people, but I also think that you pushed the envelope." Salin paused, pondering the paradox of everyday people pushing the envelope. "That's what made you feel exceptional and probably less accessible or attainable for others to model."

People were inspired by and respected the vast number of ordinary people who were able to accomplish extraordinary things, but it was the "shared control" and the "why not" attitude that most often proved dilemmas for the those who wanted to "replicate" it. Our team's ability to provide a strong process that helped us "share control" and Joe's "risk failure" approach made it simultaneously exhilarating and terrifying.

Market Creek was a contradiction — everyday AND exceptional. It was clearly both.

In his years with both the Casey Foundation and HUD, Salin has watched as institutions which have to interact with communities "lose their nerve," as he framed it. "But your team saw people as resilient, capable of confronting challenges and figuring them out. Sometimes we speak about scale in both the public and philanthropic sectors without understanding what enables action to be replicated or applied in a different context. You brought a "why not" disposition to the work that was critical to making it work. That dynamic is sorely needed in the field."

A Comprehensive and Up-Close-and-Personal Approach

"Although I met Joe Jacobs only once or twice, I enjoyed listening to resident leaders talk about him," reflected Ralph Smith from the Annie E. Casey Foundation. "In almost every respect, they were ready to invest with Joe."

Ralph would call himself a "recovering law professor," but it was obvious when our team was with him that he never really completed his twelve-step program. Mention Market Creek Partners and the Community Development IPO and Ralph would light up like someone who still wanted to be in securities law. He valued the investment residents made and the direct personal involvement of our team.

"Your whole team was visible, accessible, and engaged. Those relationships that evolved, that direct-face-to-face involvement, led to decisions, made way for financing, created the possibility for success." In talking about the enduring impact of Market Creek, Ralph continued: "Organized philanthropy has many layers of decision-makers. It might be hard to duplicate all of the elements, but Market Creek's community engagement process to close the gap between the decision-makers and community residents is one from which we can all learn. The more residents know they have direct access to the decision-makers, the more consequential and trustworthy the effort will become."

When Ralph and Salin first visited Market Creek, the idea of financing a double-bottom-line commercial project integrated into a comprehensive resident-driven community-building effort was a new concept for foundations. It was one of the Casey Foundation's earliest program-related investments.

"In the field of community change philanthropy, there has always been this false dichotomy of people- versus place-based strategies," Salin noted. "Most foundations have gravitated to people-based program support, even if they funded in a specific place. But your strategy at Market Creek was both. You considered all of the drivers of change even though that was a tougher course. I think the growth of integrated, comprehensive approaches in the field now proves that collective impact across both people-based and place-based, across both social and economic, is the way forward. Market Creek was on the vanguard of that work."

Shared Decision-Making with Residents as a Foundation for Going Far

Omowale Satterwhite is more than a community development veteran; he is a writer and storyteller, a facilitator, an urban policy scholar, and a capacity-builder that has influenced work in over 43 states. He has spent his years working vigorously to tackle racism, address the fragmentation of communities, and build structures for community control of decisions.

"Foundations often start wanting authentic engagement but typically get more prescriptive as the work moves along and the envisioned results are not achieved as quickly as desired. At this stage of a place-based initiative, foundations normally back away from the idea of shared decision-making with communities," Omowale observed.

The concept of shared decision-making is frightening. It's like giving up control of the steering wheel in the first self-driving car. For those of us responsible for philanthropy investments, we need guarantees, timelines, and master plans. We have also created a self-imposed barrier to change by allowing our need for speed to take priority over resident involvement.

"The idea of highly engaged community work is farther along, but still faces pushback and obstacles for funders," noted Victor Rubin from PolicyLink. As a leading voice in the movement for social equity, access to opportunity, and an inclusive economy, PolicyLink has pushed for a shift in the national conversation, bringing the topic of just and fair inclusion to the forefront. "With greater racial diversity among foundation staff, there is more awareness among grants officers of the importance of community engagement, but the pressure to achieve a narrower range of outcomes decreases their ability to move this as an agenda. Foundations want to get away from a medical model, but the pressure for short-term results works against it."

As a community-builder, Omowale has experienced this pressure. "Nine times out of ten," he commented, "these initiatives are thought up by foundations. They have to move right away and want to get results as quickly as possible. So when community change does not happen quickly, foundations typically set their own funding priorities and become quite prescriptive with communities. When deemed necessary, they form partnerships with big institutions and stop bringing people on the street to the decision-making table."

"Market Creek, on the other hand, was on a track of its own," Omowale continued. "It had six things aligned: 1) an engaged funder that protected the process, 2) the ability to use resources in a way that no other grants officer could do; 3) an ownership model, 4) a focus on producing tangible benefits — a grocery, jobs, other opportunities, 5) a trusting relationship with residents, and 6) the right team. You also had the ability to align corporate structures and bring in other players."

Omowale has throughout his career found himself stressing the need for community task forces. "If we want a strategy for community change, we need to create space for lots of different people to come together who share a common interest. We need to get beyond working just with people affiliated with groups. We need a critical mass of voices from a broad cross-section of the entire community."

In our decision-making about whether or not to create space for the citizens of disinvested communities to come together to grapple with and crystalize the issues, determine together what is in their collective interest, and create plans that they own and can implement, our most frightening trade-off is **fast** versus **far**. What Market Creek demonstrated, however, was by opting for far, we can very often get farther faster than moving forward without the will, wisdom, and knowledge residents bring to the table.

To understand Market Creek, you had to hold in view two opposing views of time. Richard Woo, CEO of The Russell Family Foundation, another important partner in the learning exchanges, framed it as "at once urgent and patient." Gus Newport, who consulted with us after his work with the Dudley Street Neighborhood Initiative, framed it as a guiding principle: "to go fast you have to go slow."

Omowale believes resident engagement will emerge or re-emerge as important noting: "Institutional players are now all about empirical evidence whether or not there is authentic community participation. However, the primacy of empiricism is beginning to swing back to people and connections and social networks as a central value. We must not only focus on measuring impact but also on engaging communities and building networks to magnify impact. We must move back to democracy."

A Commitment to Ownership with Organizational Values in the Pole Position

"Market Creek made a unique contribution to what it meant for residents to own their own change. But this can easily become a 'saying' within philanthropy without enough understanding of the unique experience and expertise that residents bring. They make the work in neighborhoods come alive," noted Salin Geevarghese in reflecting on the ripples from Market Creek that impacted the field. "I think it is hard for 'experts' to let go of power and privilege to make this happen, and I don't think people have enough experience to enable them to hold onto this as a core value. You were very clear about values. But in program and policy work, you don't really hear people talking about values."

The drive to assure that the work stayed grounded in shared decision-making within teams was embedded in what we called our "Four R's" — respect, relationship, responsibility, and risk. We were in a constant conversation about adhering to these values. These values shaped how we thought about our work, how we did our work, and how our staff was evaluated on their role in the work.

"We have an ecosystem that is not delivering well. I don't think we have created the conditions for sharing power in a sustainable way, acknowledging that different actors play different roles and add different value," noted Salin. "What I loved about Market Creek was the self-effacing nature of the team, their humor, and the intense focus on values and results. So often resident meetings are about 'check-the-box,' but at Market Creek you could hear people say 'they not only want me to show up, but they really want my advice.' You respected their knowledge and know-how. You took a principled-oriented approach and let your values drive impacts and outcomes. When we visited, we were seeing innovation as it was happening. It forced people to deliberate on data, share stories, challenge issues of race and class. Whatever discovery came, it emerged from those values."

In discussing the core values we worked to operationalize over time — of which risk taking was primary — Salin indicated that he believes theoretically — as do most of foundation leaders I have spoken to over the years — that the role of philanthropy "is to take risks, to test, and to demonstrate." But as he indicated, we so often "end up taking a conventional approach with conventional expertise within a conventional frame and that doesn't work. For most foundations," he continued, "this work feels too risky to stick with it over time. Risk is not something that we talk about within philanthropy enough."

What our up-close-and-personal approach showed those of us involved in the Market Creek experience was that risk needed to be measured on two fronts: what was the risk of moving forward and what was the risk of not moving?

"We don't permit ourselves to discover what will happen organically," reflected Salin. "That was another unique aspect of the Market Creek story. You permitted discovery and evolution without knowing exactly where things would end up. That was a deep belief in your values and in what you believed about people. I suspect that companies investing in R&D create the conditions for discovery, but we don't think that people in communities are capable of that same discovery. That might be an ideological barrier or filter that is operating."

To be a foundation that defined itself as R&D, we had to face this ideological barrier and opt for discovery-based learning. It was a choice we made.

After seven years working at the top levels of HUD on urban policy, Salin noted: "If we define ourselves by transactions, we are not in the change business. For the most part, however, we are more comfortable with an outcomes-oriented frame than a values-oriented frame. But this work must start with an internal barometer of change rather than what you are going to impose on others. I hope that those who saw it in Market Creek will know what is possible."

Confidence, Hope, and Courage

"In order to accelerate social justice, we have to change and that can feel like a betrayal to our theories. These neighborhoods are invisible and philanthropy is allowing this to exist. As a field we need to create visibility in places that need help," reflected Tonya Allen, President of the Skillman Foundation in Detroit. "How do we leapfrog when we are so wedded to how it's been done?"

Tonya is distinct. She is smart and self-effacing. And she is a rich conversation, whether it's in her office, a convening, or just down the street at Starbucks, and nothing is off-limits, including her sense of elitism within foundations. She is passionate about the possibility for change and the need to inspire people, and without romanticizing how hard it is, she believes that problems can be solved.

"We need to stop treating people in communities as novices," she expresses adamantly, "and treat them as professional. There isn't a public system that hasn't tried to engage resident voice, but somehow we still think it's optional. When it came to flipping the question — 'what's the get' — you pushed us to make sure people were connected and answered that for themselves."

Tonya is a native of Detroit and is unrelenting in her commitment and drive to impact the conditions created by long-term disinvestment in her hometown. She has spent two decades in philanthropy, starting as a grantee with the Casey Foundation, and has maintained her passion for the possibility of an equitable and inclusive society.

"I saw this documentary recently about Detroit 40 years ago," Tonya noted, reflecting on "Do You Think a Job is the Answer?"[186] by Gary Gilson, shown at the Detroit Institute of Arts Film Festival about the civil unrest in 1967. "What hit me hard were two things — one was that the issues of poverty, unemployment and racism are sadly the same today, and secondly, the line 'I want dignity.' People want to matter, to feel valued. This isn't just about people sustaining themselves. The underpinning to everything is that you matter and so many people don't feel that way. I don't want people seeing this film in another 40 years saying it's still relevant!"

In reflecting on her work in Detroit, she shared: "We have to be place-based, even if it's messy. This is a period of renaissance for Detroit and I'm concerned about gentrification. Two years ago, I was talking about 'New Detroit' and 'Old Detroit' but now there's a third Detroit. It's detached youth who are not exposed to opportunity, just like in Ferguson and Baltimore. We need to hear their voices. You can't build on a lie. It's time to be inclusive. People want to move away from what is messy, but we need to be courageous enough in philanthropy to figure out transformation."

For Tonya, Market Creek was what she called her "proof-point." It was evidence that resident voice mattered on multiple fronts. "It was a story with so many wins in it from social inclusion to immigrant connection to how people benefitted from construction. The complexity of the story is so important."

For many, the learning exchanges helped people feel united as part of a larger movement, expand their vision of what was possible, and accelerate the impact of community revitalization efforts through citizen action. The time at Market Creek gave people from around the country nerve and helped them overcome fear and redouble efforts.

"It gives me hope," noted a participant from Tacoma in a learning exchange with The Russell Family Foundation, "that we're not alone in the work we do."

Richard Woo, CEO of The Russell Family Foundation, in reflecting years later on those exchanges, noted that its impact can still be felt. "I have board directors, family members and staff who still refer to what they learned about community-centered development and civic engagement from our multiple visits to Market Creek Plaza many years ago. The recollections are particularly powerful for third generation family members who visited along with staff and who are now beginning to serve terms on the foundation's board of directors."

"It gave us courage," reflected Bob Welker — Dr. Bob, as he is known in Ohio's Springfield Promise Neighborhood — in talking about the impact of joining a learning exchange.

Bob is an educator who left the university, where he taught teachers, in order to work "across town" on improving educational outcomes for children at the community level. After five years of working with residents and bridging a network of funders, he knows about the need for inspiration, determination, and courage. "You have to have a level of self-forgiveness," Bob noted, reflecting on his years in working in a Promise Zone, "because this work is less about success than keeping the faith. It's as much about hope as expectation."

Growing up in "the Bottoms," an area on the west side of Columbus, Ohio, Bob has a passion for the work. "The Bottoms was where the factories were, and its immigrants were the Appalachian poor," remembers Bob. "My mom, a single-parent, had children she couldn't afford. I was passed around the family. It was hardship. This work mirrors my own history."

In reflecting on the impact of Market Creek, Bob noted, "It doesn't have the same public profile of the Harlem Children's Zone, but as a resident-led project with the notion of combining the economic and social, Market Creek was absolutely stunning! Since our visit we refer to it all the time. It demonstrated the economics of give-and-take. People had such a go-figure-it-out attitude and the celebration of business and culture was powerful."

In looking back on the Market Creek experience, many who visited it called it magical. What visitors experienced at Market Creek was the capacity of people to step into a different future — a future that was fundamentally about inclusion, creativity, and shared decision-making. One that honored all voices, regardless of income or education. One that thrived on a sense of abundance that was achieved through the power of participation. One where the richness of our relationships took the work from feeling heavy and hard to innovative and inspired.

As Victor Rubin from PolicyLink noted: "Given the opportunity, people can translate ownership not just into physical development but into a new social community."

Bob Welker could have been summarizing its impact on all of us when he poignantly noted: "It gave us courage." This courage-building was a two-way street. "If you are feeling like you are the only one to have these problems," a resident once told me, "it's discouraging. To be with residents from other communities made us feel connected to something bigger than ourselves."

Because we needed to break down fear, build trust, and affirm that all people are gifted, creative, and capable, broad civic action was essential. The scale and diversity of the civic teams gave us the courage we needed for endurance and the staying power needed to achieve change that was enduring.

And for so many people it heralded a time of being our best, most respectful, tolerant, and courageous selves.

THE
COURAGE TO
CHANGE

THE POWER OF POSSIBILITY

34

THE UTTERLY SIMPLE IDEA

*"To my mind there must be, at the bottom of it all, not an equation
but an utterly simple idea. And to me that idea, when we finally discover it,
will be so compelling, so inevitable, that we will say to one another
"Oh, how beautiful. How could it have been otherwise.""*[187]

— John Archibald Wheeler, Physicist

Three Wishes

"You loved us and you weren't afraid."

A soft, deep, low-toned voice came from the doorway. I stood up from my job of packing up my office to find Stacy Butler, from the maintenance team, standing there. He had tears welling up in his eyes. The deep scar across his neck seemed suddenly to tell the story of an age gone by. His decade behind bars had melted into his decade at Market Creek and now we were saying goodbye. After a bear-hug-sized squeeze, he just stood and stared at the boxes, packed and ready to load on the truck. He wanted to carry them for me so he could feel helpful, so he could give me something.

His words to me were unforgettable. Simple. To the point. This "old gangster" who, after leaving prison, had the courage to stand up to violence and take a stand for peace, held a mirror up and revealed what I needed to know — that this had not just been an act of will and discipline, but an act of love and courage. The courage to act and interact without being afraid of the things that keep us human that are self-generating sources of energy and inspiration.

"I used to dream in black and white, now I dream in color," I say when people ask me if I've been changed through this experience. I have 32 shades of acrylics in my drawer beckoning me to try something wild every chance I get — like the difference between the plate of food I was served once in my dorm when I was in school in England — all white, mashed potato pie and cauliflower — and a plate full of purple Samoan taro, vibrant red and green Mexican salsa, and deep brown Sudanese KOP. I want to live in living color. It makes me happy. I'm now uncomfortable in a room that is all white, in any sense of the word.

I am now fearless when it comes to food, and when I hear Islander music, I want to dance and share some storyline with the motion of my arms. When I meet someone along the street, while walking my dog, I get the urge to greet them with a big telofa, buenas noches, or as-salam, sidee tahay. I speak to cab drivers about their histories in whatever war-torn area they grew up in and about their journeys to whatever city we happen to be in. And I laugh every time I make broad sweeping assumptions about someone sitting across a room — who they are or what they are like — before actually getting to know them, acknowledging that I need to stop myself.

What didn't change is my belief that place matters. Our communities ground us, connect us, and shape who we become. I know my heart beats differently when I return to my Ohio homeland, with its small-town-clock-tower courthouse, front-porch-lined streets, vast corn fields, and scattered stone quarries where, as youth, we took dare-devil swims. And because place is capable of both nourishing and damaging our spirits, I am more passionate than ever about supporting the foot soldiers in the field of audacious dreams who stand up for other people's struggle and seek new ways to revitalize disinvested neighborhoods in the context of complexity and uncertainty.

When it comes to community change, however, I now believe that experts, while needed, should always be matched with local indigenous expertise and have become an ardent advocate for large-scale resident voice, involvement, and investment. And while I am still unwavering in my belief in financial contributions as an important part of communities of caring, I have come to believe that institutional philanthropy needs to examine itself as a structure of power and privilege and own its own change.

People ask me often if I have regrets and if I did it over, would I change something.

It is impossible from this point in time to say if there are different decisions I would make if given the chance because each challenging decision made sense only within the context and set of conditions that existed at the time. Many seem questionable or even crazy looking back. Were bad decisions made? Yes. At every turn we were doing and undoing and redoing. But the beauty of staying the course is you can correct almost anything.

When it comes to the millions of decisions we mulled, dissected, debated, and ultimately made, I can forgive myself for any and all of those that didn't work out, knowing that more did than didn't. I also know that if we had waited to get things "right," instead of good enough, without risking action, Market Creek would likely still be an industrial dump.

Lastly, people often ask me if I just generally "wish" things had unfolded differently.

Of course I do. The board's decision to "change direction" was painful and personal, and the mourning was long and deep. But when I think of wishing for things, I can only smile and let my imagination go wild to the discovery of a magical lamp in the Cave of Wonders.[188] When I release the genie, which I'm certain will rise up with the booming voice of Robin Williams and grant me three wishes, they would be:

1. That no more kids would ever be killed;
2. That we all wake up one morning truly respectful and appreciative of our differences; and
3. That the Nguzo Saba, the Seven Principles of Kwanzaa, buried by the youth in the time capsule, with its commitment to restorative healing, taking responsibility, shared prosperity, and the values of unity and purpose — the "first fruits," as they are called — actually grow, and its harvest celebrated and commemorated.

And if there is no genie, I think, perhaps concentrating on #3 can deliver the other two. Because when the commitment to restorative healing, taking responsibility, shared prosperity, and the values of unity and purpose take root and grow, the precious change we seek is possible.

To Go Far, Go Together

We need each other. In the search for "hard outcomes," we cannot overlook or under-estimate the power of citizen action, working in relationship, and taking the journey together as critical principles in achieving impact — from addressing the health of a community to the creation of new jobs.

To go far, we must go together.

The phases of our work evolved from an outreach team, open houses, and surveys in 1998, to community coordinators and a working teams council in 2002, to a strong multicultural outreach team and town hall meetings by 2006, to Project VOCAL by 2010 — a network of networks focused on collaborative leadership. Beyond our core team, the budget to support hundreds of families turning out to spend thousands of hours in volunteer work largely consisted of food, childcare, translation, space to convene, stipends, and salaries for a core cross-cultural team of five to six residents trained in organizing.

But this was not "community-organizing-lite," as Bill Traynor coined in his 2007 article "Building Community in Place: Limitations and Promise," referring to the largely undisciplined and under-resourced approaches to community building that have proven unequal to their task. On this platform, we linked expertise in social, economic, physical and political development in order to leverage action with a strong and experienced team at the top of their fields that knew process design, strategy development, and facilitation. We were a team of dot-connectors and people-linkers that truly valued new and different voices at the table.

We were able to go far because we started and stayed together. We kept our eyes on the horizon, and with Joe's care and encouragement, we were able to warmly, enthusiastically, and courageously embrace the journey.

As the pendulum swings from place-based efforts to regional approaches to federal policy as the best response to disinvestment and back again, we need to continually remind ourselves that isolated strategies are not enough. We need the both/and. Most of all, we need to remember that people live their lives, raise their families, and gain access to the opportunities first and foremost within their communities. Working in place matters.

In a Chapin Hall report on the core issues of power and race in place-based initiatives, Sandra Jibrell from The Annie E. Casey Foundation, noted: "As a group, funders of comprehensive community initiatives have to undergo significant shifts in both the assumptions that we hold and in our behavior if we are to be effective catalysts for the level of change that we envision in distressed communities." Her poignant self-reflection highlighted our inclination in the foundation world toward "being the ultimate expert and authority" on most topics and our tendency to marginalize the communities that we work in, "regarding them as 'sites' in a traditional treatment modality, rather than communities of people with the same needs and aspirations that we have."[189]

Sandra was asking, as were many of us who were leading place-based work at that time, how do we as foundations achieve a level of mutual trust and respect that would allow us to work together with people in communities on a shared commitment to change?

"We can't afford to ignore or devalue each other," noted Elwood Hopkins reflecting on his long career in community change philanthropy. "We like to celebrate heroic efforts of people whose good is predicated on someone else needing them, but this work is about our humanity. It is about melting the walls between people of power and privilege and those who struggle. Community development exposes this tension, and it's unsettling. Joe had it right to have you focus so intensely on preserving the dignity of people, trying to avoid this weird dynamic in philanthropy of people being less than."

Over the last 20 years, there have been many daring teams which undertook community initiatives to connect people and place and grow the community-building field. Many of these people took us beyond the debate about whether or not residents who might lack specialized expertise should have a voice, whether their involvement can or will derail our models, whether or not it is burdensome or difficult to get beyond "window dressing" and tokenism. They understood that working with residents as our central partners in place-based work needs to be deeply rooted in our values and DNA.

Market Creek was an effort to embrace this principle. We took the concept of resident engagement and pushed it toward resident ownership. We envisioned a different inside-outside way of coming together that was neither top-down nor bottom-up. We believed that local efforts would naturally link, as people hit barriers and had to address them, across sectors and regions or through public policy.

We believed it was important to embrace people in communities as citizens, and not clients, and to advance deep and open dialogue on race and class, power and control. And we believed that resident voice wasn't necessary for pragmatic reasons, but rather as a matter of principle — precisely because of the legacy of poor public policy that demolished neighborhoods, relocated businesses, devastated cultural communities by cutting freeways through them, and displaced people.

And while involved, creative, comprehensive, and courageous philanthropy comes hard, there is not enough money for grants to be the only way we approach the entangled network of issues that plague our historically disinvested areas. Without large-scale civic involvement woven into a web of connections capable of bridging the boundaries that divide us, we will never achieve what is truly possible.

In the closely held world of philanthropy, we must stare in the face the conundrum of money, power and control, have and have nots, and propensity toward professional elitism that limits rather than expands the playing field, and determine if we have an obligation to hear what David Mathews, President of the Kettering Foundation, calls "a public voice."

It is time to end the long-held practice of doing "about me without me" and acknowledge that inclusion starts with us. Time to elevate philanthropy out of the historical dynamic of the privileged and the underprivileged. Time to create a platform for people to work together across race, class, gender, age, economic status, and education levels on issues of common concern. Time to appreciate each other's gifts, honor each other's voices, and believe an open, respectful, inclusive, and courageous world starts with us.

And by changing our "how" — how we do our work of resourcing social change — that open, respectful, inclusive, and courageous world we seek can be our "now" and not just our ideal future.

Summarizing the Lessons

As a learning organization, there were countless lessons, but four became central to coordinating and stimulating resident-owned community change:

- Intense Dream Work: The only way to get beyond the entrenched, interconnected, and complex issues our disinvested communities face is to build a collective vision so strong, so clear, so powerful — and so fun — that people are magnetized to it, can see themselves in it, and can walk around in it long before they get there.
- Creative Team Work: If our work is to ignite people's deeply human capacity for creativity and learning, we must listen carefully and lead with questions. The most important example we set is to trust teams to grapple with and find answers and then embrace a fast and iterative rotation from planning to action to reflection. Innovation and ownership stand on this platform.
- Inside-Out Net Work: When people in a community connect, their neighborhoods become better and safer places to live. Just linking institutional partners to a collective agenda is not enough. Deep engagement that weaves a web of relationships with residents inside a community through teamwork allows critical social and economic networks to be connected in a way that more effectively deploys expertise and resources. These networks, so essential to thriving people and places, must be built and strengthened from the inside out — so responsibility for change can be shared, resident voice respected, and citizen action leveraged.
- Flexible Frame Work: The old organizational constructs, with their historical separation between funders, non-profits, businesses, and residents, have not resulted in transformational work. Because change

cannot be given, prescribed, or imposed, we must all — wherever we sit in the ecosystem — risk our own change so we can discover new structures for shared power and decision-making and create the ever-evolving mission-related set of containers needed for action.

Along with the lessons about implementation, I also came to hold these lessons as central to thriving within the experience of change:

- Real Relationships: The world does not always change the way we think it should — through grand initiatives, catalytic grants, and astute theories. Change comes from within, and more often than not, is triggered through turbulent interactions and simple acts of kindness. Meaningful and lasting change depends on the whole ecosystem working in direct relationship, staying open and real, embracing each other as people and not roles, contributing to a can-do spirit, and embracing the challenges of change.

- Culture of Risk and Learning: If social change is about shifting power and creating a new future, people need the courage to step out of what has been historical practice. This requires a culture in which people have permission to risk, the freedom to try, the constant nudge onto uncertain paths, and the team structure for deep reflection and appreciation for failure. Working inside complex social, economic, and political dynamics requires both the tools for discovery-based learning and the time for people to both mourn and celebrate.

- Collaborative and Willful Leadership: Community change work is not about organizational leadership; it's about network or collaborative leadership. This requires a very different understanding of and orientation to what we think of as leading or directing programs. And while seldom addressed in evaluations, faulty program designs and poor implementation, although common, are less likely to derail community change efforts than pettiness, politics, and the abuse of power, making it paramount that we help each other develop an indefatigable will, the ability to withstand critics, and an unsinkable spirit in the face of hurt and disappointment. Where there is will, there is always a way.

- Shared Ownership: Finally, ordinary people are capable of extraordinary things. When human creativity is unleashed, relationships nourished, and dreams nurtured, people believe that anything is possible and easily step into personal and collective responsibility for change. When people truly own change, it not only has staying power, but it can also be embraced whole-heartedly. Culture might eat strategy,[190] but ownership feeds inspired action.

Last Word on Ownership

Joe was a man perfectly at peace with risk — win or lose. For me, Market Creek was about making that peace.

From the outset, Joe — with his entrepreneurial spirit — set out an expectation that I risk failure, swing for the fences, learn-by-doing, and accept that doing things differently would make me a lightning rod for criticism. He stood by me every step of the way. Without his spirit of risk-taking, his permission to see the work as an open field of possibilities, his deep belief in human dignity and pride of ownership, and his strong conviction that failures are only moments in time, Market Creek would probably not exist today.

Joe believed deeply in people's innate abilities and wanted to discover a way to operationalize his respect for and belief in people. In the journey to discover how to be a respectful partner in community change, many other foundations took that risk with us. We all stepped out of our philanthropic safety zones — neat program designs and predetermined metrics and outcomes that have for so long led to less-than-honest reporting and the complete disregard for residents' capacity to be lead actors in changing their own conditions — to try something different. This break from historical practice was fraught with challenging dynamics, but led to rich learnings, simple structures, and bold strategies for how philanthropy can change to become more relevant to the communities we seek to support.

We launched a project that blurred the lines between the sectors in order to inspire greater innovation. It was community-building, capacity-building, and asset-building in a commercial package. It brought a new vision into view — a vision that community-owned, sustaining structures can continue the work of creating value and recycling ongoing benefit.

Our work at Market Creek was to create a culture of ownership, which took us "public" — moved us into a large-scale public process culminating in an initial public offering. Through the process, *ownership of the plans* magnitized and amplified individual will and motivation by focusing on collective decision-making and civic action. *Ownership of the implementation* connected residents to networks of opportunity for strengthening skills, building resumes, and earning income while collectively expanding the capacity for change. And *ownership of the assets,* built through forward-looking wealth-building democratic structures, gave residents a long-term voice and collective control over land, profits, and neighborhood philanthropy.

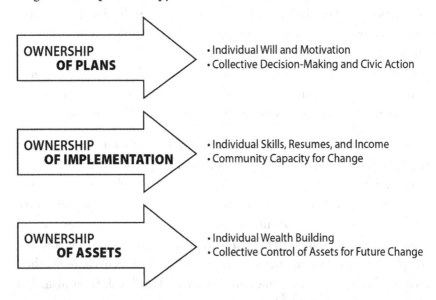

OWNERSHIP OF PLANS
• Individual Will and Motivation
• Collective Decision-Making and Civic Action

OWNERSHIP OF IMPLEMENTATION
• Individual Skills, Resumes, and Income
• Community Capacity for Change

OWNERSHIP OF ASSETS
• Individual Wealth Building
• Collective Control of Assets for Future Change

Throughout the journey, residents were involved, valued, and voiced what they believed was standing in the way of change so they could combine ideas, achieve economy of effort, and leverage action. This rode on stakeholders sharing decisions, building systems of accountability to each other, securing and managing resources, and developing a love for learning. It was about the search for something with staying power. Caring that lasts. Friendships that last. Expectations for change that endure.

Being directly accountable for change and taking a shared risk with residents on the success or failure of every piece of work changed everything.

I felt every up and every down, every win and every loss, with extraordinary personal impact. It was the school of hard knocks. There were days when I felt the big reason why comprehensive community change fails is because — it's hard.

And it was hard, no doubt about it.

But living inside so much complexity and at the edge certain disappointment, I came to see a different world — a world of courage, creativity, and the guts to reach beyond safety zones for something better. It was a world of angels, unsung heroes, caring people who worked every day to regenerate the world's shortage of hope and happiness.

I loved the spirit of people congregating for community meetings, the smiles, the hugs, the renewed energy for action, the growing expectation that trying again would be worth the effort, and the inspiring stories of human change. I came to see how this dense web of relationships — in which people combined their will, wisdom, and know-how — gave people the drive and endurance to address real issues and achieve lasting impact.

At the bottom of it all was a very simple idea: looking to people in their own communities for solutions and working together as neighbors. Igniting the spirit of people to work in relationship. Supporting people in writing a new narrative for their communities by taking charge of change. Giving people a platform for experiencing their great gifts and talents and seeing themselves — to use Maya Angelou's line — as "the miraculous...the true wonder of this world."[191]

As we work on untangling the web of issues that plague our disinvested communities, we must create strategies which shift power and create ownership where it has staying power. When stakeholders share a vision of a different future that they have shaped together, they take ownership for achieving it. When they implement, they build lasting skills and know-how. When they co-invest on a platform of shared risk, that skin in the game ratchets up responsibility for change. And when each of us — individually, as well as collectively — own our own change, that changes us all.

At the bottom of it all was this "utterly simple idea" — ownership.

35

LETTER TO THE NEXT GENERATION OF "UNREASONABLES"

"Without courage, we cannot practice any other virtue with consistency. We can't be kind, true, merciful, generous, or honest."[192]

— Maya Angelou

"You Reading This, Be Ready"[193]

"There are these 'unreasonables.' These leaders are in every community, but they are alone. They are the ones that are willing to take big risks, who exhibit courage, try to look beyond what other people think, and despite their accountability to their own organizations, realize that the 'big goal' is first and foremost."

Amy Celep sat across the table and talked about what she sees the next generation of social change leaders dealing with. She is in her 40's; I'm in my 60's. We are a generation apart, but I was her age when I started the Jacobs Center. Like Amy and her colleagues at Community Wealth Partners, I spent a career searching for the "unreasonables," the people who challenged the status quo, realized they couldn't do things alone, and saw their role in a much larger ecosystem.

"There are *satisfiers* and *maximizers*. Then there are the *unreasonables*," she continued. "The unreasonables are the ones asking the question about why we are not breaking down large-scale barriers and achieving large-scale change. They are the ones asking whether or not we have the courage to do something even if we don't know it will work."

Joe Jacobs would have liked Amy. She has welded social change and business. She watches for the people who have the courage to step up and swing for the fences. She puts teams around those with bold goals and the ability to think beyond organizational boundaries. She is both poised and approachable, warm and professional.

The group Amy heads — Community Wealth Partners — is a strategy and capacity-building organization that supports change agents in "tackling social problems at the magnitude they exist."[194] It was launched as a specialized team focused on the larger dynamic of systems or transformational change by Billy Shore's Share Our Strength, which works to address childhood hunger.

"The term 'unreasonables,' Amy noted, was spawned by Billy's book The Imaginations of Unreasonable Men: Inspiration, Vision and Purpose in the Quest to End Malaria.[195] Tackling a disease thought to be impossible, Billy shares in this book an inside look at the fearlessly bold moral commitment by a handful of scientists who decided to break with the tradition of working in isolation to find a cure for the world's most ancient and persistent disease. In the book, Billy dissected the approach these scientists adopted to deflect nay-sayers and defy reason in order to find — not incremental change — but a game-changer.

While finding a modern-day cure to an ancient scourge is the plot of many a novel, Billy's tale is something different and deeper. His story is not a romanticized version of the lives of people who take on these kinds of goals. He describes a world where success is the exception, not the rule, and the failure rate is high. It's one thing to acknowledge there will be failure and critics, and another thing altogether to live it. It requires a special personality to pull it off. In the book, Billy writes:

> "It takes someone with persistence bordering on stubbornness, confidence bordering on arrogance, the long-term patience of a cathedral builder, and the immediate impulses of an emergency-room doc. It takes leadership.

And it takes a boxer's willingness to take a punch and come up off the canvas."[196]

"They tell me — the unreasonables — that they feel more courageous when they are with someone," Amy Celep noted. She is in the courage business. She stands by the 'unreasonables' and puts a team with them to give them courage — support, information, space for break-through thinking, and confidence.

To step into the future, what we are being called to create will demand something very different of the next generation of community change leaders, but we have learned that this kind of courage is always easier to muster with someone.

So "you reading this" — as the next generation — will need to build work communities based on relationships of trust that can provide support, information, break-through thinking, and confidence. Then with this support, you will need to create a new construct for managing change that looks very different from the paradigm of *funder* ➤ *grantee* ➤ *client* in a service-delivery, inward-looking, self-preserving organization that is defined by boundaries.

As the next generation of philanthropic leaders, you will have to build strong platforms for joint action, de-silo efforts, coordinate networks of significant scale, create sacred spaces, balance individual and community interests, blend social justice and market strategies, matrix resources, and lead collaboratively. You will have to let go of thinking that the way to scale strategies for social change is by closing gaps in services, investing in projects that have guaranteed outcomes and income streams, and aligning "stakeholders" defined only as institutional partners. And you will have to engage in a very different kind of conversation — first and foremost — with everyday citizens across enormous differences.

This new landscape will call you to re-imagine the non-profit and foundation of the future — both strategically and structurally.

Darren Walker, President of the Ford Foundation, in his address to the Class of 2015 at Presidio Graduate School, reflected on his years as head of the Abyssinian Community Development Corporation in Harlem. "In those days," he commented, "many of the so-called advocates and experts — people I respected and admired — would speculate about the concerns of the community without ever so much as visiting with local residents." What he refers to as the "tragic irony" of this was that "if these experts had listened not lectured, they might have learned that the biggest issue on people's minds was not the lack of some complicated, rights-based 'theory of change,' it was the lack of a supermarket."

Listening is where courage comes in. And tapping this kind of courage is both simple and hard.

Hard because people like to avoid what is confrontational and messy, as Tonya Allen, CEO of the Skillman Foundation, framed it in a conversation about the next generation of philanthropic leadership. Having come up the ranks in the world of community change, she believes the level of elitism that exists in institutional philanthropy keeps it from creating a place at the table for all voices:

> "As the next generation, we need to stop shying away from the 'discontented'. Hear their voices. We don't want to hear them because we are exhausted with the conversation, so we never acknowledge the hurt. The future cannot be as sanitized as we might like. The work can't keep avoiding the big issues. Philanthropy has to be connected, embedded, rooted. We have to be place-based even if place is messy. People want to move away from messy, but we need to be courageous in philanthropy and figure out transformation."

Mustering the courage to hear all voices is hard, but it is at the same time simple. In discussing Market Creek Plaza, Angela Glover Blackwell framed it like this:

> "The work [at Market Creek] was so brilliantly simple. It was comforting to see it working. All you did was ask people 'what would I want for myself?' and then you asked that in a deeper and deeper way. You took a factory that was offensive when operating, even more offensive when not operating, in a community that — not surprisingly

— needed a grocery store and you got the logical response. Authentic community engagement doesn't mean leaving residents to fend for themselves and do it alone. Residents need the same things we all need to make good decisions — access to information, access to expertise, and a safe place to ask your question and feel honored. What was heartening was to see a real example of how good and smart and wise residents are when partnered with professionals."

It is time to quit avoiding the "big issues," as Tonya noted, and one of those big issues is the need for the philanthropic world to practice what it seeks to instill in our culture — inclusion, human connection, the honoring of differences, and the ability to listen, even if we don't want to hear what people have to say. This is the stuff that makes it both simple and hard.

"You had the courage to ask and act," Angela noted. To her point, this is a job description that reads: *courage required or do not apply*. It requires a team of unreasonables.

"One thing we learned the hard way was the importance of having the right staff and the right mindset," noted Garland Yates, reflecting on the decade-long foundation initiatives that led the way for the field of comprehensive community change. "This was key. This was not a job checklist saying what you are good at."

Garland was up-close-and-personal to community initiative teams placed on the ground by foundations. "We had grandiose ideas and we thought we knew what was needed. We assumed teams needed to know subject matter, so we were just looking at professional skills. It turned out there was something more than skills. There were values. Where people had been in life. What kind of relationship they had with the community. Their appreciation for diverse populations. And the ability to put people together on teams in a way that choices could be made collectively and action carried out."

When Garland and I were growing up in the world of philanthropy, there was a funder, a non-profit, and a client. In that ecosystem, the funder rarely talked to the end-user of the services provided. Our role as foundation leaders was to set the agenda, select who was at the table, and hold people accountable. We could focus on a problem or a policy and go after people <u>who believed like we believed</u> to help advance that agenda. We could maintain control, rely heavily on experts, and aim for detailed plans based on empirical evidence, highly efficient partners, and well-structured program designs.

And that was absolutely fine so long as our goal was teaching Johnny how to read. But this approach became absolutely counter-productive in trying to get at the underlying conditions that were impacting every child's chances of getting ahead.

"The transformation we need is both personal and organizational," noted Donna Stark, a long-time member of the Annie E. Casey Foundation team. "We realized that the key to success rested in the permanent connections among families. Once we had that ah-ha, we realized we needed to come to the table with a sense of humility about what can be learned, instead of us coming in and saying you need to care about what we care about. The most important work we left behind was where residents determined their own future or where we built the institutional ability to work directly with residents."

Charles Rutheiser, a cultural anthropologist who serves as a senior program officer for community change at the Annie E. Casey Foundation, remarked: "Communities are inherently complex, messy things, and we, as a field, have a hard time acknowledging or dealing with high levels of complexity or messiness. What happens," he reflected in his introspective way, "is that we often try to deal with this complexity by invoking the language, if not the practices, of an overly-reductive kind of science, talking about communities as 'laboratories' or some kind of machine that can be tuned for rationally-optimized outcomes. And at the core of our scientific model," he continued, "is our deeply mistaken notion that all of those who live in a disinvested neighborhood must be suffering from some kind of dysfunction, so we try to do the work *without* the input of those who are most affected by these designs. By over-simplifying the challenges and then excluding those most affected, we end up generating uneven and disappointing results."

How can you — as tomorrow's leaders — make better use of the expertise of residents?

By having the courage to ask. By not predetermining everything— which kills innovation. By not thinking that degrees are the only smarts needed for this work. And by not equating the hard histories that many people have experienced with a lack of capability. The historical residents of communities have the right to stay and the right to be engaged planners of the destiny of their neighborhoods.

There is no doubt that you will need outside experts working on regional market-driven opportunities and federal policy. You will need people within systems to challenge and change them. But central to community change must be residents. You must *be public* and *go public* because the public has a right to decide what is in its own best interest and have ownership of action.

To lead in this space, you must carry with you the perspective that everyone is capable of participating in civic life and recognize that what typically stands in the way of that — time, children, language barriers, discomfort, fear, and isolation — are problems that are easily solved with outreach strategies that are culturally specific and make people feel welcome and comfortable; meetings in locations that are familiar and easy to get to; hours that are convenient; support by way of food, childcare, transportation and translation; and last, but not least, agendas that are relevant to them and to their families.

As tomorrow's philanthropic leaders, you must think beyond the program grant to the building of civic capacity — creating the conditions and the platforms for people and their families to find common purpose, develop relationships, and strengthen connectedness. To do this:

- Model an inclusive society, making it a moral imperative to "not do about me without me."
- Listen carefully so that healing can happen and learning can be embraced.
- Aim, not at a problem, but at the need to move collectively toward a redefined vision of the future.
- Practice collaborative leadership and be comfortable as one leader among peers, with a strong enough process to be comfortable letting go of control.
- Work in teams - where all people own the results.

- Build networks with extraordinary reach.
- Risk action with imperfect plans.
- Learn at a high rate of speed and apply that learning in real time.
- "Resist structural containment" and build flexible evolving structures as containers for action.
- Create intentional structures for community ownership — both figurative and literal — to unleash innovation, feed endurance, and raise expectations for change.
- Become uncompromising in the need to be attentive, thoughtful, open, and respectful in how community change initiatives start, stop, or change direction, given the work's deep roots in relationships, emotional ties, and hard-earned trust that are needed for the work to continue.
- And last, but not least, let go of the intuitive belief that efficient is faster, and faster is more effective — and realize what is rooted in the African proverb "to go fast, go alone; to go far, go together."

"It's uncomfortable because people have to look at things they don't want to talk about — social justice, racism, classism, the legitimacy of people," noted Tony Iton from The California Endowment after hitting the half-way mark on a ten-year community change initiative. "You are put in high pressure situations that are make or break. It's tough sledding."

And that's the work.

As tomorrow's daring leaders, you must carry to your work a different mindset, unconstrained by how things have always been; be adept at working with a high level of uncertainty; and have the heart necessary to embrace learning, survive in a world of complexity and critics, and endure the change process itself. You must be bold and muster the courage to step up to the plate and swing without guarantees. And you must know — to quote William Stafford's poem *"You Reading This, Be Ready,"*[197] — that you can never "bring a better gift for the world than the breathing respect that you carry wherever you go..."

As for the rest of us?

Our job is to support you — the "unreasonables" — by letting you know we are at your side for the long haul because "success is not final, failure is not fatal: it's courage that counts."[198]

Toward a More Perfect Philanthropy

Parker Palmer, in an article drawn from his book Healing the Heart of Democracy, writes "American Democracy is a non-stop experiment in the strengths and weaknesses of our political institutions, local communities, and the human heart. The experiment is endless unless we blow up the lab, and the explosives to do the job are found within us. But so, also, is the heart's alchemy that can turn suffering into compassion, conflict into community, and tension into energy for creativity amid democracy's demands." In reflecting on the politics of our day, so full of false claims, half-truths, hateful rhetoric, and fear-mongering which drives out issue-oriented debate, he continues: "We need citizens with chutzpah and humility to occupy our civic space and call American democracy back to health."[199]

It is time for philanthropy to acknowledge the contradiction posed in being a structure of power and privilege, run by an elite few, determining what is in other people's best interest — "doing about me without me" — and see what a powerful role it can play in calling democracy back to health.

In James Carse's book, Finite and Infinite Games: A Vision of Life as Play and Possibility, he writes: "A finite game is played for the purpose of winning, an infinite game for the purpose of continuing the play."[200] In the game of life, community development — because it is about connection — is rich with play and possibility. In foundations it is easy to miss it because we want to be about winning. We want to claim victory. Declare success. And this might very well be possible if there is a clear-cut cause-and-effect challenge, known predictable interventions that are scientifically sound, and public agreement.

But communities aren't problems to be solved with a medical model. They are complex systems in constant change — residents move, economic factors shift, policies and laws intended to provide equal protection are adopted and then are sadly undone, and a plethora of other dynamics are always evolving. And there is generally little agreement on the underlying barriers and who is responsible for them, let alone the "right answer" for solving the myriad of interconnected issues within our communities. The path for building a just and equitable future requires debate, deliberation, our most creative spirits, our most open hearts, and our most daring acts of healing and action. It requires taking a courageous path to understanding.

In a finite game there are winners and losers. They are about glory and power. Community development, on the other hand, needs to be engaged in a way that assures the continuation of play, so that something far grander than glory and power can be achieved. An election is won or lost, but our democracy must continually be strengthened for the sake of both liberty AND justice. When we no longer work to sustain our own points of view and work toward community ownership of change as accountable partners, we will discover that what endures is the fire of inspired action.

This is more important than ever.

In a time when power and privilege set the agenda for change and everyday citizens don't believe their voices count more than money — either in the voting booth or in philanthropy — we need to shed the contradiction that those who control private wealth within foundations are building power in marginalized communities by determining what policies, what programs, and what opportunities are best for them according to research compiled at arms-length.

When we abandon silo approaches in areas of interest that perpetuate the fragmentation within our communities...when we let go of our expectations that residents should be passive recipients of "expert" knowledge and services...when we stop engaging residents in <u>our</u> work and start engaging them as creative and capable citizens on agendas they own...when we stop asking what is wrong with "these communities" and start asking how we are contributing to injustice and how can that change...and when we do not flinch in the face of the confrontations that challenge our own change — philanthropy will have bridged a divide and arrived at some new place, more courageous than ever, and, because of that, more capable than ever of moving the needle toward "We the People."

In order to create a more perfect philanthropy, you — as a new generation of philanthropic leaders — must align the work of community regeneration with the heart of democracy by lifting up the chorus of voices within neighborhoods as worthy, mindful, and equal at the table — appreciative of differences, inclusive in your approach, and able to act with courage and conviction.

This, so new teams, which are highly invested and involved and have a sense of their place in the infinite, can continue the long and arduous work of bending the "arc of the moral universe" toward justice,[201] before passing the torch.

Because, as Carse frames it: "Infinite players are...but the joyful poets of a story that continues to originate that they cannot finish."[202]

APPENDICES

TIMELINE & ENDNOTES

Timeline at a Glance
(1992-2011)

1992 - 1995
- Rodney King acquittal ignites philanthropic focus on **economic opportunity**
- Jacobs Center for Neighborhood Innovation (JCNI) is incorporated as an operating foundation with its focus on **non-profit capacity-building**
- Jacobs Team created

1996 - 1997
- JCNI moves from capacity-building to **community-building**
- JCNI enters escrow on the 20-acre Langley factory property

1998 - 2001
- **Outreach Team** and community survey launched
- **Ethnic Nights** and Cultural Village site dedication held
- Phase 1 **Creek Restoration** and site preparation launched
- **Community Contracting Program** launched
- Ten acres of the Langley site becomes **Market Creek Plaza**
- Community celebrates **Grand Opening of Food 4 Less**, Market Creek Plaza's anchor tenant

2002 - 2005
- **Community Coordinators** and **Working Teams** launched
- **Working Teams Council** launched
- Market Creek Plaza financed, fully leased, and operational
- **Youth Violence** and **Schools Listening Projects** launched
- Graff Creek Team becomes **Writerz Blok** urban art park
- **Ownership Team** uses "Theory of Thirds" to plan Market Creek Partners, LLC

2006 - 2009
- **Market Creek Partners** goes public with approval of the IPO permit
- **International Outreach Team** and **Mix-n-Match Teams** launched
- The **Prisoner Re-entry Design Team** and **Project SafeWay** launched
- **Arts & Culture Fest** becomes signature event
- Land acquisition expanded to 50 acres
- Market Creek Plaza becomes the hub for **The Village at Market Creek**

2010
- The **VOCAL Network** launched
- **Center for Community & Cultural Arts** launched
- The Village designated as **California Catalyst Community**
- **Family and Community Networks Planning Circles** launched
- **Diamond Community Investors** sub-committees on responsibilities of ownership launched
- Urban Land Institute Summit leads to **Commission on San Diego Regional Infrastructure and Equity**

2011
- Northwest Village Plan for Walgreens Drug Store launches **Comprehensive Village Plan**

ENDNOTES

1   Attributed to Peter Drucker in a speech by Mark Fields, President & CEO of Ford Motor Company (2006).
2   Robert F. Arnove, Philanthropy and Cultural Imperialism: The Foundations at Home and Abroad, (Bloomington, IN: Indiana University Press), p 1-2.
3   John Kania & Mark Kramer, "Collective Impact," Stanford Social Innovation Review, (Winter 2011) (http://www.ssireview.org/articles/entry/collective_impact).
4   Margaret J. Wheatley, Leadership and the New Science: Discovering Order in a Chaotic World, (San Francisco, CA: Berrett-Koehler Publishers), p. 173.
5   Peter Block, "Civic Engagement and the Restoration of Community: Changing the Nature of the Conversation," 2007, A Small Group Civic Engagement Series (www.asmallgroup.net), p. 19.
6   John Kao, Jamming: The Art and Discipline of Business Creativity, (New York: HarperCollins Publishers), 1996, p. xix.
7   Hector Reyes, Interview, December 1, 2016.
8   Wendell Berry, "The Real Work," Standing by Words, (Berkeley, CA: Counterpoint, 1983), p. 97.
9   "Assumptions for Innovation," The Rensselaerville Institute (2002), p. 5.
10 John Steinbeck, Cannery Row, (New York, NY: Viking Press, 1945; reprinted by Penguin Books, 1994), p. 6.
11 Marshall Ganz, "Story of Self," Address at the 4th Annual South Carolina Patient Safety Symposium, "Organizing for Health," Columbia, SC: March 16, 2011 (https://www.youtube.com/watch?v=WR2Evw4SjJE).
12 Joseph J. Jacobs, Anatomy of an Entrepreneur: Family, Culture and Ethics, (Richmond, CA: Institute for Contemporary Studies Press, 2007), p. 4.
13 Jacobs, Anatomy of an Entrepreneur, p. 223.
14 Jacobs, Anatomy of an Entrepreneur, p. 3.
15 "Assumptions for Innovation," p. 7.
16 Brené Brown, Ph.D., LSMW, Daring Greatly: How the Courage to be Vulnerable Transforms the Way We Live, Love, Parent, and Lead, (New York, NY: Penguin Group, 2012), p. 30.
17 Jacobs, Anatomy of an Entrepreneur, p. 240.

18   Bevelynn Bravo, "Notes from Bellagio," quoted in the President's Report, Jacobs Center for Neighborhood Innovation, December 17, 2004, p 21.

19   Martin Luther King, Jr., "Nonviolence: The Only Road to Freedom," Ebony, Volume 21, Issue 12, October 1966, p. 27.

20   Ephesians 4:15, Bible, All English Translations.

21   U.S. Surgeon General M. Joycelyn Elders, "Protecting the Nation's Future," (Speech Delivered at "Children and Families at Risk: Collaborating with Our Schools," The Tenth Annual Rosalyn Carter Symposium on Mental Health Policy, Atlanta, Georgia, November 2-3, 1994) p.31

22   Vickey Schubert and Rachael Baker, "Creating New Futures through Community Conversation: An Interview with Peter Block," Leverage Points, Issue 99, Pegasus Communications, June 2008.

23   H. L. Mencken, "On the Unknowable," quoted in Wheatley, Leadership and the New Science, p. 60.

24   Rainier Maria Rilke, Letters to a Young Poet, Letter #4, 1908, Translated by M. D. Herter Norton, (New York, NY: W. W. Norton & Company Ltd., 1934), p. 27.

25   Peter H. Pennekamp with Anne Focke, "Philanthropy and the Regeneration of Community Democracy," Kettering Foundation, June 2012, p. 14.

26   Mary D'Souza, "Participation: Key to Human Resources Development," (Brussels, Belgium: The Institute of Cultural Affairs, 1987), p. 7.

27   D'Souza, "Participation," p. 7.

28   John McKnight and Peter Block, The Abundant Community: Awakening the Power of Families and Neighborhoods, (San Francisco, CA: Berrett-Koehler Publishers, Inc., 2012), p. 107.

29   David Mathews, Opening Plenary Session, 2014 National Conference on Dialogue & Deliberation, December 22, 2014 (https://www.youtube.com/watch?v=jVyRb159nrk), edited for clarity.

30   David Mathews, A Public Voice That's Missing: A Cousins Research Group Report on the Public and the Government, (Dayton, OH: Kettering Foundation, 2016), pp. 2-3.

31   Toba Beta, Master of Stupidity, Goodreads, Inc., 2017, (https://www.goodreads.com/quotes/539955-vision-without-guts-is-fantasy-visi-tanpa-nyali-adalahfantasi).

32   Clayton M. Christensen, The Innovator's Dilemma, (New York, NY: HarperCollins Publishers, 1997), p. 154.

33   Peter M. Senge, The Fifth Discipline: The Art and Practice of the Learning Organization ((New York, NY: Doubleday, 1990), p. 3.

34   "Philadelphia," Directed by Jonathan Demme, released December 22, 1993, (Culver City, CA: TriStar Pictures).

35   Wheatley, Leadership, p. 8.

36 Susan Kenny Stevens, Nonprofit Lifecycles: Stage-based Wisdom for Nonprofit Capacity, Stagewise Enterprises (2001) and Judith Sharken Simon with J. Terence Donovan, The Five Life Stages of Nonprofit Organizations, (New York, NY: The Fieldstone Alliance, 2001).

37 Wheatley, Leadership

38 Wheatley, Leadership, p. 11.

39 Chrislip & Larson, Collaborative Leadership

40 Chrislip & Larson, Collaborative Leadership, p. 79.

41 Chrislip & Larson, Collaborative Leadership, p. 97.

42 Jack and Suzy Welch, "Eating and Dreaming," LinkedIn column, (https://www.linkedin.com/pulse/20130725154204-86541065-eating-and-dreaming), July 25, 2013.

43 Cartoon written by M. M. Rogers and illustrated by Ariv R. Faizal, Walyu S., Ary W. S., Creative Team for Search for Common Ground, Indonesia, first appearing "Designing for Results: Integrating Monitoring and Evaluation in Conflict Transformation Programs," Cheyenne Church and Mark M. Rogers, Search for Common Ground, Washington D.C., 2006, p. 32.

44 Clayton M. Christensen, The Innovator's Dilemma, p. 202.

45 "Assumptions for Innovation," p. 5.

46 Draw Line: Classic (Version 3.3.4, uploaded to Apple App Store), Developer: BitMango (Publisher: BitMango Corporation, 2012.)

47 Steve Jobs, Commencement Address, Stanford University, Stanford, CA, June 12, 2005.

48 Steven R. Covey, The 7 Habits of Highly Effective People, (New York, NY: Simon & Schuster, 1989), p. 102.

49 Aaron Sojourner, Prudence Brown, Robert Chaskin, Ralph Hamilton, Leila Fiester, and Harold Richman, "Moving Forward While Staying in Place: Embedded Funders and Community Change," Chapin Hall Center for Children (Chicago, IL: University of Chicago, 2004), p. 5.

50 Bill Traynor, "Reflections on Community Organizing and Resident Engagement, Rebuilding Communities," The Annie E. Casey Foundation (2002), p.28.

51 The Aspen Institute, Voices from the Field: Learning from the Early Work of Comprehensive Community Initiatives, (Washington D.C., 1997), p. 8.

52 The Aspen Institute, Voices, p. 8.

53 Prudence Brown and Sunil Garg, "Foundations and Comprehensive Community Initiatives: The Challenges of Partnership," Chapin Hall Center for Children, University of Chicago, 1997, p. 1.

54 John F. Eliot, Overachievement: The Science of Working Less to Accomplish More, 2nd ed. (New York, NY: Diversion Books, 2015), p. 91.

55 Block, "Civic Engagement," p. 7.

56 "Chicano Park, Barrio Logan, San Diego: The Takeover of Chicano Park," Kathleen L. Robles, SDSU, Project Director (http://www.chicanoparksandiego. com/history/page1.html).

57 Kao, Jamming, p. xviii.

58 "ICA-USA: Building a Just and Equitable Society in Harmony with Planet Earth," www.ica-usa.org.

59 Bill Staples, Transformational Strategy: Facilitation of TOP Participatory Planning, (Bloomington, IN: iUniverse, 2013).

60 Staples, Transformational Strategy, p. 29.

61 Staples, Transformational Strategy, p. 12.

62 Staples, Transformational Strategy, p. 54.

63 Drucker, 2006.

64 Senge, Fifth Discipline, p. 12.

65 Neil Smith, "To Build Your Business, Smash Your Silos," Fast Company On-line Newsletter, Excerpted from How Excellent Companies Avoid Dumb Things by Neil Smith with Patricia O'Connell. Copyright © 2012 by the author and reprinted by permission of Palgrave Macmillan, a division of Macmillan Publishers Ltd. (http://www.fastcompany.com/1839317/build-your-business-smash-your-silos).

66 Kao, Jamming, p. 33.

67 Valdis Krebs and June Holley, "Building Smart Communities Through Network Weaving," Appalachian Center for Economic Networks, Athens, OH (2006), p.6.

68 Diana Scearce, Gabriel Kasper, & Heather McLeod Grant, "Working Wikily," Stanford Social Innovation Review, Summer 2010, p. 32.

69 "Wikipedia: About," last modified November 17, 2015 at 21:53 (https:// en.wikipedia.org/wiki/Wikipedia:About).

70 Scearce, Kasper, & Grant, "Working Wikily," p. 33.

71 Katherine Fulton, Gabriel Kasper, Barbara Kibbe, "What's Next for Philanthropy: Acting Bigger and Adapting Better in a Networked World," The Monitor Institute (July 2010), p. 16.

72 John Kania & Mark Kramer, "Collective Impact," Stanford Social Innovation Review, (Winter 2011) (http://www.ssireview.org/articles/entry/collective_impact).

73 Kao, Jamming, p. 34.

74 Wikipedia: Pilot Plants," last modified November 10, 2015 (https://en.wikipedia. org/wiki/Pilot_plant).

75 Noel Watson, "The Story of Vicksburg," Printed Interview, "President's Report," Jacobs Center for Neighborhood Innovation, December 17, 2004.

76 Jacobs, Anatomy, p. 119.

77 Stephen Godeke with Jennifer Vanica, "Financing Change: The Social and Economic Costs of Market Creek Plaza," Rockefeller Foundation, September 2004.

78   Antony Bugg-Levine, "Complete Capital: We Need Integrated Solutions, Not Just Investment Capital, to Address Social Problems," Stanford Social Innovation Review (Winter 2013), p. 17.

79   Michael W. Sherraden, Assets and the Poor: A New American Welfare Policy, (New York, NY: Taylor & Frances Group, 1991).

80   Antony Bugg-Levine and Jed Emerson, Impact Investing: Transforming How We Make Money While Making a Difference, (San Francisco, CA: Jossey-Bass, 2011).

81   "State Asset Development Report Card: Benchmarking Asset Development in Fighting Poverty," Corporation for Enterprise Development, Washington D.C., 2002, pp. 88.

82   Katia Savchuk, "California Has More Billionaires Than Every Country Except the U.S. and China," Forbes, May 4, 2015, (https://www.forbes.com/sites/katiasavchuk/2015/03/04/california-has-more-billionaires-than-every-country-except-the-u-s-and-china/#35f2e73637c1).

83   Senge, The Fifth Discipline, p. 58.

84   Godeke with Vanica, "Financing Change."

85   "Assumptions for Innovation," p. 3.

86   Senge, Fifth Discipline, p. 57.

87   Albom, Tuesdays with Morrie: An Old Man, A Young Man, and Life's Greatest Lesson, (New York, NY: Doubleday, 1997), Time Warner Paperback/Sphere Publishing, 2003), p. 61.

88   Anne Stuhldreher, "The People's IPO: Lower-Income Patrons of Market Creek Plaza Can Now Invest in the Shopping Center," Stanford Innovation Review (Winter 2007), (https://ssir.org/articles/entry/the_peoples_ipo).

89   Janet Yellen, "Improving the Outcomes of Place-Based Initiatives," Keynote Address, Federal Reserve Bank of San Francisco (San Francisco, CA, February 9, 2010).

90   Yellen, "Improving Outcomes."

91   Yellen, "Improving Outcomes."

92   Aristotle Onassis, (https://www.brainyquote.com/quotes/quotes/a/aristotleo1190 69.html).

93   Marion Weber, "How the Flow Fund Circles Began," Speech Delivered at Bioneers, 2006.

94   Jacobs, Anatomy of an Entrepreneur, p. 147.

95   Jhon Goes in Center, Science and Native American Communities, quoted by Cynthia-Lou Coleman and Douglas Herman in "Ways of Knowing: Naked Science or Native Wisdom," Smithsonian National Museum of the American Indian Magazine, Winter 2010, p. 33.

96   David Mathews, The Ecology of Democracy: Finding Ways to Have a Stronger Hand in Shaping Our Future, (Dayton, OH: Kettering Foundation Press, 2014), p. 18.

97   Mathews, Ecology, p. 84.

98   Mathews, Ecology, p. 82.

99   Mathews, Ecology, p. 84.

100 Dennis Martinez, "The Value of Indigenous Ways of Knowing to Western Science and Environmental Sustainability," The Journal of Sustainability Education, May 9, 2010, (http://www.susted.com/wordpress/content/the-value-of-indigenous-ways-of-knowing-to-western-science-and-environmental-sustainability 2010 05/).

101 Ray Barnhardt & Angayuqaq Oscar Kawagley, "Indigenous Knowledge Systems and Alaska Native Ways of Knowing," Anthropology and Education Quarterly, 36 (1), pp. 8-23, (updated and posted online 4/29/2005).

102 Coleman and Herman, "Ways of Knowing," pp. 31-33.

103 Sylvia L. Lovely, Introduction to Lori Silverman's Wake Me Up When the Data is Over: How Organizations Use Storytelling to Drive Results, (San Francisco, CA: Jossey-Bass, 2006), p. xxvii.

104 Patricia Auspos, Mark Cabaj, "Complexity and Community Change: Managing Adaptively to Improve Effectiveness." The Aspen Institute Roundtable on Community Change, September 2014, p. 57.

105 Lovely, Wake Me Up, p. xxv.

106 Merv Griffin, creator, Jeopardy! is a registered trademark of Jeopardy Productions, Inc., Sony Pictures Entertainment, 2018.

107 Chuck Barris, creator, The Dating Game is a registered trademark of Sony Pictures Television, 2008.

108 Zoe Clayson, "Market Creek Partners, LLC Ownership Strategy: Community Development Initial Public Offering (CD-IPO) Pathway Analysis," Abundantia Consulting, with contributions from Allio Consulting and Philliber Research Associates, December 1, 2008, p.21.

109 Victor Rubin and Lisa Robinson, "Participatory Evaluation Design: The Outcomes Expected as a Consequence of the Market Creek Resident Ownership Strategy," PolicyLink, July 2004.

110 Mathews, Ecology, p. 115.

111 Michael Quinn Patton, Developmental Evaluation: Applying Complexity Concepts to Enhance Innovation and Use (New York: The Guilford Press, 2011), p. 9

112 Quinn Patton, Developmental Evaluation, p. 5

113 Quinn Patton, Development Evaluation, p. 9.

114 Quinn Patton, Developmental Evaluation, p. 5.

115 Patricia Auspos and Mark Cabaj, "Complexity and Community Change: Managing Adaptively to Improve Effectiveness," The Aspen Institute Roundtable on Community Change, September 2014.

116 Auspos and Cabaj, Complexity and Community Change, p. 13.

117 Quinn Patton, Developmental Evaluation, p. 11.

118 David Mathews, For Communities to Work, (Dayton, OH: Kettering Foundation Press, 2002), p. 14.

119 Mathews, For Communities to Work, p. 14.

120 Mathews, Ecology, p. 61.

121 Mathews, Ecology, p. 115.

122 Robert Giloth, "Failure Fuss," Blog, July 23, 2014, 9:53 a.m., (http://www. robertgiloth.com/2014/07/failure-fuss.html).

123 Omowale Satterwhite & Shiree Teng, Honor the Work: Building Capacity for Social Change in Communities of Color (Oakland, CA: National Community Development Institute, 2010), p. 53.

124 Mathews, Ecology of Democracy, p. 139.

125 Peter Block, Community: The Structure of Belonging, 1st ed., (San Francisco: CA Berrett-Koehler Publishers, Inc, 2008), p. 30.

126 Block, "Civic Engagement, p. 5.

127 Block, "Civic Engagement," p. 9.

128 Block, "Civic Engagement,", p. 8.

129 Block, "Civic Engagement, p. 7.

130 Sir Ken Robinson, Out of our Minds: Learning to be Creative (Chichester, West Sussex, UK: Capstone Publishing Ltd., 2011), p. 47.

131 Wheatley, Leadership, p. 174.

132 Brown, Daring Greatly, p. 43.

133 Brown, Daring Greatly, p. 2.

134 Brown, Daring Greatly, p.54

135 Brown, Daring Greatly, pg. 16.

136 Gloria Steinem, "Am I helpful?," O Magazine, April 2014.

137 Bill Traynor, "Building Community in Place: Limitations and Promise," April 2007, p.1, accessed at http://www.trustedspacepartners.com/uploads/7/7/3/4/77349929/building-community-in-place--traynor_0.pdf; A version of this article was published in the Community Development Reader, edited by Susan Saegert and James DeFillipis, (New York, NY: Routledge), 2008, p. 214.

138 Kao, Jamming, p. 19.

139 Vanessa Daniel, "Conference on Welfare Ignites Protests in DC," Z Magazine, April 1, 2001.

140 Tamara Copeland, "Philanthropy Must Understand Racism Is Not Dead," Chronicle of Philanthropy, January 21, 2016.

141 Brown, Daring Greatly, p.120.

142 Tiny Fey, Bossypants, (New York, NY: Reagan Arthur Books, 2011), p. 123.

143 Joe Robinson, "The 7 Traits of Successful Entrepreneurs," Entrepreneur, January 10, 2014, accessed online (http://www.entrepreneur.com/article/230350).

144 Martha E. Bray, The Sweet Far Thing (New York, NY: Delacorte Press, 2007 (Quoted in: https://www.goodreads.com/work/quotes/3072872-the-sweet-far-thing).

145 Elizabeth Gilbert, Eat Pray Love: One Woman's Search for Everything Across Italy, India and Indonesia (New York, NY: Penguin Books, 2006), p. 334.

146 Gilbert, Eat Pray Love, p. 18.

147 Paraphrased reference to Gilbert, Eat Pray Love, p. 149.

148 Maya Angelou, A Brave and Startling Truth, (New York, NY: Random House, 1995).

149 Paraphrased from Erma Franklin, "Piece of My Heart," Sony BMG Music Entertainment, 1967.

150 Robert Giloth, "Failure Learning," Blog, December 5, 2012, 9:53 a.m., (http://www.robertgiloth.com/2012/12/failure-learning.html).

151 "Achieving Impact and Sustainability through Market-Based Approaches," (Washington DC: Community Wealth Ventures), Published March 2008 Documenting Conventing on October 27, 2007.

152 Elizabeth Alexander, "Praise Song for the Day: A Poem for Barack Obama's Presidential Inauguration," January 20, 2009 (St. Paul, MN: Graywolf Press), 2009.

153 President Barack Obama, Speech, 50th Anniversary of Bloody Sunday, March 7, 2015, Selma, AL (https://youtu.be/gvAIvauhQGQ).

154 Eddie S. Glaude, Jr., "America's Racial 'Value Gap': A Two Part Conversation with Bill Moyers," Part 1, May 2, 2016, http://aas.princeton.edu/publication/americas-racial-value-gap/.

155 Nikki Giovanni, "Nikki-Rosa," The Collected Poetry of Nikki Giovanni, 1968-1998, (New York, NY: Harper Perennial, 2007), p. 53.

156 Richard C. Harwood and John A. Creighton, "The Organization First Approach: How Programs Crowd Out Community," The Kettering Foundation and The Harwood Institute for Public Innovation, 2009, p 13.

157 Harwood and Creighton, "The Organization First Approach," p 13.

158 Ramon E. Daubon, "A Civil Investing Strategy for Putting Communities in Charge," Kettering Foundation, 2007, p. 5.

159 Daubon, "A Civil Investing Strategy," p 17.

160 Daubon, "A Civil Investment Strategy," p. 18.

161 Daubon, "A Civic Investing Strategy," p 19.

162 Mathews, Ecology, p. 165.

163 Mathews, Ecology, p. 165.

164 Mathews, Ecology, p. 26.

165 Mathews, Ecology, p. 28

166 "Resident-Centered Community Building: What Makes It Different?" Connecting Communities Learning Exchange, San Diego, CA, June 2012, The Aspen Institute and the Jacobs Center for Neighborhood Innovation, p. 23.

167 Alice Walker, as quoted in The Best Liberal Quotes Ever: Why the Left is Right (Source books, 2004) by William P. Martin, p. 173.

168 Commission on Social Determinants of Health, "Closing the Gap in a Generation: Health Equity through Action on the Social Determinants of Health," World Heath Organization, 2008.

169 Ronald A Heifetz and Marty Linsky, Leadership on the Line: Staying Alive through the Dangers of Leading, (Boston, MA: Harvard Business School Publishing, 2002), p. 41.

170 Heifetz and Linsky, Leadership on the Line, p. 12.

171 Megan Burks, "A Case of 'Planning Fatigue' in City Heights," Voice of San Diego, May 16, 2013 (http://www.voiceofsandiego.org/neighborhood-growth/a-case -of-planning-fatigue-in-city-heights).

172 Gilbert, Eat Pray Love, p.22.

173 Corinne Wilson and Vladimir Kogan, "Investing in Our Future: Infrastructure and Equity in Chula Vista, National City and San Diego," Center for Policy Initiatives, July 2012, p. 7.

174 "Community Campaigns for Infrastructure Equity: A Review of Four Case Studies," prepared for the Commission on San Diego Regional Infrastructure & Equity, PolicyLink, July 2012, p.1.

175 Elwood Hopkins, James Ferris, "Place-Based Initiatives in the Context of Public Policy and Markets: Moving to Higher Ground," The Center on Philanthropy and Public Policy and the Sol Price Center for Social Innovation, University of Southern California, March 2015.

176 Jacobs, Anatomy of an Entrepreneur, p.147.

177 Gilbert, Eat Pray Love, p. 277.

178 Pierre Teilhard de Chardin, The Phenomenon of Man [Le Phénomène Humain] (New York, NY: Harper Perennial 1955); Quoted by Stephen Covey in The 7 Habits of Highly Effective People: Powerful Lessons in Personal Change, (New York, NY: Simon and Schuster, 1989), p. 330.

179 Thomas Homer-Dixon, "Leadership Captive," Toronto Globe and Mail, Published Friday, November 24, 2000, 12:00AM EST; Last updated Saturday, March 21, 2009 7:12PM EDT (http://www.theglobeandmail.com/globe-debate/ leadership-captive/article771093).

180 Darrick Hamilton, Interview with Courtney Hutchison, "New Narratives, Bold Ideas: A Conversation on Race and Inequality with Economic Darrick Hamilton," PolicyLink Equity Blog, April 7, 2016.

181 Brené Brown, Ph.D., L.M.S.W., The Gifts of Imperfection: Let Go of Who You Think You're Supposed to Be and Embrace Who You Are, (Center City, MN: Hazelden Publishing, 2010), pp. 65-66.

182 Bruce Fairchild Barton, (https://www.brainyquote.com/authors/bruce_barton).

183 Daubon, "A Civic Investment Strategy," p.18.

184 Dr. Maulana Karenga, "Nguzo Saba: The Seven Principles," (http://www. officialkwanzaawebsite.org/NguzoSaba.shtml).

185 Steve Forbes, quoted by Alex A. Lluch, Simple Principles to Becoming a Millionaire, (San Diego, CA: WS Publishing Group, 2008), p. 34.

186 "Do You Think a Job Is the Answer," Documentary Produced and Directed by Gary Gilson, Public Broadcast Laboratory, March 1969.

187 John Archibald Wheeler, as referenced by Wheatley, Leadership, p. 2.

188 "Aladdin," dir. by Ron Clements and John Muster. Burbank, CA: Walk Disney Pictures, 1992.

189 Sandra Brock Jibrell, "Changing Foundation Assumptions and Behavior," Core Issues in Comprehensive Community-Building Initiatives: Exploring Power and Race, Chapin Hall Center for Children, (Chicago: University of Chicago, 2000), pp. 79-80.

190 Drucker, 2006.

191 Angelou, Brave.

192 Maya Angelou, Interview, USA TODAY, March 5, 1988.

193 William Stafford, "You Reading This, Be Ready," The Way It Is: New and Selected Poems (St. Paul, MN: Graywolf Press, 1998), p 45.

194 "Tackling Social Problems at the Scale that They Exist," Community Wealth Partners, (http://communitywealth.com/our-work).

195 Bill Shore, The Imaginations of Unreasonable Men: Inspiration, Vision and Purpose in the Quest to End Malaria, (New York, NY: Public Affairs/Perseus Books Group, 2010).

196 Shore, The Imaginations of Unreasonable Men, p.90

197 Stafford, "You Reading This," p. 45.

198 Winston Churchill, as referenced by John Wooden, They Call Me Coach, with Jack Tobin, Epigraph of Chapter 17, (New York, NY: The McCraw-Hill Companies, Inc., 2004), p. 114.

199 Parker Palmer, "Five Habits to Heal the Heart of Democracy," The Global Oneness Project, (https://www.globalonenessproject.org/library/articles/five-habits-heal-heart-democracy).

200 James P. Carse, Finite and Infinite Games: A Vision of Life as Play and Possibility, (New York, NY: Free Press, 1986), p 3.

201 Martin Luther King, Jr., "Sermon at Temple Israel of Hollywood," Delivered February 26, 1965.

202 Carse, Finite and Infinite Games, p.149.

Printed in the United States
By Bookmasters